ACCOUNTING ETHICS

ACCOUNTING ETHICS

Iris Stuart
Bruce Stuart
Lars J. T. Pedersen

WILEY

ISBN 978-1-118-54240-8 (pbk)
ISBN 978-1-118-88018-0 (ebk)
ISBN 978-1-118-88020-3 (ebk)

A catalogue record for this book is available from the British Library

Set in 10/12pt New Caledonia by Thomson Digital, Noida, India
Printed in Great Britain by CPI Antony Rowe, Chippenham, Wiltshire

CONTENTS

PREFACE

Accounting Ethics grew out of the teaching experiences of the three authors, especially their efforts in a basic course in accounting ethics taught the Norwegian School of Economics in Bergen, Norway. The book blends features of moral philosophy, insights from business ethics, and practical experience in accounting and audit practice. It builds upon basic knowledge of international accounting principles and standards, realistic assessments of individual behavior in organizations, and a firm grasp of sound accounting practice in the modern business environment.

The diverse backgrounds of the authors and their search for appropriate technical and ethical resources for their course on accounting ethics has inspired their collaboration on this project. The research foundations of the book, the structure of its chapters, and the formulation of its "end of chapter" cases and questions have been determined by the teaching responsibilities of the accounting ethics course. To address specific learning challenges, the authors have constructed a textbook that is designed to supplement the classroom lectures and interactive exercises among students and teachers.

The book seeks to balance a concern to teach (or remind) students of the basic vocabulary, concepts, and decision-making processes of accounting *and* to introduce the elements of ethical sensibility both as an intellectual enterprise (to learn about ethics) and most importantly, as a foundation for moral commitment and consistent ethical behavior (to be ethical). The authors think that contemporary accounting education has adequately dealt with technical matters – identifying and resolving accounting problems in accordance with sound principles and contemporary standards. They seek – by means of the textbook and through teaching – to enhance students' skills in addressing issues that are likely to be encountered in their future practice of accounting and to empower their ability to produce and/or use financial statements and other accounting reports.

As the authors develop their informal "accounting theory" in first section of the textbook, they focus attention on the fundamental purpose of accounting to produce and communicate business knowledge to a variety of stakeholders – both within and outside particular business entities. Continuing demonstrations of accounting proficiency and ethical sensibility, the book argues, are the marks of accounting competency. This "dual competency" is an appropriate goal of accounting education; indeed, it is the basic duty of the professional accountant. Given our commitment to fostering this competency, the book supports the technical and moral development of what we call "the virtuous accountant." In other words: we aim for the skillful application of contemporary accounting standards for the communication of accounting knowledge to various stakeholders and the realization of sound accounting principles in decision making.

The core of accounting ethics is the ability to address accounting and ethical problems by making decisions that express sound accounting principles and also demonstrate the accountant's integrity and commitment to public service through ethical behavior. The core of this book is its presentation of the authors' decision model for directing intellectual and moral resources to accounting practice. Introduced in Chapter 2, the decision model anchors the discussion of each succeeding chapter. The elaboration of the decision model and its step-by-step application to numerous accounting cases provide ample opportunity for students to rehearse and improve their own decision skills.

Technically proficient and ethically sensible decisions do not come easily. The book recognizes this, but it also assumes that both technical skills and ethical decision making can be developed through education, mentoring and work experience. In the book, the specialized accounting and ethics concepts and decision processes are introduced, illustrated and explained – assuming the readers to be in early stages of professional education. Accounting principles and specific standards are introduced as they are appropriate for accounting decisions within particular situations; the concepts of several traditions of moral philosophy are made available so that beginning students can make use of them in the cases and business circumstances that are described.

Learning is facilitated as the chapters "remind" the reader of earlier treatments of the decision model or key features of the accounting and business organizational environment. The chapter discussions highlight the main points in clear, logical patterns, with numerous examples and definitional "reminder boxes" at strategic places within the text. Philosophical elements are themselves treated in specific relation to accounting principles and "real-world" practice – in view of contemporary situations of business organization and activity, government regulation, and professional responsibilities.

While the primary focus of the book is to treat accounting decision making as the task of the individual accountant who is duty-bound to make technically appropriate and ethical choices, each chapter also places the accounting decision making in social contexts. Accountants produce their specialized texts and communicate their business reports in a complex social environment of businesses and firms, in the context of globalized markets, monitored by professional organizations and government regulators. Moral issues and ethical dilemmas arise within corporate offices, in the marketplace and other social settings. And while there is a concluding section on "Accounting in Society" (with "Auditing Ethics" and "The Accountant in Society"), almost every chapter develops some discussion of the social dimensions of technically proficient and ethically sensible decision making.

ACKNOWLEDGMENTS

The authors want to acknowledge the mutual support they have received from their colleagues and to express their appreciation to one another for "time well spent" in conversation and teaching, and even in research and writing! We also owe debts beyond measure to our families. Need we say more?

PART I

PURPOSE, BACKGROUND, AND APPROACH

CHAPTER ONE

The Technical and Ethical Responsibilities in Accounting

LEARNING OBJECTIVES

By the end of this chapter you should be able to:

1. See ethics as a key feature in accounting reforms.
2. Describe recent debates and research about accounting ethics in education.
3. Explain the dual competence of the accountant as technical proficiency and ethical sensibility.
4. Describe the ethical dimensions of competency, giving attention to moral philosophy as an intellectual resource for the accountant's moral education.
5. Explain the authors' accounting theory: they see accounting as a cooperative enterprise that produces business knowledge and communicates it to interested users.
6. Understand accounting as discourse.
7. Understand accounting as a practice.

ACCOUNTING, ETHICS REFORM, AND YOU

By the time you open this book, you've probably taken several accounting courses. You have a basic practical grasp of what accountants do. You know that accounting is a profession that serves various stakeholders by communicating crucial business information. Accountants' work, you have seen, is important for business decision making, market activity, and the economic vitality of modern society. In the classroom, you've solved accounting problems by applying current accounting standards and struggled through exercises to apply rules in rational decision procedures. You've experienced the complexity of accounting practice and faced demands for technical competency and skillful problem-solving. You've become acquainted with accounting standards and principles and probably understand accounting as a rules-oriented activity within the contemporary business environment.

STAKEHOLDER

For a number of fields, including business ethics, a stakeholder is a person or organization that influences a decision or is influenced by the outcome of that decision. For accounting: a stakeholder is a person, group or organization that may use the knowledge that is communicated in financial statements and reports. Stakeholders can be considered as "insiders" or "outsiders" to the company whose financial status is described. Insiders are those who have access to company information in addition to its financial statements – management, board of directors, employees. Outsiders include: creditors and lending institutions, stockholders and prospective investors, and regulators.

It is likely that by now, you have an image of an accountant: a respected, well-paid professional, conservatively dressed, a "numbers-crunching," hard-working employee. Accountants create a company's financial statements by reviewing invoices, spreadsheets and computer print-outs of company transactions and complicated business deals. Accountants contribute to the publication of monthly, quarterly and year-end reports on "how a company is doing" – all this to satisfy management and stockholders, analysts and potential investors or creditors, even lurking government regulators or tax collectors. Accountants are valued employees, members of an honorable profession, steady fellows and solid citizens – accountants are rarely cast in a heroic mode, but in most people's eyes neither are they villains.

But you have also heard of business fraud and mismanagement where accountants played a major role. The media and the courts have exposed significant scandals that demonstrated accountants' failure to serve the public interest. Corporate accountants failed to provide clear, accurate pictures of the companies' financial performance, and public accountants working in audit firms failed to notice this during the yearly audit. These accountants and auditors failed their profession and the public because they did not tell the truth about companies' transactions. They did not disclose relevant and reliable business information that could be used by "stakeholders" for decisions to invest, loan money, or buy and sell stock. Auditors and accountants did not report large-scale fraud or warn the public that creative accounting techniques hid millions in debt as financial statements deceived the public. Auditors and accountants deliberately violated professional standards and government regulations and acted "with malice aforethought" to "cook the books" and fool the public.

AUDIT FAILURE: KPMG AUDITORS ALTER WORK PAPERS OF TENET AUDIT, CHARGES THE SEC

The US Securities and Exchange Commission (SEC) found improper professional conduct by a KPMG partner and a senior manager for making after-the-fact modifications to audit working papers, to create a false impression that an audit of Tenet Healthcare

Corporation for the fiscal year 2002 had been properly conducted. These modifications included adding substantive comments to the working papers, backdating documents and creating audit documentation after the fact. "By failing to perform a proper audit and then altering documents, thereby concealing their audit failures, the KPMG auditors were derelict in their most basic gate keeping functions . . . The KPMG auditors' misconduct in this case undermined the very integrity of their audit and impeded our ability to determine whether a proper audit was conducted." The audit report had been released, stating that KPMG had performed an audit in accordance with Generally Accepted Auditing Standards. But the KPMG auditors knew, or should have known, that the audit team had not completed procedures involving Medicare revenues. Later the audit team changed audit papers, to leave an impression that the audit procedures were complete. These alterations, involving more than 350 working papers, continued into 2002. In addition, audit evidence was falsified and documents were backdated. The SEC found that these actions were improper professional conduct, "unreasonable conduct, each resulting in a violation of applicable professional standards . . . ". The auditors engaged in this conduct were denied the privilege of appearing or practicing before the SEC as accountants. (SEC News Release 2006-45, March 30, 2006)

You can now join with the authors of this book and ask: "How did such things happen? Why didn't the auditors and the accountants do their jobs properly, follow their own rules, act responsibly and protect the public interest?" We wonder: "Were the company accountants and the auditors incompetent; were they simply deceived by dishonest managers or confused by complicated business deals? Were the techniques of accounting simply unable to address the complexities of business organizations and activities?" We ask: "Does the profession need new and improved rules? Do accountants need better technical training or more effective incentives, including higher pay and more public recognition, so they will work harder to detect fraud?" At the personal level, we ask: "Did these accountants lack character and have no integrity?" At the institutional level, we wonder: "Were accounting systems inadequate to deal with the rapid changes in business technology, the international scope of trade and finance, and the tremendous variety of business services and products in the market?"

To ponder these questions and consider what accountants ought to do about fraud, deception and dishonesty, to ask about the kind of persons accountants ought to be and the types of decisions they ought to make: these are the issues of morality and ethics. These questions and the answers they generate go far beyond technical matters – beyond merely focusing on rules and principles. They force us to ask about the fundamental purposes of accounting and the basic motives that influence accountants' behavior. The scandals draw us into the complexities of accountants' work environments and compel us to think about the structures and systems that support accountants' activities. In particular, we note factors in the business environment that influence accounting practices, including the pressure of time constraints, pressures to cut expenses, and the desire for firms to increase their profit margins. We are challenged to consider the basic features of modern business, where accountants face the pressures of profit-taking, are tempted by the lure of professional ambition, and their own desire sometimes to pursue selfish interests even if others are harmed and public interests are ignored. Reacting to accounting failures and faced with these pressures, we remind ourselves of the goals and purposes of accounting.

The public spectacle of major business scandals and accounting failures forces our attention toward the flawed character of some accountants and auditors and to the misdeeds of particular firms. The sheer scope of fraud raises questions about whether institutional regulation is adequate to deal with unethical behavior on a grand scale. These scandals raise calls for reform and "more ethics" in the institutions involved in such affairs.

Concern about ethics, however, is not to be associated only with the special circumstance of business fraud and high-profile deception. Neither does accounting ethics, in particular, merely focus on scandal and wrongdoing. Nor does ethics simply alert us to bad behavior, dishonesty, and deception (however important these warnings may be). For clear thinking about the type of persons accountants ought to be and reflection on what they ought to do in their distinctive practice inspire us to affirm the highest ideals for accounting practice. As ideals for practice, ethics – the values worth pursuing, the principles and rules for decision making, the assessment of the consequences of actions, the individual's character traits (virtues) and aptitude for moral judgment – forms the core of accounting practice itself.

We believe that honesty, integrity and a passion to exercise thoughtful, well-informed judgments and do right things are the appropriate virtues of the accountant. Accountants have the duty to tell the truth about financial matters. Given this view, we want you to think clearly about the morality of accountants and the moral choices they must make. We have high hopes that you will learn and adopt the ethical responsibilities of accounting practice. Indeed, we have a grand vision on your behalf, a sweeping agenda for your well-being. We hope that you will be motivated to act ethically, to behave as "a virtuous accountant" (as well as a technically proficient accountant). This book's message is a call for reflection and inquiry about accounting ethics, to inspire you to reason clearly about accountants' duties and their character, and the expectations for their ethical behavior in performing their tasks. What is more, we want you to become motivated, fully committed to acting ethically as an accounting professional.

The next sections recall the recent history of debate about accounting ethics in higher education. They present the authors' perspective on the importance of accounting standards and the accountant's dual competency of technical proficiency with regard to accounting standards and ethical sensibility with regard to the ability to recognize moral issues and resolve ethical dilemmas. The sections then treat accounting ethics education as a high priority, introducing moral philosophy as a useful resource for the moral development and education of accountants.

After these discussions, the chapter outlines the authors' "accounting theory," our understanding of the basic purposes of accounting – the foundation for our understanding of the accountant's ethical responsibilities. This description of accounting identifies accounting as a form of discourse, wherein knowledge is produced and communicated to potential stakeholders. We also describe accounting as a practice, a cooperative endeavor with specific purposes where the creation of specialized accounting texts "embodies" or "realizes" the accountant's distinctive virtues. The production of financial statements depends on specific character traits and intellectual skills that are crucial for professional practice. This part of the chapter reminds us that accounting as discourse and practice are supported by accounting standards and by particular accounting institutions, as well as the cultivation of distinctive accountant's virtues.

A BRIEF HISTORY OF ACCOUNTING ETHICS IN HIGHER EDUCATION

Accounting ethics courses and the inclusion of accounting issues within business ethics courses pre-date the recent wave of international business scandals and accounting failures. One scholarly article, sketching a history of reform, begins its study in the mid-1980s, calling for ethics reform in the profession and advocating ethics training in accounting education (Loeb, 2006). That study, along with others that review the past quarter-century, summarizes debates about accounting ethics in undergraduate and graduate curricula and comments on teachers' credentials and teaching strategies. Other studies assess the effectiveness of particular courses of study and consider methods of evaluating the students' learning of ethics. In recent decades, academic researchers and accounting professionals pose questions about who ought to teach accounting ethics courses; most prominently, there is even significant debate on whether ethics can be taught effectively within the modern university or business school.

Reviewing recent developments within the United States and Europe, accounting scholars note reform efforts in the profession and acknowledge the increased attention to ethics training in accounting education. Several professional commissions advocate programs of ethics training in undergraduate and business school education. In the past two decades, several dozen studies have reviewed these educational changes and discussed their key elements. These articles reveal an important debate about ethics training as they examine the sophisticated, highly technical educational process now deemed necessary to prepare each generation of accountants for professional practice. As major scandals rock the business world and fraud and mismanagement in large corporations involve company accountants' and auditors' failures, the issues of accounting ethics have become matters of public debate. These scandals have prompted a public outcry not only for new regulations and change in the accounting profession, but also for educational reform. There is a call for more course work in accounting ethics and for research to determine how classroom education can be an effective means to motivate ethical decision making (Stuart, Stuart & Pedersen, 2011; Levy and Mitschow, 2008).

Several articles by Stephen Loeb, Mary Armstrong, J.E. Ketz, and Dwight Owsen provide a good sketch of the recent debate (Loeb, 2006; Armstrong, Ketz & Owsen, 2003). Their reviews note that since the late 1980s, professional accountants and scholars consider whether or not ethics can even be taught in the classroom. As this key issue is debated, researchers discuss educational goals for accounting curricula and the types of instruction that may be effective. Other articles describe various methods of assessing faculty performance and student learning. Both researchers and working accountants debate the impact of ethics training on professional practice – especially focusing on whether coursework enhances the ability to recognize ethical issues and resolve ethical dilemmas in "the real world," in actual business settings (Loeb, 2006). Many articles assess teaching techniques and evaluate classroom activities designed to increase knowledge about ethics, with some scholars arguing that it is essential to go beyond just "learning about ethics" to find effective ways of encouraging ethical behavior so that students enter accounting practice with a determination to behave ethically (Mintz, 2006; Low, Davey & Hooper, 2008; Armstrong, Ketz & Owsen, 2003).

Empirical studies examine student responses to ethics education. Many studies employ the ethics concepts introduced in James Rest's (1994) ethics model – ethical sensitivity, judgment, motivation, and character. Their authors investigate whether students are learning to think critically about moral issues. Most importantly, they ask whether students are given the proper education to become motivated to act ethically. Armstrong and her colleagues, for example, frame their review of recent research with their own variation of Rest's four-part model. They argue that more ethics education should focus on student motivation and the enhancement of student commitment to ethical behavior. In this way, the authors seek to expand upon earlier classroom emphases on lectures, dialogue, and case studies that narrowly focused only on the recognition of moral issues and showed too little concern for empowering ethical action by students. To be sure, these authors support the development of the skills of moral reasoning, but they also seek better ways to encourage ethical behavior (Armstrong, Ketz & Owsen, 2003).

JAMES REST: COMPONENTS OF MORALITY

In the late 1970s and early 1980s, James Rest, University of Minnesota, developed a four-part model to identify the main elements of morality. This model has been used in thousands of articles and books that treat the cognitive aspects of moral decision making: (1) moral sensitivity – ability to recognize the moral/ethical issues in a given situation; (2) moral judgment – capacity to determine the ideal course of action among several alternatives; (3) moral motivation – skill of selecting valued outcomes and ability to take action that is deemed moral; and (4) moral character – skills and perseverance to make moral decisions and maintain morality over a long-term, throughout a lifetime. (James R. Rest, "The Major Components of Morality," in W.M. Kurtines and J. Gewirtz (eds) *Morality, Moral Behavior and Moral Development*, New York, Praeger, 1984.)

Additional literature treats classroom teaching, outlining proposals of curriculum reform and revisions of educational goals for accounting ethics, as well as teaching strategies and various methods of assessment (Cheffers & Pakaluk, 2005; Mintz, 1995, 2006). Scholars examine the relationship between business ethics courses and more specialized courses in accounting ethics, with attention given to professionalism and the ethical responsibilities within public accounting (Jennings, 2004; Levy and Mitschow, 2008; Williams, 2010). Efforts to link the specialized courses in business, accounting ethics and professional ethics to the several traditions of moral philosophy reveal a lively debate on whether a focus on moral philosophy is particularly helpful when accounting ethics is understood as "applied ethics" (Dolfsma, 2006).

THE AUTHORS' PERSPECTIVE

The authors of this book participate in these debates over accounting ethics. We review research on business and accounting ethics courses and the development of several professional codes of conduct. We also consider numerous international proposals for change in the governmental regulation of accounting. This book emerges from our perspective that accounting is a type of applied ethics, grounded in principles, expressed in standards and rule-oriented behavior, and aimed at particular beneficial consequences for businesses and society. The main message of this book is to highlight the ethical features of accounting and to equip students for making ethical decisions and taking ethical actions in accounting practice.

Competency in accounting practice, we maintain, presupposes technical knowledge and skills, ethical awareness, and steadfast motivation for ethical behavior. In short: for the working accountant, technical proficiency and ethical sensibility go hand in hand. By technical proficiency, we mean knowledge of the vocabulary, concepts, and decision procedures of accounting and stated principles and rules as this knowledge is applied in making accounting decisions. Knowledge of the accounting standards and the methods of making decisions recognized as authoritative by the standards setting institutions are learned in the classroom and through the early stages of the accountant's working experience. This knowledge comes into play when accountants use the skills they have learned and employ practical judgment to apply standards in making appropriate accounting decisions.

TECHNICAL PROFICIENCY

The technically proficient accountant has gained the knowledge of accounting standards and learned the skills of accounting decision making. This knowledge includes the basic vocabulary and concepts of accounting, its fundamental principles and specific rules for recording financial information, and the decision procedures of accounting practice. To be technically proficient means having the ability to apply accounting standards and exercise knowledge-based (knowledge-informed) judgment to making accounting decisions.

By ethical sensibility, we mean the accountant's ability to recognize moral issues that are encountered in business circumstances and the capacity to identify the key features of a moral problem and grasp the significant aspects of ethical dilemmas. Ethical sensibility further involves the skill of judgment to identify options for resolving ethical dilemmas. This judgment includes the ability to choose among these alternatives. Finally, the ethically sensible accountant is empowered to act ethically. Combining knowledge of standards with practical judgment and the capacity to choose among alternatives, the accountant is motivated and acts with integrity. In brief, the accountant's discernment of the key features of moral problems plus the ability to make decisions results in ethical actions.

ETHICAL SENSIBILITY

The ethically sensible accountant makes use of several intellectual and moral capacities: (1) an ability to recognize moral problems and dilemmas in accounting situations, (2) insight to identify the key features of an ethical dilemma, (3) capacity to determine and choose among alternatives in resolving ethical dilemmas, and (4) motivation to act ethically; that is, "to do the right thing" as the fulfillment of one's own responsibility.

This understanding of the accountant's dual competency assumes that the technical aspects of accounting practice are very important and are closely linked to the ethical demands of accounting. This textbook is itself a resource for technical training as it presents ethical issues in relation to the technical matters of professional practice – its regulations, rules, and prescribed patterns of decision making. Indeed, the book assumes the fundamental necessity of technical proficiency as a key mark of professionalism. Accountants should comply with the standards of accounting practice and follow its principles and rules in their most up to date form. The authors believe that one of the professional's most important ethical obligations is to comply with the standards of accounting.

Some Examples of Technical Knowledge, Knowledge of the Relevant Accounting Standard

Consider, for example, that an accountant reviews a company's transactions and notes that specific products are sold, to be shipped one month from the date of purchase. When is the revenue expected from the sale to be recognized in the financial statements? There is an accounting standard to address this question. The technically astute accountant will know that revenue is recognized when a *service is provided or a product is shipped* and *the company expects to be paid*. (Recognize revenue, then, on the date the products are shipped.) In another situation: an auditor notices that a financial statement lists as "current liabilities" the moneys owed to a company due in 18 months. He or she wonders: "Is this money a current liability or might it be a long-term liability?" Technical knowledge of the relevant accounting standard will give the answer. "Current liabilities are moneys owed, to be recorded at the cash to be paid – within one year. Moneys owed as a result of borrowing cash or purchasing goods or services, to be paid in more than one year, are long-term liabilities. They are recorded at the present value of the future cash flow." (So the money owed for 18 months is a long-term liability!)

Accounting standards require the company to distinguish between operating leases and capital (financing) leases. Knowledge of the standards and knowledge about the terms of a given lease must be part of the technical knowledge of the accountant. Operating leases are recorded as expenses: the asset used by the company based on the lease agreement is not recorded on the financial statements of that company. By contrast, capital or financing leases are recorded as if the company had purchased the asset. The asset is recorded on the balance sheet under long-term assets. A capital (finance) lease asset is depreciated over the life of the lease.

A brief note on ethical sensibility in relation to accounting standards: the accountant is responsible for knowing and following the accounting standards in each of the above situations. In effect – these decisions are ethical, as well as technical, responsibilities. If the accountant were pressured by management or by some desire to misrepresent the financial situation of the company and then chose to violate the accounting standard, that action would be unethical.

The authors think that the technically proficient accountant needs also to be the ethically sensible accountant. We might say: "The technically good accountant should also be a virtuous accountant; that is, an ethically sensible accountant." By this we mean that the accountant who performs his or her tasks skillfully by technical standards does this at the same time he or she acts virtuously (i.e., reveals the admirable quality of his or her character by taking ethical actions within the accounting decisions). For the competent accountant, both technical skill and ethical sensibility will be demonstrated in accounting decisions that produce accounting texts. As an obligation placed upon the accountant by the practice itself, the technically proficient accountant will always strive to make ethical judgments and act with integrity.

We develop the themes of the book to emphasize first and foremost that accountants and auditors adhere to the standards of accounting practice and follow its principles and rules. In this context, learning the standards, developing the skills to apply them, and exercising judgment in decision making will necessarily include both technical elements and an ethical dimension – with competency for the accountant demonstrated as technical proficiency and ethical sensibility put into practice.

COMBINING TECHNICAL PROFICIENCY AND ETHICAL SENSIBILITY: FOUR TYPES OF ACCOUNTANTS

Our perspective on accounting ethics claims that the accountant's competency has two dimensions – technical proficiency and ethical sensibility. Assuming this: a given accountant may be technically proficient or not and may be ethically sensible or not. Taken together, this means that we envision four types of accountants based on the degree to which the accountant is technically proficient and ethically sensible.

		ETHICAL SENSIBILITY	
		−	+
TECHNICAL PROFICIENCY	−	The Destructive Accountant	The Good-hearted Accountant
	+	The Opportunistic Accountant	The Virtuous Accountant

The Destructive Accountant is characterized as lacking both technical and ethical competence. If such an accountant enters the practice, he or she is surely the opposite of what accounting education aims to produce. Such an accountant is neither able nor willing to act in accordance with accounting standards.

The Good-hearted Accountant is characterized by ethical sensibility, but lacks technical competence. Such an accountant is essentially well meaning, but has a *knowledge problem*, in the sense that he or she is not able to act in accordance with standards. This problem can be overcome by increasing the accountant's knowledge and skill in applying the accounting standards.

The Opportunistic Accountant is characterized by being technically proficient while not being ethically sensible. This means that he knows the standards well enough to use them well, but he is willing and able to exploit loopholes to benefit himself or those whom he favors. Such accountants are in a narrow sense competent, but they have a *motivation problem*, in the sense that they do not place the common good ahead of their own self-interest. This is a problem that can be addressed either by strengthening the moral character of the accountant, or by putting control measures in place that will hinder him from acting unethically.

The Virtuous Accountant is characterized by being technically proficient and ethically sensible. This means that he or she integrates technical and ethical knowledge in accounting decisions. Such an accountant will follow standards and act to promote the common good.

This book originates from the authors' criticism of their own profession. Despite the many calls for reform and the introduction of ethics in accounting programs over the past decades, we see that scholars and practitioners often give highest priority to the technical aspects of the profession – its standards and prescribed procedures – to the relative neglect of research about ethics and the encouragement of ethical commitment on the part of accountants. We want to change educational priorities to remedy this shortcoming. We think technical proficiency must be matched with ethical behavior. Accounting practice is a type of applied ethics; accordingly we criticize scholars and accountants for their all-too-frequent failure to acknowledge and appreciate the ethical dimensions of accounting practice. The ethical nature of accounting practice is not yet emphasized enough in the training of accounting professionals. The recent accounting scandals and subsequent calls for reform in education and accounting practice do indeed suggest that scholars and accountants must continue to give high priority to refining technical standards. There is much need to construct rules appropriate for addressing the complexities of businesses that are large in scale, engaged in international trade and finance, and equipped with rapidly changing technologies. But such efforts must also be matched by comparable emphases on honing the skills of ethical decision making and motivating the present generation of accountants to be ethically aware as well as technically skillful. In brief, we need more support for developing competence in both technical matters and in ethical decision making.

ACCOUNTING EDUCATION: TRAINING FOR COMPETENCY AND MORAL PHILOSOPHY AS A RESOURCE

Accounting is a cooperative enterprise – a practice – that is crucial for business and society. Accountants create business knowledge and communicate it to various individuals and groups (stakeholders) who use this knowledge in business decision making. In this practice, accountants are guided by standards (principles, rules, and codes of conduct) and supported by professional societies, legislation and regulatory bodies. Adherence to these principles and compliance with the rules of practice includes both a technical and an ethical dimension; competency in accounting is the demonstration of technical proficiency and ethical sensibility in the completion of the distinctive tasks of the practice.

ACCOUNTING STANDARDS

Accounting standards establish the guidelines and formats for preparing financial statements and reports, thus governing accounting practice at the practical level. The standards establish the appropriate manner of recording financial transactions in the financial statements. Standards include the prescribed rules, procedures, and criteria for measurement that determine appropriate accounting practice, including broad guidelines (principles) and detailed procedures (rules). Accounting standards are established in the US by the Financial Accounting Standards Board (FASB). Internationally, the standards are set by the International Accounting Standards Board (IASB).

In response to recent accounting and audit failures, many have advocated reforms in accounting education and changes in the regulation of accounting practice. Technical matters predominate in these reform efforts as new laws, rules, and prescribed procedures are introduced. By contrast, the authors of this book respond to the crisis of business scandal by highlighting the significance of accounting as a form of "applied ethics". We emphasize that accounting decision making includes not only technical compliance to standards and rules but also ethical sensibility – awareness of moral issues, capacity to resolve dilemmas, and a commitment to behave ethically. The book supports this attitude: we hope that students develop both technical and ethical competences as they prepare to enter the accounting profession so that they will "tell the truth" about financial matters by demonstrating technical knowledge of accounting standards, steadfast integrity and persistent commitment to ethical behavior throughout their practice.

It is a complicated process to learn the technical skills of accounting practice and to develop the intellectual judgment to identify accounting issues, recognize moral problems, and resolve dilemmas. The issues and study questions presented in the following chapters are intended to assist you in identifying moral issues in accounting situations and to support moral reasoning and making ethical judgments. The authors believe that moral education in accounting includes both "learning about ethics" (developing moral discernment – the capacity to recognize moral issues and the skills of moral reasoning) and supporting efforts to "act ethically" (developing habits of moral commitment and the ability to do "the right things for the right reasons").

This book expresses faith that accounting ethics education will "make a better person out of the student"; that is, study and engagement in the classroom will enhance students' capability to fulfill the distinctive tasks of accounting practice. Students should develop the competency of technical proficiency and ethical sensibility. This dual competency is crucial for producing accounting knowledge and communicating clear, accurate and truthful financial information to stakeholders who will then use that accounting knowledge for their own business decision making.

Within the accounting classroom, the engagement of students with each other and their teachers continues an initiation into the professional duties of accounting practice. By means of reading, discussion, and problem-solving exercises, the educational program will blend the learning of technical standards – principles, rules, and decision procedures – and the skills of ethical sensibility. Our approach to these tasks will make use of the history of ethics inquiry, as well as current discussions within moral philosophy. The intellectual tradition of philosophical inquiry in ethics – concepts, issues, decision making – can become a significant foundation for students' ethical decision making. Within the classroom setting, students and their mentors will address historical and contemporary philosophical studies to learn how various moral traditions have conducted ethics inquiry. This learning strategy assumes that aspects of philosophical ethics can be useful as a "toolkit" of concepts, arguments, and moral reflection that can guide accounting decision making.

Philosophical ethics provides a valuable resource for recognizing and addressing ethical issues that arise within the special domain of accounting practice. By gaining some awareness of its several traditions, accountants will not "have to reinvent the wheel" whenever they grapple with moral dilemmas communicating business knowledge. As they encounter business complexities and try to construct clear, accurate financial reports, acquaintance with the philosophical traditions can frame the manner in which they approach ethical issues. The authors believe that this introduction to moral philosophy will help student-accountants to work their way toward practical solutions to moral dilemmas in accounting. The philosophical background will inform their reasoning processes and support their efforts to act with integrity and to persist in ethical behavior. Such study should equip them to resist the pressures to break rules, manipulate financial reports, and deceive the public.

MORAL PHILOSOPHY

Moral philosophy or philosophical ethics is the branch of philosophy concerned with inquiry into the nature of human action-behavior in particular situations and conduct over the long term. Ethics offers rational argumentation on how people "ought to live their lives". Ethics considers questions of right and wrong, principles and rules for behavior, and the consequences of actions.

It must be emphasized that the intellectual and practical exercises of the classroom are not intended simply for the sake of "studying about ethics". The primary objective of ethics education in accounting is to develop a practical capacity for judgment which will inform and motivate ethical behavior in accounting tasks. Ethics education should inspire accountants and auditors to serve their companies, clients and the public interest. Using the toolkit of moral philosophy, students will recognize moral issues, resolve dilemmas, make ethical decisions in a process of moral education in the classroom. In this practically oriented educative process, actions shaped by technical knowledge and expressing the student's integrity will form the habits of sound judgment and thus provide the moral foundation for acting ethically. As one of the traditions of moral philosophy (virtue ethics) describes the process: the student will gain important intellectual and moral virtues (character traits and skills) vital to professional practice. Emerging from this process, the accountant will be able to act virtuously, taking the character traits and skills that are learned to perform the special duties of accounting practice.

For accountants, the domain of ethical activity is the preparation, review (auditing and assurance services) and communication of financial information to potential users. The principal goal of accounting practice is the transmission of clear, accurate, and trustworthy information to people who depend on such knowledge for their business decision making. Within this domain of ethical activity, accountants are expected to adhere to the principles of their profession, comply with its rules "in service to principles," and exercise judgments (technical and ethical), so that financial knowledge can be conveyed impartially to those who would make use of it. By subordinating his or her own interests to the task of serving others, the accountant fulfills a moral obligation that is critical for business and society. In the ethical performance of accounting tasks, the accountant and auditor will likely earn the trust and respect of those who depend on this crucial service.

ACCOUNTING THEORY AND ETHICS

A few scholars research the history of accounting, the origins and development of its distinctive vocabulary, key concepts, principles and rules. They describe accountants' historical and current methods of recording and reviewing financial information. They analyze the functions of accounting institutions – audit firms, professional societies and regulatory agencies. These scholars examine the role of accounting in capital markets, manufacturing and trade.

As part of their description and analysis of the place of accounting in modern business and society, the scholars evaluate accounting. In effect, they criticize the ideals of the practice – the goals and purposes of the accounting enterprise – and they assess the rules and decision-making procedures that shape everyday accounting actions, for better or worse. Most significantly, these researchers and critics offer prescriptions for accountants and their activity; that is, they advocate specific ideals which accountants should institutionalize, "best practices" that ought to shape accountants' decisions. They often suggest agendas of reform to address the complexity of the marketplace and remedy accounting failures. The systematic presentation of such issues by accounting scholars forms a special subfield of research called accounting theory.

Accounting theory is the systematic, logical analysis of the history and current practice of accounting. It describes the purposes, ideals, and principles of accounting, as well as the actual practice of accountants. Accounting theory discusses how the rules and prescribed decision procedures of accounting apply to particular business circumstances; theorists examine specific accounting practices to determine whether or not they reflect principles, rules, and prescribed procedures. Accounting theory elaborates on the institutions that set accounting standards and regulate, monitor, and support accountants in their work. The field of study describes the role played by accounting in business and society and assesses the effectiveness of current practice. Following contemporary research, theorists discuss alternatives to current practice, addressing the limitations and problems of accounting in the contemporary business environment. They offer explanations of how accounting information is used by various stakeholders. Accounting theory not only describes, but it also criticizes, evaluates and prescribes changes for the field of accounting. This means that theorists are not content only to describe aspects of current practice, but they also suggest what ought to happen; they advocate reform and suggest possible changes in practice.

ACCOUNTING THEORY

Accounting theory is the systematic, logical description of the origins, development, and current status of accounting in business and society. It considers the purposes of accounting, its vocabulary and key concepts, accounting standards and decision procedures. Theorists analyze the interests of various stakeholders, in seeking and using accounting information. Accounting theory studies accounting institutions and regulatory agencies and analyzes the role of accounting in business and society. Theorists examine current accounting practices, identifying problems and reviewing disagreements over financial reporting (and auditing) methods. As they review research literature, theorists sometimes advocate reforms in accounting practice and prescribe specific changes in accounting standards and financial reporting procedures.

The authors' participation in the debate about accounting ethics reflects their understanding of the nature of accounting as a modern business enterprise. Their concerns about ethics in accounting education are based on the crucial role that accounting plays in the modern marketplace. In effect, this perspective represents a key aspect of the authors' accounting theory. In making the argument that ethics is important in accounting, the authors think it essential to examine the ideals of accounting and to consider accountants' actual practice, their behavior in relation to accounting standards – the principles, rules, and decision procedures that are supposed to guide accountants in the performance of their duties.

Here we do not offer a lengthy account of theoretical matters, but we do want to examine the ideals of accounting and elaborate on specific accounting practices as a necessary introduction for describing the ethical responsibilities of the accountant. In this context, we maintain that the basic purpose of accounting prescribes a dual competency for the accountant. Every accountant should first possess the knowledge of accounting standards and the skills to apply these standards in decision making. They should also be competent to recognize moral issues and resolve dilemmas they will be encounter in business circumstances. In short: our accounting theory prescribes the accountant's dual competency as technical proficiency (in "following the rules") and as ethical sensibility that supports ethical judgment and motivates ethical behavior. This ethical sensibility includes an intellectual and emotional disposition that commits the accountant to behave ethically in the performance of accounting tasks.

What follows, then, is our own modest version of "accounting theory". We describe the place of accounting in business and society, its principal goals and purposes, and the relationship of its ideals and prescriptions for best practice. When this task is completed, we will sketch out our understanding of the professional responsibilities of accountants in terms of their dual responsibility of acting on the basis of the technical standards of their profession and fulfilling their ethical duties in decision making and action (i.e., demonstrating technical proficiency and ethical sensibility).

ACCOUNTING DISCOURSE: KNOWLEDGE PRODUCTION AND COMMUNICATION

As we have seen: accounting has technical and ethical dimensions. Accounting is a technical enterprise bound to accounting standards. These principles, rules, and prescribed decision procedures set the patterns for appropriate accounting practice. Company accountants should record financial information according to contemporary technical standards. Auditors review these specialized financial statements and seek evidence to verify their accuracy. Auditors determine whether or not companies have prepared financial statements that comply with accounting standards, even as the auditors themselves are expected to follow the laws, regulations, and professional codes that govern auditing as a special field of accounting.

In addition to its technical demands, ethical decision making is crucial to accounting. This expectation of ethical sensibility is set by law, accounting regulations, and professional codes. The accounting standards not only establish the technical guidelines for accounting but also provide the basis for ethical decision making. Because accounting is both a technical and an ethical enterprise, individual accountants must exercise a dual competency in their accounting tasks. As we stated earlier: they must demonstrate both technical proficiency and ethical sensibility as they produce and transmit accounting texts.

This book calls for balancing the extensive practical attention now given to technical proficiency in accounting with thoughtful treatment of the ethical sensibility needed in the normal course of accounting duties. In this context, we believe that recent studies of accounting have often missed the mark. Scholars have not adequately analyzed the role of accounting in society or described the responsibilities of the accountant. They have also neglected ethical concerns. Despite the widespread public debate about accounting ethics in the wake of business scandals, ethics research has not yet become a high priority for scholars. Even today ethics education plays but a minor role in business school and accounting curricula: technical training prevails.

By contrast with the prevailing scholarship, the authors believe that professional conversation about accounting and research and their role in business and society should highlight ethics as a key aspect of accounting's social responsibility. What is more, ethics training should play a more central role in accounting education. This agenda emerges from our accounting theory, an understanding which emphasizes the ethical dimensions of professional ideals and best practices. This ethics-oriented conversation and an expansion of practical ethics training is likely to lead to a richer, more realistic understanding of accounting's role in business and society; that is, a richer and more realistic assessment of accounting than can be expressed when concern for ethical sensibility is neglected.

Our understanding of the ethical dimensions of accounting motivates this book project in ethics education. As a primary objective, we seek the development of technically skillful and virtuous accountants who are able to demonstrate technical expertise and moral insight in the contemporary business environment. Our educational agenda for the classroom presupposes that the enterprise of accounting is already embedded with an ethical dimension which is presupposed by accounting standards and regulatory institutions. Indeed, along with the technical demands, the ethical obligations at the center of accounting ought to drive the decision making of individual accountants.

To summarize: the authors of this book call attention to the fact that ethical concerns are not yet a high enough priority for academic research or accounting education. Even with the recent, widespread debate about accounting ethics, the curriculum expansion of ethics training in business education, and public concerns about ethics in the wake of accounting scandals, there is still significant need for more emphasis on the ethical dimensions of accounting practice. To overcome this deficiency in research and education, we advocate building upon technical knowledge and supplementing technical training with ethics education. For even as there are critical demands for technical skill – for accountants to follow technical principles, rules, and procedures – so also are there ethical responsibilities in the day-to-day practice of accounting. This point will be developed throughout the following section as we treat accounting as discourse and as practice.

Let us now consider accounting as a type of discourse. Accounting is one of the languages of the business world (Morgan, 1988). Through concepts, narratives, and, most commonly, numbers, accountants represent business realities by producing knowledge and communicating it to others. In producing and transmitting business knowledge accounting can be understood as a community-oriented discourse. Engaging in this discourse, accountants produce knowledge and communicate it so it can be received by stakeholders. The stakeholders can then use the knowledge to make business decisions; in effect, they can decide to alter human experience and transform society according to their own goals and purposes. Accountants play a distinctive role in producing specialized forms of knowledge about business entities from financial data; auditors review these statements and gather evidence to affirm the reliability of statements' by publishing their own special texts, called audit opinions, for stakeholders. In this discourse, accountants and auditors create specialized texts that communicate accounting knowledge in accessible modes for stakeholders' analysis and use. Accountants and auditors through their specialized discourse serve the public interest and the interests of business stakeholders, including companies, current and prospective investors, lenders, and creditors.

This book assumes that accounting is a specialized discourse crucial for modern business and society (Arnold & Oakes, 1998; Llewellyn & Milne, 2007). In their discourse, accountants create knowledge and communicate it through distinctive forms to stakeholders – company managers, investors and creditors, government regulators. The book emphasizes that accounting follows a standards-based framework for the construction of knowledge, with particular technical and moral claims on accountants who are responsible for providing usable, unbiased information to various stakeholders (Morgan, 1988). In other words, accounting discourse in its content and specialized formats communicating knowledge should follow sound technical procedures as established by accounting standards. In addition, the (accountant) creators of such knowledge will find themselves bound to an explicitly ethical outlook that is mandated by those same accounting standards. The book will illustrate how the accounting standards and institutions support technical and ethical decision making as accountants demonstrate their dual competency.

DISCOURSE

Discourse is the language used by members of a specific intellectual discipline, field of inquiry or practice. It includes the development of a special language – vocabulary, concepts, numbers, and measurements – used by members of a discipline or practice to produce knowledge and communicate this knowledge to those who will use it. In accounting, the discourse includes the specialized written texts of financial statements, reports, and audit opinions that communicate accounting knowledge of business entities to interested users (stakeholders).

Both accountants and auditors participate in accounting discourse. As decision-making agents within business entities, company accountants construct specialized texts – financial statements (income statements, balance sheets, and statements of cash flow) – while other accountants, namely, auditors, review these specialized accounting texts (analyze and critique these forms of knowledge). These auditors gather evidence and record their findings in the special language of work papers. The auditors then issue audit opinions that are, in effect, an evaluation of the discourse of the company accountants and its management. Such knowledge production and its review, with the communication to stakeholders, are governed by accounting and auditing standards (the principles and rules of a distinctive practice). The discourse is subject to legislation, the regulation of professional associations, and the oversight of government agencies.

A generation of critical and mainstream scholars has characterized accounting as a creative discursive practice, a cooperative enterprise wherein accountants process financial information to produce knowledge (Francis, 1990; Hines, 1988). Accountants are responsible for creating intelligible forms to represent business realities – transactions and the financial status of companies. Accountants order information into clear, meaningful patterns expressed in written texts so that this communication of business knowledge can become useful for decision making (Arrington, 2007; Llewellyn & Milne, 2007). Using specialized forms – that is, financial statements, quarterly and annual reports, and audit opinions – accountants examine and classify financial data in the process of creating explicit knowledge about the tangible and intangible assets of business entities. Viewed as a complex process oriented to modern industrial society, accounting discourse takes place within a social and institutional context that encompasses business entities, government institutions, professional societies, and voluntary associations (Burchell *et al.*, 1980). The agents of this discourse – accountants as creators of financial statements and stakeholders as recipients of the mediated accounting texts – can be described as the "producers" and the "consumers" of accounting knowledge. This discursive interaction is community-oriented, as the accountant "knowledge-producers" and the stakeholder "knowledge-consumers" make decisions that will not only change the behavior of individuals but will also influence groups and institutions throughout society (Arrington & Francis, 1993).

Accountants gather information about the financial status of an entity (company, government agency or social organization). Ordering and classifying data into useful knowledge, they determine how best to represent the structures and the activities (the assets and transactions) of the entity they address. To guide accountants in this process, regulatory institutions create standards – principles and rules – to establish appropriate patterns for the specialized texts – financial statements and accounting reports. These institutions also set the standards for the auditors of this discourse, the texts that are to represent the financial reality of the companies under consideration. In brief, these accounting principles and rules provide the technical and ethical framework for proper accounting decision making to produce and transmit financial information.

ACCOUNTING AS PRACTICE: THE REALIZATION OF INTERNAL GOODS AND VIRTUES

Alasdair MacIntyre, an American student of virtue ethics, provides us with a good way to deepen our reflection about accounting as the discourse of a community of specialized craftsmen (accountants) and their interested audience (stakeholders of various kinds). In a widely cited section of *After Virtue* (1984), he elaborates the nature of a practice:

> By a "practice" I . . . mean any coherent and complex form of socially established cooperative human activity through which goods integral to that form of activity are realized in the course of trying to achieve those standards of excellence which are appropriate to and partially definitive of, that form of activity, with the result that human powers to achieve excellence, and human conceptions of the ends and goods involved, are systematically extended. (MacIntyre, 1984, p. 187)

For MacIntyre, a practice is a socially constructed, cooperative enterprise in which people realize intellectual and moral virtues. Individuals within a practice express particular predispositions of character and attitude – distinctive character traits – as they act to fulfill the goals of the practice. As an arena of purposeful activity, a practice supports the intellectual and moral capabilities of practitioners, their capacities to think, evaluate, act, and accomplish the particular purposes of their common endeavor.

A practice, created to fulfill particular social purposes, reveals itself through the actions of its participants in the realization of their intellectual and moral capacities in the particular "internal goods" which they create. Internal goods are the things produced that contribute to the ultimate realization of the community goals, created in order to fulfill the goals of the practice. The members of a practice associate themselves in a cooperative relationship as a contemporary generation of colleagues. These practitioners find themselves linked together by common purposes, by standards of thought and conduct and by supportive institutions. Members of a practice are also linked in historical association with the previous generations of practitioners, earlier members of the enterprise who worked for its common purposes. The members demonstrate their personal virtues through their activity of producing the internal goods of their practice and achieving the purpose of their group. In this manner, the practice as a communal enterprise extends itself through time and establishes itself in a particular society. The practice creates and sustains its own history. Within a practice, there develops a living tradition, consisting of authoritative standards, shared beliefs, and significant institutions that extend from one generation of practitioners to the next.

PRACTICE

A practice is a cooperative enterprise with distinct goals and purposes. Members follow a practice as they use their intellectual (and moral) skills to pursue its goals. They use their intellectual judgment and exercise their moral sensibility to seek excellence, high-quality achievement, in the various tasks that are vital to fulfillment of the practice's goals. Football, for example, is a practice. Players on a team develop their physical and mental abilities through training to play well in games and gain victories in competition. Team members learn to trust each other, cooperate, and become proficient in the skills of kicking and passing and positioning themselves to play defense and offense. To play well and to win, the teammates master the different aspects of the sport, playing by its formal (and informal) rules. To succeed, players persevere in the heat of competition, blend their individual abilities into a team effort, and – as they collectively demonstrate excellence in the various parts of the game – show appreciation for the beauty and complexity of the game; in effect, they play well (show their "virtues" as footballers) and likely gain victories.

To adopt MacIntyre's insight: accounting is a discursive practice. In this practice, the accountants' specialized texts realize or illustrate what MacIntyre calls "the twofold excellences" (the intellectual and moral virtues) of accounting practice. For our purposes, the "internal goods" of accounting can be understood as the decisions made and the specialized texts created by the competent accountant in producing and diffusing accounting knowledge. The accountant uses technical skills and ethical sensibility – expressed in his or her judgment – to classify financial transactions and record them according to accounting standards. This is the proper activity of the accountant.

The items written into the balance sheet or income statement by the accountant constitute the products of the discourse created by the accountant to communicate useful knowledge to stakeholders. Guided by accounting standards deemed authoritative, the dutiful accountant has processed financial information and expressed it in the special, systematic forms of the financial statements, thus rendering it as appropriate accounting knowledge. In this process, each part of the financial statement is integral to the overall purpose of the accountant to provide useful knowledge to facilitate stakeholders' decision making. In MacIntyre's language: as accountants perform their distinctive tasks related to the preparation of financial statements, they manifest intellectual and moral virtues by creating the internal goods of accounting practice (the specialized texts), and thus they engage in the practice of accounting discourse. By thus doing their job, accountants faithfully pursue the goals of accounting practice.

Each of the accounting standards established by law, regulation, and professional code, as well as the institutions that monitor accounting discourse and the decision processes through which the accountant's intellectual and moral virtues are embodied in financial statements, is significant for our description of accounting as a discursive practice. In accounting practice, technical proficiency and ethical sensibility are expressed through the accountant's judgment, and this results in the written accounting texts. The exercise of judgment and the creation of properly written texts (the production of the internal goods of accounting, to use MacIntyre's terms) are required by accounting standards and the institutions that monitor accounting practice. In this way, the standards and institutions hold the accountant responsible for technical and ethical decision making. In MacIntyre's language, the intellectual and moral virtues of the accountant are realized as "internal goods" of accounting practice, with institutional standards supporting their expression in financial statements and audit opinions. As internal goods these judgments and the resultant accounting texts represent crucial stages in the discursive practice. In the proper production of the specialized texts of accounting and auditing, the ethical expectations and purposes of the practice itself are achieved. We elaborate on this below.

Because of the great potential of accounting knowledge to influence business decision making – with its capacity to shape society and create opportunities for human development – accountants cannot "do as they please" when representing companies' activities and status to stakeholders (Schweiker, 1993; Arrington & Francis, 1993). Accounting practice and discourse must conform to the spirit and the letter of accounting standards. In other words, there are "prescriptions" for what is to be represented and how; there are rules to obey and "codes" to follow (Llewellyn & Milne, 2007). In addition, institutions have been created to regulate accountants' discursive activity. When accountants join their practice, they bind themselves to these accounting standards (principles, rules, codes, exemplary models) and to various mechanisms of legislative, governmental, and professional regulation.

Accountants' judgments and actions are answerable to these institutions that constrain their knowledge production and its diffusion. Institutions – by their standard-setting and the monitoring of accountants' texts – support accounting discourse and shape its practice. Accounting standards and institutions set the appropriate forms of textual expression for accountants' communication. In essence, accounting standards are the authoritative principles and rules that guide accounting discourse in its communication about financial transactions. In brief: accounting standards mark the technical limits and the ethical expectations of accounting practice. The standards set the ethical restraints and moral patterns for proper discourse, so that accountants may fulfill their responsibilities to stakeholders – be they management, investors, creditors, or the general public. In following the standards, making technical and ethical judgments, and creating financial statements, accountants achieve the goals of their practice.

CHAPTER REVIEW QUESTIONS

1. (LO1) Briefly explain how and why ethics has come on the agenda in accounting.

2. (LO2) Describe some key issues related to the integration of ethics in accounting curricula, and why these are important for how and why ethics should be taught to accountants.

3. (LO3) The chapter states that accountants need a dual competency – technical proficiency and ethical sensibility. Write a couple of paragraphs to explain what this means.

4. (LO3) The chapter claims that accounting has both a technical orientation and an ethics-oriented practice. Write a couple of paragraphs to explain what this means.

5. (LO6) Accounting is a discourse that communicates financial information to stakeholders and speaks of the financial status of business entities. Why is ethics important for this discourse?

6. (LO1) Accounting has standards – principles, rules, and standardized decision procedures – for making financial reporting decisions. Why are ethics important for its practice? (Aren't accounting standards adequate, in and of themselves?)

7. (LO3) What benefits to business and society are gained when accountants act ethically and are technically competent? Who benefits? Is anyone harmed? Explain your answer.

8. (LO3) The chapter suggests that the twofold competency of the accountant (technical proficiency and ethical sensibility) implies that there are four types of accountants. Briefly account for each type and explain how these four are different from each other.

9. (LO3) Consider the four types of accountants, the destructive accountant, the good-hearted accountant, the opportunistic accountant, and the virtuous accountant. Explain which accountant made the following decisions and describe how these accountants might become a virtuous accountant if they are not.

   a. Cedric is an auditor for Stuart LLP working on the audit of Pedersen Enterprises. He knows that Pedersen Enterprises needs a bank loan to continue in operations the following year. Pedersen Enterprises is a small landscape company and he knows how hard the employees have worked to build the business. If they do not get a loan, they will have to close. This means that he will lose an audit client. Cedric decides to allow the company to recognize revenue early for contracts that will be done after year-end, so the company appears to be more profitable. The early recognition of revenue should allow Pedersen Enterprises to receive the loan they need to stay in business.

b. Dominyka is an accountant for Scott Company. She receives stock options from the company as part of her salary. She benefits from the stock options when the stock price increases, because she can then sell the options for more than they cost at the grant date. She knows that the company should include an estimate of bad debt expense on the financial statements, but, if they do so, net income will decline, and the price of company stock is likely to fall. If this happens her stock options are worthless. She decides to prepare the financial statements without the reduction for bad debt expense, to report net income higher than the previous year. This should increase the stock price and then she can exercise her options.

c. Fumika is an accountant for BCS Inc. She is one of the executives who receives a bonus if net income increases by 6%. She does not understand the accounting rules for recognizing revenue related to leased office space, but she believes that all revenue recognized during the life of the lease should be recognized in the current year, even though the length of each lease is five years. She knows the accounting rules permit the company to recognize revenue when the service is provided and her company allowed the clients leasing the office space to begin using it immediately.

10. (LO3) Consider the four types of accountants, the destructive accountant, the good-hearted accountant, the opportunistic accountant, and the virtuous accountant. Describe what is missing from each accountant's experience. How can you transform the destructive accountant, the good-hearted accountant, and the opportunistic accountant into a virtuous accountant?

11. (LO4) Explain why accounting is so important to societies and why there is a need to make sure that accountants "play by the rules".

REFERENCES

Armstrong, M.B., Ketz, J.E. & Owsen, D. (2003) Ethics education in accounting: Moving toward motivation and ethical behavior. *Journal of Accounting Education*, 21(1): 1–16.

Arnold, P. and Oakes, L. (1998) Accounting as discursive construction: The Relationship between Statement of Financial Accounting Standards No. 106 and the dismantling of retiree health benefits. *Accounting, Organizations and Society*, 23(2): 129–153.

Arrington, C. (2007) A prolegomenon to the relation between accounting, language, and ethics. *Australasian Accounting Business and Finance Journal*, 1(2): 1–12.

Arrington, C. and Francis, J. (1993) Accounting as a human practice: The appeal of other voices. *Accounting, Organizations and Society*, 18(2–3): 105–106.

Burchell, S., Clubb, C., Hopwood, A., Hughes, J. & Nahapiet, J. (1980) The roles of accounting in organizations and society. *Accounting, Organizations and Society*, 5(1): 5–27.

Cheffers, M. & Pakaluk, M. (2005) *A New Approach to Understanding Accounting Ethics: Principles, Professionalism, Pride*. Manchaug, MA: Allen David Press.

Dolfsma, W. (2006) Accounting as applied ethics: Teaching a discipline. *Journal of Business Ethics*, 63(3): 209–215.

Francis, J. (1990) After virtue? Accounting as a moral and discursive practice. *Accounting, Auditing, and Accountability* 3(3): 5–17.

Hines, R. (1988) Financial accounting: In communicating reality, we construct reality. *Accounting, Organizations and Society*, 13(3): 251–261.

Jennings, M. (2004) Incorporating ethical and professionalism into accounting ethics and research. *Issues in Accounting Education*, 19(1): 7–26.

Levy, D. & Mitschow, M. (2008) Accounting ethics education: Where do we go from here? *Research on Professional Responsibility and Ethics in Accounting*, 13: 135–154.

Llewellyn, S. & Milne, M. (2007) Accounting as codified discourse. *Accounting, Auditing and Accountability Journal*, 20(6): 805–824.

Loeb, S. (2006) Issues related to teaching accounting ethics: An 18 year retrospective. *Research on Professional Responsibility and Ethics in Accounting*, 11: 1–30.

Low, M., Davey, H. & Hooper, K. (2008) Accounting, scandals, ethical dilemmas and educational challenges. *Critical Perspectives on Accounting*, 19(2): 222–254.

MacIntyre, A. (1984) *After Virtue: A Study in Moral Themes*, 2nd edn. Notre Dame, IN: Notre Dame University Press.

Mintz, S. (1995) Virtue ethics and accounting education. *Issues in Accounting Education*, 10(2): 247–267.

Mintz, S. (2006) Accounting ethics education: Integrating reflective learning and virtue ethics. *Journal of Accounting Education*, 24(2/3): 97–117.

Morgan, G. (1988) Accounting as reality construction: Towards a new epistemology for accounting practice. *Accounting, Organizations and Society*, 13(5): 477–485.

Rest, J.R. (1994) Background: Theory and research. In Rest, J.R. & Narvaéz, D.F. (eds) *Moral Development in the Professions: Psychology and Applied Ethics*. Hillsdale, NJ: Lawrence Erlbaum Associates, pp. 1–26.

Schweiker, W. (1993) Accounting for ourselves: Accounting practice and the discourse of ethics. *Accounting, Organizations and Society*, 18(2–3): 231–252.

Stuart, B., Stuart, I. & Pedersen, L.J.T. (2011) Accounting discourse: Technical proficiency and ethical sensibility. Unpublished manuscript. Bergen: Norwegian School of Economics, NHH.

Williams, P.F. (2010) The focus of professional ethics: Ethical professionals or ethical profession? *Research on Professional Responsibility and Ethics in Accounting*, 14: 15–35.

CHAPTER TWO

Decision Making in Accounting

LEARNING OBJECTIVES

By the end of this chapter you should be able to:

1. Understand the general features of decision making.
2. Explain the basic purpose of accounting: the preparation of financial statements.
3. Describe the technical requirements to present high-quality information in financial statements. Understand the fundamental qualitative characteristics of financial statements: relevance and fair representation and the enhancing qualitative characteristics: comparability, verifiability, timeliness, and understandability.
4. Understand that the accounting standards support the technical competency of the accountant.
5. Understand a "working definition" of ethics/morality as reasoned reflection on "how one ought to live," judging right from wrong behavior, choosing good over bad (evil), and seeking the well-being of other people instead of harming them.
6. Describe several traditions of ethical reasoning within moral philosophy.
7. Understand accounting ethics in terms of an ethics of duty and an ethics of virtue.
8. Understand a decision model for accounting ethics.
9. Describe key problem-solving resources for accounting ethics.
10. Explain who the stakeholders of a decision are; explain what a conflict of interest is.
11. Understand sources of pressure in the decision environment.

ACCOUNTING AS DISCOURSE AND PRACTICE, COMPETENCY, DUTY, AND VIRTUE

Reminder: Accounting is a discursive practice; accountants produce business knowledge and communicate it to stakeholders, who use this knowledge to make business-related decisions.

Reminder: Accountants should exercise a dual competency: technical proficiency – knowledge of accounting standards and capacity to apply them in practice – and ethical sensibility – capacity to recognize moral issues, resolve ethical dilemmas, and demonstrate the motivation and commitment to do the right thing; that is, act ethically.

THE GENERAL NATURE OF DECISIONS AND DECISION MAKING IN ACCOUNTING

Because you have already taken a number of accounting courses and may have work experience as accountants (and have read Chapter One!), these "reminders" of the authors' accounting theory and their basic approach to accounting ethics should be familiar to you. This chapter will build on what you have already learned and on your experience as accounting students. It will confirm what you already know about accounting: accounting is about making decisions; decision making is the central task of being an accountant.

This chapter focuses on making accounting decisions and will address a variety of topics important for understanding how accountants make decisions. The chapter opens with a few ideas on the topic of decision making, sketching a brief "decision-making case" and commenting on the general features of decision making. It assumes that accounting decisions should be made in relation to the general purpose(s) of accounting practice. We first give special attention to the technical expectations for the primary accounting discourse, looking at how accounting standards shape the preparation of financial statements. In our view, particular accounting decisions are efforts to apply contemporary accounting standards to the challenge of communicating knowledge about the financial activities and financial status of business entities. This knowledge is conveyed to stakeholders who are affected by the activities of those businesses (and to those who may chose to influence the financial affairs of the company by their investment or credit decisions). Along with the duty to apply accounting principles and rules while making decisions comes the accountant's responsibility to address moral issues that arise in accounting situations and to take ethical actions. At the core of the accountant's decision making is the dual obligation to be technically proficient and ethically sensible.

Viewing this dual responsibility of technical proficiency and ethical sensibility at the center of accounting practice, the chapter introduces features of decision making with a focus on morality and ethics. Its discussion illustrates how the accountant's decision making expresses ethical sensibility. The authors assume that accountants express their ethical sensibility whenever accounting situations are addressed and that accounting knowledge must be communicated in accordance with accounting standards. This part of the chapter treats historical and contemporary discussion in moral philosophy in order to introduce a "working vocabulary" of ethics. We then argue that ethics decision making is one of the principal duties of the practicing accountant.

The authors will briefly describe several traditions of moral philosophy and suggest how aspects of these approaches to ethics decision making can be significant resources for accounting practice: moral philosophy conversations can support accountants in their exercise of ethical competency. The chapter discussion expresses the authors' view that accounting discourse and practice calls for an applied ethics within the domain of contemporary business. By this we mean that the production and communication of accounting knowledge is how accountants show their moral virtues and demonstrate the ethical quality of their decisions. To elaborate: through their applied ethics, accountants exercise their *duty* of adhering to accounting standards and their *virtues*; that is, they exhibit their intellectual skills and their traits of moral character.

As they engage in the distinctive tasks of accounting practice, accountants are "to do ethics"; that is, they are to express their ethical sensibility. Whenever accountants review business transactions, prepare financial statements, and communicate knowledge about the financial status of business entities, they engage in continuous decision making. As these decisions conform to accounting standards, they express the values, principles, and patterns of judgment that are key elements in accounting ethics, a specialized form of applied ethics that is intended to be suitable for "the real world" of contemporary business and society.

MAKING A DECISION UNDER CONDITIONS OF UNCERTAINTY

Imagine that you rent a small, fourth-floor apartment and ride an old bus a long distance to work each day. Your upstairs neighbors stay up late and are noisy; the apartment is poorly-lit and the laundry room is at the far end of the building, in the basement. The bus is hot in the summer and has no heater for the winter months. You have just received a sizable inheritance and are looking for more comfort and convenience in your daily living. You wonder: should I buy a car or maybe buy a new apartment? *You have a decision to make.*

A goal or purpose: Decisions are conscious, voluntary and goal-oriented.

The inheritance money permits you to think about changing your daily life. You can now consider new possibilities and set a goal of more comfort and convenience. (No more long bus rides; no more noisy neighbors!)

Alternatives: Decisions involve options, with choices to make.

I could buy a car and not have to ride the bus to work. I might get a new apartment, big enough for a clothes washer and dryer.

Evaluations: The alternatives can be considered in terms of their worthiness for meeting a goal, fulfilling a purpose.

With a car, I can get to work more quickly (convenience); I can have an air conditioner and a heater (comfort). But I will have gasoline and insurance expenses and have to maintain the vehicle; I'll have to pay attention as I drive instead of sleeping on the bus (inconveniences). Are comfort and convenience more important for the working day or for when I am in my apartment?

Choices: Alternatives, once weighed, call for a decision to act.

If I cannot both buy a car and get a new apartment, I must choose between alternatives. Should I choose the option for more comfort or choose for convenience? Do I want to improve my life at home or should I decide for a better work-day?

Action: Decisions lead to actions being taken.

If a car, then go to the dealer and make the purchase. If an apartment, contact the realtor. (And now you face a new decision!)

This simple case illustrates the basic elements of a decision-making process as they apply to a situation that could occur in someone's "real life". The features of the case are realistic. The structure of the decision process is orderly, logical and should suggest widespread applicability; that is, fit a wide variety of circumstances. For our purposes, it focuses your attention and encourages you to think about the nature of decision making.

ELEMENTS OF A DECISION

1. The goal of the decision.
2. The alternatives; options to consider.
3. Evaluation of the options.
4. Choice of a particular option; the decision.
5. The action that is taken.

THE LEARNING OF TECHNICAL COMPETENCY IN THE CLASSROOM AND MENTORED WORK EXPERIENCE

As you know from earlier coursework, the student learns the basic purpose of accounting, its vocabulary, key concepts and patterns of decision making through reading, lecture-discussion, practice exercises and problem solving. You become acquainted with the task of producing financial statements to provide knowledge useful to stakeholders, so that they can make investment and credit-related decisions about the business whose reports are communicated to them. This creation of financial statements is governed by accounting standards – principles, rules, decision, and measurement procedures – put forth by standards-setting organizations, sometimes set into law, and monitored by regulatory organizations. These standards express both legal and professional expectations. In brief: as an accountant, you find yourself constrained by rules and regulations, with specific reporting duties to stakeholders and the general public. In the course of training, these technical obligations become key components of the knowledge base of the individual accountant. First-hand awareness of these technical expectations and practical skill in their application to particular accounting problems form the intellectual foundation for accounting practice.

To a great extent, your accounting courses and your on-the-job training concentrate on intellectual exercises and practical tasks designed to teach the basic vocabulary, concepts, and decision procedures of accounting. You have been introduced to the conceptual framework of accounting practice. Course readings, mentored dialogue and classroom conversation, and problem-solving exercises – these are all intended to provide you with the foundational skills of accounting decision making. These "lessons" communicate the values, norms, and attitudes that will distinguish you as an accountant. Through this learning, you will become an accounting specialist, trained to engage in accounting discourse and practice. You are taught that the primary work of financial accountants is to prepare financial statements so they can be useful for stakeholders. Your accounting education directs your attention to accounting standards and calls for your own commitment to comply with the values and norms of accounting practice. In decision-making language: the goal of accounting education is to prepare a person to make accounting decisions in accordance with accounting standards. You are to embrace the goals of accounting practice, become committed to accounting standards and their application, and also demonstrate technical proficiency and ethical sensibility as you practice.

THE GOAL OF ACCOUNTING: THE PRODUCTION OF FINANCIAL REPORTS FOR VARIOUS STAKEHOLDERS

To understand the importance of technical proficiency for the accountant, it is crucial to call attention to the basic purpose of accounting as that purpose is declared by the accounting standards. The foundation of the conceptual framework for financial reporting identifies "general purpose financial reporting" as the primary form of

THE BASIC PURPOSE OF FINANCIAL REPORTING

"The objective of general purpose financial reporting is to provide financial information about the reporting entity that is useful to existing and potential investors, lenders, and other creditors in making decisions about providing resources to the entity. Those decisions involve buying, selling, or holding equity and debt instruments and providing or settling loans and other forms of credit." (FASB: *Statement of Financial Accounting Concepts No. 8, Conceptual Framework for Financial Reporting*; IFRS: Chapter 1: *The Objective of General Purpose Financial Reporting, Conceptual Framework for Financial Reporting* – hereafter known as *The Conceptual Framework*.)

the accountant's discourse. The primary task of accounting is the production of general financial reports that communicate knowledge about the financial activities of a business entity and present a picture of the financial position of that enterprise. This communication is directed toward those who may use its business knowledge, toward the stakeholders who will make their own business-related decisions.

The international and the American standard-setting organizations that identify the main purpose of accounting assume that specific information about a business identity can be helpful to outsider stakeholders for assessing the company's past performance and current financial position. They further assume that this accounting knowledge can be useful for stakeholders' predicting "net future cash inflows" to the company. In particular, stakeholders seek to learn about the company's resources and the claims against the company. Stakeholders also want to acquire accounting knowledge about the changes in the company's cash flows in a given period. For stakeholders, it is reasonable to think that knowing this information will help them to understand the company's financial position and assess its past performance because these accounting evaluations of a company can be useful for predicting the company's future net cash inflow.

Because the reports and the picture of the company they represent are used by stakeholders to make their own business decisions regarding that company, accountants have responsibilities with regard to the form and the contents of these financial reports. Of crucial import, the skills and judgments of the accountant exercised in creating these reports, which are based on "estimates, judgments, and models rather than exact depictions" (*The Conceptual Framework*, Chapter 1, Section OB11), should be directed toward expressing "high-quality" information that fairly represents as knowledge the economic matters it purports to represent. The reports should publish specific information that depicts the financial position and the transactions of the business reported.

Let us briefly consider the technical requirements for the general financial reports produced by accountants and communicated to stakeholders. Standards-setting organizations set these technical requirements on how to present the financial position, financial performance and cash flows of the company reported in the financial reports. International standards set requirements for four general financial reports: The Statement of Financial Position, The Statement of Profit or Loss and other Comprehensive Income, The Statement of Changes in Equity, and The Statement of Cash Flows. (These statements correspond to the following US statements: the Statement of Financial Position, the Statement of Earnings and Comprehensive Income, the Statement of Investments by and Distribution to Owners, and the Statement of Cash Flows.) The standards include guidelines for the structure of the financial statements and minimum requirements for their content. Standards also establish the principles governing the quality of information published in the financial statements. Accountants are duty-bound to comply with these accounting standards.

While a more lengthy treatment of financial statements will follow in a later chapter, we make a few preliminary remarks concerning the functions of financial statements in communicating financial knowledge about companies. We take note of particular standards governing their creation. These remarks identify some of the company activities and economic phenomena that are reported – taking the four financial statements in their entirety. We also elaborate on the standards with regard to the quality of information that is presented in the statements.

Stakeholders make use of the information presented in the financial statements concerning the company's financial position, its financial performance, and its cash flows. Knowledge about the company's current position, past performance and estimates of future cash flows (in and out of the company) will help stakeholders predict the company's future performance and thus shape their investment and credit-related decisions regarding the company. Keeping in mind the stakeholders' use of financial statements, the standards employ a specialized vocabulary, with distinctive concepts and definitions. The standards put forth principles and rules that set the patterns for communicating financial knowledge. They prescribe how the elements of financial statements are to be presented, how the broad classes of financial and economic phenomena are to be identified, measured, and recognized in the special-ized texts we call financial statements.

The technical education you received in your previous coursework in the accounting curriculum has focused on teaching the specialized vocabulary, the key concepts and definitions, the means of appropriate measurement, and ways to categorize features of company position and performance so these can be recognized in the financial statements. These lessons supported the development of your technical competency for accounting practice and "pushed" you toward acknowledging the authority of the accounting standards over your own practice of accounting. Whether it is through reading, problem-solving exercises, or mentoring by teachers and peers, the practical dimension of this education consistently derived its lessons from the current standards of accounting practice. You have learned – through reading, reflection, practice, and feedback from others – how information is to be presented in the financial statements in accordance with accounting standards. You have learned how accounting knowledge is best produced and communicated to stakeholders. In effect, you have become acquainted with your personal duty to function within a standards-driven accounting practice.

Accordingly, the accounting "problems" you now face in preparing financial statements have primarily to do with making judgments about how the business activities of a given company and the economic phenomena that affect the company can be identified and appropriately fitted into the concepts, definitions, and measure-ment categories set by accounting standards. Accounting decisions to produce financial statements are made with "one eye" on the company's activities or on economic phenomena that may affect that company; with the "other eye" searching for the accounting standard appropriate for the item and circumstance.

Consider how accounting standards shape the preparation of financial statements. In the financial statements, the accountant presents information as broad classes of the financial effects of transactions and other events ("the elements of the statement"). In this presentation, the accountant follows the definitions of the elements as established by the accounting standards. The accountant reports them – recognizes them in the financial statements – according to criteria for their recognition set by the standards. The key elements of financial position, for example, are assets, liabilities and equity. For financial performance, the key elements are income (revenue and gain) and expenses (operating expenses and loss). The accountant makes decisions on whether and how to recognize (identify, describe, and measure) a particular item in the financial statement, by using the definitions of the financial statement elements to determine what type of transaction/event is being considered. The accountant then recognizes it in accordance with the standards. The accountant turns to the standards in order to answer many questions: Does this transaction count as having the effect of an expense? Does this property or piece of equipment get recognized as an asset or an expense? When should that revenue be recognized? Is that contract a lease?

The process of determining how to recognize a transaction/event is complicated by the fact that distinctions are made within the classes of financial statement elements, and decisions must be made regarding the distinct category to be assigned to a particular item. In addition, criteria for recognition may involve estimates and judgments that are not neatly prescribed by existing rules (and circumstances may suggest that differing overarching accounting principles may come into play), so a decision process is used to determine which accounting principle to follow.

The accounting standards govern the form of presentation for financial statements by setting the patterns for how transactions/events are to be identified as significant elements and recognized in the financial statements. In addition, the standards go beyond these basic concerns. The standards also set guidelines for the quality of the information. Financial statements with high-quality information are presumed to be more useful to stakeholders than statements with lower quality information, so accountants are expected to communicate high-quality information. The quality of information in a financial statement is determined with regard to its usefulness for stakeholders. With regard to quality, the standards mandate that the information presented in financial statements must be *relevant* and must *fairly represent* that which it purports to represent (in the US accounting standards, this concept is referred to as reliability). For information to be of high quality, to be useful to stakeholders, the presentation must both be relevant and fairly represent the financial position, performance, and cash flow of the business reported. The usefulness of financial information is also thought to be enhanced if it is comparable, verifiable, timely, and understandable.

RELEVANCE AND FAIR REPRESENTATION

"If financial information is to be useful, it must be relevant and faithfully represent what it purports to represent. The usefulness of financial information is enhanced if it is comparable, verifiable, timely, and understandable." (*The Conceptual Framework*, Chapter 3, QC4)

The qualitative characteristic of relevance has to do with whether the information is capable of making a difference in the users' decision making. Relevant information may be predictive, useful for projecting possibilities about future performance of the company, or confirmatory, useful in assessing previous evaluations of the financial information. Stakeholders make use of past performance and previous evaluations of financial information as they attempt to predict future performance. These assessments influence their decisions on whether to invest, or extend credit, or take other financial actions.

Fair representation of a financial or economic phenomenon has to do with whether the phenomenon is depicted in an accurate way, whether the representation depicts what the report says it depicts. Such representation includes a clear identification of the item and a complete representation, with no significant aspect omitted. The depiction should not be slanted toward a favorable or an unfavorable reception by stakeholders (the representation is neutral). The presentation should be free of errors. As a rule of thumb, the financial or economic phenomena represented in the financial statements should be presented as clearly and accurately as possible. Their description and the decision process that produces specific information about the items should be free from error.

The standards note that usefulness is also enhanced by several other qualitative characteristics: comparability, verifiability, timeliness, and understandability. Comparability refers to the identification of an aspect of business life and the making clear of its similarities with and differences from another phenomenon. Verifiability assures stakeholders that information faithfully represents what it purports to represent. A test of verifiability is whether "different knowledgeable and independent observers" can reach a consensus that the depiction is a faithful representation. Information that is available to influence the stakeholder's decision is timely information. By understandability, the standards mean information that can be understood by a person who has reasonable knowledge about business and economic matters and who reviews/analyzes information in a diligent way.

Because financial and economic phenomena are diverse and sometimes complicated to describe, the fundamental and enhancing qualitative characteristics are projected by the standards as goals for the accountant to achieve. Financial statement producers should maximize the quality of the information they produce. And this goal is achievable only if numerous decisions are made.

To produce high-quality financial statements presupposes numerous decisions – analyses of financial and economic phenomena, applications of appropriate standards to accounting problems, judgments regarding the identification, classification, and measurements of financial data, decisions on how to present information in the most clear and accurate ways. This brief introduction of the expectations of the accounting standards for the preparation of financial statements, standards about the form and contents of the primary discourse of accountants, and the goals for the clarity and accuracy of the knowledge communicated to stakeholders (information of high quality), frames the basic context for accountant decision making in its technical aspect.

EXAMPLES OF TECHNICAL DECISIONS AND ACCOUNTING STANDARDS

1. When and how is revenue recognized in the financial statement? Revenue is recognized when a service is provided or a product is shipped and the company expects to be paid. The amount of revenue recognized is equal to the amount of cash the company expects to receive.

2. What is the accounting standard for liabilities? Current liabilities are money owed as a result of purchasing goods or services. Current liabilities will be

paid within one year. They are recorded at the cash to be paid. Long-term liabilities are money owed as a result of borrowing cash or purchasing goods or services. Long-term liabilities will be paid in more than one year. They are recorded at the present value of the future cash flows.

3. How are leases recognized in the financial statements? Accounting standards require a company to distinguish between operating leases and capital (IFRS refer to them as finance) leases. Operating leases are recorded as expenses as the lease payments are made. The asset used by the company based on the lease agreement is not recorded on the books of that company. Capital (finance) leases are recorded as if the company had purchased the asset. The asset is recorded on the balance sheet under long-term assets, and the liability for the lease payments is recorded as a long-term liability on the balance sheet. A capital (finance) lease asset is depreciated over the life of the lease.

To summarize: the preceding section has identified the basic goal of accounting and focused on accounting standards for producing financial reports that represent the financial position, performance, and cash flows of the entity reported. We have seen that the forms of presentation and the specific contents of the financial statements are intended to help stakeholders find the statements useful for decision making. The definitions, concepts, and decision processes – including standards for measurements – that are set forth by the accounting standards constitute the knowledge base for a technically competent accountant. The accountant is duty-bound to present high-quality information to the stakeholder, useful because it is relevant and faithfully representative. Information that is comparable, verifiable, timely, and understandable enhances its usefulness to stakeholders.

Up to this point we have spoken of the accountant's responsibility to make technical decisions by following the rules set forth in the accounting standards. Facing accounting decisions on how to recognize transactions and economic phenomena in the financial statements, the technically competent accountant chooses to follow the appropriate accounting standard – considers alternatives, chooses, and then acts to communicate high-quality information to stakeholders. We now shift gears to the second aspect of the accountant's competency: the capacities we call "ethical sensibility".

Just as accountants have numerous technical responsibilities established by accounting standards; they also have an ethical obligation to identify and deal with moral issues that arise in the course of their practice. These obligations, like the technical expectations, arise when accountants provide service to stakeholders, including the general public. And as we shall see, these ethical expectations are also set forth in the accounting standards, most notably in the professional codes of conduct as the principles of accounting and the accountant's virtues (or qualities of character) that equip him or her to meet the responsibilities of practice, the duties of accountancy.

These ethical duties are particularly important because of the complexity of modern business organizations and transactions. The competitive pressures, and the uncertainties of the global marketplace, and the drive for profit and high stock prices tempt management to hide, even distort, financial information from other stake-holders. Accounting decisions have the potential either to benefit or to harm stake-holders, whether these are "outsiders" or "insiders" of the company whose financial information is reported. While even clear disclosure and high-quality information may harm some stakeholders, deliberate harm to stakeholders may result from the manipulation and distortion of financial statements, from the unethical actions of management and the willingness of unethical accountants to deceive stakeholders. To limit the possibility of such harm, the conceptual framework of financial accounting and the particular principles and rules set forth in the accounting standards call for the accountant's integrity, diligence, and fair-mindedness in the preparation of financial statements, their review, and their communication to others.

In effect, the standards call for a technically competent accountant and an ethical practice of accounting. Indeed, as accounting scholars Thomas and Mary Doucet have argued, the standards-setting organizations have created US and international codes of conduct for accountants. These codes not only set forth rules, regulations, and decision procedures, but they also present the fundamental purposes of accounting. They mandate general principles for accounting practice. They call for the development and exercise of intellectual and moral virtues on the part of the individual accountant. The decision making necessary to produce financial statements of high quality – to meet the basic goal of providing useful accounting knowledge to stakeholders – demands technical competence, to be sure. But such decisions must also be ethical in nature. In other words, for the creation of financial statements, the technically competent accountant must also be the virtuous accountant. The Doucets describe these ethical responsibilities and personal abilities of the accountant as the accountant's "ethics of duty" and the "ethics of virtue" (Doucet & Doucet, 2004).

A WORKING DEFINITION OF ETHICS

In Chapter One, we spoke of moral philosophy or philosophical ethics as a potential resource for accounting ethics. We defined ethics as "the inquiry into human action . . . " that offers rational arguments on "how people ought to live their lives – behave in specific circumstances and conduct themselves over a long term." This ethical reasoning focuses on questions of right and wrong, examines the principles and rules that govern behavior, and considers the consequences of human action. In the following section, we will continue to describe key aspects of ethics and offer a working definition of ethics. We emphasize that knowledge of moral philosophy perspectives should support your own accounting decision making and help you to address the moral issues and dilemmas you'll face in accounting practice.

As you will quickly discover, there is a wide variety of approaches to ethical reasoning in the history of philosophy. Because of this, it is actually quite difficult (if not impossible) to offer a "definition" of ethics that will escape criticism and controversy. For our immediate needs, however, this book puts forth a "working definition" to establish a common vocabulary for our conversation about ethical decisions and "virtuous action" in practice. We will then discuss features of ethical thinking that fit into our special treatment of accounting ethics.

First, we emphasize that our treatment of accounting ethics is part of a long history in Western thought, an aspect of "good conversation" about "the life well-lived (or lived well)." In language this book has already used: ethics is a *discourse* oriented to real world *practice*. Men and women have long considered the questions: what kind of person do I want to be and what ought I to do in the situation I now face? how shall I conduct myself in the long run, over a long period of time? Most often, thought about ethics is for the sake of shaping actions, influencing behavior. As the ancient Greek philosopher Aristotle stated in *Nicomachean Ethics*, a person's ethics conversation is "for the sake of practical wisdom and deliberation on conduct in the concrete circumstance in which he lives." Continuing in the spirit of Aristotle (1985), we also want to emphasize that our treatment of ethics has the goal of supporting ethical actions; it is not merely an exercise in abstract "thinking about ethics" without putting thought into action.

Secondly, this text uses the terms, morality and ethics, interchangeably (Some thinkers distinguish the two concepts, giving them contrasting meanings). For us, morality/ethics is reasoned reflection on how one ought to live life well – the task of judging right from wrong, choosing good over evil, deciding to do good for others rather than doing them harm.

Ethics is the use of logic and reason to distinguish right from wrong and to choose to do good rather than bad (or evil). Ethics involves decision making and the use of judgment to determine what is good in a situation. At its best, ethics discussion should support a commitment to do "good things" rather than "bad things". Ethics seeks the well-being ("the flourishing") of the self and, most importantly, the welfare of others, asking: "How might I seek their good and avoid doing them harm?" Ethics as reasoned inquiry examines the principles and rules that shape behavior: "What makes for good behavior and how can we behave well?"

Finally, because there is so much variety in how philosophers and other social thinkers understand the main issues in ethics and the reasons they give for acting ethically, we want to show you important examples of how ethics reasoning has been done. These examples demonstrate that the accountant's ethics reasoning does not "start from scratch" and that there is no reason "to reinvent the wheel" when it comes to conversations about right and wrong, good and bad behavior, doing good rather than harm. In other words: because some of the discussion within the history of moral philosophy can support ethics decision making in the special domain of accounting, this chapter will introduce several philosophical ethics traditions. A later chapter will expand on this treatment, to highlight philosophical discussions. We do this because these questions, concerns, and reasoning can provide "tools" to assist the accountant in his or her own ethics decision making.

JUDGMENT AND SOUND REASONING IN ETHICS

The contemporary philosophers, James and Stuart Rachels' claim: "Moral philosophy is the effort to understand the nature of morality and what it requires of us – in Socrates' words, to understand 'how we ought to live' and why." Their publications elaborate on Socrates' idea by examining how morality arises from judgment and arguing that ethics decisions are defended by using logic and reason, by giving good reasons for what one does. (Rachels & Rachels, 2009, p. 1)

The following section will introduce four traditions or approaches of moral philosophy and sketch out the main features of these "schools of thought" for ethical reasoning: utilitarianism, deontology, virtue ethics and social contract theory. Through this introduction, you'll become acquainted with key concepts and ways of posing ethics questions and will also gain insight into the various ways that ethics conversation has taken place in the past and continues in our own day. Hopefully, you will see how intellectual conversations within moral philosophy may serve as a "toolkit" for your own reasoning as accountants whenever you face moral issues and encounter dilemmas.

Before our discussion of the four traditions of moral philosophy, let us consider a few basic elements common to ethics reasoning within all the traditions. First, each tradition considers the human person as a *"moral agent,"* a human being who decides how to act within particular situations, as well as how to conduct himself or herself over a long period of time. Moral agents find themselves caught up in confusing *circumstances* and *situations* that are messy. These situations present uncertainties and call for decisions on how the person ought best to act in the given situation. In such situations, *moral issues* arise and the moral agent faces *dilemmas* (situations where deciding what to do is difficult because aspects of the circumstance make it difficult to tell whether a given action is right or wrong, good or evil, helpful to others or harmful). In a dilemma, confusion may be so great that finding good reasons to do one thing may conflict with other good reasons to do something else, and even "correct decisions" may lead to some negative consequences.

Moral agents, facing issues and dilemmas, have a number of *resources* for their ethics decision making. Some resources are aspects of their character: character traits – intellectual abilities and moral aptitudes, natural talents and learned skills, emotional and intuitive qualities. The moral agent possesses virtues gained through experience – formed through habit. Other resources are external to the person, aspects of the social and institutional environment in which the moral agent lives. These resources include *values* and life-models to be admired, social and institutional *norms* that establish standards for actions and long-term conduct, *institutional patterns* of decision making, systems of rewards and punishments. In effect, the moral agent can make use of many resources: social and institutional expectations, general principles to shape conduct and influence particular behaviors, specific rules and prescribed procedures for special circumstances, and various conventions (customary means) for sorting out acceptable courses of action.

A final basic element for ethics decision making: each tradition of moral philosophy calls for an account of the *consequences of the decision*, an evaluation of what happens after an action-choice, results that can be linked to the choices made and actions taken by the moral agent.

Each of the moral traditions gives attention to these foregoing elements. At the same time, each tradition approaches ethics decision making in its own distinctive fashion and weighs these elements according to its own intellectual priorities. What is more, within the scope of moral philosophy, numerous questions are raised and many different answers are given: Who is the relevant moral agent in a situation? Which features of a dilemma are crucial; which aspects are of lesser import? How much emphasis should be placed on the moral agent's personal traits, interests and motives; how much weight is to be given to social and institutional norms? Are decisions to be guided by principles that are external to the moral agent, determined by specific rules, constrained by threats of punishment or hopes of reward? And since predicting consequences is a tricky business and "things just seem to happen," how does one evaluate an action by a later happening? And who is to measure the responsibility of a moral agent after the fact of his or her decision?

Whew! Such an introduction of moral philosophy also expresses the authors' view that dealing with moral issues and resolving moral dilemmas are not likely to be easy tasks. Speaking about ethics decisions and giving good reasons for one's actions may not be easy either. At first glance, it may even seem to you that lessons learned about moral philosophy cannot possibly become useful resources for decision making in accounting! It is our task to convince you otherwise: moral philosophy can be an excellent resource for accounting decisions.

UTILITARIANISM

When a person faces a moral issue and attempts to resolve a dilemma, utilitarianism argues that the right answer is the one that promotes happiness for those affected by the decision. The moral agent considers alternate courses of actions, trying to decide which option will lead to benefits that will satisfy those involved in the issue. The moral agent evaluates alternatives by asking: which action-choice will have the result of causing happiness, which action will promote well-being and satisfaction? This goal for decision making is not to be pursued merely for the sake of one's own happiness, but also for the well-being and satisfaction of other people. Indeed, the action should result in happiness for many or as some say: "the greatest happiness for the greatest number" (Rachels & Rachels 2009).

For utilitarians, the rightness of an action-choice lies in its results or consequences. This "consequentialist" mode of thinking directs the attention of the moral agent to consider how a given action may influence events. Will this action bring about something good? In evaluating actions, the moral agent anticipates possible futures, trying to predict what will happen if one choice is made, another avoided. Will the circumstances that are now changed by the action-choice benefit people later; will there be a "net gain" in their well-being, an increase in their level of satisfaction? In a contrasting, but related consideration: the moral agent may ask whether an alternative might cause more harm or lead to increased unhappiness. If that is the assessment, that action should not be taken.

The goal of utilitarian decision making is to increase the well-being of the self and others conceived as an aggregate; indeed, action-choices should maximize happiness for all concerned in the decision – including the moral agent considered as part of those affected by the action. Decisions should add value in an objective fashion to the society. This means that the decision produces a real good, actually improves the circumstances of society, with the sum total of "utility" higher than it had been prior to the decision. It is very important, too, that individuals within the group affected by the decision be treated impartially, with the assumption that each person is equal to any other as potential beneficiaries of increased happiness. A utilitarian decision brooks no favorites.

In another aspect of utilitarian thought on moral issues and dilemmas, the moral agent need not consider only specific actions and their consequences. He or she may well consider a standard – a principle or a rule – as a structured resource to assist in the evaluation of action alternatives. We imagine that others have in the past encountered circumstances and dilemmas similar to our own. If so, the decisions they made, expressing their unique judgment and insight, may have become formulated as rules that are now put forth as guidelines for our contemporary decisions. These standards and rules stand as short-hand accounts of successful decision making from the past. They represent procedures and patterns of decision making that led to more happiness (or less harm) when previous actions were taken. With this mind: the moral agent can ask: which rule, which standard, applied in my situation will now lead to happiness for the people involved in my moral issue and for those affected by my decision?

This consideration of rules and guidelines moves our attention from particular actions that are appropriate to a given circumstance, from "act-utilitarianism," where the focus is on how those actions may cause happiness (create utility), to a focus on "rule-utilitarianism," where the question is whether a given rule applied in a situation (and other similar situations) may cause the most happiness. In the latter case, the moral agent anticipates a future shaped by the rule-based decision, predicting a result of the action-choice within the framework of the rule. But as with any decision focused on a single action, the rightness of a given rule is still determined by results and is evaluated as right or wrong according to the happiness caused (or unhappiness avoided.)

The utilitarian approach has much appeal for us. It seems almost commonsense to think of ethics decisions in terms of choosing to do whatever makes us happy, gives us satisfaction. It is no big stretch, either, to believe that people often do make ethics decisions to make others (not just themselves) happy. Individuals do, indeed, act to benefit others. In addition, for those of us in the business world, engaging in "cost–benefit" analysis is a common aspect of decision making. Such calculation is seen in many decisions: in the process of determining which products, which "goods," might be bought or sold, deciding how to "satisfy" customers, or when to enter a market with a new product or service. And who would downplay the importance of results in ethics decisions; aren't results "the proof of the pudding"? Results are important!

DEONTOLOGY

Yet results take a back seat to other concerns in the next moral philosophy tradition we consider: deontology. In this philosophical approach, moral principles guide ethical decision making. At the core of these principles is the idea that human beings are rational, free, and autonomous with regard to their own life's goals. The moral agent is expected to respect the dignity of others, honor and promote their rights and liberty. He does this by following moral principles: this is his duty. Addressing moral issues and resolving dilemmas bring these core principles into play. "What should I do? What action-choice ought I to make?" These questions are answered in terms of the moral agent's duty to observe the core principles, to honor and promote their application within any given situation. The question of what to do in a situation is answered by appealing to an over-arching "moral law," which states "an imperative" to obey.

One principle, for example, may be the imperative to: "Tell the truth," with its counterpart, "Do not lie." Another is: "Do not steal," with its companion, "Support others in protecting their property." A third: "Show respect for the humanity of each person and for the human community as a whole." Or: "Do not undermine the dignity, freedom, and autonomy of another person."

With little regard for the specific consequences of a decision, the moral agent should discern the core principle at stake in a situation and then act in accordance with that principle. *Do your duty: act on the basis of the core principle*. This duty-oriented decision will then be evaluated by identifying the principle and determining whether that the action-choice was actually made on account of that principle. That is, was the moral agent's reason for action the purpose of honoring and promoting the moral principle? Evaluating the action, it is asked: Did the moral agent identify the relevant principle and follow his duty by acting on behalf of that principle (with duty being the only motive to observe the principle – the moral agent having no other motive in mind)?

In this tradition, the rightness of an action depends on the moral agent's reason for the action. If the action is done because of the moral principle, then the action is right. If the decision is not grounded in a principle, or if the action is taken for reasons other than following one's rational duty to observe the principle, then the action is not right. An unreasonable or unprincipled choice does not express a good thing to do. (In terms of moral value, it is not sufficient to take action on the basis of one's inclinations or feelings, or because external pressures push you to follow the principle, or because you're afraid of being punished or you seek a reward for your choice.) For deontology, the right thing must be done for the right reason. That is what counts.

With deontological ethics, there is a moral obligation, a duty, for the moral agent to promote the well-being of others, to affirm their dignity and freedom. This duty means that the moral agent must respect the rights of others, including the right "to personal space" where the person can decide for himself to pursue goals and take actions to fulfill his own purposes. In this tradition of ethical reasoning, the moral agent finds him or herself constrained or limited by the core moral principles and the demand for a reasoned compliance to these standards. Moral agents are to use reason and logic to do their duty of following the moral law.

In this way of thinking, the results of a reasoned action-choice are not of much importance; the reasonable carrying out of a duty is what matters most. It is crucial to emphasize "reason and logic" in the pursuit of one's duty. It is the motive of the moral agent, not the result of his decision, that is given highest priority in this tradition of ethics. In the moment of decision making, feelings and emotions, inclinations to follow conventional social standards, thoughts of punishment or reward – all these are considered to be "temptations". They are distractions that draw the moral agent away from reason, undermine genuine demonstration of respect for others, and threaten the serious effort to live a principled life. The sole motive of the moral agent is supposed to be the reason-driven desire to do one's duty. The moral demand to seek the well-being of others is addressed primarily by reasonable efforts on the part of the moral agent. Whether the well-being or the happiness of other people is actually achieved seems to be a lesser concern within this tradition of moral philosophy. When faced by a dilemma, I want to know what core principle is at stake, then I do my duty by choosing a reasonable action that fits that principle.

VIRTUE ETHICS

The utilitarian and the deontological traditions emphasize the results (utility-happiness) or the goal and motivation (reasonable observance of moral duties) of ethical decision making. Virtue ethics presents a different approach. This tradition focuses on the character traits and mental-emotional capacities of the moral agent. Given that each person plays a number of roles and performs various functions within society, the virtue ethicist asks: "What intellectual and moral capabilities must the person possess (have within himself or herself) 'to live well,' to meet successfully his social or work-related responsibilities? What abilities and talents must lie 'ready to hand,' within persons for them to thrive ('flourish') personally and perform social and work tasks well?"

Concentrating on the person, rather than moral laws or the consequences of actions, virtue ethicists look beyond the particular decision making circumstance to focus on qualities of character possessed by the moral agent. They speak of the character traits, or "virtues," of a person that enable him or her to thrive within the community and function as an admired citizen. The ethical thinker considers the intellectual and moral virtues necessary for a person to play a role in a family or a profession, to be excellent in a social endeavor, and "do a job well" – whatever that job may be. The moral agent may possess virtues that benefit himself or herself – like courage, cool-headedness in a crisis, diligence – or character traits that may benefit others – generosity, honesty, integrity. In this context, the challenge of resolving a moral dilemma is, however, not the task of producing something good for the self and others (collectively adding happiness to society) or the responsibility of doing one's duty with regard to a moral law or a core principle of behavior. Virtue ethics reasoning focuses first on the character of the person, and it does not give the highest priority to achieving good results or to the requirements of duty.

By contrast to the utilitarian and the deontological approaches, virtues ethics addresses the moral issues that arise from social roles and the workplace by giving primary attention to the qualities of character of the moral agent – considering virtues possessed by people and looking for the realization of those virtues in actions they take. In brief: as one faces action-choices to resolve a moral dilemma, virtue ethicists first want to speak about the qualities of character of a moral agent as the potential intellectual and moral resources for decision making. In evaluating action, they then look to see whether particular virtues are embodied (become realized) in the decisions made. They ask: does the person possess the virtue of honesty or integrity; is she courageous, does she have practical wisdom about human nature? Is the person of moderate temperament, well disciplined, and diligent in work habits? Faced with a dilemma, they inquire: "How might specific actions in this circumstance show the signs of these virtues, demonstrate the virtuous character of the moral agent?"

As a general approach for evaluating an action-choice in a dilemma, this question is asked: "Is the decision process and resulting action in a given situation what a virtuous person would do?" For example, does the decision process show diligence and disciplined thinking; does the moral agent resist temptation and pressures from others to act with integrity, to show honesty or to tell the truth? Does the decision express the type of thought produced by a moderate temperament – avoiding impulsiveness and strong emotion? Does the action express generosity or altruism, insight about the power of peer pressures or the temptations of greed and selfishness? In brief, the evaluation of the action-choice is achieved by turning toward issues of character and the nature of the virtues brought into play in the circumstance. A decision is right because a virtuous person would have made the same choice; an action is correct because it is what a virtuous person would do in this situation.

At first glance, it may appear that virtue ethics does not offer a great resource for decision making in real-world situations; it is difficult to discern useable guidelines for choosing between different courses of action, sorting through various option alternatives. We can ask: "How can we tell a virtuous person when we meet one, which of many character traits are admirable? How can we make the right action-choices, if we are not ourselves virtuous?" In another perspective, a results-oriented ethics such as utilitarianism and a principle-centered, rule-oriented ethics such as deontology may have great appeal to us because of our understanding of how businesses function and because we have already seen how principles and rules play such an important role in accounting. But consider this: is not the character of an accountant important; isn't it crucial whether the accountant possesses and uses the special intellectual and moral traits (skills, talents, attitudes, and insights) necessary for demonstrating technical, as well as ethical, competence on the job? Can we not identify the traits and qualities of character of the good accountant? What is more: doesn't it take specific virtues for accountants to commit themselves to "follow the rules," "seek the good for other people," "treat all individuals equally," and "persist in doing the right thing against temptations and pressures"? If these questions seem important; if you wonder about the relationship between the accountant as a person and the duties he performs in order to achieve the primary purpose of accounting practice, then virtue ethics reasoning – like that of utilitarianism and deontology – may well provide "tools" useful for your practice of accounting.

SOCIAL CONTRACT THEORY

The fourth ethics tradition we consider has had great importance for social thought, Western political theory and aspects of business ethics, but the tradition is not treated extensively by most specialists in accounting ethics. We want to overcome that deficiency. We will introduce its key features here and later expand our treatment of the theory in a separate discussion of professionalism and the public service dimensions of accounting practice.

Our previous introduction to the three traditions of moral philosophy revolved around a "case" where a moral agent faced a dilemma. We discussed key features of each tradition in relation to a decision making process. Here we take a different starting point.

The social contract theory presupposes that a moral agent acts as a citizen within a specific type of society. In this theory, the society itself is formed through the voluntary consent (choices) of its citizens. These individuals bind themselves in obligation and support one another for the sake of everyone's protection against the threat of violence. Individuals form a *social contract* with one another. The combination of cooperative power and consensus of purpose that emerges from the consent of many individuals forms a defense against violent action. The contract protects the life, liberty, and property of any and all citizen-individuals. Alone and isolated, individuals are vulnerable to aggression; they are prey for murderers, thieves, conquerors. In combination, the individuals constitute a community that creates laws and can marshal the force necessary to protect each of them as citizens of the community.

By giving consent and joining in the social contract, the individual voluntarily submits to constraints on his own freedom and accepts limitations on his own self-interest.

Individuals do this in exchange for social protection and security. Acknowledging, in effect, that the pursuit of untrammeled self-interest by individuals may threaten the lives and well-being of others, the citizen agrees to follow the laws and rules of society. He assumes that other citizens will do this, as well. With this self-limitation and trust in others, the self-constrained rights of each citizen are secured through the social cooperation of his fellows. In the framework of the social contract, each citizen finds himself or herself obligated to protect the rights of others in the society and acknowledges the society's laws and rules as appropriate means of protection for themselves and others.

We can now turn to the situation of a moral agent (citizen) who faces a dilemma. His action-choices are to be shaped by an explicit awareness of his social duties to protect and not violate the rights of others. The moral agent can turn to the laws and regulations of society for guidance and support in decision making – assuming that these codes of conduct not only serve his own interests but also provide the means by which his own obligation to support others can be expressed. In practical terms, the moral agent can follow an ethics of duty and strive to meet his obligations as a law-abiding citizen. Using reason to apply laws and rules to particular circumstances and affirming his "social responsibility" to other individuals (and society itself), the moral agent-citizen makes his decisions about how to behave.

In the context of this social contract, the moral agent may be asked why he took a particular action which affects others. As an aspect of social responsibility, the moral agent is duty-bound to explain himself, and, in effect, submit his decision and actions to the judgment of others. Such explanations and judgments, to be successful in an ideal sense, will lead to a consensus of opinion. The action and explanation, by consensus, would be deemed reasonable. They would be acceptable as marks of a good citizen who fulfilled his obligation to protect the rights and interests of others, as well as by satisfactorily constraining his own selfishness. This would constitute a "right action".

If, however, the action and public defense (explanation) by the moral agent are disputed and no consensus is reached on their reasonableness, and if the question remains of specific citizen rights being violated, then the action is thought to be wrong. In the more extreme case where public consensus determines that people's rights were violated and that an action harmed fellow-citizens, the action is rejected and condemned as wrong.

The appeal of this approach to ethics is that it is grounded in the "real world" (even if the theory seems abstract). The moral agent lives within a particular society and takes into account the interests and the rights of real people. His decisions affect other people, real human beings with whom he has significant associations. And not only that: in choosing to act, the moral agent quite realistically finds his actions evaluated by others, and these fellow-citizens can rightfully push on him, seeking consensus on how he has acted. If his actions harm someone, he is likely to find this out in the social conversation that follows the action. If his actions are acceptable, he may find approval and praise from fellow-citizens. If consensus is not readily reached, quite possibly the civic evaluation and dialogue may afford the moral agent the chance to change his mind and take a different action in order to "set things right".

Building on this "decision, dialogue, consensus-building" pattern, one appeal of the social contract theory is that it makes it possible to demonstrate that many different individuals and groups (many "fellow citizens") may be affected by the moral agent's decision. Potentially there are numerous stakeholders, so the impact of a given decision should not be understood too narrowly. Another feature of this philosophical approach is that it reminds us that decision making within the framework of a particular social role (policeman, school teacher, carpenter) or as a professional (doctor, lawyer, accountant) does not set aside the individual's social responsibility for protecting the interests and rights of others. The professional person or the specialist, who plays a distinctive role in the society, still has the obligation to serve the wider public interests of that society.

A DECISION MODEL FOR ACCOUNTING ETHICS

This chapter has thus far introduced the decision making perspective on accounting ethics upon which this book is based. Our emphasis on accounting ethics as decision making expresses our belief that the practical task of accounting ethics is to promote ethical awareness, reflection and judgment of ethical issues in accounting, as well as to enhance the ability of the individual accountant to act on his or her judgments. We think that accounting ethics education should be oriented toward the decision making of accountants in practice.

For this reason, our book is based on – and structured along the lines of – a decision model for accounting ethics. In this section, we will introduce our decision model and briefly outline its main components. In the following sections of this book these components will be treated in detail, so in this chapter we present only a brief overview of the model. We then indicate the chapters where each component of the model is further elaborated. Accordingly, the following pages serve as an outline for the remainder of the book.

It is well established that people differ with regard to how they make decisions. For instance, some individuals are rule-followers while others approach problems more intuitively. It should be noted that we do not claim that our decision model is a concise description of how contemporary accountants actually approach ethical issues; neither do we think the model presents a normative solution for neatly resolving every ethical dilemma encountered in accounting practice. The intention of our decision model is twofold. First, it offers a structured approach to ethical decision making for accountants to use as a framework for addressing ethical issues. As the accountant gains experience in identifying, judging and managing ethical issues, he or she will likely develop their own approach to ethical decision making and the need for such a structured decision model will diminish. Second, the model serves a pedagogical purpose as it summarizes and draws together key stages of ethical decision making. The model identifies key resources that may support decision making, and it points out relevant environmental characteristics that may influence the decision process. These features of the model allow us to communicate "the parts and the whole" of accounting ethics in an accessible and useful structure that can be used both for analyzing situations and making practical action-choices in accounting discourse.

The decision model (see Figure 2.1) comprises five stages of decision making from the identification of a problem to taking an action that follows a deliberative process. The first stage of the ethical decision-making process is *defining the problem*. The

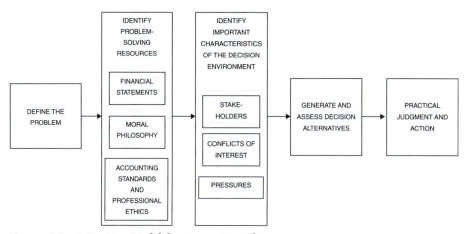

Figure 2.1 A Decision Model for Accounting Ethics

second stage discusses the *identification of relevant problem-solving resources* that are available to the decision maker (i.e., the accountant as *moral agent*). The third stage involves *identifying important characteristics of the environment within which the decision takes place*. The fourth stage is *generating and assessing decision alternatives* (options) that are feasible. The final stage of the decision-making process considers the *practical judgment of the moral agent and how this judgment leads to action*. One final note: we see this process as having a feedback loop. This means that the moral agent, the practicing accountant, uses his or her concrete experiences from a given decision-making process to enhance the ability to deal with other moral issues and dilemmas that may arise later; that is, to improve subsequent decision making.

In the following section, we will briefly illuminate each component of the decision model outlined above using a simple case example to illustrate how such a decision-making process can be carried out in practice.

Defining the problem is a crucial part of any decision-making process. Problem definition (or problem *formulation*) means identifying what the problem actually entails. We typically think of problem formulation as identifying "the gap between the current state and the ideal state". By this we mean that there is something undesirable or unsatisfactory in the current situation with regard to how we would like things to be. For instance, a person may consider his poor physical shape a problem; that is, he considers the current state ("I am in bad shape") to fall short of the ideal state ("I would like to be physically fit"). This problem formulation expresses his understanding of a situation as containing a problem, and thus it serves as the point of departure for problem-solving measures (e.g., working out on a regular basis).

For the purposes of this book in accounting ethics, we distinguish between two types of problems that are related, yet distinct. For the first part, we are concerned with *identifying (or defining) the accounting problem*. This means figuring out what is wrong with a given decision or what is not yet resolved in a particular situation *from an accounting point of view*. This means that "the ideal state" must be considered from an accounting point of view; that is, with reference to accounting purposes and accounting standards. For the second aspect of the problem situation, we are concerned with *identifying (or defining) the ethical problem*. This means determining what is wrong with the decision or what is left unresolved in a situation *from an ethical point of view*; for instance, by assessing the positive and the negative consequences of a particular decision or asking whether the decision complies with relevant duties or moral principles. Typically, the problem formulations from the accounting and the ethical perspectives will be related, but these formulations will highlight differing aspects of the ambiguous situation that need to be addressed by the practicing accountant.

Let us consider a simple example: Imagine that in an accounting ethics course, there is an attendance requirement of 80%, and students must sign an attendance list that is circulated in every lecture period. The attendance list, in effect, serves as an accounting system for student attendance. Let us also imagine that the lecturers discover that students are taking turns skipping class and faking each other's signatures, so that the list shows perfect attendance for students even when this is, in fact, not the case. These absences and the forged signatures can be seen both as an accounting problem and as an ethical problem. If we define the problem from an accounting point of view, we would emphasize that the attendance list does not, in fact, reflect the underlying reality or fairly represent what it purports to represent. The signed attendance list does not fairly represent actual attendance. We have an accounting for attendance that gives information of poor quality with regard to whether the students on the list were actually present for a given lecture. The gap between the current state and the ideal state, then, is that the attendance list currently gives the wrong information about which students were present and which were absent. Ideally we want a list that gives correct information about each student's attendance.

If we define the problem from an ethical point of view, however, we would highlight the practice of the students' faking each other's signatures. This is an ethical problem because the students are forging documents and deliberately giving wrong information to deceive their lecturers. The students who participate in this fraudulent behavior do not act with integrity. Their actions violate the pedagogical standards of the course and contribute to a practice that undermines trust in the classroom.

This example shows that the accounting problem and the ethical problem are certainly related; they reflect the same issue – absenteeism and deliberate, willful acts of deception. The students are engaged in the manipulation of the accounting system for recording attendance, and their undisciplined absenteeism is supported by explicit lying intended to deceive the course lecturers. Our decision model encourages us to examine this situation from two perspectives; to take two different angles on a problem. When we define the accounting problem, we are looking for *relevant issues from an accounting point of view*. Does the student practice of signing the list provide high-quality information? Does the attendance list format provide adequate mechanisms of internal control to lower the risk of manipulation? Are there rewards and punishments for compliance to the signature-attendance policy? When we define the ethical problem, we are looking for *relevant issues from an ethical point of view*. Does the policy reward virtuous behavior? Can we remind the students of the logic and fairness of signing only on the days they attend? Is there, in effect, a social contract that binds the students to a pattern of behavior, with fitting punishment for those who violate this code? Together, these two perspectives provide us with the combined insight we need in order to deal with the problem from a comprehensive perspective, the point of view of *accounting ethics*. We will revisit this example in a number of ways later in the book, but let us first describe the next stage in the decision-making process in the specific terms of accounting practice.

We see the *identification of problem-solving resources* in terms of the moral agent's pursuit of suitable tools or frameworks that may be helpful for understanding the situation and identifying the problem – especially for understanding how the situation at hand differs from how we might want things to be. Considering a "real world" accounting dilemma, we suggest that there are three broad categories of such problem solving resources available to the moral agent (i.e., the accountant). First, the accountant may consult the *guidelines for the preparation of financial statements*, which is the relevant framework for determining the acceptable form and content of financial accounting according to the relevant regulatory bodies. These guidelines (accounting standards) show how the accountant is supposed to present accounting information, recognize financial and economic information in the financial statements. Second, the accountant may assess the situation and make a decision in light of *perspectives from moral philosophy*, such as duty ethics, virtue ethics or utilitarianism. These resources enable the accountant to analyze a situation and make a decision from relevant ethical points of view. Third, the accountant may consult *professional codes of ethics (or similar documents that set forth the professional ethics for accountants)*. This consultation of the codes will enable the accountant to familiarize himself or herself with relevant standards that guide the preparation and communication of financial knowledge to stakeholders. The code of ethics will provide information about the standards of conduct that are required for professional accountants, even standards that extend beyond the preparation of financial statements – to maintain public respect for the profession and secure trust that supports the functions of the financial markets.

Let us revisit the attendance list example in order to discuss the relevant problem-solving resources that can be identified in the case. If the students are to consider relevant resources to determine how they should use the attendance list, they could listen to the standards communicated by the lecturers ("sign the list when you are present in class"). In our example, this is the equivalent of having a guideline for preparing financial statements, a rule set forth by the accounting standards. In addition, the students might consult ethical theories within the moral philosophy traditions. The three ethical theories we employ in this book are deontology, virtue ethics and utilitarianism. A principled, duty-based ethics perspective could inform students in this case ("I should not lie, because it violates the norm of truthfulness"). They might also approach the attendance policy from a virtue ethics perspective, which emphasizes character and community ("I don't want to lie, because it is not the kind of person I want to be" or "lying will not support my community's efforts to flourish"). They could also approach decisions on class attendance and signing the list from a utilitarian point of view ("I won't skip class, because it affects the classroom activities negatively, and my inappropriate signature may contribute to a culture of lying and cheating"). Finally, students could consult the code of ethics for students, which most business schools have. Therein, they could find standards of conduct for such cases. Typically, such codes would include guidelines like: "Students are expected to take part in mandatory activities and only be absent when there is a justifiable reason to do so."

These three problem-solving resources from the lecturers, moral philosophy and school codes of conduct inform the students in our example so they might analyze the situation, identify both the accounting and the ethical problems and determine how to make their decisions. In the language of problem formulation introduced above, we could say that the students are given information about "the ideal state" (i.e., how things should be done) by consulting these three sources. In a comparable fashion, an accountant can consult the three types of problem-solving resources presented in the second column in Figure 2.1 whenever they face an ethical issue in accounting practice.

After identifying problem-solving resources that enable the accountant to conceive of the *ideal state* (i.e., how things should be), the accountant should attempt to *understand the decision environment*. This means gaining insight into relevant situational, institutional and environmental features that influence the decision making of the accountant. We identify three broad categories of factors in the decision environment that are particularly salient for the accountant's purposes: stakeholders' power, and legitimacy, potential conflicts of interest, and pressures on decision making. Examination of these three features of the decision environment will lead to insights about the situation and illuminate the nature of the ethical problem. In the language of "problem formulation," analysis of these three aspects of a situation provides the student in our attendance list example and practicing accountants with relevant information about the "actual state" (how things really are) of the decision environment.

First, the accountant should identify which *stakeholders* are influenced by the decision (or may aim to exert influence on the decision-making process). This means determining which individuals, groups, or organizations have a stake in the decision at hand. Following the identification of stakeholders, the accountant may attempt to *characterize* those stakeholders based on relevant aspects of their roles or policy positions. As we will see later, important characteristics include the degree to which the stakeholder has power and whether the stakeholder has a legitimate role in the situation. Second, the accountant can scrutinize the decision environment to identify potential *conflicts of interest*. This follows from the stakeholder identification, because one needs to have an interest in the decision at hand (i.e., be a stakeholder) in order to have a conflict of interest. It should be noted that the moral agent (accountant) may have a conflict of interest in the situation, but it may also be the case that the conflict of interest lies with another stakeholder (e.g., the manager to whom the accountant is accountable). Third, the accountant may "scan" the environment for relevant pressures that can influence decision making. Pressure comes in many forms. For example, it may include direct attempts from managers or others to *coerce* the accountant into acting on behalf of their own agendas. In addition, business organizations are prominently characterized by *time pressure*, such as the ticking clock towards a deadline, the end of the fiscal year, and so on. Finally, there is considerable *social pressure* in organizations, for instance, to act in accordance with the expectations of peers to "help out" your co-workers by taking their interests into account or to conform to "the way things are done in this organization".

Let us again return to the attendance list example in order to discuss the relevant characteristics of the environment in that case. In the attendance example, the primary group of *stakeholders* includes the students and the lecturers. In addition to these stakeholders, we should include the school itself, since the course is "owned" and managed by the school, and whatever happens in the course is the business of the school. We may also include students from other courses as stakeholders, since students typically make assessments of fairness across different courses ("in the accounting ethics course, the students don't have to attend class, but in our strategy course we are required to attend class each time"). Future students may also be considered as stakeholders, since their decision of whether to take the accounting ethics course next year will be based partly on the information they get from former students in the course. There is also a unique *conflict of interest* within the case. In the case, the students are the "accountants," since they fill in the "data" in the attendance list which serves as the accounting system for the class. If students take turns skipping class and writing missing students' names on the list, a situation is created where private interests ("helping each other out" and "getting out of class once in a while") clashes with the interest of acting "professionally" as a student (writing your name when you are present and refraining from having someone else cover for you when you are absent). Finally, there is considerable *pressure* in the situation. There may be strong social pressure to take part in the practice, since the system only works as long as the students who are present at a given time are willing to write the names of those who are not present. Such a system, with its peer pressure, makes it difficult to refuse to take part. Moreover, there is the pressure of managing student life alongside extracurricular activities (e.g., a part-time job, cleaning one's apartment, and suchlike). It is well-known that students in the contemporary educational system struggle to make ends meet – financially and with regard to time – and some may skip class whenever possible in order to work. This creates a pressure to participate in falsifying the attendance list.

To summarize: the moral agent can use these three characteristics of the decision environment (stakeholders, conflicts of interests and pressures) to gain information about the "actual state" (i.e., how things really are). By analyzing these three characteristics, the nature of the ethical problem can be clarified and steps taken to select action alternatives that address specific features of the problem. And like the students in the attendance list example, accountants can analyze these three characteristics of their decision environment in the decision process. These characteristics are listed in the third column in Figure 2.1, when they are faced as aspects of ethical issues in accounting practice.

Once the accountant has identified problem solving resources (and thus created a mental image of "the ideal state") and examined the key features of the decision environment (and thus created a mental image of "the current state" of affairs in the situation), the search for alternative courses of action may begin. The accountant can *generate and assess decision alternatives*. At first, this is an open-ended process that expands the "action space" of the accountant; that is, it is desirable to conceive as many action alternatives as possible before weighing their costs and benefits, seeking to arrive at the best solution given the constraints of the situation. Following the generation of alternatives, the accountant then determines which alternatives are relevant to a course of action. In principle, any action alternative might be assessed, but in practice, the accountant narrows the list to close the gap between the current state and the ideal state. This means that the relevant decision alternatives follow from the initial definition or formulation of the problem and that the main criteria for assessing the alternatives are also related to the problem formulation. The accountant wants to make a decision that (1) solves the problem, i.e. brings him closer to "the ideal state," while at the same time (2) being feasible, given the constraints of the situation (e.g., pressures, the degree of power held by the accountant, and suchlike). Following the logic of the model (and recalling the discussion in previous chapters), this assessment will combine the accountant's professional knowledge (technical proficiency) with his competence in assessing the problem from a moral point of view (ethical sensibility).

Let us illustrate by returning to the attendance list example. If we take a broad approach to the problem, a given student has several choices at his disposal. He may quit the class and thereby remove himself entirely from the problem. This will, however, have the undesirable side-effect of giving up the credits for the course. He may also engage in the practice of faking the attendance list, thereby freeing up time for other activities while (potentially) passing the course. This creates the risk of getting caught and suffering the consequences of school discipline. Another option for the student is to "blow the whistle," to notify the lecturers or the school about the practice, either openly or anonymously. This will end the problem, but it may also have significant negative effects for the student since the social costs of being a whistle-blower may be substantial. In another response, he could confront his fellow students and suggest that the class abandon the practice of faking the list. This is likely to result in conflict between the student and his peers. Finally, the student may simply choose not to engage in the practice, while at the same time keeping quiet about what the other students are doing. But even this could result in negative reactions from other students, since the student's actions would not conform to their behavior.

After conceiving these action alternatives, the student can assess them using the resources at hand. Broadly speaking, three assessment approaches from moral philosophy can be distinguished – a principle-oriented (deontology), a consequentialist (utilitarian), and a character-based (virtue ethics) assessment. The former would mean assessing the alternatives with regard to whether they involve violations of important principles or norms (e.g., "do not lie" or "follow guidelines for professional practice"). The second approach assesses the alternatives with regard to whether they lead to positive, rather than negative, outcomes for the broader community (e.g., "trust breaks down" or "the teaching environment suffers from student absences"). The third assessment approach suggests assessing the alternatives with regard to whether they are in harmony with or contradict the individual's ideals for the kind of person he would like to be (e.g., "truthful," "deceptive" or "always acting with integrity").

Finally, when all alternatives have been assessed, the accountant as moral agent will judge the problem and select a course of action that (1) he considers to be rationally and ethically justifiable; for example, an action that emerges from combining his professional and ethical judgments, and (2) he commits himself to act on this judgment. It should be noted that these two elements, judgment and action, do not necessarily go hand in hand. That is, the accountant may act in a way that is not in accordance with his judgment. If, for instance, he is pressured to act but does not have the means, competence or power to realize his judgment in action, or if the preferred action alternative is, for some reason or another, unavailable to him. The difficulty with acting in line with one's convictions should not be underestimated – in fact, it is quite common that people know what the right action is, but they fail to act accordingly. Judgment and action, as we can see, comprise two difficult tasks for the accountant. First, the accountant must arrive at a justifiable assessment of the course of action he should follow. Second, the accountant must be able to realize this in practical action and to implement the decision despite obstacles.

Let us return one last time to the attendance example. After assessing the action alternatives with regard to relevant rules, guidelines and ethical standards, the student needs to make a decision on how to proceed, how to act. He needs to judge the situation in order to arrive at a wise solution to his problem. As we will elaborate in the following chapters, a wise solution would combine the technical proficiency of the student (e.g., his or her ability to act in accordance with his best knowledge about how to act rationally and effectively in the given situation), and his or her ethical sensibility (the ability to act in accordance with relevant ethical principles, values or standards). In the attendance case, then, he or she should select the alternative that best complies with the professional expectations of the student and the relevant ethical standards that enable him or her to realize important values in practice. In the case, it would be possible to argue that the student should choose *not to engage* in the practice of faking the list but yet not "blow the whistle". This would enable the student to act with integrity while at the same time allowing him to respect the value of loyalty to his peers. Similar arguments, however, could be made for other options, for instance, the option of anonymously blowing the whistle or confronting the students about the practice. Whatever the judgment, the student must realize the decision by taking action. It is quite likely that obstacles to action may arise. For instance, the student could face social pressures or reactions that are personally costly. The moral agent may be publicly criticized, friendships may be strained. These consequences could possibly derail the intentions to carry out an appropriate decision. Given these pressures and possible consequences, realizing one's judgment in action becomes a matter of character and steadfast attitude.

This overview of the components of our decision model and the practical illustration provided by the attendance list case shows a stylized picture of how an ethical decision-making process may be carried out in practice. As the previous discussion illustrates, ethical decision making involves perception, reflection, judgment and action. It comprises a series of choices and brings into play a comprehensive toolbox of resources that the individual may use to support his decision making.

As indicated by the arrows in the decision model, we anticipate the decision process to move through these steps in a linear fashion. Yet, it is certainly possible that the process can move back and forth among the parts of the model and that the starting point for an individual's problem-solving could emerge from any of the stages of the model. For instance, it could be that the accountant experiences pressure to act in a specific manner (cf. stage 3), and this pressure leads the accountant to assess the situation as being ethically problematic. He realizes, responding to the pressure, that he faces an ethical issue and confronts a dilemma. In that case, this pressure will be the impetus that shapes the accountant's definition of the problem. Our subsequent discussion will treat the decision process in the form presented by the model, but later in the book we will return to this issue of how problems can arise from any point of the model.

With reference to our definition of a problem as the gap between "the ideal state" and "the current state," we can see how "the ideal" and "the actual" are reflected in the model. First, the accountant must define the problem (column 1). Thereafter, the problem-solving resources at his disposal – guidelines for preparing financial statements, moral philosophy and accounting standards and codes – express "the ideal"

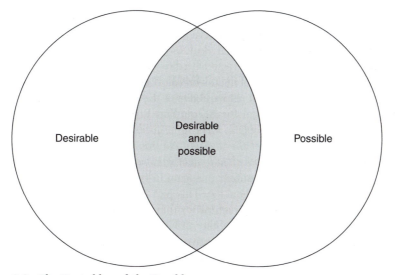

Figure 2.2   The Desirable and the Possible

(column 2). That is, they formulate the standards for *how things ought to be*. But the characteristics of the decision environment also reflect "the actual" (column 3). That is, these characteristics demonstrate the constraints on the moral agent and obstacles to achieving the ideal outcome. Finally, practical judgment and action reflect the accountant's challenge of acting in a way that approaches the ideal as closely as possible, given the constraints of the actual situation (column 4). We may say that the problem-solving resources in column 2 indicate *the desirable ways of deciding and acting*, while the characteristics of the environment in column 3 are constraints on the *possible ways of deciding and acting*.

This relationship between desirable action alternatives and possible action alternatives is illustrated in the Venn diagram in Figure 2.2. The circle on the left represents all possible decision and action alternatives that are consistent with the technical and ethical requirements the accountant should take into account. The circle on the right represents the possible decision and action alternatives, those that are available to the accountant given the constraints of the situation (e.g., pressure, lack of power, knowledge or authority, and suchlike). The intersection of the two circles represents the alternatives that are both possible and desirable, alternatives that are consistent with standards, codes and requirements and the accountant finds it possible to realize them. To conclude: this book aims at supporting the accountant's analysis of complex situations and decision environments that have both technical and ethical requirements, so that he may arrive at decisions and take feasible actions that are desirable.

OUTLINE OF THE BOOK

The book is structured along the lines of the decision model outlined here. In this section, we outline the remainder of the book and the content and purpose of its sections and chapters. Part II includes chapters that follow the structure of the decision model; in these chapters we account in depth for each component of the decision model and show how the model (in its parts and in the whole) is relevant for decision making in accounting ethics. Part III includes topical chapters that deal with issues of particular significance for accounting ethics but which are not treated in a direct decision-making approach. Instead, these chapters focus on questions of the relationship between accounting, society, and the environment, including the social responsibility of the practicing accountant.

Part II – A Decision Model for Accounting Ethics – deals with the decision-making model: *defining the problem, identifying problem-solving resources, identifying important characteristics of the decision environment, generating and assessing decision alternatives*, and *practical judgment and action*. It is aimed at giving the reader an idea of how the accountant may gain insight into the nature and scope of ethical problems in accounting practice. This part also gives the reader insight into situational and environmental characteristics that may influence or distort the individual accountant's decision-making ability and integrity, as well as suggesting how the accountant may generate decision alternatives and subsequently assess them based on relevant criteria. Finally, another aim of Part II is to give the reader insight into how practical judgments are made and then put into action. Several challenges to this judgment–action process are discussed.

In Chapter 3 – Defining the Problem – From an Accounting and Ethical Point of View – we illuminate the role of problem formulation for accounting ethics. We focus both on how to define the accounting problem and how to formulate the distinct ethical issue at hand. In Chapter 4 – Accounting Standards for Financial Statements: Resources for Decision Making – we provide the guidelines for preparing financial statements and discuss how these guidelines serve as important resources for recognizing and analyzing ethical problems in accounting. In Chapter 5 – Moral Philosophy and Ethical Reasoning: Resources for Decision Making – we outline several ethical theories that can serve as normative frameworks for ethical decision making in accounting. Finally, in Chapter 6 – Professional Ethics as a Resource for Decision Making – we treat the third category of problem-solving resources, namely accounting standards and professional ethics, and discuss their role in supporting the accountant's effort to resolve ethical issues. In Chapter 7 – Stakeholders in Accounting Ethics: Pressures and Conflicts of Interest – we present stakeholder theory and a framework for assessing and evaluating the significance of stakeholders for decision making. This stakeholder theory relates to the individuals, groups and entities whose interests are influenced by the decisions of the accountant and specifies their importance for the accountant's decision making. Moreover, we illuminate the nature of conflicts of interest and how they pertain to the role of the accountant, and we discuss various types of pressure experienced by the accountant in the decision situation. In Chapter 8 – Generating and Assessing Decision Alternatives: Practical Wisdom and Action – we shed light on how the accountant, based on the problem-solving resources and situational and environmental characteristics outlined thus far, can generate action alternatives and assess them with regard to appropriate criteria. In Chapter 8, we discuss the nature of practical judgment in order to explore how the accountant may arrive at a well-grounded decision that is in line with both his professional and his personal judgment. We also outline issues related to the implementation of this judgment, namely the problem of putting one's decision into practical action.

Part III – Accounting in Society – deals with current themes concerned with the relationship between the accountant and society. The section aims to provide the reader with insight into the role of accountant in modern society. In Chapter 9 – Auditing Ethics – we illuminate the ethics of auditing, based on the particular role of the auditor in ensuring that financial information is produced and presented in a justifiable fashion. Finally, in Chapter 10 – Accounting in Society – we focus on the role of the accountant in society.

CHAPTER REVIEW QUESTIONS

1. (LO5) Write a brief definition of "ethics".
2. (LO6) According to the utilitarian tradition, what is the highest priority in making an ethical decision?
3. (LO7) Make a brief list of virtues that may support the activities of an accountant. (Consider the types of tasks performed by an accountant and the responsibility to act ethically.)
4. (LO3) Explain why the accountant should present high-quality information in financial statements. (Think of who uses these statements and possible consequences of low quality information.)
5. (LO6) According to deontological ethics, the person should make ethical decisions that are reasonable and in accordance with "moral principles". Briefly explain what this means.
6. (LO2) Explain "relevant" information and information that "fairly represents".
7. (LO9) Explain why a stockholder is considered a "stakeholder" when a company's financial statements are prepared. Why a bank may be a stakeholder. Why an assembly line worker may be a stakeholder, a management executive. Could "the general public" be a stakeholder? Explain your answer.
8. (LO11) Identify some "pressures" and give examples of how they may influence decision making for an accountant.

REFERENCES

Aristotle (1985) *Nicomachean Ethics*, translated by T. Irwin. Indianapolis, IN: Hackett Publishing Company.

Doucet, M. & Doucet, T. (2004) Ethics of virtue and ethics of duty: Defining the norms of the profession. *Research on Professional Responsibility and Ethics in Accounting*, 9: 147–168.

Rachels, J. & Rachels, S. (2009) *The Elements of Moral Philosophy*, 6th edn. New York: McGraw-Hill.

A DECISION MODEL FOR ACCOUNTING ETHICS

CHAPTER THREE

Defining the Problem – From an Accounting and an Ethical Point of View

LEARNING OBJECTIVES

By the end of this chapter you should be able to:

1. Understand the concept of problem-definition.
2. Deepen your understanding of how problem solving requires both finding and formulating problems.
3. Understand the nature of problems as the gap between the current and the desired state.
4. Understand the difference the and relationship between the accounting problem and the ethical problem.
5. Understand how problems can be found and addressed or even prevented.
6. Understand principles that may enhance your ability to detect and define ethical problems in accounting.

ACCOUNTING AS DECISION-MAKING

Reminder: The purpose of financial accounting is to prepare financial statements with high quality information to be communicated to various stakeholders. The accounting standards establish the guidelines for preparing financial statements, and professional codes of ethics express the basic principles for accountants' long-term conduct and specific practices.

Reminder: Decision-making is a crucial feature of accounting practice. Competent decision making includes both technical proficiency and ethical sensibility.

Reminder: Understanding accounting ethics as decision-making implies seeing the ethical problem faced by accountants as consisting of a series of challenges throughout the decision-making process (from problem-definition to action).

INTRODUCTION

In the first part of this book, we introduced our understanding of accounting ethics. In Chapter Two, we introduced our decision-making perspective on accounting ethics. This is summarized in the decision model upon which the next sections of the book are based. In the following chapters, we will provide a step by step discussion of the key stages of the ethical decision-making process in accounting.

The problem treated in this chapter is the most fundamental decision-making problem: *finding* and *formulating* the problem itself. The chapter thus deals with the first step of any decision-making process, which is to figure out what the decision to be made actually entails. This is arguably an overlooked aspect of decision making – especially in educational contexts. Often we are presented with problems to be solved as pre-defined and pre-labeled. Yet a key feature of decision-making in real-life situations is that the task of finding and understanding problems and making decisions is often left to the individual. In the real world, decisions do not come pre-labeled; therefore the first challenge faced by the decision maker is to identify the problem that must be solved and define its key features. This requires attention, effort, skill, and motivation.

In this chapter, we address the first step of the decision-making process – defining the problem. As indicated in the chapter title, ethical problems in accounting have a dual nature. On the one hand, they are *accounting problems* that need to be understood within the framework of accounting knowledge and accounting principles. On the other hand, they are *ethical problems* in their own right, yet within the accounting context. This means that they have ethical implications for a business environment and in the wider society. These ethical dimensions should be considered as an integral part of the problem to be addressed in the decision-making process.

In order to make an appropriate and justifiable decision, the decision maker needs to understand a given problem clearly and define its particular features in a manner that renders the problem manageable for the decision maker. This chapter deals with the process of finding, understanding and defining problems in accounting ethics. In our decision model (reproduced in Figure 3.1), this chapter is represented by the first box on the left-hand side of the model: *Defining the Problem*. As the model illustrates, this step is the entryway into the decision-making process. The way in which the problem is identified and defined serves as a "frame" for the individual's decision-making effort: this frame determines which characteristics of the situation and its environment should be considered, as well as which problem-solving resources are

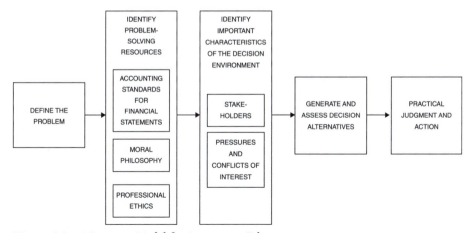

Figure 3.1   A Decision Model for Accounting Ethics

appropriate to apply. This frame influences the decision alternatives that are considered, thus it affects the final decision. Each of these steps is treated in the following chapters.

The chapter is structured as follows. First, we explore the nature of problem-definition and its place in the decision-making process. Second, we outline the two problem dimensions in accounting ethics and illuminate the distinction between the accounting problem and the ethical problem. Third, we discuss the challenge of *identifying the problem*. Fourth, we discuss the challenge of *formulating the problem*. Finally, we summarize the chapter and point forward to the following chapters.

PROBLEM-DEFINITION: FINDING AND FORMULATING THE PROBLEM

Any decision-making or problem-solving process begins with the decision maker noticing a problem and then making sense of what the problem actually entails. This step of decision-making is typically called the *problem-definition*. The authors' view of problem-definition assumes an active and conscious approach to problem-definition. Yet it should be noted that all-too-often decision makers take the nature of the problem as given and do not spend enough time reflecting on the precise nature of the problem or defining its features clearly. This failure to reflect adequately carries the risk of misunderstanding the problem and can lead the decision maker to *solve the wrong problem*.

Problem-definition involves identifying the nature of the problem in its key features and refers to the process whereby the decision maker makes sense of the decision to be made. Hence, there are two distinct processes that are part of problem-definition: (1) realizing that one is faced with a problem, and (2) understanding what the problem entails. A common understanding of problem-definition is that it involves identifying "the gap between the current state and the ideal state". By this we mean that there is something undesirable or unsatisfactory in the current situation with regard to how we would like things to be. This does not necessarily mean that one is faced by a problem in the negative sense – it may only mean that there is something that needs to be addressed and handled well. Someone must take care of the problem; that is, solve it. For instance, if a company is expanding its sales staff, we may consider the process of finding candidates and selecting new staff as "a problem" without implying that this is a negative circumstance for the organization. Yet until the task of hiring has been completed, the expansion constitutes a problem that needs a resolution.

PROBLEM-DEFINITION

Problem-definition involves identifying the nature of the problem in its key features and refers to the process whereby the decision maker makes sense of the decision to be made. Problem-definition involves both (1) finding the problem (i.e., identifying that one is faced by a problem) and (2) formulating the problem (i.e., understanding what the problem entails).

Problem-definition is a crucial part of decision-making, because during the stage of definition the boundaries of the problem are constructed. This means that we are "framing" the problem in a particular way so that we emphasize particular features of the problem while overlooking its other aspects. This framing step is commonly referred to as "constructing the problem space". The problem space may be narrow or broad, and the boundaries we conceive "around the problem" determine how we approach the special features of the problem. Since the definition of the problem builds on an initial understanding that a certain situation poses a problem, this stage of defining the problem serves as the point of departure for the subsequent problem-solving measures.

Consider, for example, the current climate crisis. It is common to think of climate change as a problem of high emissions (for instance, of CO_2). If we set the boundaries of the climate change problem as those of high emissions, it follows that our problem-solving measures will be tailored to reduce emissions (i.e., they will be directed at those who emit). This leads us to search for solutions that can entice businesses and governments to change their practices in order to reduce emissions. If, by contrast, we define the climate change problem in a different way – for example, defining the problem more broadly than that of producers' emissions and instead as a problem of a widespread consumerist lifestyle – this suggests that individuals' social behavior must be addressed in solving the problem. This opens up new possibilities, alternative solutions, for managing the problem. In this instance, rather than attempting to influence airline companies into reducing their emissions (through legislation or economic incentives), individuals might be encouraged to change their habits of consumption and reduce their travel by airplane. How we construct the problem space, define the problem, then, is crucial for how we address and solve that problem.

As indicated, problem-definition comprises two distinct aspects; it is fruitful to treat them separately, since they involve distinct issues and give rise to different challenges. First, problem-definition involves what is commonly referred to as *problem finding*. Second, problem-definition further involves *problem formulation*. Later in the chapter we outline each component of problem-definition. First, however, we must distinguish between what we call the "accounting problem" and the "ethical problem". These two types of problems are key aspects of the difficulties that an accountant decision maker may encounter in the accounting situations. The identification and definition of any given problem in the accounting situation will likely need to make such a distinction. In brief, this distinction will be crucial for framing the problems that emerge in the domain of accounting ethics.

THE ACCOUNTING PROBLEM AND THE ETHICAL PROBLEM

We have already characterized a problem as "the gap between the current state and the desired state". Given this view, a principal characteristic of problems in accounting ethics is their dual nature. On the one hand, there is a gap between the current and desired states in relation to accounting. For example, look back at earlier accounting decisions: there may be something in the way that accounting decisions were made that deviates from the relevant accounting standards and principles. Or in another circumstance, looking ahead to an accounting decision yet to be made: the financial situation may be complicated and confusing to the accountant, or he will experience pressures within the circumstance that will make it difficult to follow the rules of the profession or act with integrity in the situation. In such cases, the decision maker is challenged in the accounting decision and may struggle with how to act. Resolving these problems – largely technical in their nature – requires knowledge and skill related to the rules of accounting; it requires *technical proficiency*.

On the other hand, there may also be a gap between the current and desired states in relation to ethics. In such a circumstance, something is being done that violates shared principles, standards or judgments of what is considered right, good or wise – principles likely shared by the accountant and those whom he or she serves. In another instance, the accountant decision maker faces a situation in which important values are at stake for the various stakeholders and these particular values may be in conflict or the interests of the different stakeholders may collide. These problems are ethical in nature, and dealing with such dilemmas requires knowledge and skill related to ethical judgment; such circumstances call for *ethical sensibility*.

It follows from this brief description of both accounting problems and ethical problems that both types of problem may be either *retrospective* or *prospective* in nature. In this book, we deal with both types of problems. When we talk about problems that are retrospective in nature, we are referring to situations in which something has already been done, and this has given rise to a problematic situation. Often this forces an issue of accountability, meaning that the individual has to account for what he or she did in the past and must now act to rectify the situation. By contrast, when we speak about problems that are prospective in nature, we refer to situations in which the decision maker has not yet decided or acted. This means that the problem relates to a decision yet to be made. Retrospective problems, then, generate questions of what was done, what this led to, who is to blame, and how to avoid this problem in the future; prospective problems are questions of *what to do*.

In ethics, we are concerned with both retrospective and prospective problems. In order for individuals and organizations to improve their ethical conduct, it is important to be able both (1) to recognize when something ethically problematic has already occurred, and (2) to recognize when you faced an ethically challenging decision before that decision is made. Both challenges involve the finding and formulation of problems; that is, the individual needs to be able to identify the presence of a problematic situation and to make sense of what the problem entails. In the dual context of problems relating both to accounting and ethics, these challenges require specific knowledge and skill in two separate domains. In addition, problem-solving needs to be integrated by a simultaneous assessment of the problem from both perspectives of accounting and ethics. We treat each type of problem in the following section.

The Accounting Problem

Any accounting ethics problem has its basis in accounting-related content matter. At the core of the problem, then, is an accounting issue. For the purposes of this book, we think of accounting problems as *problems related to the practice of accounting, in which accountants aim to prepare financial information properly for users of information, but in which the quality of information may be threatened or undermined by the accountant's decision or by other parties' attempts to influence the accountant's decision.*

When we talk about accounting problems, we refer to situations wherein the accountant has to make an accounting-related decision and there is a gap between the current state and the desired state. This gap may be *knowledge-based*; that is, it may be that the accountant faces an issue for which he or she does not have adequate knowledge or skill to make a good decision. The gap may be *motivation-based*; that is, it may be that the accountant faces an issue in which he or she is not motivated to do what is required by accounting standards or what is to be expected from a sound judgment grounded in accounting principles. One possible reason for lack of motivation may be that the accountant does not perceive there to be clear sanctions (positive or negative) in response to either the ethical or the unethical behavior.

> ### THE ACCOUNTING PROBLEM
>
> Accounting problems are problems related to the practice of accounting, in which accountants aim to prepare financial information for users of information, but in which the quality of information may be threatened or undermined by the accountant's decision or by attempts by other parties to influence that accountant's decision.

Let us consider two examples related to the practice of auditing to illuminate this distinction between an accounting problem and an ethical problem. An auditor may be faced by the task of auditing a firm that sells products in bulk, and there are nuanced differences between their different products that otherwise appear similar to the naked eye. In such a setting, the auditor may overlook these differences due to his or her lack of knowledge about the products in question. This could lead the auditor to fail to reveal misstatements in the valuation of the company's inventory at year-end. In this situation, the auditor's knowledge is the problem, and the problem could have been solved by the auditor if he or she had acquired more knowledge about the products and their valuation prior to the audit. Alternatively, we can envision an auditor in the same situation realizing that there were, in fact, such nuanced differences in quality and value of the products, but the auditor chooses to overlook this in order to avoid making the necessary inquiries and tests to value the products properly. (The accountant may be trying to save time.) In this situation, the auditor's motivation is the problem and to solve this personal problem, it may require providing the auditor with the incentives (i.e., reward or punishment) to conduct the task in a manner consistent with the accounting standards. This simple example shows that it is important to understand the nature of a problem in order to find an appropriate solution.

As discussed above, accounting problems can be either retrospective or prospective in nature. An example of a retrospective problem is one that relates to misstatements in financial reporting or failures to disclose information in financial statements already published. For example, in our class list case, a student discovers that one of his friends has forged a signature. Now what does the student do: report the forgery, warn the friend not to do it again, or ignore the situation? In such cases, the problem concerns previous decisions. In another example, the accounting problems are seen in a current situation where a decision is yet to be made. In the class list example, what should a student do with regard to the continuing forgeries: tell the instructor, report the matter to other school officials, or keep quiet? In another example from a business setting a decision may involve the choice of how to estimate bad debts for the company. In general, estimates are an example of accounting problems where there is considerable potential for making problematic decisions, since the accountant has considerable freedom in making estimates.

On many occasions in this book, you will be asked to reflect on accounting problems. The nature of those problems will differ with regard to whether they are retrospective or prospective. This will influence the features of the problems we ask you to consider, the definition of the problems. The retrospective or prospective nature of the problems you face will influence which features of the problem may be of most importance and the types of reflection you should use to resolve the issues. For problems that are retrospective in nature, questions like "What has been done that is problematic?" "What allowed this to happen?" and "What can be done to remedy the negative effects of what was done?" will be appropriate. For problems that are prospective in nature, other questions will be appropriate and helpful. Examples include: "What are the action alternatives of the accountant?" "How would the different alternatives differently influence the stakeholders in the situation?" "What is the quality of information stakeholders receive in each alternative solution?"

Thus far we have provided a broad overview of the nature of accounting problems. In Chapter Four, we give an in-depth presentation of the resources that are necessary for properly understanding accounting problems – the frameworks for preparing financial statements and how to judge the quality of accounting information. These sources serve as the resources for our insight into the desired state – the ideal manner for presenting accounting information – and these serve as benchmarks that may allow us to recognize accounting problems when information is prepared without regarding the standards or accounting principles, or when there is uncertainty regarding how to present a specific item to users of information.

The Ethical Problem

In addition to the accounting-specific issue, any accounting ethics problem involves content-matter that has a prominent ethical dimension. Such problems have to do with issues of right or wrong, good or bad, wisdom or foolishness. For the purposes of this book, we think of ethical problems as *problems where multiple values are at stake, and in which the various decision or action alternatives of the individual have different value implications for the parties influenced by the choice.*

When we speak about ethical problems, we refer to situations wherein the individual (the accountant) has to make a choice or engage in action that has ethical significance, and there is a gap between the current state and the desired state. We make a similar distinction as above. On the one hand, there are *knowledge-based gaps* (i.e., the individual does not know what is right or wrong, good or bad, in the situation). On the other hand, there are *motivation-based gaps* (i.e., the individual knows what is right and what is wrong, but is not sufficiently motivated to act in accordance with his or her ethical judgment).

THE ETHICAL PROBLEM

Ethical problems are problems where multiple values are at stake, and in which the various decision or action alternatives of the individual have different value implications for the parties influenced by the choice.

Ethical problems, as we have seen, can be either retrospective or prospective. In ethics, the retrospective view is typically about ascribing accountability. By this we mean making assessments of praise or blame on the basis of what someone has done – relative to shared conceptions of what they *should have done*. Accountability is a central aspect of behavior in all organizations, and it has prominent ethical dimensions. Accountability deals with justifications of why someone did what he or she did, and the extent to which this is seen as acceptable behavior. The retrospective view thus deals with making ethical assessments *after the fact*, as well as trying to understand how a given transgression could have occurred and whether something can be done to fix the problem. By contrast, the prospective view in ethics is largely about responsibility in the present circumstance: it deals with the question of what to do in the current situation. This is a question *before the fact* of arriving at a justifiable choice and action.

Two general questions are central to any ethical problem: (1) *What is at stake?* (2) *For whom?* These questions aim at revealing two central aspects of the problem: who are the involved parties that are affected by the decision and in what way are they affected; that is, which values or interests are at stake in the decision. For instance, in a situation where a company is considering whether to understate its debt in order to secure a loan, there is a trade-off between the moral value of truthfulness and the economic value of securing the loan. In addition, the interests of the company (secure financing) and the bank (manage risk) are at stake. The two questions – what is at stake and for whom? – can help the decision maker identify key characteristics of the decision from an ethical point of view. Making an ethical decision means ensuring that decisions are made in an ethically sensible manner either by reducing harm to involved parties or by making decisions and taking actions that comply with relevant norms and principles. The starting point for such assessments is to understand what is at stake and for whom. An essential part of formulating the ethical problem, then, is the identification and "mapping" of these aspects of the problem.

Thus far, we have provided a broad overview of the nature of ethical problems. In Chapter Five, we give an in-depth presentation of resources that are appropriate for helping us to understand ethical problems – several prominent theories of moral philosophy. These resources serve as guidelines for our insight into the desired state – allowing us to recognize ethical problems and to distinguish between that which is or is not ethically justifiable.

Similar, Yet Differing: Accounting Problems and Ethical Problems

In the previous sections, we have shed light on what characterizes the accounting problem and what characterizes the ethical problem. In this book, we are concerned with the specific type of problems that integrate both accounting-based features and those aspects related to ethics in a given situation. We have argued that finding and formulating the accounting problem is about discerning the accounting-relevant features of the current situation as well as of the desired state; that is, what one is trying to achieve as an ideal solution. Formulating the ethical problem, in comparable fashion, is about discerning what is ethically relevant in the situation at hand, the features of the situation and characteristics of the decision to be made that are relevant from an ethical point of view. As we will see in Chapter Five, different ethical perspectives within the moral traditions lead us to arrive at various answers to such questions. This means that the formulation of the ethical problem may well be grounded in different understandings of ethics.

We have previously stated that problems in accounting ethics comprise an accounting dimension and an ethical dimension. These two perspectives of the problem are partially overlapping; despite their differences, they express some similarities with one another. The reason for this is that accounting principles and rules carry within them ethical judgments that are seen as appropriate from an accounting point of view. We might say that accounting theory and its relevant frameworks are based on a particular type of ethics. Let us consider a concrete example. A fundamental principle for auditors is that they have a duty to maintain confidentiality vis-à-vis their clients. That is, they are not to disclose information obtained through the auditor–client relationship unless this is authorized by the client or it is ordered by the relevant regulatory bodies (for instance, the SEC). If we look at the decision of whether or not to disclose information from an accounting point of view, the clear conclusion is that the auditor should not disclose information, since doing so would be a violation of the auditor's professional responsibility. From an ethical point of view, however, what is the problem with violating confidentiality? This question brings us deeper into the justification of the technical rule. One ethical justification may be that it would inflict harm on the client, since sensitive information could end up in the public domain, giving advantage to a competitor or threatening the profitability of the client's business. Another, and quite different, justification would be that violating confidentiality would undermine public trust in the audit process, thus threatening the professional legitimacy of the auditing profession. And other ethical perspectives could inform us as we seek to justify the decision.

This simple example illustrates how the accounting problem and the ethical problem are intertwined; they both express aspects of a larger issue, yet when we view the problem through the lens of accounting, we highlight different features of the problem than when we view it through the lens of an ethical perspective. Because of the nature of the situation and the duality of the problems contained within it, analyzing it from both points of view may lead us to a deeper understanding of its features, increase our *knowledge* of the ethical dimensions of the accounting decision and *motivate* us to take ethically justifiable behavior in accounting practice. In addition, taking ethics into account may lead the decision maker to act in a different manner than if he had not made an ethical assessment of the situation.

In this context, we typically employ two different vocabularies when we talk about accounting problems and ethical problems. In this book we draw on sources from accounting theory, its conceptual framework, and current accounting standards and also from moral philosophy and professional ethics. This combination of perspectives and languages provides the reader with resources that allow for in-depth analyses of ethical issues in accounting, both from an accounting point of view and from an ethical point of view. Ultimately the purpose of this approach is to enhance the reader's ability to identify and manage problems with this dual nature in a way that accords with professional accounting standards and sound ethical judgment (to demonstrate technical proficiency and ethical sensibility).

Up to this point, we have explored the two components of accounting ethics problems – the accounting problem and the ethical problem – and illuminated some important characteristics of these types of problems from each perspective. In the remainder of the chapter, we discuss the distinct challenges of (1) finding the problem and (2) formulating the problem in accounting ethics.

FINDING THE PROBLEM IN ACCOUNTING ETHICS

As we argued in the chapter introduction, problem-definition involves both finding and formulating the problem. It consists both of the challenge of identifying that one faces a problem (finding the problem) and the challenge of understanding what the problem actually entails (formulating the problem).

When we introduced the decision model in Chapter Two, we used the simple example of an attendance list in an accounting ethics class to illustrate the steps of the decision model. The case described a situation wherein an attendance list is the "accounting system" for student attendance, but the reliability of the system is threatened by students faking each other's signatures in order to skip class occasionally. In that context, we asked: "What should a student do, if asked to participate in this practice?"

In the situation, we might distinguish between four broad categories of student response:

1. Student 1 recognizes that this is an ethical issue and abstains from joining in the practice of faking signatures.
2. Student 2 recognizes the ethical issue, but still joins in the practice.
3. Student 3 does not recognize that this is an ethical issue, but does not join in the practice.
4. Student 4 does not recognize the ethical issue and joins in the practice.

This overview shows that student 1 and student 2 are able to *find the problem*, but they arrive at different decisions from each other, while student 3 and student 4 actually *do not find the problem* in the first place, although they also arrive at different decisions from one another.

An important characteristic of our moral psychology is revealed in this simple distinction between the four students: We differ in the degree to which we are able to identify that we are faced by an ethical issue. This is very important, for being able to identify an ethical issue is a presupposition for making a *consciously ethical* decision. It is, of course, possible to act ethically without consciously thinking about one's act as ethical: If we consider not joining the signature-faking practice as being an ethical decision, student 3 acts ethically without consciously trying to do so. In order for an individual to make an informed decision related to accounting ethics, however, it is a necessary requirement that the individual be able to *find the problem*.

The ability to recognize when one is faced by an ethical problem is referred to as *moral sensitivity,* and individuals differ in the degree to which they are sensitive to the moral dimensions of situations. In an accounting context, this is an important part of the accountant's ethical competence. Moral sensitivity is fundamentally a question of awareness: is the accountant "tuned into" the moral dimensions of accounting practice? While individuals may differ in their natural inclination to conceive of moral issues, there are cognitive strategies that can be employed to enhance one's ability to identify ethical issues, and knowledge about ethics and the nature of ethical transgressions can support the accountant's effort to recognize situations that have a prominent ethical dimension and subsequently identify its features.

Awareness, Discernment, and the Ability to Find the Problem

As indicated above, finding the problem is largely a matter of awareness and discernment. By this we mean that finding the problem requires (1) awareness of specific types of features within situations (accounting-relevant and ethically relevant) and (2) the ability to discern between situations in which there are significant threats from an accounting point of view or from an ethical point of view and situations in which this is not the case. In Chapter Six, we will discuss codes of ethics in accounting and auditing and how they support the ethical decision making of accountants and auditors in practice. In such professional codes, there is a heavy emphasis on the distinction between significant and non-significant threats; that is, where to draw the line between those ethical issues which are so important that they need to be specifically addressed and the ethical issues which are only of minor importance.

Awareness and discernment are distinct skills, and both are important factors that promote the individual's ability to *find the right problems*. Awareness has a conscious side as well as an unconscious one; that is, individuals differ in the degree to which they are attuned to different aspects of life, but they can also work consciously at becoming more aware of any given object. This also means that experience and knowledge can be important drivers of knowledge, since it is easier to become aware of things that correspond with our existing framework of knowledge and experiences. Discernment is also in an important sense related to the individual's knowledge and experiences, since we learn to make distinctions – between relevant and irrelevant, important and unimportant, problematic and unproblematic – largely through experiences with concrete cases and structured reflection on the similarities and the differences among the case features.

The difficulty of finding the problem is exacerbated by the fact that individuals in general and professionals in business practice in particular have *limited time, effort, and attention*. This threatens the ability to find problems, since the scarcity of these resources implies that time, effort, and attention spent on "searching for" ethical problems in one's professional practice comes at the expense of spending these resources on other tasks. The upshot, however, is that by improving one's ability to become aware of (and give attention to) ethical dimensions of accounting practice, accountants may in fact improve their ability to find the right problems without expending too much time and effort in the long run.

To promote this end, simple heuristics or rules of thumb can be used by the individual to promote one's awareness of ethical problems in accounting, to become better at finding such problems in everyday practice. We suggest two such rules of thumb which can serve as "warning signs" or indicators that the accountant is facing a situation of ethical significance. These suggestions can thereby serve as entryways into further ethical reflection to make sense of the problem and reach a sound judgment to handle it.

Following Kvalnes, we refer to the two "rules of thumb" as *the principle of equal treatment* and *the public principle*, respectively.[1] These two principles can serve as simple indicators of whether or not a decision or situation has ethical significance. They are both intuitive and simple to use, yet powerful in the sense that they serve as clear tests to indicate whether one is faced by an ethical problem.

The Principle of Equal Treatment

The principle of equal treatment can be stated as follows: *similar cases should be treated similarly, and if two similar cases are treated dissimilarly, it should be possible to point out an ethically relevant difference between them*. This principle is based on a value that arguably characterizes the majority of ethical theories, namely *impartiality*. Equal treatment is a cornerstone in accounting and auditing, and it is an important principle in financial accounting that financial reports should provide all users of information with similar information about the financial performance and position of the company.

As is evident from how the principle of equal treatment is stated, there are certainly exceptions from equal treatment that can be justified on ethical grounds. In such cases, however, it is necessary that the unequal treatment can be justified with respect to differences that are seen as relevant from the perspectives of those affected by the treatment.

THE PRINCIPLE OF EQUAL TREATMENT

Similar cases should be treated similarly, and if two similar cases are treated dissimilarly, it should be possible to point out an ethically relevant difference between them.

Let us revisit the case of the attendance list, in order to illustrate the principle of equal treatment. In this case, a relevant question might be: is it appropriate from an accounting point of view and from an ethical point of view that both students who are present and those who are not have their signatures on the list? Quite clearly, this is not appropriate – either from an accounting point of view (improving quality of information in the list) or from an ethical point of view (students truthfully representing whether or not they are present). There is a clear inequality in giving credit to both the attending and the non-attending students. Could we, however, with regard to the principle of equal treatment conceive of a situation where it would be justifiable that students not in attendance were accounted for on the attendance list? One justifiable example could be if a group of students were away from class on the given day in order to collect information for a classroom project. In this case, the students would be given credit for attendance, and thereby be on the list, while not actually being present in the lecture. The point is that both from the accounting and the ethical points of view, equal treatment suggests similar treatment of similar cases, while particular and relevant differences may justify different treatment between otherwise similar cases.

Before making a decision, asking yourself if you would treat any other person, situation or problem in a similar way (and if not, why) can be a powerful rule of thumb that may prevent you from making a decision that is ill-advised. In addition, the principle of equal treatment is a useful first step in reflection on the ethical issue at hand, because it necessitates some preliminary ethical analysis with regard to what constitutes ethically relevant differences in different cases. In these ways the principle not only relates to awareness and defining the problem, but also to subsequent stages in the ethical decision-making process.

The Public Principle

The public principle is stated: *you should be comfortable explaining your decision or act in public, and to inform all involved parties of what you have done*. The public principle is often also referred to as "the TV test," referring to the principle that you should always be willing to justify any choice you make on national television. Perhaps the most powerful aspect of the public principle as a test of a given decision or action is that it calls for an assessment of whether you would be willing to justify your act to the face of those who are influenced by the decision. Unethical decisions are easier to make when there is distance between the actor and those affected by the act, and the public principle encourages the decision maker to visualize those affected by the decision prior to making the choice.

THE PUBLIC PRINCIPLE

You should be comfortable explaining your decision or act in public, and to inform all involved parties of what you have done.

Consider again the concrete example of the attendance list. The student faced with the offer of signing for another student could use the public principle as a test of whether or not it is justifiable. He could envision having to explain his choice in the school newspaper, or perhaps, more personally, getting up in front of the class and the lecturers to give account for his choice. Using a simple test such as the public principle here clearly indicates that this would not be comfortable. Considering the scenario, the student can ask himself why this would be uncomfortable and thus explore the question of *"what is the problem* with forging a signature?"

Before making a decision, asking yourself whether you would be comfortable explaining it or your subsequent action can be a powerful rule of thumb that may prevent you from making unprofessional or unethical decisions. As with the case of the principle of equal treatment, we see how the public principle may trigger further reflection that is useful for ethical analysis.

Obstacles for Finding the Problem

We have shed light on the process of finding the problem in accounting ethics, and we have argued that it involves both awareness and discernment. As we have also indicated, there are obstacles to finding the problem which may prevent accountants from recognizing that they are faced by an ethical issue.

We emphasized that time, attention, and effort are scarce resources and that when individuals are under pressure they may miss important problems. Research in psychology has demonstrated the phenomenon of *inattentional blindness*, which happens when individuals focus their attention on one or more specific things and thereby miss other important features of problem or situation at hand. This could be because they are not asked to be attentive to these features, because they are not trained to be attentive, or simply because their capacity for attention is overloaded. To the extent that ethics is not emphasized as crucial for the accountant – as part of his role or as important for the company in which he works – there is a risk that ethical dimensions of accounting decisions may be overlooked through intentional blindness. The upside of this discussion is that by actively focusing on ethical dimensions – for instance, by using tools such as the two principles outlined above – the individual may move beyond this blindness and enhance situational and ethical awareness.

A second challenge that may hinder the finding of ethical problems in accounting practice is lack of knowledge about the nature of ethical inquiry and decision making. In Chapter Five, we will explore the theories of moral philosophy that may aid the individual accountant in becoming aware of ethical issues and of discerning between the ethically relevant and the ethically irrelevant. The reason for a book like this one and for courses in accounting ethics is that expanding your knowledge about ethics may stimulate consciousness about ethics in your practice. Without a proper vocabulary to talk about ethical issues or lacking perspectives to help the accountant grasp that important values may be at stake for stakeholders in any given accounting decision, the accountant is inadequately equipped to recognize that a decision has ethical significance. This obstacle may be overcome by increasing the accountant's ethical competence, by developing a wider base of knowledge and encouraging ethical motivation.

Finally, another challenge that may be an obstacle for finding ethical problems in accounting practice is the accountant's motivation (or lack thereof) for doing so. This means that accountants may fail to recognize that they are faced by an ethical issue simply because they do not place importance on such issues. It is well established that individuals have so-called *motivated cognition*; that is, that we notice things that are important to us but not things we consider to be unimportant. This suggests that it matters whether or not ethical sensibility is emphasized as a crucial competence for accountants, since emphasizing this sensibility may influence their self-understanding as professionals to make them more inclined to pay attention to ethical issues.

FORMULATING THE PROBLEM IN ACCOUNTING ETHICS

In the previous section, we treated the decision maker's ability to identify problems, and we spoke of obstacles to such identification. Becoming aware of a problem, however, is only a first step of problem-definition. Problem finding can take many forms: it can be an intuitive sense or a "gut feeling" that something is not quite right, it can happen through the conscious use of tools such as the public principle, or other indicators in the situation may suggest to the accountant that he faces a problem. Following the awareness of a particular problem, however, he needs to make sense of it. What does the problem entail? He needs to formulate the problem.

As the word "formulate" suggests, problem formulation concerns how the problem is stated, the wording that expresses how to understand the problem. When the accountant realizes that he faces a problem, he must clarify to himself the precise nature of the problem. In effect, this formulation is the individual's representation of the gap between the current state and the desired state. This means that the formulation is based on (1) the accountant's understanding of the important characteristics of the current situation, with particular emphasis on the problematic features that he has "found" in the situation, and (2) the accountant's understanding of the ideal state, a preferred state of affairs; that is, what would be a desirable outcome of the situation after action is taken. Problem formulation is important because the manner in which the problem is stated is crucial for understanding the gap between the actual and the ideal and determining the subsequent movement toward solutions and action-choices by the accountant.

Consider a simple illustration. An individual may "find" a problem in his own life, related to the fact that he is "out-of shape" physically. This problem can be formulated in a multitude of ways, each suggesting a specific understanding of what the problem entails and how it might be solved. The following statements are alternative problem formulations that partially overlap, but each focuses on features of the problem thought to be particularly salient and therefore suggests different solutions as appropriate: "I am overweight," "I have too high a body mass index," "I eat too much," "I don't exercise enough". As is evident from this short list of problem formulations, these statements suggest different understandings of what the problem entails (or at least different aspects of the same problem), and they suggest different solutions for each problem formulation. For instance, it is possible to solve the problem of being overweight with or without exercise, which implies that these two problems are not merely different phrasings of an identical problem, but rather different variations of problem formulation of the related issues.

Problem formulation, then, has to do with how the individual represents the problem to himself: which features of the current situation are highlighted, which goals or aspirations are implicit in the problem formulation, and what the particular formulation suggests with regard to an action-choice, suggestions of what might be done. A fundamental idea in our book is that accountants can improve their ability to formulate problems both from an accounting point of view and from an ethical point of view by being proficient in accounting knowledge and skills and also by employing ethical perspectives relevant to accounting. Embedded in this accounting knowledge are the profession's assessments of problematic practices as well as the ideals and standards that should guide accounting decisions and practice. In this context, the problem formulation for a virtuous accountant will be informed by knowledge of how accounting information should be prepared and transmitted and by knowledge of the values, norms and principles that guide accounting practice.

Let us revisit the attendance list example to explore how the problem of that situation might be formulated. As we recall, a student in the accounting ethics class has been asked to join in the practice of signing the list for another student, thus permitting other students to take turns skipping class. What is the problem for this student? The problem space in this situation is, in fact, quite broad. The student might ask: "Wouldn't my joining in the practice contribute to creating a poorer learning experience for the students?" In this formulation, the problem is related to how the practice may create a gap between the current and the desired state with regard to learning quality. By contrast, she reasons: "This practice has to be stopped. Would it be acceptable for me to inform the lecturers?" In this case, the problem formulation relates not to whether she should join – this is not a question for her. Instead, she sees the problem as a question of how to prevent the practice of faking signatures. A third formulation of the problem might involve the student asking: "How can I refuse taking part in this practice without offending my fellow students?" In this case, her formulation of the ethical problem relates to the social dimension of the problem. We could state several other formulations of the problem, but the point here is that embedded in this single situation are several ethical dimensions of a larger complex problem. How the student formulates the problem depends on how she *sees* the problem and determines which features of the situation are most significant in relation to the values that are most important to her.

As the example shows, formulating the problem is not a simple task with a simple right or wrong pattern. Instead different people might see the same problem in different ways and conceive of a variety of ways to describe the gap between the current and the desired state. Of course, it is possible that most accounting problems will lend themselves to a more one-dimensional problem formulation than is the case in this situation. Yet the accountant may also face more complex problems that can be formulated in several different ways. For instance, consider a situation where an accountant is asked by his boss to recognize revenue early in order to achieve a sales target. The accounting issue itself is quite straightforward, and it is clear to see that there is an ethical gap between complying with the accounting rules and not doing so. However, the *situation* in which the accountant finds himself may have additional values at stake than just the question of rule compliance. The accountant knows what negative circumstances may develop for the company if this misstatement is detected, and he will also be aware that not following orders may have serious consequences for himself. How, then, should he act in this situation, where multiple values are at stake for multiple stakeholders – including himself, his boss, the company and other users of accounting information? There are several ways in which he can formulate this problem, each of which leads him to understand the situation differently and possibly to make different action-choices.

In order for accountants to have the resources necessary to address ethically challenging situations – both with regard to the actual practice of preparing financial statements and to the potential pressures that may influence decision making – accounting knowledge and ethical competence are useful. In the following, we briefly point to such resources that are presented in subsequent chapters and to how awareness of these resources may influence problem formulation.

Resources for Sound Problem Formulation

For problems related to accounting ethics, the current situation and the desired situation can be described both in accounting terms and in ethical terms. To do this, the accountant needs knowledge about the technical requirements of the practice and about ethics; he or she needs perspectives through which he can understand situations, problems, and decisions, and he needs an appropriate vocabulary for discussing these issues. For this reason, the next three chapters of the book are devoted to those resources that can aid the accountant in understanding and formulating the problems he or she might face. These resources should enable him or her to understand problems and to talk about how things should be, that is, in an ideal situation.

The frameworks for preparing financial statements and for assessing the quality of accounting information (Chapter Four) are necessary for understanding the goals of accounting which are to be sought as the ideal in a given accounting decision. In addition to the foundational standards of accounting practice, the accountant needs the appropriate perspective to discern between ethically relevant and ethically irrelevant features in situations where the quality of accounting information is threatened. He needs intellectual and moral resources to formulate desirable outcomes which embody worthwhile values and sound ethical principles (Chapter Five). Finally, in order to make accounting decisions that can be justified from both technical and ethical standpoints, and thus to act in a justifiable manner in accounting practice, knowledge of the codes of professional ethics and the formal statements of professional principles is crucial for accountants and auditors (Chapter Six). These resources form the knowledge base and foundational values upon which the accountant can make decisions and take actions.

In Chapter Four we will describe the framework for quality of information in accounting. This discussion outlines the characteristics that *should* be conveyed by accounting information. This means that these characteristics are critical sources for understanding the ideal state of accounting communication. Deviations from this state are then understood to constitute an accounting problem as well as an ethical problem. In such a situation a problem can then be formulated as the expression of a threat to the quality of accounting information at both a technical and an ethical level. For example, the problem formulation might be stated in this way: "The decision I am being asked to make would threaten the *relevance* of the financial statements. How can I avoid this?"

Similarly, in Chapter Five we will outline ethical perspectives that might inform accountants in decision making, such as utilitarianism and deontology (and duty ethics). These perspectives serve as analytical frameworks for understanding problems. They also suggest ideal states for a situation. As we will see, utilitarianism holds that *good* decisions maximize the positive consequences and minimize the negative consequences of an action for all involved parties. Deontology argues that the *right* decisions are in line with rational and universal principles. Based on such perspectives, a given problem might be formulated in the following ways: "Does the decision I am about to make seem to create more harm than benefit for the involved parties? How can I act differently in order to create a better outcome for them?" or "The decision I am about to make is hard to justify in light of the ethical principles that ought to govern my decisions as an accountant. How can I comply with the appropriate principles?"

Finally, in Chapter Six we will discuss the codes of ethics and the professional responsibilities that are embedded in the professional roles of accountants and auditors. These codes and principles can serve as the framework for assessing situations and identifying problems faced by the accountant. The codes give fairly clear directions about the values on which accounting practice should be based. The accountants' codes of ethics indicate the fundamental values and principles of accounting and suggest how threats to or violations of these norms should be handled by the accountant. Among other things, this involves assessing the significance of the threats (as we have already discussed as part of the section on finding problems) and finding safeguards that can dampen the problems. The codes of ethics may aid the accountant's problem formulation in several ways: by pointing out typical threats to professionally responsible action, by formulating the ideals of the profession, and by suggesting approaches for safeguarding against problems (this final issue, in fact, also goes beyond the task of merely formulating the problem, since safeguarding is part of problem solution.)

Obstacles to Problem Formulation

We have just discussed obstacles to finding the problem, which largely have to do with factors that undermine the ethical awareness and discernment of the accountant. Many of the same factors can interfere with the accountant's ability to formulate the problem, but the challenge here is largely about grounding an understanding of the problem, a grasp of the situation, within a relevant knowledge framework. Three particular challenges are salient in this regard.

First, as we have emphasized, an appropriate formulation of the problem depends on the ability of the accountant to phrase his understanding of the problem in an appropriate manner. This involves using relevant concepts and perspectives to highlight the central features of the problem and, in effect, to represent the gap between the current state and the desired state. To the extent that the accountant does not have an adequate vocabulary with regard to either accounting or ethics, his effort to formulate the problem may be undermined. This is similar to our earlier discussion of the obstacles encountered in finding the problem.

Second, the accountant's ability to formulate problems in accounting ethics depends on a knowledge of the frameworks we have outlined above – with regard to preparing financial statements of high quality, understanding the ethical dimensions of accounting, and affirming the professional responsibilities of the accountant and their implications for decision making and action. To the extent that the accountant lacks the knowledge to accompllish his ability to understand and represent the gap between the current and the desired state in situations related to accounting ethics may be undermined.

Finally, the accountant's effort to formulate an issue relevant to accounting ethics may be hindered by stakeholders who are trying to influence the decision. In Chapter Seven, we will discuss the various types of pressure aimed at influencing accounting decisions. These pressures may have a great impact on how accountants act in a given situation. These influences can include time pressure (as we discussed in relation to awareness), social pressure, and the blatant exertion of power by superiors in the organization. Just as problem-solving measures can be influenced by actors other than the individual himself, the individual's understanding of the problem can also be distorted by others. These people may exert various forms of influence to make the individual see the problem in ways that advance their own interests to the harm of others. One way that this may happen is through efforts to convince the accountant to see a significant ethical problem as if it were merely a technical issue without importance for stakeholders. Stakeholders may also try to influence the accountant's understanding of the ideal state. For example, if a company is under grave financial pressure, managers may try to persuade the accountant to formulate the problem as one of saving the company (as the ideal state) rather than as a problem of acting in accordance with standards – within relevant accounting frameworks, and according to cherished values and time-honored principles (an alternative ideal state that conflicts with the former emphasis on the fate of the company). In this way, the managers' undue influence hampers the accountant's ability to formulate the problem.

SUMMARY

In this chapter, we have shed light on the task of defining problems in accounting ethics. We have seen how problem-definition involves both finding and formulating ethical problems in accounting practice. This necessitates awareness, discernment, and knowledge on the part of the accountant, as well as the ability to understand the accounting point of view, the ethical point of view, and the relationship between them.

This chapter has explored the first step in our decision model. As we have seen, this step is crucial in the decision making process, since it shapes the subsequent stages of the decision process. How the accountant defines the problem is closely related to his goals and aspirations, as well the manner in which he construes the relevant features of the situation. Finally, problem-definition is crucial because it shapes the problem space within which the remaining decision-making process takes place.

In the following three chapters, we explore the various resources to which the accountant may turn to develop appropriate problem solving measures. In so doing, we turn to the question of how accountants approach and manage ethical problems in accounting practice.

CHAPTER REVIEW QUESTIONS

1. (LO1) Why and how is problem-definition central to decision making in accounting ethics?

2. (LO2) Explain what is meant by the distinction between finding and formulating problems in decision making.

3. (LO3) Explain what we mean by "a problem," and how our understanding of the problem depends on our view on how things are as well as of our goals or ideals.

4. (LO4) Explain how problems in accounting ethics are at the same time two types of problems – accounting problems and ethical problems.

5. (LO5) Discuss some of the things that interfere with the accountant's ability to identify that he is faced with an ethical issue.

6. (LO5) What might stand in the way of the accountant's ability to formulate an ethical issue in accounting?

7. (LO6) Explain the principle of equal treatment and the public principle and how they may help the accountant find and formulate ethical problems in accounting practice.

CASES

8. Estimating a Future Expense[2]

The cost associated with mothballing a nuclear power plant at the end of its useful life, approximately 20 years in the future, will be paid by the utility company when the plant is obsolete at the end of the 20 year period. When should the expense be recognized for this expenditure? Current utility users receive the benefit of this plant. Do accounting rules require them to pay the cost in terms of increased utility rates by including the expense of the future mothballing in their rates, or should the expense be delayed for 20 years, until the cash is actually paid out?

Required:

a. What are the accounting problems and the ethical problems in this situation?

b. How can the principle of equal treatment be used in this case, and what would it suggest?

    c. What are the options of the accountant? Assess them in light of the public principle.

9. Year-End Shipments

24 Karat Caramels is a new candy company specializing in flavored caramels. The company has advertised widely in catalogs and has received more orders than IT can ship on a daily basis. Elizabeth Hutchinson, the president, has instructed the shipping department to work overtime the last two weeks in December to ship as many orders as possible by year-end. Elizabeth says: "It is important for the company to show a profit in the first year of operations to obtain a bank loan to expand. We can recognize revenue on each sale as soon as we ship the caramels to the customers. At the end of the year, we will just recognize revenue on all the remaining orders, even if we have not shipped the goods."

Required:

    a. What is the accounting issue discussed in this problem? Can 24 Karat Caramels recognize revenue on the orders received or on the items shipped?

    b. Is there an ethical issue in this situation? Is the directive given by Elizabeth unethical or is it simply clever business advice?

    c. Assess Elizabeth's statement in light of the principle of equal treatment and the public principle.

10. Contingent Rental Fees

Allied Insurance Company, the owner of West Acres Mall, charges Software Etc. a rental fee of $25,000 per month, plus 5% of yearly profits over $5,000,000. Lee Grant, the owner of Software Etc., directs her accountant, Roger Harrison, to increase the estimate of bad debt expense, warranty costs, and depreciation on store equipment in order to keep profits at $4,900,000.

Required:

    a. What is the ethical problem facing Roger Harrison?

    b. Who is harmed if the estimates are increased? Who benefits?

    c. Based on your accounting knowledge, what should Roger do?

    d. What would you do? Explain your reasons to Lee Grant.

11. Debt Covenants

Tom Anderson, the controller for Plains Software, is in the process of reviewing the financial statements for the previous month. He is preparing the report to the insurance company that holds the bonds payable issued to finance the plant expansion. This report must be completed by the fifth of each month. Tom is horrified to find that the cash balance dropped below $3,000,000 the previous month, so technically the company is in default on its loan. This violation is serious, because now the $100,000,000 in long-term debt becomes a short-term liability that bondholders might decide to collect immediately. Tom suggests that Jason, the accountant in charge of cash receipts, hold the books open until November 1 to include these cash receipts in the October 31 cash balance. This extra day's receipts would increase the cash balance to the desired $3,000,000 mark.

Required:

    a. What is the accounting problem for these accountants?

    b. Consider two heuristics for recognizing ethical problems: does either the principle of equal treatment or the public principle suggest that the accountants have an ethical problem?

    c. What is the ethical problem for these accountants? What is at stake in this decision and for whom?

    d. Explain how defining the problem helps you resolve the problem.

12. Classifying Notes Payable

Chris Sanderson and Jeremy Ulster are working on the statement of cash flows for the Oak Grove Management Company. It is their responsibility to determine the cash flow from operations to calculate the yearly dividend payment to the twenty shareholders of the company. The board of directors specified that dividends can be paid only when the cash flow from operations is at least $50,000,000. The owners of the company expect to receive a sizable dividend each year and may fire management if the company fails to produce the required cash flow. On January 15, 2015, Sanderson and Ulster calculate the cash flow from operations to be $45,000,000. Their supervisor, Julia Kremer, suggests several ways to increase operating cash flow above the $50,000,000 mark. Her most forceful suggestion is to reclassify a two-year note payable taken out on November 1, 2013, as a short-term note payable. The change will increase cash flow from operations to $52,500,000 and will permit the payment of the dividend.

Required:

    a. Does the reclassification of the long-term note payable to a current liability account have the desired effect on the statement of cash flows? Explain.

    b. What is the accounting problem for these accountants?

    c. Consider two heuristics for recognizing ethical problems: does either the principle of equal treatment or the public principle suggest that the accountants have an ethical problem?

    d. What is the ethical problem for these accountants? What is at stake in this decision and for whom?

    e. Explain how defining the problem helps you resolve the problem.

NOTES

    1. See Øyvind Kvalnes (2006) *Se Gorillaen: Etikk i Arbeid*. Oslo: Universssitesforlaget.

    2. This case will be presented in several chapters with different questions for each chapter. This will illustrate how each of the tools can be used to help the accountant make a decision that reflects both technical proficiency and ethical awareness.

CHAPTER FOUR

Accounting Standards for Financial Statements: Resources for Decision Making

LEARNING OBJECTIVES

By the end of this chapter you should be able to:

1. Understand that the objective of financial statements is to provide useful information about a company to outsiders.

2. Explain the role of the conceptual framework and the accounting standards as resources to provide guidance to the accountant for making accounting decisions that reflect technical competence and ethical awareness in the preparation of financial statements.

3. Describe the financial statements required by regulators and the technical requirements to recognize and value financial statement elements in these statements.

4. Explain how the qualitative characteristics of information in the financial statements: relevance and fair representation and the enhancing qualitative characteristics: comparability, verifiability, timeliness, and understandability are related to decisions made about how information is presented in the financial statements.

5. Describe ethical issues related to preparing the statement of financial position and the profit or loss statement.

6. Explain two types of fraud and the conditions typically associated with the occurrence of fraud in the financial statements.

ACCOUNTING AS A VEHICLE FOR OBJECTIVE FINANCIAL INFORMATION

Reminder: Accounting is a discursive practice; accountants produce business knowledge and communicate it to stakeholders, who use this knowledge to make business decisions.

Reminder: Accountants should exercise a dual competency: technical proficiency – knowledge of accounting standards and capacity to apply them in practice – and ethical sensibility – capacity to recognize moral issues, resolve ethical dilemmas, and demonstrate the motivation and commitment to do the right thing, that is, act ethically.

Reminder: Accountants have an ethics of duty – obligations to adhere to principles and obey rules (follow accounting standards) – and an ethics of virtue – to gain and realize virtues, that is, to possess the distinctive intellectual and moral traits of character of the virtuous accountant and to use these virtues in the particular activities of accounting practice.

THE OBJECTIVE OF FINANCIAL STATEMENTS

The objective of financial statements is to provide financial information about a company that is useful to current and potential investors, to lenders, and other creditors (known as outsiders) in making decisions about the company. Because you have already taken a number of accounting courses and may have work experience as accountants, this "reminder" of the objective of financial reporting should be familiar to you. This chapter will build on lessons that you have already learned and on your experience as accounting students. It will confirm what you already know about accounting: accounting is about preparing useful financial information that is needed by outsiders to make decisions about the company.

THE BASIC PURPOSE OF FINANCIAL REPORTING

"The objective of general purpose financial reporting is to provide financial information about the reporting entity that is useful to existing and potential investors, lenders, and other creditors in making decisions about providing resources to the entity. Those decisions involve buying, selling, or holding equity and debt instruments and providing or settling loans and other forms of credit. (FASB: *Statement of Financial Accounting Concepts No. 8, Conceptual Framework for Financial Reporting*; IFRS: Chapter 1: *The Objective of General Purpose Financial Reporting, Conceptual Framework for Financial Reporting* – hereafter known as *The Conceptual Framework*.)

This chapter focuses on the guidance given by the conceptual framework as a resource for an accountant to use for making decisions that are technically sound and express the ethical awareness of the accountant. The chapter opens with a discussion of the conceptual framework and how accountants use this framework as a resource to make accounting decisions. The purpose of concept statements is to set forth objectives and fundamental concepts that are the basis for developing new financial accounting standards. The fundamental concepts guide the selection of transactions and other events to be accounted for in the financial statements. Concept statements are not part of the accounting standards, but they present and elaborate the concepts that underlie guidance for the formulation of accounting standards. Because of this, they are a resource for accountants in the decision-making process; they give accountants information about the purpose, content, and characteristics of information to be reported in financial statements. The chapter concludes with a discussion of fraud in the financial statements and an examination of how fraud might occur in the preparation of financial statements.

Along with the duty to apply accounting principles and rules while preparing financial statements comes the accountant's responsibility to address moral issues that arise in accounting situations and to take ethical actions. In other words: at the core of the accountant's obligation to provide objective financial information is the dual obligation to be technically proficient and ethically aware.

When accountants prepare objective financial information, they demonstrate their intellectual and moral virtues. Let us explain this: through their applied ethics, accountants exercise their *duty* of adhering to accounting standards and they express their *virtues*; that is, they exhibit their intellectual skills and their traits of moral character. Whenever they engage in the distinctive tasks of accounting practice, accountants are "to do ethics"; that is, the decisions they make should reflect their ethical awareness. Whenever accountants review business transactions, prepare financial statements, and communicate knowledge about the financial status of business entities to an interested public, they are engaged in continuous decision making. As these decisions conform to accounting standards, they also express the values, principles, and patterns of judgment that are key elements in accounting ethics, the specialized form of applied ethics that is intended to be suitable for "the real world" of contemporary business and society.

USING RULES FOR FINANCIAL STATEMENT AS A RESOURCE TO MAKE ACCOUNTING DECISIONS

Chapter Three introduced the decision model that we use in this book, which is reproduced in Figure 4.1. We now review the place of this chapter within the model. Its contents elaborate the first box in column two, labeled *Identify Problem-Solving Resources: Accounting Standards for Financial Statements*. In this chapter we speak about the use of the accounting standards and the conceptual framework as resources for shaping accounting decisions that are technically correct and demonstrate ethical awareness. To achieve this goal, we must understand the rules related to the preparation of financial statements. In Chapter Three we developed the idea that accounting ethics decisions are responses to two types of problems, accounting

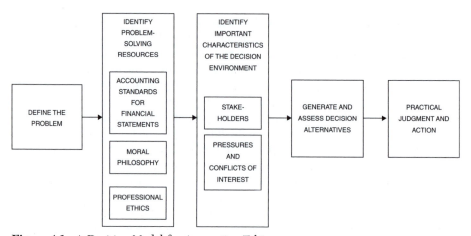

Figure 4.1   A Decision Model for Accounting Ethics

problems and ethical problems. The conceptual framework and the standards of accounting serve as primary resources for addressing the accounting problem in many circumstances, but these resources are also available whenever ethical problems and moral dilemmas arise in accounting practice.

THE CONCEPTUAL FRAMEWORK

Let us first consider how the conceptual framework can be used as a resource in preparing financial statements. As previously stated, the objective of financial reporting is to provide financial information about the company to outsiders – current and potential investors, lenders, and other creditors – so outsiders can make decisions about whether to provide resources to the company. Decisions by current and potential investors about buying, selling, or holding debt or equity investments depend on the returns these stakeholders expect to receive from their investment. In similar fashion, decisions by current and potential lenders about providing loans depend on the return their lenders expect. The return expected by potential lenders and creditors is related to the assessment of the amount, timing, and uncertainty of future cash flows for the company. In short, investors, lenders, and creditors need information to help them assess the likelihood of future cash flows for the company.

Information about a company's cash flow helps users to assess the company's ability to generate cash in the future. A cash flow statement shows how the company gets and spends cash, including information about dividend payments, borrowing and repayment of debt, issuance or repurchase of capital stock and purchase or sale of long-term assets. This information permits users to understand a company's operations, including its financing and investing activities, and to assess the liquidity or solvency of the company.

To assess future cash flows, current and potential investors, lenders, and other creditors need information about the resources of the company, the claims against the company, and how efficiently and effectively the company's management and governing board meet their responsibility to use the company's resources. Management provides this information to outsiders in the financial statements. Financial statements also provide information about the effects of transactions and other events that change the company's economic resources and claims. These types of information provide useful information for decisions about providing resources to a company.

Information about the economic resources and claims on the company can help outside investors and creditors assess the company's liquidity and solvency, its need for additional financing, and the probability of its success in obtaining that financing. Financial information about the payment requirements and priorities of current claims can help users to predict how future cash flows may be used. Some transactions have a direct effect on cash flows (such as accounts receivable), while other transactions lead to the production of goods or services which can be sold to customers (such as raw material inventory and building and equipment used in manufacturing goods for sale). Sales activity results in changes in economic resources and in claims against resources, as does issuing debt or equity securities. To assess properly the future cash flows associated with these events, outsiders need to distinguish among the changes. Information about the company's sales activity helps outsiders to understand the return the company has generated on the assets it has available for this purpose. This indicates to outsiders how well management has done in generating a return on the resources available to them. Information about a company's financial performance may also indicate the extent to which events such as changes in market price or interest rates have altered the company's economic resources and claims.

The financial performance of a company is reported according to accrual accounting. This means that the effect of a transaction on the economic resources and claims on the resources is reported in the time period when the transaction occurs, even if the cash flow occurs in a different time period. Accrual accounting provides a better basis for assessing the company's past and future performance than does information based on cash receipts and payments.

THE FINANCIAL STATEMENTS

Regulators usually require companies to issue four financial statements. These are:

1. A Statement of Profit or Loss
2. A Statement of Financial Position
3. A Statement of Cash Flows, and
4. A Statement of Changes in Equity.

Companies are also required to prepare footnotes for the financial statements. These footnotes include a summary of significant accounting policies and other explanatory information. Regulators typically require either the statement of profit or loss or the statement of financial position to include "other comprehensive income".[1] The information found in the four statements and their footnotes is information given to outsiders to make decisions about the company. It is the only information available to outsiders that is audited by an independent source – the external auditor. If this information is of poor quality (e.g., not objective, biased towards management), or if the information does not represent the future cash flow associated with the transactions then outsiders might make bad decisions about the company. These bad decisions include: selling stock when they should keep it, buying stock when they would not buy stock if they had better information, lending money to companies at lower interest rates than appropriate for reflecting the risk in the transaction, and doing business with a company expecting to be paid when they would not have done business with that company if more accurate information had been available to them.

Auditors are required to audit these four financial statements and the footnotes on a yearly basis and to issue an opinion on whether the financial statements have been prepared in accordance with the accounting standards. Before management in a company can prepare the financial statements for the auditor to audit, its accountants must understand the requirements of the accounting standards. A separate set of standards (the auditing standards) provides rules for the auditor in auditing the financial statements. Accountants who are technically proficient and ethically aware will use the conceptual framework and the accounting standards as the starting point for making decisions regarding how information is presented in the financial statements. Let us consider the information presented in two of the financial statements and the conceptual framework behind each of these statements.

The financial statements list the financial effects of transactions and other events by grouping them into broad classes (referred to as elements) according to the economic characteristics of the transaction. Basic definitions of each element are found in the conceptual framework and may be used as a resource to the accountant in making decisions about reporting transactions and events in the financial statements. The elements used to measure the financial position of the company in the balance sheet are assets, liabilities and equity. Elements used to measure performance in the profit or loss statement are income and expenses. The statement of changes in financial position reflects both income statement elements and changes in balance sheet elements. The statement of cash flows and the statement of changes in equity are prepared based on the transactions reported in the profit or loss statement and the statement of financial position. If either the income statement or the statement of financial position (balance sheet) is incorrect, the statement of cash flow and the statement of changes in equity will also be incorrect. For this reason, we will focus on the technical proficiency and ethical awareness necessary to permit the accountant to make good decisions for the profit or loss statement and the balance sheet. If the accountants get those two statements right, the statement of cash flows and the statement of equity are also likely to be correct.

A Statement of Profit or Loss

The basic format of a statement of profit or loss follows. Remember, the statement of profit or loss (also known as the income statement) is a statement to measure the performance of the company for the year.

Statement of Profit or Loss
For the Year Ending 20XX

Sales Revenue

– <u>Cost of goods sold</u>

= Gross Profit

– <u>Operating expenses</u>

= **Income from continuing operations**

± Gains or Losses

± Non-operating income or expense

– <u>Tax expense</u>

= **Net income**

Income is defined in the conceptual framework as an increase in economic benefits during the year: (1) in the form of inflows or (2) enhancements of assets or (3) decreases of liabilities that result in increases in equity, other than those increases relating to contributions from equity participants. Income includes both sales revenue and gains. Expenses are decreases in economic benefits during the year: (1) in the form of outflows or (2) depletions of assets or (3) incurrence of liabilities that result in decreases in equity, other than those relating to distributions to equity participants. Expenses include both expenses related to the normal course of business (cost of goods sold and operating expenses) and losses.

The distinction between continuing operations and non-continuing operations is important. In general, management is evaluated based on their decisions related to "income from continuing operations" because this is the only income they control. Outsiders also make their estimates of future cash flows from the company based on income from continuing operations because the income reported that is related to non-continuing operations is income based on one-time events. The most important number on the income statement for outsiders is "income from continuing operations," but in recent years, sales revenue has also been an important number for outsiders. In particular, growth in sales revenue, whether or not it is accompanied by growth in income from continuing operations, is viewed by outsiders as an important element of the income statement in terms of evaluating the potential of the company for generating future economic resources.

A Statement of Financial Position

The basic format for a statement of financial position (also known as a balance sheet) is shown below. This statement measures the financial position of the company for one day in time, the last day of the accounting year.

In the conceptual framework an asset is defined as a resource controlled by the company as a result of past events from which future economic benefits are expected to flow to the company. Liabilities are present obligations of the company arising from events in the past, the settlement of which is expected to result in an outflow of resources with economic benefits from the company. Equity is the residual interest in the assets of the company after deducting all liabilities. In determining whether a

Statement of Financial Position
At December 31, 20XX

Assets:	Liabilities:
Cash	Accounts payable
Accounts receivable	Salaries payable
Inventory	Total current liabilities
Total current assets	Long-term Debt
Land	Total liabilities
Building	Common stock
Equipment	Additional paid in capital
Intangible Assets	Retained earnings
Total assets	Total Liabilities and Owners' Equity

transaction meets the definition of an asset, liability, or equity, the underlying substance and economic reality of the transaction must be considered instead of the legal form of the transaction. For example, a company cannot make its capital (finance) leases into operating leases by producing a lease agreement that labels the lease an operating lease if the terms of the agreement indicate that the substance of the lease is a capital (finance) lease.

The conceptual framework defines the elements of financial statements and general recognition rules for the elements. The accounting standards for particular elements (inventory, intangible assets) provide more specific rules.

ACCOUNTING RULES FOR RECORDING TRANSACTIONS AND VALUING ACCOUNTS

Companies use the accrual method to record all transactions and events that are reported in the financial statements. Accrual accounting information provides a better basis for assessing the company's past and future performance than information based on cash receipts and payments. The requirement to use accrual accounting, however, makes it easier for management to manipulate the financial statements. For example, management might recognize sales revenue at the end of the year for items that will not be shipped until the following year. Because the cash is normally not collected until after the sale is recorded, the auditor may not notice that sales revenue has been recognized early without testing year-end sales.

A second requirement for financial statements is that financial statements must be prepared using consistent accounting standards. Consistent standards mean consistency from year to year for one company and consistency from company to company for one year. If the accounting standards are not consistent, the auditor's report must include an explanatory paragraph describing the change in accounting and the impact of the change on the financial statements. Ethical issues for accountants sometimes involve the lack of consistency in financial reporting. One place where companies may be inconsistent is with the reporting of operating and non-operating income. Companies may include some transactions in non-operating income one year and include the same type of transaction in income from operations the following year. This leads to a lack of consistency in the accounts between the two years reported in the profit or loss statement. The most important information outsiders receive about the company usually comes from the financial statements. They use revenue and expense for the current year to predict next year's revenue and expense. Their prediction will be wrong if income from operations for the company includes income that should have been classified as non-operating.

A third requirement for financial statements is the matching concept. This requires all companies to match expenses to revenue. This means that if revenue is recognized, the company must recognize all expenses associated with generating the revenue. A failure to do so means that financial statements have not been prepared in accordance with the accounting standards. In this situation, the accountant has failed to demonstrate technical proficiency.

To prepare the statement of financial position, the accountant must consider whether the company is expected to be in business in the near future, usually defined as one year. If the company meets the "going concern assumption," the assets held by the company should be valued as if they will continue to be used by the company. If the company does not meet the going concern assumption, the assets will be valued as if they will be sold. This usually results in a change in asset valuation from cost to market value (the exception to this would be a company using market value for its long-term assets under international accounting standards).

Accounting standards provide rules for recording transactions. Consider how these rules shape the preparation of financial statements. In preparing the financial statements for stakeholders, the accountant makes decisions on how to recognize (identify, describe, and measure) and value a particular item in the financial statement. To do this, the accountant uses the definitions of the financial statement elements to determine what type of transaction is being described. The accountant reports the transactions – recognizes them in the financial statements – according to criteria for their recognition also set by the standards. The accountant also values them – recognizes the year-end value of the elements – according to criteria for valuation set by the standards. In producing financial information for the stakeholder, the accountant also indicates the interrelationship of the elements. The interrelationship of the elements means that if an item meets the definition and recognition criteria for a particular element, recognizing the first element will mean that a second element also is recognized (double-entry accounting). Financial statement elements should be recognized when: (1) it is probable that any future economic benefit or cost associated with the item will flow to or from the company and (2) the item has a cost or value that can be measured with reliability. Criteria for recognition and valuation may involve estimates and judgments that are not neatly prescribed by existing rules, so a decision process must be used to determine which accounting standard to follow.

THE ACCOUNTING PROBLEM OF ESTIMATES

A situation in which an item may call for an estimate is, for example, a circumstance with an "accounting problem," to use the language of earlier chapters. Reference to the conceptual framework and to the accounting standards will provide guidelines on how to make the particular estimate. Estimates, however, may also pose an ethical problem – whenever the estimate may arbitrarily advance the interests of one stakeholder at the expense of another.

Measurement is the process of determining the dollar amounts for the elements of the financial statements that are to be recognized and carried in the balance sheet and income statement. There are four measurement bases that might be used in the financial statements. They are:

1. *Historical cost*   Elements are recorded at the amount of cash or the cash equivalent paid or the fair value of the consideration given to acquire the asset or paid to satisfy the liability in the normal course of business. Historical cost is an *objective* measure of the value of the asset or liability. Two individuals would not disagree on the amount of historical cost.

2. *Current cost*   Assets are valued at the amount of cash that would have to be paid if the same or an equivalent asset was acquired currently. Liabilities are carried at the undiscounted amount of cash that would be required to settle the obligation currently. Current cost is also known as market value. Current cost or market value is a *less objective* measure than historical cost. The current cost or market value of an asset or liability usually must be estimated. Any account that must be estimated can be estimated using several different methods. Two individuals could disagree on the current cost or market value of an asset or liability, sometimes quite dramatically.

3. *Realization or settlement value*   Assets are carried at the amount of cash or cash equivalent that would currently be obtained by selling the asset in an orderly disposal. Liabilities are carried at their settlement values (the undiscounted amount of cash expected to be paid) in the normal course of business. The settlement value of an asset or liability is usually estimated, so two individuals could disagree on the settlement value of an asset or liability. It is a *less objective* measure than historical cost.

4. *Present value*   Assets are carried at the present discounted value of the future net cash inflows that the item is expected to generate in the normal course of business. Liabilities are carried at the present discounted value of the future net cash outflows that will settle the liabilities in the normal course of business. The present value of an asset or liability is an *objective* measure of the value of an asset or liability. The only issue that might cause two individuals to disagree about the present value of an asset or liability is the situation where the interest rate used to determine the present value is not specified in the contract.

In terms of the quality of information categories of relevance and faithful representation, cost is both a relevant and faithful representation of the benefits of the transaction at the point when the transaction occurs. Most transactions enter the financial statements at historical cost. Historical cost is an objective measure of the transaction at the point when the transaction occurs. Asset accounts including accounts receivable, inventory, investment securities, and land, building, and equipment are all recorded at cost when the original transaction is recorded on the books of the company. Using historical cost for recording short-term asset transactions at the point of origination is *relevant* because it measures the amount of cash the company expects to receive from the asset (it predicts the cash flow associated with the asset). Using historical cost for long-term assets is also *relevant* at the point the transaction is recorded, because it measures the amount of cash the company has used (or plans to use) to obtain an asset to generate revenue in the future. Historical cost *faithfully represents* the value of both short-term and long-term assets held by the company because it is an unbiased, objective measure of the value of an asset at the point of origination.

Historical cost, however, may not give outsiders a relevant measure of the value of an asset as time passes. For this reason, many assets are revalued at year-end to give outsiders more relevant information about the future cash flow of the asset. For example, accounts receivable is revalued at the end of the year to the amount of cash the company expects to collect on the accounts receivable balance. At year-end historical cost is not a relevant measure of the cash flow the company expects when the accounts receivable is collected for the accounts receivable balance outstanding at the end of the year. Because cost does not allow outsiders to accurately measure the future cash flow of the accounts receivable asset, the company revalues the accounts receivable balance so it correctly reflects the cash flow expected when the accounts receivable is collected. There are few ethical issues regarding historical cost. In some instances, the ethical issues in accounting arise when management changes from historical cost to another measurement base. Since both the current cost and the settlement value are estimated amounts, there is room for management to estimate these amounts to favor their interests instead of the interests of outsiders.

The balance sheet contains current and long-term assets, current and long-term liabilities, and owners' equity. Current assets are recorded at cash value. Inventory is recorded at cash paid to purchase the inventory, accounts receivable is recorded at the cash you expect to collect on the receivable and cash (of course) is recorded as the cash value. Long-term assets are recorded at cost when purchased (assets given up plus the present value of the liability assumed in the purchase, if applicable). Current liabilities are recorded at the cash to be paid. Long-term liabilities are recorded at the present value of the future cash payments. Common stock and additional paid in capital are recorded at the cash received from the sale of the stock. Retained earnings is the net income or loss for all years the company has been in existence, less the dividends paid.

The accounting standards require some elements of the financial statements to be revalued at the end of the year. This revaluation is done so outsiders have information that is more relevant than the original cost for the financial statement element. Accounts receivable are valued at the net receivable value at year-end (accounts receivable less the allowance for uncollectible accounts). This is the amount of cash the company expects to receive after adjusting the balance for the customer accounts that are likely to be uncollectible. At the end of the year, inventory is valued at the lower of cost or net realizable value (the amount the company would receive if the inventory was completed and sold) for companies using international accounting standards and at the lower of cost or market value (the cost to replace the inventory) if US accounting standards are used. If US accounting standards are used, long-term assets are valued at cost less accumulated depreciation. International accounting standards (IFRS) allow a company to choose between cost less accumulated depreciation and fair value less accumulated depreciation.

QUALITY OF INFORMATION

The accounting standards determine the form of the financial statements by setting the patterns for how transactions are to be recognized and valued in the financial statements. In addition, the standards go beyond these basic concerns. The standards also set guidelines for the quality of the information. Financial statements with high-quality information are presumed to be more useful to stakeholders than statements with lower quality information, so accountants are expected to communicate high-quality information. In effect, the quality of information in a financial statement is determined with regard to its usefulness for stakeholders. With regard to quality, the standards mandate that the information presented in financial statements must be *relevant* and must *fairly represent the economic phenomena purported.*

The qualitative characteristic of relevance has to do with whether the information is capable of making a difference in the users' decision making. Relevant information may be predictive, useful for projecting possibilities about future performance of the company, or confirmatory, useful in assessing previous evaluations of the financial information. Stakeholders make use of past performance and previous evaluations of financial information as they attempt to predict future performance. These assessments influence their decisions on whether to invest, extend credit, or take other financial actions.

Fair representation of a financial or economic phenomenon has to do with whether the phenomenon is depicted in an accurate way (i.e., the representation depicts what the report says it depicts). Such representation includes a clear identification of the item and a complete representation, with no significant aspect omitted. The depiction should not be slanted toward a favorable or an unfavorable reception by stakeholders (the representation is neutral). The presentation should be free of errors. As a rule of thumb, the financial or economic phenomena represented in the financial statements should be presented as clearly and accurately as possible. Their description and the decision process that produces specific information about the items should be free from error. If two decision choices are equally relevant and provide a fair presentation of the economic phenomena, the enhancing qualitative characteristics of comparability, verifiability, timeliness, and understandability should be considered. The qualitative characteristics of accounting information were discussed in more detail in Chapter Two.

ETHICAL ISSUES ASSOCIATED WITH THE PROFIT OR LOSS STATEMENT AND THE STATEMENT OF FINANCIAL POSITION

Let's consider the financial statements presented at the beginning of the chapter to see if we can determine how ethical decisions related to the financial statements arise. Consider the statement of financial position beginning with the unadjusted balance in the accounts before the year-end adjustments are made. Transactions related to the current assets have all been recorded based on the historical cost of the transaction. Long-term assets have been recorded based on historical cost or market value.

Statement of Financial Position
At December 31, 20XX
Unadjusted Balances

Assets:	Balance	Cost basis
Cash	20,000	historical cost
Accounts receivable	50,000	historical cost
Inventory	75,000	historical cost
Total current assets	145,000	
Land	2,000,000	historical cost (US), market value or historical cost (IFRS)
Building	400,000	historical cost (US), market value or historical cost (IFRS)
Equipment	600,000	historical cost (US), market value or historical cost (IFRS)
Total assets	3,145,000	
Liabilities:		
Accounts payable	140,000	historical cost
Salaries payable	25,000	historical cost
Total current liabilities	165,000	
Long-term Debt	1,000,000	present value
Total liabilities	1,165,000	
Common stock	100,000	historical cost
Additional paid in capital	1,200,000	historical cost
Retained earnings	680,000	historical cost
Total Liabilities and Owners' Equity	3,145,000	

Statement of Profit or Loss
For the Year Ending 20XX
Unadjusted Balances

Sales Revenue	2,000,000
– Cost of goods sold	1,200,000
= Gross Profit	800,000
– Operating expenses	300,000
= Income from continuing operations	**500,000**
± Gains or Losses	0
± Non-operating income or expense	0
– Tax expense	120,000
= Net income	**380,000**

Consider what accounts need to be adjusted at year-end so the financial state-ments are prepared according to the accounting standards. When accounts require adjustment, accountants have three choices: (1) to adjust the accounts in a manner required by the accounting standards, (2) not to adjust the accounts in any way, even though it is required by the standards, or (3) to adjust the accounts according to their interests. Note that these decisions of adjustment address both an accounting problem and an ethical problem. Outsiders receive high-quality information with choice (1) and information that is not relevant or faithfully presented with choice (2) and (3). Accountants have met the requirements of the profession to be technically proficient and ethically aware with choice (1), but not with choice (2) or (3).

First, consider the assets on the balance sheet. Accounts receivable must be valued at the amount of cash the company expects to receive at the end of the year, so an allowance for uncollectible accounts must be estimated so accounts receivable is reduced to the amount of cash collectible the following year on the year-end balance. Let's say that based on past experience, the company has found that 2% of the accounts receivable balance at year-end will not be collected. So, accounts receivable must be valued at $50,000 − (50,000 × 0.02). The correct valuation for accounts receivable at year-end is $49,000, not $50,000. The journal entry to adjust accounts receivable to the correct amount according to the accounting standards will also recognize bad debt expense in the amount of $1,000. Net income is reduced by $1,000 due to this adjustment.

(1)   Bad debt expense   1,000
                     Allowance for uncollectible accounts   1,000
To recognize bad debt expense for accounts receivable estimated to be uncollectible at year-end.

Inventory might also need adjustment at year-end. Inventory is recognized on the balance sheet at historical cost. The accounting standards require inventory to be valued at lower of cost or net realizable value for companies using international standards and lower of cost or market value for companies using US accounting standards. Net realizable value is the estimated selling price less the estimated costs of completion of the inventory and the estimated costs needed to make the sale. So, the company must determine the net realizable value of its inventory at year-end and if this cost is less than the cost recorded on the balance sheet, the inventory must be written down. Let's say that the net realizable value (or the market value) of the inventory at year-end is $60,000. Since this is lower than the cost recorded on the balance sheet, an allowance must be created to write-down the value of the inventory. Inventory must be valued at $60,000. The journal entry to adjust inventory to the correct value according to the accounting standards will also recognize an expense in the amount of $15,000. Net income is reduced by $15,000 due to this adjustment.

(2)   Inventory write-down expense   15,000
                     Allowance to write-down inventory   15,000
To adjust the cost of inventory at year-end because the net realizable value (or the market value) is lower than cost.

For companies using US accounting standards, long-term assets are not adjusted at year-end. Companies using international accounting standards which choose to use market value for their long-term assets might write the value of long-term assets up or down to market value. If long-term assets are written up, it has no effect on net income. If assets are written down, net income decreases. If previous write-downs are adjusted upward, then net income increases. Let's say that a company using international accounting standards uses market value for land and buildings and cost for equipment. The market value of the land has increased to $2,100,000 and the market value of the buildings has decreased to $350,000. The increase in the value of the land has no effect on net income. The decrease in the market value of the buildings reduces net income by $50,000. This is the first revaluation of land and buildings the company has done[2].

(3)	Land	100,000	
	Asset revaluation reserve (owners' equity)		100,000
	Asset revaluation reserve (loss)	50,000	
	Buildings		50,000

To record year-end adjustments in the market value of land and buildings.

Adjustments (1), (2), and (3) all require the accountant to estimate the correct value for the financial statement accounts according to the accounting standards. The accounting standards tell you only that the correct value is the net realizable value or the market value; they do not tell you what the amount should be. In our language: this estimate does not involve an accounting problem. It does, however, pose an ethical problem of considering stakeholders' interests in the decision process and determining whether or not a given estimate may unduly harm one stakeholder or another. Determining the correct amount of an estimate is where ethical decisions must be made. To properly make this estimate, the accountant is required to use the skills of technical proficiency and ethical awareness. That is, to demonstrate awareness of the technical requirements of the standards and also show insight on how stakeholders are affected by changes in the size of balance sheet accounts requiring estimation.

Now, let's consider how liabilities need to be adjusted at year-end on the balance sheet. The ethical decisions related to liabilities differ from the decisions for assets. For assets, the ethical decision is usually whether the asset is *valued correctly* at year-end. For liabilities, the ethical decision is one of *completeness*: have all liabilities that should be recorded according to the accounting standards been recorded? The valuation standards do not help us here. What does help us is to refer to the rules for recognizing liabilities and expenses. The auditor has the same three choices when adjusting liabilities at year-end: (1) to adjust the accounts in a manner required by the accounting standards, (2) not to adjust the accounts in any way, even though it is required by the standards, or (3) to adjust the accounts according to their interests. With liability accounts, choice (2) is the easiest thing to do because it allows the accountant to do nothing.

According to the conceptual framework and the accounting standards:

- The financial performance of a company is reported according to accrual accounting. This means that the effect of a transaction on the economic resources and claims on the resources is reported in the time period when the transaction occurs, even if the cash flow occurs in a different time period.
- Financial statements are prepared according to the matching concept. This requires all companies to match expenses to revenue. If revenue is recognized, the company must recognize all expenses associated with generating the revenue.
- Expenses are decreases in economic benefits during the year: (1) in the form of outflows or (2) depletions of assets or (3) incurrence of liabilities that result in decreases in equity, other than those relating to distributions to equity participants. Expenses include both expenses related to the normal course of business (cost of goods sold and operating expenses) and losses.
- Liabilities are present obligations of the company arising from events in the past, the settlement of which is expected to result in an outflow from the company of resources with economic benefits.

With these rules in mind, let's see how ethical issues arise in connection with the current and long-term liability sections of the balance sheet and how the rules for preparing financial statements help us resolve the ethical issues when they arise.

How does the accountant determine that all liabilities have been recognized according to the accounting standards in the year-end financial statements? Consider first the current liabilities and look at two common current liabilities as an example of how to resolve ethical issues related to current liabilities. Consider accounts payable and salaries payable as two current liabilities that are found on the financial statements of most companies. There are several procedures the accountant might use to determine if current liabilities have been recognized in the financial statements according to the accounting standards. The logic behind these procedures is the fact that a company might avoid recording the liabilities related to these items at year-end, but they cannot avoid paying out cash related to the liability for very long because vendors will stop supplying goods to them and employees will stop working if the bills are not paid. These procedures include:

- The accountant reviews the transactions recorded in accounts payable a few days before and a few days after year-end (e.g., five to fifteen days before and after year-end). For each transaction the accountant determines if the liability should have been recorded at year-end (according to the accounting standards) and whether the liability has been recorded at year-end. Items that should be recorded and have not been recorded are added to liabilities on the balance sheet.

- The accountant reviews the file of unmatched receiving documents (a file of receiving documents that have not been recorded because the vendor invoice has not been received) to determine whether the liability has been recognized for goods received at year-end. All of these items should be recorded as accounts payable at year-end because the goods have been received.

- The accountant reviews payroll records to determine when employees were last paid at year-end and how many days of payment is owed to employees on the basis of the work they performed. Let's say the company pays its employees every two weeks on Friday for work in the prior two weeks. If Friday fell on December 26 this year, the company would owe employees for three days' work, assuming that December 27 and 28 are weekend days when no one works and employees work on December 29, 30, and 31. So the company has a liability to the employees for three days' salary plus fringe benefits (fringe benefits include liabilities like pension contributions, healthcare costs, employment tax).

This discussion of the procedures for recognizing these particular liabilities illustrates the technical accounting problem that must be solved and suggests an ethical dimension of the situation, as well. Resolution of each type of problem is achieved by reference to the accounting standards and the requirement of the conceptual framework to provide high-quality information to the users of financial statements. The technical requirement to record liabilities at the end of the year comes from the accounting standards requiring companies to recognize liabilities and expense as they receive the economic benefit from the goods or the services. The ethical awareness the accountant is expected to show with regard to this requirement is the commitment to follow the rules of the profession, ensuring that outsiders receive information that is both relevant to the decisions of the user to predict or confirm future cash flows of the company and provides information that faithfully represents the economic phenomenon reported when the liability is recorded (a debt to be paid within one year).

After performing the procedures listed above to discover unrecorded liabilities related to accounts payable and salaries payable at year-end, the accountant finds that $20,000 of expense is unrecorded at year-end. This $20,000 is for electricity for the month of December. Salaries owed to employees for work done the last week of December are $30,000; fringe benefits related to this salary expense are 25%. Recording these liabilities will also increase expenses and reduce net income by $57,500 on the profit or loss statement.

(4)	Operating expense	20,000	
	Accounts payable		20,000
	Salary and fringe benefit expense	37,500	
	Salaries payable		37,500

To record liabilities at year-end related to expenses incurred in December.

Now, let us consider how an accountant might find missing liabilities in the long-term liability account. This account contains liabilities requiring cash to be paid in the time period of more than the current year. There are usually only a few transactions recorded in this account, but each transaction is significant because of its size. Each transaction in long-term liabilities is represented by a legal contract between the lending party and the company. So the best way to find missing liabilities in this account is for the accountant to review the legal documents related to long-term debt and to talk to the attorneys working for the company.

Some of the ethical issues related to this account involve related parties to a company. Related parties are parties with an economic link to the company. Sometimes related parties lend money to a company and the debt associated with this loan is not recorded in the financial statements (to hide the debt from outsiders). This type of liability is quite difficult to find because there may not be a legal contract associated with the debt.

Assume that the accountant found that a loan from a director of the firm in the amount of $200,000 had not been recorded. This loan originated on July 1 and has an interest rate of 12%. Interest expense on long-term debt from a prior year also has not been recorded. This debt is $1,000,000 with an interest rate of 8%. No payments were made on long-term debt during the year. Recording the long-term debt contract with interest and the interest on the outstanding debt reduces net income by $92,000.

(5)	Cash	200,000	
	Long-term Debt		200,000
	Interest expense	12,000	
	Interest payable		12,000

To recognize a loan in the amount of $200,000 that originated on July 1 with an interest rate of 12%.

| | Interest expense | 80,000 | |
| | Interest payable | | 80,000 |

To accrue interest on long-term debt of $1,000,000 with an interest rate of 8%.

Let's take a look at the statement of financial position after adding the adjustments related to the accountant's review to determine whether the statement had been prepared according to the accounting standards.

Statement of Financial Position
At December 31, 20XX
Adjusted Balances

Assets:		Adjustments	Cost basis
Cash	20,000	+ 200,000	historical cost
Accounts receivable	50,000		historical cost
Less allowance for uncollectible accounts		+ (1,000)	adjustment needed at year-end
Net accounts receivable	49,000		net realizable value
Inventory	75,000		historical cost
Less allowance for LCM adjustment		+ (15,000)	adjustment needed at year-end
Inventory at LCM	60,000		lower of cost and net realizable value
Income tax asset		+ 51,720	adjustment needed at year-end
Total current assets	145,000	+ 235,720	
Land	2,000,000		historical cost

Assets:		Adjustments	Cost basis
Allowance for market value		+ 100,000	adjustment to market value
Building	400,000		historical cost
Allowance for market value		+ (50,000)	adjustment to market value
Equipment	600,000		historical cost
Total Assets	3,145,000	+285,720	
Total Assets adjusted balance			3,430,720

Liabilities:			
Accounts payable	140,000	+ 20,000	historical cost
Salaries payable	25,000	+ 37,500	historical cost
Interest payable	0	+ 92,000	historical cost
Total current liabilities	165,000	+ 149,500	
Long-term Debt	1,000,000	+ 200,000	present value
Total liabilities	1,165,000	+ 349,500	
Common stock	100,000		historical cost
Additional paid in capital	1,200,000	+ 100,000	historical cost
Retained earnings	680,000	+(163,780)	historical cost
Total Liabilities and Owners' Equity	3,145,000	+ 285,720	
Total Liabilities and Owners' Equity adjusted balance			3,430,720

Statement of Profit or Loss
For the Year Ending 20XX
Adjusted Balances

		Adjustments	Adjusted Balance
Sales Revenue	2,000,000		2,000,000
– Cost of goods sold	1,200,000	15,000	1,215,000
= Gross Profit	800,000		785,000
– Operating expenses	300,000	1,000 + 57,500	358,500
= Income from continuing operations	**500,000**	**73,500**	**426,500**
± Gains or Losses	0	(50,000)	(50,000)
± Non-operating income or expense	0	(92,000)	(92,000)
– Tax expense (24%)	120,000	(51,720)	(68,280)
= Net income	**380,000**	**(163,780)**	**216,220**

The accountant needs to make one last adjustment. Tax expense is 24% of income before tax. Before the financial statements were adjusted, tax expense was $120,000 (on income before tax of $500,000). After adjustments, income before tax is now only

$284,500. Tax expense on this income is $68,280. Since tax of $120,000 has been paid, the company is due a tax refund of $51,720. The entry to record the tax refund is given below.

(6)   Income tax asset   51,720
                   Income tax expense   51,720
To reduce the tax expense owed based on a reduction in net income.

As we can see, the balance sheet (assets and liabilities and owners' equity) were understated by $285,720 before the accountant adjusted the financial statements to conform to the accounting standards. If the accountant fails to make some or all of these adjustments, the financial statements would not reflect the technical proficiency and ethical awareness of the accountant. But perhaps more importantly, income from operations is overstated by $73,500 and net income is overstated by $163,780. When income from operations or net income is overstated, outsiders will estimate that the company has more cash flow than it will have. Outsiders will also view the company as more profitable than it really is. The quality of information available to outsiders when this happens is not a relevant or faithful representation of the transactions that have occurred. Relevant information should predict or confirm. When income from operations and net income are overstated, the information provided to outsiders does not either predict the amount of cash flow for the following year or confirm the correct amount of cash flow for the past year. Overstated income does not faithfully represent the performance of the company. If you look at the adjustments made on the income statement, you can see that reporting a gross profit of $800,000 when the correct gross profit is $785,000, reporting operating expenses of $300,000 when the correct operating expense is $358,500, and failing to report a loss of $50,000 when revaluing the building account and interest expense (non-operating expense) of $92,000 from long-term debt does not faithfully represent the transactions affecting the profit or loss statement for the company.

Technical and Ethical Decisions in Preparing Financial Statements: A Summary

This brief introduction of the accounting standards for the preparation of financial statements (standards about the form and contents of the primary discourse of accountants, and the goals for the clarity and accuracy of the knowledge communicated to stakeholders' information of high quality) frames the basic context for accountant decision making in its technical aspect. The production of high-quality financial statements calls for numerous decisions – analyses of financial and economic phenomena, applications of appropriate standards to accounting problems, judgments regarding the identification, classification and measurement of financial data, decisions on how to present information in the most clear and accurate ways. To make these decisions accountants have numerous technical responsibilities established by accounting standards.

To this point we have spoken of the accountant's responsibility to make technical decisions by following the rules set forth in the accounting standards. Facing accounting decisions on how to recognize transactions and economic phenomena in the financial statements, the technically competent accountant chooses to follow the appropriate accounting standard – considers alternatives, chooses, and then acts to communicate high-quality information to stakeholders. We now shift gears to the second aspect of the accountant's competency: the capacities we call "ethical sensibility".

The accountant's decisions also have an ethical component. Accountants have an ethical obligation to identify and deal with moral issues that arise in the course of their practice. These obligations, like the technical expectations, arise as accountants provide service to stakeholders, including the general public. And as we shall see, these ethical expectations are also set forth in the accounting standards, most notably in the professional codes of conduct as the principles of accounting and as the accountant's virtues (or qualities of character) that equip him or her to meet the responsibilities of practice, the duties of accountancy.

These ethical duties and the sensibility to fulfill them are particularly important because of the complexity of modern business organizations and transactions. The competitive pressures, and uncertainties of the global marketplace, and the drive for profit and high stock prices tempt management to hide, even distort financial information from other stakeholders. Accounting decisions have the potential both to benefit and to harm stakeholders, whether they are "outsiders" or "insiders" to the company whose financial information is reported. While even clear disclosure and high-quality information may harm some stakeholders, deliberate harm to stake-holders may result from the manipulation and distortion of financial statements, from the unethical actions of management and the willingness of unethical accountants to deceive stakeholders. To limit the possibility of such harm, the conceptual framework of financial accounting and the particular principles and rules set forth in the accounting standards call for the accountant's integrity, diligence, and fair-mindedness in the preparation of financial statements, their review, and their communication to others.

FRAUD AND ETHICS

We now have some idea how misstatements can enter into the financial statements. They might be a result of accountants failing to act or acting in a manner that is inconsistent with the accounting standards. Accountants can make these decisions deliberately to benefit themselves or the company or the accountant can uninten-tionally fail to follow the accounting standards. When accountants intentionally misstate the financial statements, this is referred to as fraud. When accountants unintentionally misstate the financial statements, this is called an error. The term misstatement refers both to error and fraud. For our purposes, outsiders fail to receive high-quality financial information when either fraud or errors occur. Fraud, however, carries a heavier ethical burden than a mere error, because with fraud the accountant sets out to benefit himself or herself or the company and to deceive outside users of the financial statements. We will consider fraud briefly in this chapter and then speak more extensively about it in a later chapter.

Management is responsible for preventing and detecting fraud in a company. To achieve this objective, management should place a strong emphasis on fraud prevention, which reduces the opportunity for fraud to occur, and fraud deterrence which persuades employees not to commit fraud because the likelihood of detection and punishment is great. One way to achieve this objective is for management to create a culture of honesty and ethical behavior in the company. Management should consider the potential for the override of controls or other influences which may inappropriately influence the financial reporting process such as the effort to manage earnings to meet earnings targets or to influence the perceptions of outsiders as to the performance of the company.

When fraud is present in the financial statements, someone in the company has made an unethical decision in the preparation of the financial statements, because an ethical decision would require the accountant to prepare the financial statements in accordance with the accounting standards.

There are two types of fraud that might occur: (1) fraudulent financial reporting and (2) misappropriation of assets. Fraudulent financial reporting involves intentional misstatement of amounts or disclosures in the financial statements for the purpose of deceiving financial statement users. Fraud occurs because of efforts by management to "manage earnings" to deceive users about the performance or profitability of the company. This happens when management, due to the pressure to meet the expectations of outsiders, a desire to maximize their compensation or to secure outside financing, *intentionally* takes actions that lead to fraudulent financial statements. Fraudulent financial reporting can be accomplished by the following methods:

1. Manipulating, falsifying, or altering accounting records used to prepare the financial statements.

2. Misrepresenting or intentionally omitting transactions or significant information from the financial statements.

3. Intentional misapplication of accounting principles related to the amount, classification, or disclosure of financial statement elements.

Fraudulent financial reporting often involves the situation where management overrides internal controls that appear to be working effectively. Some of the techniques used by management to accomplish this override of controls include the following methods:

1. Recording fictitious journal entries to manipulate operating results (which is often seen at the end of the accounting time period).

2. Inappropriately changing assumptions used to estimate account balances.

3. Omitting, advancing, or delaying recognition of events that have occurred during the year.

4. Concealing or not disclosing facts that could affect the amounts recorded in the financial statements.

5. Engaging in complex transactions structured to misrepresent the financial position or financial performance of the company.

6. Altering records and terms related to significant and unusual transactions.

Misappropriation of assets, the second type of fraud, involves the theft of the company's assets. When misappropriation of assets occurs, the financial statements may also be fraudulent, so misappropriation of assets often leads to fraudulent financial reporting. Misappropriation of assets can be accomplished in the following ways:

1. Embezzling cash to personal bank accounts.

2. Stealing assets or intellectual property (stealing inventory, stealing scrap for resale, providing technological data to a competitor for payment).

3. Causing a company to pay for goods or services not received.

4. Using a company's assets for personal use.

An employee engaging in misappropriation of assets often accomplishes the task by preparing false or misleading documents to hide the fact that the assets are missing.

Three conditions are present when either type of fraud occurs: (1) the pressure to commit fraud, (2) the opportunity to do so, and (3) the ability to rationalize the fraud. These factors are identified as the "fraud triangle" (Figure 4.2); when they are present, the likelihood of fraud is high. The pressure to commit fraud may arise when management is under pressure from sources within the company or outside the company to achieve a particular financial outcome (i.e., growth of 5%, meeting analysts' earnings forecasts). Employees may face pressure to misappropriate assets if they need cash for personal reasons. The opportunity to commit fraud exists when an employee believes that internal controls can be overrode or when internal controls do not exist. The ability to rationalize committing fraud means that the individual possesses an attitude, character, or set of ethical values that allows them to commit fraud.

The elements in the fraud triangle do not always exist at the same level, but in most instances of fraud, it is easy to see how one of these factors contributed to the performance of fraud in the company. We will come back to the fraud triangle in a later chapter. Several of the cases at the end of the chapters will ask you to identify how the components of the fraud triangle contributed to fraudulent financial reporting or the misappropriation of assets in the company.

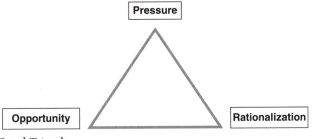

Figure 4.2   Fraud Triangle

Source: After Wells, J.T. (2008) *Principles of Fraud Examination.* New York: Wiley.

CHAPTER REVIEW QUESTIONS

1. (LO1) Briefly explain the objective of financial statements and why this objective is important to outsiders. How does an accountant act in accordance with the objective?

2. (LO2) Describe how the accountant can use the conceptual framework and the accounting standards to make accounting decisions that reflect technical competence and ethical awareness.

3. (LO3) What financial statements do regulators require accountants to prepare? What information is available to outsiders in each of the statements? Describe the financial statement elements reported on the financial statements.

4. (LO4) What are the qualitative characteristics of information in the financial statements? What is the accountant's duty to produce financial statements consistent with these characteristics?

5. (LO5) Describe two ethical issues associated with preparation of the statement of financial position. How does the accountant resolve the ethical issues?

6. (LO6) What types of fraud occur when financial statements are misstated? How does the accountant avoid engaging in fraudulent actions?

7. (LO6) Describe the fraud triangle and how it is useful to the accountant.

CASES

8. Estimating a Future Expense[3]

The cost associated with mothballing a nuclear power plant at the end of its useful life, approximately 20 years in the future, will be paid by the utility company when the plant is obsolete at the end of the 20 year period. When should the expense be recognized for this expenditure? Current utility users receive the benefit of this plant. Do accounting rules require them to pay the cost in terms of increased utility rates by including the expense of the future mothballing in their rates, or should the expense be delayed for 20 years, until the cash is actually paid out?

Required:

a. Consider the profit or loss statement of the company owning the power plant. Explain how the definitions of financial statement elements from the conceptual framework and the rules for when to record transactions could be used to help the accountant decide how the accountant should report the expense transactions.

b. Evaluate the quality of information received by outsiders if the company decides to delay the recognition of the expense compared to the quality of information received by outsiders if the company decides to estimate the expense and recognize it over the 20 year life of the power plant. Which decision gives outsiders higher quality information?

9. Investment Securities

Matt Adams, the controller of Plunkett's Furniture Store, and Becky Williams, the staff accountant, are working on the year-end financial statements. Adams wants to transfer some of the trading securities in the investment account to the available-for-sale account, because he does not want to reduce net income by the decline in fair value of these securities. Williams asks Adams how long the company intends to hold the securities, "Whatever it takes to get these securities out of the trading account. Even if we have to borrow money instead of selling the securities, it would be worth it to avoid reporting the decline in value on the income statement."

Required:

a. Consider the balance sheet and profit or loss statement of this company if the securities are reported in the available-for-sale security account instead of the trading securities account. Explain how the conceptual framework's definitions of financial statement elements and the rules for when to record transactions could be used to help the accountant decide how these two assets should be reported in the financial statements.

b. Evaluate the quality of information received by outsiders if the securities are moved from one account to the other.

c. What is the accounting problem facing Adams and Williams? Why does Adams want to transfer the securities from the trading to the available-for-sale account? Why does Williams ask Adams how long the securities will be held?

d. Consider the two heuristics for recognizing ethical problems: does either the principle of equal treatment or the public principle suggest that the accountants have an ethical problem in this transfer?

e. What is the ethical problem for these accountants? What is at stake in this decision and for whom?

10. Selling Investment Securities

Jose Garcia and Sergio Mendes are reviewing the year-end financial statements. Garcia is concerned about net income because the owners of the company had hoped for a 15% increase from 2014 to 2015 and the numbers support only a 9% increase. Garcia is afraid that the raises and bonuses for management will not be very good unless he thinks of a way to increase net income. Mendes suggests selling the available-for-sale securities that have increased in value and keeping the securities that have decreased in value. Garcia is unsure whether this approach of selectively selling securities is ethical.

Required:

a. Consider the balance sheet and profit or loss statement of this company if the securities are sold. Explain how the conceptual framework's definitions of financial statement elements and the rules for when to record transactions could be used to help the accountant decide whether it is appropriate to sell these securities.

b. Evaluate the quality of information received by outsiders if the securities are sold. Is it different than if the securities had not been sold?

c. What is the accounting problem facing Garcia and Mendes?

d. Consider the two heuristics for recognizing ethical problems: does either the principle of equal treatment or the public principle suggest that the accountants have an ethical problem?

e. What is the ethical problem for these accountants? What is at stake in this decision and for whom?

11. Sale of Investment Securities

Sam Clauson, president of Computer Software, exclaims, "Net income is too high. I never thought I'd say that! But if we grow 20% this year, the parent company will expect us to grow 22% next year. There is no way we can sustain that kind of growth. Everything just fell into place this year, but with the economy worsening, there is no way we can duplicate this year's sales. We must reduce our net income to a more manageable growth rate this year, or we'll never meet our targets next year and the company will not give us a raise. Do you have any ideas about how to lower net income?" Jennifer Korsmo, the controller of the company, replies, "We have several large available-for-sale securities that have decreased in value over the year. It would be a good time to sell the securities, realize the loss, and lower our net income in the process. We can always use the cash from the securities sales to purchase additional securities. The market is at a low, and it is a good time to buy securities at rock-bottom prices. This is the best way to lower net income."

Required:

a. Consider the balance sheet and profit or loss statement of this company if the securities are sold. Explain how the conceptual framework's definitions of financial statement elements and rules for when to record transactions could be used to help the accountant decide whether it is appropriate to sell these securities.

b. Evaluate the quality of information received by outsiders if the securities are sold. Is it different than if the securities had not been sold?

c. What is the accounting problem for these accountants? Will the security sale have the desired effect on net income? Might Korsmo also recommend this sale for the trading securities?

d. Consider the two heuristics for recognizing ethical problems: does either the principle of equal treatment or the public principle suggest that the accountants have an ethical problem?

e. What is the ethical problem for these accountants? What is at stake in this decision and for whom?

f. Explain how defining the problem helps you resolve the problem.

12. Classifying Liabilities as Short Term or Long Term

ABC Construction Company has a $100 million long-term note payable. The loan covenants relating to this note require the company to maintain a current ratio of

2 to 1. Paul Anderson, the controller for the company, is currently working on the financial disclosure report for the insurance company that holds the note. He notices that the current ratio has dropped below 2 to 1, based on a short-term loan negotiated with the bank for operating expenses. Paul is concerned about the $100 million note being due immediately if the company violates the loan covenant. The company does not have the money to pay off the $100 million note. This might be a serious problem for the company unless they can improve the current ratio. The treasurer of the company has suggested that they reclassify the note they just took out as long term rather than short term, even though it has a payment date of nine months. He also suggested paying off a portion of the short-term liabilities with cash to reduce the amount of the current liabilities.

Required:

    a. Consider the balance sheet and profit or loss statement of this company if the debt is classified as short-term versus long-term. Explain how the conceptual framework's definitions of financial statement elements and rules for when to record transactions could be used to help the accountant decide whether which classification is appropriate.

    b. Evaluate the quality of information received by outsiders if the debt is classified as short-term. Is it different than if the debt had been classified as long-term?

    c. What is the accounting problem for these accountants?

    d. Consider two heuristics for recognizing ethical problems: does either the principle of equal treatment or the public principle suggest that the accountants have an ethical problem?

    e. What is the ethical problem for these accountants? What is at stake in this decision and for whom?

13. Parmalat

Parmalat, an Italian company with revenue of $10 billion and income from operations of $1 billion, sells dairy products around the world. In 2003, the company employed 36,000 employees in 30 countries. On December 24, 2003, Parmalat filed for bankruptcy protection in Italy and a few days later the court in Parma, Italy, declared Parmalat insolvent. Parmalat's stock traded on the Milan stock exchange and its debt instruments were sold in the United States.

    On December 9, 2003, Calisto Tanzi, Parmalat's chairman and chief executive officer, and Stefano Tanzi, a senior Parmalat executive, met with representatives of a New York City private equity firm regarding a possible buyout of Parmalat. The Tanzis were interested in a buyout of Parmalat due to liquidity problems at the company. A representative of the equity firm questioned how the company could have a liquidity problem when they had a large amount of cash on their balance sheet. Stefano Tanzi stated that the cash was not there and that the company had only about $600 million in cash, instead of the $4.9 billion reported on the balance sheet. And furthermore, Parmalat's debt was nearly $18 billion, much higher than the $2.3 billion the balance sheet showed.

$15.7 billion of the debt had never been reported. In addition, the profit or loss statement reported earnings that were more than five times their actual size. According to reports in the financial press, the company had systematically falsified its accounts for 15 years.

Parmalat entered into fraudulent transactions to hide the financial position of the company. The fraud perpetrated at Parmalat was simple. Parmalat forged documents on a scanner; ran the documents through a fax machine to make them look authentic and forged signatures from old documents and simply copied them on the new agreements. Parmalat entered into fraudulent transactions four times a year to inflate the financial statements when the quarterly results were due. Managers admitted that they misstated transactions on the financial statements, prepared fake documents, and destroyed evidence, with the orders to do so coming from Mr. Tanzi. Mr. Tanzi ordered the document falsifications while he was trying to find a way to reverse the company's financial problems. At times the inflated results were unreasonable, including the report that claimed a unit of Parmalat sold enough milk to Cuba for each person to drink 55 gallons of milk a year.

From 1997 to 2003, Parmalat transferred at least €800 million to the family's tourism business run by Francesca, the daughter of Mr. Tanzi, the owner. More money is believed to have been transferred to Parmalat's soccer team, run by Mr. Tanzi's son Stefano. The Tanzi family company (La Coloniale SpA) owns 51% of the stock of Parmalat.

The Parmalat fraud is the largest fraud to occur in Europe and one of the largest financial frauds in history. Calisto Tanzi, the founder of the company, his son, Stefano Tanzi, and Fausto Tonna, the company's chief financial officer, all face indictment on charges in the Parmalat case. The fraud surprised many people. Until 2003, Parmalat received a clean audit opinion from its auditor, Deloitte & Touche, borrowed money from many international banks, and issued bonds with the assistance of investment bankers on Wall Street. One might ask how so many outsiders missed the signs of Parmalat's deception.[4]

Required:

    a. Consider the balance sheet of Parmalat with $4.9 billion of fictitious cash and $15.7 billion of debt that was not reported. Explain how the conceptual framework's definitions of financial statement elements and rules for when to record transactions could be used to help the accountant decide how cash and long-term debt should be reported on the balance sheet.

Statement of Financial Position
At December 31, 20XX
Adjustments Needed

Assets:		Liabilities:	
Cash	−$4.9 billion	Accounts payable	
Accounts receivable		Salaries payable	
Inventory		Total current liabilities	
Total current assets		Long-term Debt	+ $15.7 billion

Land	Total liabilities
Building	Common stock
Equipment	Additional paid in
	capital
Intangible Assets	Retained earnings
Total assets	Total Liabilities and Owners' Equity

b. Evaluate the quality of information received by outsiders from a balance sheet where cash is overstated by $4.9 billion and long-term debt is understated by $15.7 billion.

c. What type of fraud did Parmalat commit? Who was harmed by the fraud?

14. Royal Ahold, NV

Ahold, the world's third largest supermarket group after Wal-Mart Stores Inc. of the US and Carrefour SA of France, with headquarters in the Netherlands, was charged with filing false and misleading financial statements with the Securities and Exchange Commission (SEC) in the United States because of its treatment of promotional allowances. This incorrect treatment allowed Ahold to overstate net sales (gross profit) by $41 billion for 2000–2002, operating income by $4.5 billion, and net income by $1.1 billion.

Before the accounting fraud, Ahold NV was regarded as one of Europe's most successful companies. Founded in 1887, it operated as a family business for many years selling fishing nets, clogs, and other Dutch staples. It became a public company in November 1994 and continued to expand by acquiring other companies. In 2001, it reported net sales revenue of $82.7 billion and net income of $1.4 billion. The company operated in 27 countries and had almost 250,000 employees. In 2002, when earnings were lower than anticipated and the prospect for bonuses appeared slim, managers of US Foodservice, a division of Ahold, announced a new strategy to increase income and gain bonus payments. The company began ordering large quantities of food and paper products from manufacturing companies such as Sara Lee Corp, Kraft Foods, Inc., Georgia-Pacific Corp., and Nestlé SA. The manufacturers had agreed to pay large rebates ranging from 8% to 46% for the inventory purchases.

Rebates should be recorded as reductions in cost of goods sold and recognized when goods are sold. However, the rebates were recorded immediately as reductions of cost of goods sold to increase 2002 earnings. All the inventory was not sold in 2002, so the rebates on the unsold portion should have been recorded in the year of the sale. A year later the company still had not sold the inventory and cut prices below cost to get rid of the excess purchases. This sales strategy allowed the company to meet earnings targets for 2002 but violated accounting principles and provided false and misleading filings with the SEC.[5]

a. Consider the profit or loss statement of Ahold. Explain how the definitions of financial statement elements from the conceptual framework and rules for when to record transactions could be used to help the accountant decide how the vendor allowances should be reported on the profit and loss statement.

Statement of Profit or Loss
For the Years Ending 2000–2002
Misstated Balances

	Adjustment needed
Sales Revenue	
– Cost of goods sold	+ 41 billion
= Gross Profit	–41 billion
– Operating expenses	
= **Income from continuing**	–4.5 billion
operations	
± Gains or Losses	
± Non-operating income or expense	
– Tax expense	
= **Net income**	–1.1 billion

b. Evaluate the quality of information received by outsiders when gross profit is overstated by $41 billion, income from continuing operations is overstated by $4.5 billion, and net income is overstated by $1.1 billion.

c. What type of fraud did Ahold commit? Who was harmed by the fraud?

15. WorldCom, Inc.

In 2002, WorldCom, Inc., a telecommunications company based in the US in Mississippi, with more than $30 billion in revenue and $104 billion in assets, was one of the world's largest telecommunications companies, with 20 million customers, thousands of corporate clients, and 62,000 employees.[6]

However, in June 2002, WorldCom announced a $3.8 billion earnings restatement due to expenses that had been improperly recorded as capital expenditures. By July 1, the stock had dropped to $0.05 from a high of $64.50 in June 1999.[7] WorldCom filed for bankruptcy shortly thereafter.

The accounting errors were discovered during a routine investigation by the internal audit department at WorldCom. The information was turned over to the board of directors' audit committee and to the independent auditor KPMG, which had replaced Arthur Andersen as auditors in May 2002. After the investigation, WorldCom issued a statement announcing the accounting improprieties: "certain transfers from line cost expenses to capital assets" were not made in accordance with the accounting standards. In August 2002, WorldCom revised the amount of the earnings restatement from $3.8 billion to $7.2 billion.[8] The restatement is related to a time period when insiders were selling company stock. For example, former WorldCom chief financial officer, Scott Sullivan, sold shares valued at $18.1 million during 2000. In September 2002, WorldCom announced a further restatement of about $2 billion, to be added to the $7 billion total, making the "largest accounting fraud ever" even bigger. The new restatement was said to be related "in part to the company's accounting for the results of a foreign subsidiary". WorldCom appears to have consolidated the results of one of its subsidiaries, Embrated Participacoes SA, when it was profitable (contributing 8.6% of WorldCom's revenues in 2000) but did not consolidate results when it was unprofitable.[9] The restatement eventually grew to an earnings restatement of $11 billion.

In September 2002, David F. Myers, the former controller of WorldCom, pleaded guilty to three felony counts, saying he helped manufacture profits at the request of senior management as part of an attempt by management to defraud investors and meet Wall Street expectations. At the court hearing, Myers said he was: "instructed on a quarterly basis by senior management to ensure that entries were made to falsify WorldCom's books, to reduce WorldCom's reported actual costs and thereby increase WorldCom's reported earnings." Myers told the court that he made the entries even though he "knew there was no justification or documentation".[10]

The US House Energy and Commerce Committee also investigated the accounting practices of WorldCom. The committee released documents gathered during the investigation that showed WorldCom employees had tried to question the accounting practices but were told to keep quiet. A WorldCom executive also notified Arthur Andersen, the company's auditor, more than two years prior to the restatement that the company was inflating net income but the practice of recording expense as capital assets continued.[11]

The documents released provide detail about Steven Brabbs, a London-based WorldCom executive responsible for Europe and Asia. In March 2000, Brabbs questioned a $33.6 million reduction in expense for his division. This charge made his profit numbers look better than they were. When Brabbs questioned corporate headquarters about the entry, he was told it was made "because of a directive from Sullivan" (the chief financial officer). When Brabbs persisted in following up on the directive by sending a letter to Arthur Andersen and senior financial executives at WorldCom, he received an e-mail from David Myers, WorldCom controller, saying, "Do not have any more meetings with Arthur Andersen for any reason. Don't make me ask you again."[12] Brabbs was asked to record the expense adjustment on his books. He refused even when pressured from Sullivan's office to record the entry. Brabbs finally agreed to create a "management company" and record the entry there. The explanation for the entry reads: "late adjustment as instructed by Scott Sullivan".[13]

Troy Normand, a member of the accounting department, also questioned the capitalization of the operating expenses. When he discussed his concerns with Sullivan, he assured Normand that "everything would be OK".[14] According to the documents released by the House Committee, Normand "didn't communicate his concerns regarding prepaid capacity or relieving line-cost accruals to external or internal audit because he was concerned for his job and had a family to support".[15]

Required:

    a. Consider the statement of financial position and the profit or loss statement of WorldCom. Explain how the definitions of financial statement elements from the conceptual framework and rules for when to record transactions could be used to help the accountant decide how the accountant should report the expense transactions that the company capitalized to assets.

Statement of Financial Position
At December 31, 2002
Balances Needing Adjustment

Assets:	Adjustment needed	Liabilities:	Adjustment needed
Cash		Accounts payable	
Accounts receivable		Salaries payable	
Inventory		Total current liabilities	
Total current assets		Long-term Debt	
Land		Total liabilities	
Building		Common stock	
Equipment		Additional paid in capital	
Intangible Assets	−11 billion	Retained earnings	−11 billion
Total assets	−11 billion	Total Liabilities and Owners' Equity	−11 billion

Statement of Profit or Loss
For the Years Ending 2000–2002
Balances Needing Adjustment

	Adjustment needed
Sales Revenue	
– Cost of goods sold	
= Gross Profit	
– Operating expenses	+ 11 billion
= **Income from continuing operations**	−11 billion
± Gains or Losses	
± Non-operating income or expense	
– Tax expense	
= **Net income**	−11 billion

b. Evaluate the quality of information received by outsiders when net income is overstated by $11 billion.

c. What type of fraud did WorldCom commit? Who was harmed by the fraud?

d. Compare the behavior of Brabbs to that of Normand. Who, in your opinion, acted in the more ethical fashion?

16. Bristol-Myers Squibb

Bristol-Myers produces and distributes medicines and healthcare products. In 2002, the company experienced one of its worst years in its 100 year history. Three of its top-selling drugs lost patent protection and sales dramatically declined due to generic substitutes produced by other companies. The share price of Bristol-Myers stock declined by nearly two-thirds (from about $75 in September 1999 to $25 in September 2002).

From 2000 to 2002, Bristol-Myers engaged in an earnings management program where it sold excessive amounts of pharmaceutical products to its wholesale customers ahead of demand. The company also used "cookie jar" reserve funds to meet its earnings targets and analysts' earnings forecasts.

In 2000 and 2001, Bristol-Myers inflated its earnings results each quarter by stuffing its distribution channels with excess inventory sold to wholesalers ahead of demand, and improperly recognizing $1.5 billion in revenue from these sales. This revenue recognition was contrary to generally accepted accounting principles. When its earnings still fell short of the earnings forecasted by analysts, the company improperly created divestiture reserves and reversed portions of those reserves into income to inflate its earnings. The company took both actions without disclosing that it was inflating its results through channel stuffing and improper accounting or that excess wholesaler inventory would be a material risk to the company's future sales.[16]

Bristol-Myers agreed to pay $150 million to settle the fraud charges levied by the SEC.

Required:

    a. Consider the profit or loss statement and the balance sheet of Bristol-Myers. Explain how the definitions of financial statement elements from the conceptual framework and rules for when to record transactions could be used to help the accountant decide how to report the adjustments to the reserve account and the excess shipments to wholesale customers.

    b. Evaluate the quality of information received by outsiders when management engages in channel stuffing and manipulating reserves to manage earnings.

    c. What type of fraud did Bristol-Myers commit? Who was harmed by the fraud?

17. Merck-Medco

Between 1999 and 2001, Merck-Medco, the second largest pharmacy-benefits manager in the US, recorded $12.4 billion in revenue that it would never collect.[17] Merck's Medco unit included as part of revenue the co-payments collected by pharmacies from patients, even though Medco did not receive these funds. For the three year period, the co-payments accounted for nearly 10% of Merck's total revenue.

Merck first disclosed the revenue recognition policy in an April 2002 SEC filing in preparation for selling 20% of Medco in an initial public offering (IPO). Merck maintains that the revenue recognition was consistent with GAAP. The company said the accounting choice had no impact on net income because the company subtracted the same amount as an expense.

The $12.4 billion in revenue was paid directly to the pharmacies by consumers using a prescription drug card to cover their portion of the prescription cost under an insurance plan. The co-payment was typically $10–15 per prescription. The pharmacies kept the entire co-payment, but Medco recorded the co-payment as revenue, despite the fact that Medco did not bill the pharmacy or the patient for the co-payment, or ever see the funds.

Required:

    a. Consider the profit or loss statement and the balance sheet of Merck-Medco. Explain how the definitions of financial statement elements from the conceptual framework and rules for when to record transactions could be used to help the accountant decide how the co-pays should be reported on the financial statements.

    b. Evaluate the quality of information received by outsiders when a company overstates its revenue in the manner used by Merck-Medco.

    c. What type of fraud did Merck-Medco commit? Who was harmed by the fraud?

NOTES

    1. We will not discuss "other comprehensive income" in this textbook because it is not relevant for a basic discussion of financial statements.

    2. Buildings and equipment would also be adjusted at year end to reflect the depreciation expense for the year. This example does not adjust depreciation for the buildings and equipment, because the amounts are not estimated. The calculation for depreciation is usually quite simple. For example, equipment might be depreciated for seven years and the yearly depreciation expense for the equipment is the cost of the equipment divided by 7.

    3. This case will be presented in several chapters with different questions for each chapter. This will illustrate how each of the tools can be used to help the accountant make a decision that reflects both technical proficiency and ethical awareness.

    4. SEC Litigation Release No. 18803, July 28, 2004; SEC Litigation Release No 18527, December 30, 2003; H. Sender, D. Reilly & M. Schroeder, "Parmalat investors missed red flags," *The Wall Street Journal*, January 7, 2004; A. Galloni, D. Reilly & C. Mollenkamp, "Skimmed off: Parmalat inquiry finds basic ruses at heart of scandal," *The Wall Street Journal*, December 31, 2003; Alessandra Galloni, "Scope of Parmalat's woes emerges," *The Wall Street Journal*, January 27, 2004; Alessandra Galloni & David Reilly, "Auditor raised Parmalat red flag," *The Wall Street Journal*, March 29, 2004; SEC Litigation Release No. 18527, December 30, 2003; A. Galloni, & D. Reilly. "Two Italian partners at Deloitte may face charges over Parmalat," *The Wall Street Journal*, May 13, 2005.

    5. Ania Raghavan, "Ahold and SEC settle with no fine," *The Wall Street Journal*, October 14, 2004; Steve Stecklow, Anita Raghavan & Deborah Ball, "How a quest for rebates sent Ahold on an odd buying spree," *The Wall Street Journal*, March 6, 2003.

6. "Key facts for WorldCom, Inc.," *The Wall Street Journal*, September 25, 2002.

7. Jared Sandberg, Rebecca Blumenstein & Shawn Young, "WorldCom internal probe uncovers massive fraud," *The Wall Street Journal*, June 26, 2002.

8. Jared Sandberg & Susan Pulliam, "WorldCom finds more errors; restatement will be $7.2 billion," *The Wall Street Journal*, August 9, 2002.

9. Susan Pulliam & Jared Sandberg, "New WorldCom report to SEC will acknowledge more flaws," *The Wall Street Journal*, 2002.

10. Deborah Solomon, "WorldCom's ex-controller pleads guilty to 3 counts," *The Wall Street Journal*, September 27, 2002.

11. Yochi J. Dreazen & Deborah Solomon, "Andersen ignored warnings on WorldCom, memos show," *The Wall Street Journal*, July 15, 2002

12. Yochi J. Dreazen, "WorldCom's Myers attempted to stifle accounting questions," *The Wall Street Journal*, August 27, 2002.

13. Yochi J. Dreazen & Deborah Solomon, "Andersen ignored warnings on WorldCom, memos show," *The Wall Street Journal*, July 15, 2002

14. Dreazen & Solomon, "Andersen ignored warnings on WorldCom, memos show," *The Wall Street Journal*, July 15, 2002

15. Dreazen & Solomon, "Andersen ignored warnings on WorldCom, memos show," *The Wall Street Journal*, July 15, 2002

16. SEC Press Release 2004-105, "Bristol-Myers Squibb Company agrees to pay $150 million to settle fraud charges," Washington, DC.

17. Barbara Martinez, "Merck books co-payments to pharmacies as revenue," *The Wall Street Journal*, June 21, 2002; Barbara Martinez, "Merck recorded $12.4 billion in revenue it never collected," *The Wall Street Journal*, July 8, 2002.

CHAPTER FIVE

Moral Philosophy and Ethical Reasoning: Resources for Decision Making

DECISION MAKING, COMPETENCE, AND THE PURPOSE OF FINANCIAL ACCOUNTING

Reminder: The purpose of financial accounting is to prepare financial statements with high-quality information to be communicated to various stakeholders. The accounting standards establish the guidelines for preparing financial statements, and professional codes of ethics express the basic principles for accountants' specific actions and long-term conduct.

> *Reminder:* Decision making is a crucial feature of accounting practice. Competent decision making includes both technical proficiency and ethical sensibility.
>
> *Reminder:* Accounting decision making encompasses identification of accounting issues and the appropriate technical standards for dealing with them, as well as recognition of moral issues and their resolution by ethical behavior.

TOWARD AN ETHICAL FRAMEWORK IN ACCOUNTING PRACTICE

Chapters Two through Four have introduced several resources for accounting ethics decision making: Chapter Two introduced general features of decision making, a working definition of ethics, aspects of four traditions of moral philosophy, a decision model for identifying accounting issues and ethical issues within given situations, a brief description of the accountant's preparation of financial statements and reference to the requirements for the form and content of these financial statements as set by accounting standards. Chapter Three expanded our treatment of a decision model to distinguish accounting problems from ethical problems and to identify moral issues and ethical dilemmas encountered in accounting practice.

Chapter Four discussed the conceptual framework of financial accounting and the basic features of preparing financial statements of high-quality information. The chapter also illustrated a number of ways that financial statements might be manipulated to distort financial information and to deceive stakeholders, preventing them from gaining relevant and faithfully representative information about business entities. Chapter Four also treated several business challenges to the accountant's competence. Cases and examples showed that some managers and stakeholders pressured accountants to distort financial statements and deceive those who use them. Other cases highlighted efforts to hide the misuse of company assets. In this context of managerial pressures, stakeholder distractions, and business challenges to the accountant's competence (especially in its ethical dimensions), the present chapter will continue the discussion on moral philosophy as a resource for decision making.

Our discussion of ethical decision making in accounting now builds on our earlier presentation of the basic purpose of financial accounting: accountants are expected to prepare and communicate financial statements of high-quality knowledge to a diverse audience of stakeholders. This task (the production of accounting knowledge and its communication) calls for technical and ethical competence on the part of the accountant. Accounting standards – expressed in principles and codified in rules and decision procedures – have established guidelines for preparing financial statements. These standards also prescribe acceptable professional relationships between accountants, their clients, and stakeholders. In brief: the expressed goals of accounting and the practical responsibilities established by accounting standards set the distinctive ethical domain of accounting practice. Further discussion of this ethical domain and the distinctive task of ethical decision making in accounting can make good use of moral philosophy.

The accountant who turns to moral philosophy for assistance in moral reasoning and ethical decision making will find rich resources. In this context, we have already presented a working definition of ethics and introduced features of four traditions of moral philosophy. We proceed on the assumption that some aspects of the traditions may be useful to accountants, but we see no need to develop a systematic, coherent "theory of accounting ethics" ourselves. We do not believe that any one of these traditions of moral philosophy (or combination of them) should be thought of as a comprehensive moral theory to be integrated into accounting practice. There are too many significant differences among the traditions and too many unresolved difficulties in their patterns of moral reasoning. What is more, the debates among moral philosophers – in their selection of topics and with their level of abstraction and complexity – are often quite far removed from the practical concerns of accounting decision making (the business circumstances, the professional standards and the qualities of personal character that provide the mix for everyday accounting activities).

Chapter Five will expand the discussion of moral philosophy and ethical reasoning and illustrate how the concepts and decisions of moral philosophy – with its history of rational inquiry and argument – can support decision making in the specialized field of accounting practice. Particular attention will be paid to how accounting practice reflects features of the moral philosophy traditions and makes use of ethics concepts and patterns of ethical reasoning. To highlight moral philosophy as a useful resource for reflecting about the distinctive features of accounting ethics, Chapter Five will repeat and expand features of previous discussions. We repeat the claim that accounting ethics encompasses both an "ethics of duty" and an "ethics of virtue". The discussion then will point to elements of three moral traditions that are recognizable within the standards and practice of contemporary accounting. Our treatment of these philosophical elements within accounting serves to clarify and expand what we authors mean when we speak of the "duty–virtue" duality of accounting ethics. The philosophy materials will be used to illustrate the specific significance of duties and virtues in accounting.

Accounting competence includes both technical proficiency and ethical sensibility. We can now speak of the accountant's "duty" to be competent in this twofold manner. The accounting principles and standards project this duty of dual competence as the accountant's ethical obligation. The fundamental purpose of financial accounting is to communicate high-quality information to stakeholders. The conceptual framework, the specifications of accounting standards, and the codes of conduct project, in effect, the principles and rules of accounting practice as "moral laws". These "moral laws" of accounting bind and constrain the individual accountant: they express the particular ways through which the accountant's dual duty of technical and ethical competence is fulfilled.

Accounting practice calls for competency as the technical and ethical duties of accountants. We refer to these duties as "moral laws" for the accountant. This way of speaking blends the language of accounting with that of moral philosophy. In this chapter, the language of moral philosophy about duty and virtue will be brought into our discussion about the accountant's decision making. This philosophical language will help us to assess particular circumstances wherein accountants must identify accounting problems and make proper recognition of accounting elements in the financial statements. The language will be employed to determine whether moral issues are part of the circumstance and to assist in resolving any ethical dilemmas that may be posed. In addition, the language of moral philosophy will enable us to discuss the accountant's intellectual and moral traits of character (virtues) to show how they support conduct over the long term. Ethical decision making in specific cases and the habits of virtue to guide behavior over the long term are key components of the professional responsibilities of those who can be called "the virtuous accountants".

USING MORAL PHILOSOPHY PRINCIPLES AS A RESOURCE TO MAKE ACCOUNTING DECISIONS

Chapters Two and Three introduced the decision model that we use in this book, which is reproduced in Figure 5.1. Let us see where this chapter fits in the model. The chapter contents fit in the second box of column two, labeled *Identify Problem-Solving Resources: Moral Philosophy*. In this chapter we speak about the principles from several moral philosophy traditions as resources for determining how to make accounting decisions that are technically correct and demonstrate ethical awareness. To achieve both of these goals, we must understand how moral philosophy can be a useful resource for accounting ethics decision making.

We refer to several traditions of moral philosophy to help us understand the ethical dimensions of accounting practice and to define the ethical problems that we encounter in accounting situations. Elements within these traditions of moral inquiry support our efforts to weigh the importance of ethical matters in relation to the main purposes of accounting. In addition (and surprising as it may seem), important elements of each tradition are already present in contemporary features of accounting practice. Since this is the case, discussion of moral philosophy and the language of philosophical ethics help us better to understand and speak about the business and social responsibilities of accounting as ethical matters (and not just technical matters.)

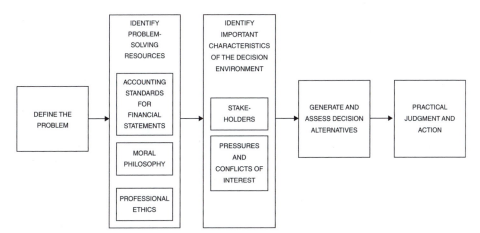

Figure 5.1 A Decision Model for Accounting Ethics

A brief examination of the conceptual framework of accounting (with its outline of accounting purposes and definitions of key concepts) and an appraisal of the key paragraphs of several professional codes show that accounting standards express some ideas and argumentation similar to those of the moral philosophy traditions. In this context, discussion of the norms and values of accounting and the treatment of its principles, rules and approved decision procedures can best be illuminated with reference to each tradition of moral philosophy. What is more important: an understanding of moral sensibility that calls forth the accountant's commitment to ethical action can be gained through discussion of the distinctive approaches of moral philosophy as they relate to accounting.

THE PHILOSOPHICAL TRADITIONS, DUTIES, AND VIRTUES

Until the past quarter century, the deontological and the utilitarian approaches had dominated modern ethical inquiry (with the social contract theory largely confined to discussion of political theory and civic duties). Recently, however, there has been a resurgence of interest in a community-centered ethics first developed in ancient Greece and extensively elaborated by Aristotle. This approach, now labeled "Virtue Ethics," encourages philosophers not only to focus on moral agents and their decision making in specific circumstances but also to consider the qualities of character possessed by these individuals. These character traits, called virtues, are influential in shaping personal motivation for taking action. Virtue ethics is also interested in how moral character is developed through education and experience, through reflection, exemplary behavior and habit formation.

You may recall, from Chapter Two, the distinction between the accountant's "ethic of duty" and the "ethic of virtue". The treatment of these two interrelated facets of accounting ethics suggests how recent developments within moral philosophy have influenced the ethical analysis of accounting practice. Thomas and Mary Doucet examined the relationship of accountants' duties and virtues by borrowing ideas from moral philosophy to present their own understanding of contemporary accounting ethics. In the language used by the Doucets, accountants fulfill their duty by exercising distinctive virtues which they possess as aspects of their personal character (Doucet & Doucet, 2004). We agree with the Doucets' approach of linking accounting duties and virtues. Their reflection on professional duties arising from accounting codes and their closely related treatment on how accountants are empowered by virtues to make technically proficient and ethically sensible decisions have influenced our own approach to accounting ethics.

In the present chapter, we elaborate on the interrelationship between accountants' ethics of duty and their ethics of virtue. In order to clarify this idea about accountants' ethical obligations as the "virtue-empowered realization of their duty," we tap into the rich resources of moral philosophy. Our discussion combines analysis of accounting standards and codes of conduct and reflects on taking personal responsibility ("doing one's duty"). It also involves examining features of deontology, utilitarianism, and virtue ethics. In effect, both the Doucets and we authors of this book acknowledge the influence of deontological and utilitarian moral reasoning in the establishment and application of accounting standards and codes. And like the

Doucets, we see the language of virtue ethics in the professional codes of conduct that guide accounting practice.

In this chapter, we take into account the new prominence of virtue ethics and recent theories of moral development to emphasize the significance of accountants' personal motivation and character traits. We examine how intellectual and moral traits support accountants' commitment to strive for excellence in their distinctive tasks. We explore how accountants express their virtues in the intellectual and moral judgments made during accounting decision making. Finally, we show the close linkage between the duties prescribed by accounting standards and the intellectual and moral virtues that are crucial for the working accountant.

To summarize: in Chapter Two, we described the ethical obligations of accounting as duties to follow the principles and the rules set by the accounting community – the accounting standards established by the standards-setting organizations. We also saw that accountants need intellectual and moral virtues as components of their character in order to fulfill these accounting duties. In this chapter, we turn to the rich storehouse of philosophical language – vocabulary, concepts, and argumentation – as well as the long tradition of inquiry and debate within moral philosophy. We do this in order to elaborate on two facets of accounting ethics: an ethics focused on professional *duties* and an ethics concerned with the accountant's personal *virtues*. These qualities of the accountant's character are crucial to practicing in a virtuous manner as the accountant fulfills his or her duty with technical proficiency and ethical sensibility in decisions.

THE ELEMENTS OF MORAL PHILOSOPHY EMBEDDED IN ACCOUNTING PRACTICE: UTILITARIANISM

The frequent references to accountants' duty throughout the book remind us of deontological and utilitarian features among the demands of accounting discourse and practice. Indeed, these two philosophical approaches are the prevailing moral systems in accounting; their key elements are seen in professional codes and specific accounting standards. Let us first consider utilitarianism. Recall that this moral tradition stresses that appropriate decision making – the best ethical choice in a situation – leads to an increase of utility among those affected by the decisions. The basic purpose of accounting reflects this utilitarian perspective: accountants are supposed to produce financial statements of high-quality information so that these reports can be useful to stakeholders.

Usefulness

According to accounting standards, relevant financial information that fairly represents the economic activities and status of businesses is considered "high-quality information". It is high quality *because it will be useful for stakeholders' decision making*. The communication of high-quality knowledge benefits stakeholders (and is, therefore, a crucial mark of a free and open market) because it permits stakeholders to pursue their own financial interests. The preparation and transmission of high-quality financial statements, in effect, is to be evaluated in their "happy" results, in the usefulness of the communication – to stakeholders, to the markets, and to the general public. This is a utilitarian criterion of value.

From a utilitarian perspective, the basic purpose of accounting to provide high-quality information is advanced by applying the principles, rules and approved decision processes that are established by contemporary accounting standards. The utilitarian asks: "Will compliance to these standards produce useful information to stakeholders, information that will benefit all the interested parties?" This question points out how any given accounting decision is to be evaluated: adhering to particular principles and following the rules of decision making is intended to support the production and communication of high-quality financial information to those who would use it. In this context, the best accounting decision is the one that most increases utility for stakeholders.

Impartiality

For such communication to take place – that is, for relevant and faithfully representative accounting knowledge to be conveyed to stakeholders – the accountant must assume an impartial stance with regard to each and every group of stakeholders. No stakeholders should be favored or discriminated against as the financial statements are prepared, economic phenomena recognized, and reports conveyed. In the process of giving account (or attesting for them), the accountant is to strive for objectivity and neutrality, to avoid favoritism to particular stakeholders and guard against discrimination (deliberately shortchanging stakeholder groups of crucial information). This impartial stance is mandated because the accountant provides a service to many stakeholders (a company or clients, shareholders, "outside" creditors or lending agencies, potential investors, the general public, the regulators, and suchlike). As complicated as it may be, the accountant has duties in relation to each of these groups. In utilitarian terms, the maximum utility can only be realized if the accountant's service is rendered impartially and if financial information is not skewed to benefit or harm any particular stakeholder.

This argument linking the purpose of accounting with the duty to be impartial in relation to stakeholders presumes that accounting standards are best perceived as supportive of the development and communication of high-quality information. From a utilitarian perspective, this is the highest possible evaluation of the standards, establishing the ideal for their authority over the actual practice of accounting. (In general, the authors adopt this positive appraisal of accounting standards.)

ACCOUNTING STANDARDS: USEFUL AND IMPARTIAL INFORMATION

The accountant standards require the financial accountant to produce and communicate useful information to stakeholders and to present this information in an impartial manner – not favoring one stakeholder over another. The accountant is expected to be neutral with regard to those who use the financial knowledge communicated to them. These requirements have a utilitarian function; that is, the standards and the accountant's decision to follow them should result in useful information, information that contributes to the happiness (or satisfaction) of the stakeholder – a benefit that supports the stakeholder's decision making.

Accrual Accounting

As the basis for providing high-quality information to stakeholders, knowledge useful for stakeholders' financial decision making, the profession has constructed a system of accrual accounting. In this accounting theory, the technical (and ethical) standards prescribe that economic events are recognized by matching expenses with revenue. In accrual accounting, the accountant recognizes what revenues generate what expenses. In this accounting method, expenses are recognized in the period when revenues are recognized. That is, revenues and expenses are recorded at the time in which the transaction occurs rather than when payment is made. In this method of giving account, current cash inflows and outflows are to be combined with future expected inflows and outflows. According to this basic principle of recognition, specific standards – rules and decision processes – have been established to determine how transactions are recognized. For example: in a credit transaction, revenue is recognized when the goods are shipped or the service provided – before cash is received; for expenses, when products or services are received – before payment is made to the supplier or employee.

The accrual accounting system sets the pattern of accounting responsibilities: the accountant's duty is to honor its principles and comply with its rules. Whenever the accountant evaluates an economic event; that is, whenever the accountant faces an accounting problem about how to assess a transaction and considers alternatives for recognizing the economic event, the accrual theory prescribes the accountant's duty. All exercise of professional judgment is to follow (represent and affirm) the accrual method. The accountant honors and advances its basic principles in any decision made, in any action-choice taken. From a utilitarian perspective, then, by following the rules and methods of accrual accounting, the accountant provides useful, high-quality information to stakeholders, and with this knowledge the stakeholders can make their financial decisions. The accrual means of communication thus supports the utility of business knowledge that is communicated to these stakeholders.

SUMMARY

Earlier we gave attention to how accounting principles and specific rules have established duties to be fulfilled whenever the accountant faces accounting problems. These obligations include both technical and ethical duties. We focused on accountants' behavior – the action-choices they made in particular circumstances. As we described this in Chapter Two: the accountant is a moral agent engaged in a business-related circumstance where his or her judgment generates an accounting action. We presented several examples of how the principles and rules that govern accountants' activities might be discussed in the language of utilitarianism. In these utilitarian terms, the accountant/moral agent is to do "the right thing" by bringing into play the appropriate rule or decision process that generates utility for stakeholders. The accountant's decision is evaluated in relation to a particular rule: does the action-choice to apply the rule in a given circumstance result in useful information communicated to the stakeholders? If so, the utilitarian criterion of "the good action" is met!

Assume that the financial duty of the accountant is to provide useful, high-quality information to stakeholders. Given this obligation, the accountant's "ethic of duty" can thus be understood as a utilitarian responsibility. That is, the logic of utilitarian moral reasoning can be employed to evaluate the accountant's effort to "do his duty" in a given circumstance. We can ask: "Does the accountant's action-choice in this instance (how to recognize a lease arrangement) result in useful knowledge for stakeholders?" (Or, better: "Does the decision result in more knowledge, or more useful knowledge, for stakeholders than the knowledge communicated through a different accounting choice?") In similar fashion, the accountant's use of an accrual method for giving account (e.g., recording revenues and expenses associated with a product's sale) can also be assessed in utilitarian terms as the accountant's moral duty. We can ask: "Does giving an account in this manner result in greater utility for stakeholders – more relevant knowledge that fairly represents the economic events – than using, let us say, an accounting method that recognizes economic events on the basis of cash transactions only?"

THE ELEMENTS OF MORAL PHILOSOPHY EMBEDDED IN ACCOUNTING: DEONTOLOGY

We now shift our attention to deontological elements that are common within accounting practice. In this perspective, we are again reminded that accounting practice calls for numerous decisions and advocates many principles and rules intended to shape accountants' decision making. To support accounting purposes and guide accountants' decisions, the accounting standards impose duties on accountants. Within this now-familiar framework about how decision making is guided by principles and rules, the basic elements and patterns of deontological reasoning should also seem familiar to you.

Our earlier discussion in Chapter Two showed that, in deontological reasoning, ethics is primarily a matter of deciding which actions conform to moral principles and then taking these actions *because it is the reasonable thing to do*. In brief: individuals who confront moral issues use their reasoning ability to determine which moral principle ought to guide their action. They then exercise their human freedom to act in accordance with this moral principle. Let us now expand on this central theme of deontology.

Once again, we consider the moral agent who faces a moral issue. In deontological reasoning (to contrast with utilitarianism), focus is not directed merely toward the consequences of the agent's action, nor does one concentrate solely on the results of the agent's decision. Instead primary attention is given to the moral agent's motivation to act within the framework of specific moral principles. The correct motivation of an ethical decision is the intent to honor and advance a moral principle through a particular action *because it is rational to do so*. In the deontological perspective: the moral agent's motive for adhering to a principle or obeying a moral rule expresses a rational purpose (or, better: the underlying motivation for a decision should be dominated by reason. In the appropriate decision process, rationality outweighs all other incentives or inclinations). The rightness of the decision is measured in terms of its rational basis, in the reason-motivated duty to adhere to a principle (or to obey a rule that expresses a moral principle).

Deontology thus emphasizes a particular relationship between general moral principles and individual ethical responsibilities: correct ethical decisions must be reason-driven efforts to follow moral principles. When the moral agent faces an ethical dilemma or recognizes a moral issue, he or she is expected to identify the moral principle at stake in the circumstance – "Tell the truth"; "Be honest"; "Do not lie"; "Do not steal". Motivated by reason and logic, the moral agent willingly decides to adopt the guidance of the principle in making the decision. In brief: the moral agent exercises his reason and logic to make an action-choice that fits the moral principle. In a deontological perspective, then, the correct ethical decision in the situation will be a reason-driven action that is consistent with an appropriate moral principle.

DEONTOLOGY: MORAL LAWS AND REASON

This moral philosophy emphasizes that the moral agent should "do the right thing, for the right reason". This means that decision-choices should conform to moral principles and the decision should be motivated by reason, rather than by any other motivating factor. "I adhere to the principle because it is the reasonable thing to do."

In ethical terms, we have already seen that accounting is a principles-driven and rules-oriented practice and that accountants are duty-bound to comply with contemporary accounting standards. In light of this claim, the logic of deontological moral reasoning is a useful tool for thinking about the role of principles and rules in accounting practice. Typically we discuss the specific duties of the accountant in terms of adhering to the principles and following the rules established by the standards-setting organizations of the profession. In the following section, we treat the accountant's obligation to accounting standards as an example of the accountant's acting within a deontological perspective – as a rational decision to follow moral principles.

THE DEONTOLOGICAL VIEW OF HUMAN NATURE: REASON, FREEDOM, AND AUTONOMY

To understand how moral principles are linked to decision making in the deontological tradition, we take a close look at several intellectual assumptions made within the tradition. These assumptions concern the nature of human communities and the individuals who live and work within them. This examination will help us think more deeply about the basic decision scenario that we have been using: where a moral agent, facing an ethical problem, weighs alternatives and makes action-choices. Let us now consider this scenario in terms of the common bond shared by the moral agent and those affected by his decisions.

Deontological thinkers emphasize the common humanity shared by individuals and those affected by their decisions. This humanity is found in the rationality, personal freedom and autonomy of decision making that is claimed for every person in the situation. Individuals – by virtue of their humanity – are presumed to be rational and essentially free creatures that thrive best when they are autonomous; that is, given space to make their own decisions. People flourish when they are not manipulated, deceived or coerced as they make decisions. They have the right to enjoy freedom of thought and action. The individual's capacity to use reason and to act freely is the intellectual and moral foundation for deontology. The primary ethical duty of each individual is to make rational decisions to conform one's actions to moral principles.

The most famous version of deontology – developed by Immanuel Kant, an eighteenth-century German philosopher – elaborated at great length these ideas about human reason, freedom, and individuality. Kant (1981) thought that each individual is supposed to make decisions as a rational, free, and autonomous creature. Although a distinct individual, the moral agent shares these uniquely human traits with the other people affected by the action-choices taken in the circumstance. In Kant's understanding, moral agents and (those whom we now label as) stakeholders are rational – capable of logically grasping moral principles and reasonably adhering to them. All human individuals are free to think and act with purpose – able to discern the salient features of a moral issue and weigh decision-alternatives. Each is capable of taking effective actions that conform to a moral principle. These rationally considered, freely chosen actions taken by the individual have moral worth; that is, they fulfill the person's ethical duty with regard to moral principles. Of key importance: throughout this process of judgment and action, the moral agent is to be autonomous (a "law onto oneself") in determining his or her own purposes; that is, each individual sets his own goals, chooses the ends to achieve, and the means to do the tasks necessary to fulfill these goals.

Within deontology, then, what counts as *human* activity is marked by rationality and the freedom expressed by autonomous individuals. Accordingly, any situation that calls for an ethical decision is a circumstance where the humane quality of individual life is at stake. This is because moral principles and ethical decisions affect personal lives and shape human relationships. The choices made by a moral agent can have an impact on other individuals' goals and purposes. In the deontological ideal, moral principles prompt reason-driven, duty-inspired choices by individuals to "do the right thing for the right reason". What is more, as circumstances make it possible for reasonable, dutiful adherence to moral principles (expressing human rationality, freedom, and autonomy), the well-being of individual members of the community can be promoted. Through the exercise of principled decision making, the moral development of the agent is enhanced. The autonomy of the other individuals affected by the decision is also respected and promoted.

DEONTOLOGY: HUMANITY IN ITS FREEDOM, RATIONALITY AND AUTONOMY

For deontological thought: the distinctive marks of being human are the characteristics of freedom, rationality and autonomy in decision making. Applying this assumption to accounting: the accountant as moral agent and the stakeholders who are affected by the accountant's decision share a common humanity. Each individual possesses the traits of freedom and rationality and is capable of autonomous decision making. Decisions, then, should acknowledge and affirm the humanity of all concerned in the decision; that is, ethical decisions will honor and promote these human traits.

Individuals with their distinctive traits of rationality, freedom, and autonomy become entangled in ethically significant circumstances. In these situations, they have the power to take effective ethical actions. It is, therefore, vital to acknowledge the rich possibilities for human progress inherent to decision making. The moral agent's decision can make a real difference in others' lives and also promote the wellbeing of the community. This means that examination of ethical decision making must take into account both the possibility of the self-improvement of moral agents and the well-being of stakeholders. Given the possible outcomes of reason-driven, principled ethical decisions (their potential impact on individuals' lives and the well-being of society), ethics discussions ought to highlight duties and support actions which conform to moral principles.

The Rational Moral Agent, Free to Conform to Moral Principles

In the deontological tradition, the moral agent who faces a moral issue is presumed to have the intellectual tools necessary for addressing the perplexing situation. In Kantian language, the individual's rational, free, and autonomous will is fully capable of identifying the crucial elements of the circumstance, weighing decision-alternatives, and making a decision to conform with an appropriate moral principle. In the language of Chapter Three, the individual can find and define the problem. The autonomous individual has the capacity to solve the problem that is defined. The following paragraphs will discuss a deontological perspective on decision making to illustrate how the tradition understands ethical obligations and the individual's capacity to fulfill moral duties.

First, we emphasize that each human being has intrinsic moral worth. As a rational, free, and autonomous creature that lives and works within a human community, each individual is to be accorded high status by everyone who faces moral issues and attempts to resolve moral dilemmas. In brief, the high moral value of each individual is the basis of the moral obligation to promote the well-being of other individuals. This is achieved by affirming their capacity for rational thought, their freedom of thought and action, and their autonomy to choose their own ends and seek personal goals without manipulation or coercion by others. In short, we have a moral duty to support others as they express their humanity through reason, free thought, and voluntary action. We are obliged to promote their non-coerced (untrammeled) pursuit of happiness as they conceive it.

This is a tall order, a demanding obligation, one that gives highest priority to those aspects of human nature and personal development associated with reason, making logical choices, and the pursuit of goals and purposes. Deontology promotes the exercise of human will ("a good will") to conform to moral principles. In short, each moral agent is supposed to affirm his own dignity as a human being and also respect the moral worth of other free, reasonable, and self-determining individuals (persons who decide for themselves the ends – short term and long term – they pursue).

The moral agent seeks to conform to moral principles because it is reasonable to do so. The assumption that human beings are rational, free, and autonomous leads to another feature of the demand to conform to principles. By freely choosing to conform to appropriate principles, the moral agent affirms his own dignity and seeks his own self-improvement and the well-being of others. By following moral principles because it is reasonable, the moral agent uses reason, freedom, and personal autonomy to demonstrate the humane quality of his decision. Quite as importantly, the moral agent also promotes the well-being of others – supports their ability to make free, rational choices and pursue their own purposes (and thus express their humanity).

In this perspective, humanity – in its essential characteristics and most noteworthy features – is conceived in terms of rational expression, reason-driven analysis, and decision making. Humanity is revealed in the individual's capability of exercising effective free choices – to live and act in freedom. This moral obligation to promote and protect reason in its free exercise ranks as the core challenge for deontology; this constitutes its key ethical duty.

To be sure, Kant and other deontological thinkers recognize that individuals possess non-rational traits and that people have needs, desires, and passions that are not grounded in reason. Communities populated with these complex individuals generate material demands and social behaviors that cannot be construed as rational. These various non-rational aspects of human life play significant roles in particular decisions. A person has many appetites and inclinations that draw him toward one decision option or another. People express many emotions, and any given emotion may weigh prominently in a particular decision. Material desires and hopes for security, prestige, and social acceptance are powerful factors in some human decisions. Various incentives – promises of reward and threats of punishment – play important roles, as well. Yet in deontology, these non-rational aspects of life and society do not carry significant moral weight: what counts most are reason, freedom, and autonomous decision making. Deontological thinkers claim that only those decisions that express these human traits have moral worth. And the ability to exercise these distinctive human traits is to be protected through ethical decision making, and promoted in all moral choices.

THE INNER CONFLICT OF THE MORAL AGENT

The moral agent should make action-choices (decisions) that conform to moral principles. In this process, the freedom, reason, and autonomy of the individual are often challenged by conflicting appetites and inclinations. Emotions, material desires, and hopes for security and prestige may distract from the reasonable pursuit of moral principles. Promises of reward or threats of punishment may tempt the moral agent, making it difficult to choose a reasonable, principle-guided course of action. But only a reasoned conformity to moral principles has moral worth in the deontological tradition.

The deontological features of accounting practice are: freedom, rationality, and autonomy of the moral agent and the stakeholder.

In Chapter Two, we discussed the deontological claim that the moral agent is "to do the right thing for the right reason". The moral agent should be motivated by reason to conform to moral principles. This perspective emphasizes moral principles and gives highest priority to duty and reason in decision making. When such a view is applied to accounting practice, it encourages us to examine how accountants understand their relationship to the standards and rules of the practice. Deontological language is useful for describing accounting ethics in terms of principles and compliance to rules. Because accounting is a principles-shaped and rules-driven practice, it makes sense to identify deontological features in the application of the principles and rules of accounting. For example, consider the conceptual framework of accounting, with its statement of the basic purpose of financial accounting as the production of high-quality information. This fundamental statement of purpose projects an ethical duty for the accountant. The accountant has a moral obligation to shape specific financial communications to stakeholders to achieve the goal of conforming to this high standard. In a second example, the adoption of the methods of accrual accounting can be evaluated in deontological fashion by asking whether the particular methods are reasonable means of communicating high-quality financial information. Do accrual techniques respect the stakeholders' right of access to knowledge; do they generate information that fairly represents the financial positions of a business entity, transparent and clear information that does not deceive or manipulate the stakeholder? In deontological terms, does such communication respect the autonomy of the stakeholders' decision making and their freedom to pursue economic goals by exercising reason and logic? In a third example, we can also see the deontological dimensions in the professional demands for auditors' independence from those whose financial statements are attested. Such a principle proclaims the moral duty for the auditor to avoid even the appearance of a conflict of interest, thus to ensure the trustworthiness of the audit process and its resulting audit opinion.

We should also consider how the deontological ideas about human nature deserve a prominent place in accounting ethics. Accountants would be well-served to adopt the insight that human nature is expressed in freedom, rational thought, and autonomous decision making. Considering the accountant as a moral agent and stakeholders as those to whom he or she is responsible, we should highlight the basic humanity both of the accountant and the stakeholder.

This intellectual and moral assumption supports two important claims: (1) the accountant is capable of taking responsibility for his action *because* he is free, rational, and autonomous in decision making and (2) working within the framework of accounting standards and principles, the accountant has a fundamental duty to honor and respect the freedom, rationality, and autonomy of all stakeholders. In the context of these two deontological claims, the production and communication of financial information are human activities that presuppose and should support the humanity – the freedom, rationality, and autonomy – of all those who engage in discursive accounting practice.

In view of the first claim regarding the taking of responsibility: the moral agent can be held responsible for demonstrating technical proficiency and ethical sensibility (dual competency) in a given situation. This is *because* he has reason, *because* he can act freely, and *because* he can assert autonomy against various temptations, pressures, and incentives that threaten the faithful performance of professional duties. As a free and decisive human being, the accountant is capable of analyzing a situation and exercising judgment that conforms to the guiding standards of accounting. As a moral agent, the accountant can make choices to affirm and achieve the goals of the accounting practice to serve stakeholders.

In view of the second claim, we speak about the accountant's adherence to accounting standards that focus on stakeholder interests. In deontological terms, conformity to the standards supports and protects the humanity of the stakeholders. Consider, for instance, the standards that affirm the independence of stakeholder interests from those of the accountant or make the ethical demand for impartial and equal treatment of each stakeholder group, or those that warn against favoritism and personalized preference. Adherence to these standards demonstrates an ethical sensibility and professional discipline on the part of the accountant to "guarantee the stakeholders space" to pursue their own purposes. The moral agent, in choosing to follow the principles of accounting practice, honors and respects the stakeholders' basic humanity – their freedom, rationality, and autonomy. This commitment to make rational choices to achieve the fundamental purpose of financial accounting and follow standards that support stakeholders in their exercise of freedom, rational thought, and autonomy demonstrates the accountant's technical proficiency and ethical sensibility. In deontological language: the accountant fulfills his ethical duty.

Finally, by emphasizing the accountant's taking responsibility for action-choices and showing respect for the stakeholder's freedom to make decisions, we affirm the moral worth of both; the essential humanity of accountant and stakeholder is honored and advanced in the decision process. Freedom, rationality, and autonomy – as deontology characterizes the key features of human identity – are expressed as moral principles guiding decision making. Such a claim is an acknowledgment that both the accountant and the stakeholder deserve consideration as individuals of high moral worth and dignity, each possessing rights and each called to account for his choices and actions.

THE MORAL WORTH OF AGENTS AND STAKEHOLDERS

By making free and rational action-choices to conform to moral principles, the accountant as a moral agent affirms and supports the stakeholders. Such decisions respect the stakeholder's humanity by providing information that can be used in pursuing his or her own ends and in supporting stakeholders' goals in financial decision making. In effect, the decisions by accountant and stakeholder have the potential to enhance the human community of which both are a part.

Universal Principles (Categorical Imperatives) and Conditional Duties (Hypothetical Imperatives)

Given this view of human freedom and autonomous decision making, deontological reasoning elaborates the criterion for evaluating actions and conduct. In a given instance, does the action-choice express a reason-dominated motivation to follow a moral principle? To be sure, philosophers recognize that while people are free, rational, and autonomous, they are also creatures who exhibit non-rational attitudes, express emotions, and demonstrate desires, inclinations, and even compulsions that cannot be considered rational. (And this description encompasses accountants and stakeholders!) With this in mind, the deontological criterion of right behavior and conduct focuses on doing one's duty in compliance with moral principles, while *motivated by reason*. The influence of non-rational factors is to be limited as a "distraction". What is more, deontology asks whether the moral principles themselves are reason-based imperatives that the moral agent can intend (in Kant's language, "will") as universal guides to action. Can the statement of the principle that shapes a given action be extended to every free and equal individual? Does the action-choice conform to a moral law fitting in all circumstances similar to the one in which the moral agent (the accountant) is currently engaged? If it does, the action represents the decision of the agent's good will. It has emerged from a reason-guided intention, and thus the moral principle that underlies the action can be called a "categorical imperative".

The deontological treatment of categorical imperatives is specifically connected to the tradition's emphasis on the role of human freedom and rationality in decision making. As we have seen, the tradition emphasizes the free exercise – indeed the primacy – of reason in making ethical decisions. Its philosophers argue that human reason directs ethical action toward moral laws. Because of this emphasis, deontology is aptly described as an ethics of duty grounded in human reason, a duty that is fulfilled in actions that conform to moral law.

This philosophical discussion about the relationship of reason and moral law and of how individuals ought to determine (and evaluate) ethical actions is complicated and extensive. However a brief sketch of Kant's view should fit our purposes. According to Kant, a categorical imperative is an absolute moral law that commands practical action. It places a demand on an individual to use his powers of reason to guide his will (his intention) to conform to the moral law. Considering the action to be taken, the individual should ask: "What is the statement of the moral law which guides my action (in Kant's terms, 'the maxim')?" Then it must be asked: "Am I willing, can I intend, that this moral law should also be a universal law for each and every person, (all) other people?" The assumption here is that moral laws arise within an intelligible world that is rational. As a rational creature (and through a rational process), the individual can recognize and state these laws and shape his own action in accordance with them. And as a final stage, the individual can advocate his maxim, his own statement of the moral law, as one that other free and equal individuals should follow.

Kant distinguishes categorical imperatives from another class of imperatives which he calls "hypothetical imperatives". In simple terms, these latter commands are not absolute, but limited, conditional on the individual's personal values and specific goals. If a person, for example, desires a particular object, seeks a goal, or wants to affirm a distinctive value, then his choices are determined and evaluated in terms of that desire, goal or value. And such "inclinations" are normally pursued through a mixture of rational and non-rational means and incentives. For example, "If I wish to lose weight, then I will follow a low-calorie diet"; "If I want to become a better football player, then I will practice more"; "If I want to get a high mark in school, I will study and participate in classroom discussions". These actions (and the statements to describe the principles behind them) are not universal or absolute. While there is a certain logic that underlies them, the imperatives are not grounded in reason – the specific goals may reflect a wide variety of motives (not reason alone), and the particular actions may be taken in view of various incentives (desires for prestige, financial reward, praise from a teacher, competitive advantage over a fellow student). Because of this mixture of rational and non-rational motives and incentives, fulfilling such conditional imperatives has little moral worth. Accordingly, Kant and those who follow his tradition devote their primary attention to categorical imperatives and the reason-driven motives to follow them. They are little concerned with hypothetical–conditional principles and laws.

In Kant's thought, then, human beings as rational creatures can only fulfill their duty when they use their reason to conform to categorical imperatives – moral laws that are absolute and universal. This responsibility is not easy to fulfill. This perspective presupposes that a moral law places a demand on an individual who has the freedom to reject it, to disobey and fail to conform. The person's intentions can be directed away from the moral principle by non-rational inclinations, desires, and incentives. These "distractions" challenge the exercise of reason and compete with it for control over the person's will, contesting for the power to shape his intentions and determine his actions.

In spite of these distractions and pressures weighing against the exercise of reason (pressures which may originate either within or outside the person), the successful functioning of reason will turn the person's will toward conforming to the moral law. The individual conforms because it is reasonable to do this. And, what is more, the individual can now will (or intend) that the principle that has guided his action should also be the principle that guides the actions of other people. In the individual's willingness to act ethically and to advocate a moral principle and reason-based action to others, reason has prevailed and respect for the moral law is expressed. The action taken shows itself to have moral worth. To summarize this pattern of thought: in Kantian language, the categorical imperative is concerned with the mental disposition of the individual; the rational commitment to an absolute moral law, universal in its application, expressed in choosing a particular ethical action.

It may appear that such reasoning is far removed from the practical actions of an accountant who is attempting to follow the standards of the profession. To be sure, there is much in Kant's discussion that is abstract and too dense to follow, but we call attention to the fact that there are indeed important principles in accounting that are comprehensive in scope. These principles have great significance for the performance of the accountant's duties. Yet it is important to recognize that few accounting standards seem to be "categorical imperatives".

Accounting standards include numerous rules and guidelines that are conditional – not universal in intention or scope. This means that most of the prescribed procedures and decision processes – as they are applied in accounting – have the form of "if–then" statements. For example, if a financial transaction has such and such characteristics, then it is to be recognized as income; if these other characteristics are seen, then record the transaction as a cost. If a sale is made in this period, then it is to be recognized in the same period, regardless of when cash is received. If the owner of a business is your close relative, then as an auditor you cannot audit his business (you are not, in fact, independent). The accounting standards contain hundreds of pages of such conditional rules and prescriptions.

Accountants voluntarily adopt the principles and rules promulgated by their professional standards. As these men and women address accounting issues in their practice, most of the relevant standards, as we have already noted, take the form of "hypothetical categorical," or conditional commands – often in the "if this, then that" form. Yet, despite the conditional nature of these rules, as explicit standards of the practice, accountants have the duty to follow these rules.

Yet within the codes of conduct of accounting practice, as well as in the conceptual framework of financial accounting (for examples), there are also statements of moral principles that can be universalized. These also have generalizability and can be construed as fitting within a wide variety of circumstances. These moral principles (moral laws, in deontological terms) can be construed as (fit the definition of) "categorical imperatives" for the accountant. The profession, in effect, projects certain ideals onto its members. These principles are not expressed only as conditional commands; in Kant's terms, they can be called "the moral laws" of accounting. Even as they are to obey the conditional commands within the accounting standards, accountants are duty-bound to conform to these principles. These ideal expectations are to shape practical activities that contribute to the production and communication of financial statements (and to the audit work that reviews them).

For example, as a general principle, the financial accountant has an absolute duty to prepare financial statements of high quality that are useful to groups of stakeholders. As a comprehensive standard, the accrual method is indeed appropriate, reasonable for widespread application, and should be chosen as a dutiful response to provide such high-quality information. The important principle of auditor independence is also a rational approach for establishing the reliability of financial statements. The principle of auditor confidentiality protects clients and maintains the possibility of company's permitting access to its financial information, vital to outsiders' decision making. In addition, the codes of professional conduct assert the high significance of accountants' integrity and objectivity, as well as their neutrality in relation to the forms of financial knowledge communicated to various stakeholder groups – both insiders and outsiders. These principles present powerful ideals for accountants (moral laws!) and the moral worth of accounting activity can be weighed against these standards.

VIRTUE ETHICS AND ACCOUNTING

Reminder: The accountant should exercise a dual capacity that includes technical proficiency and ethical sensibility. Accounting standards hold accountants to principles, rules and normative patterns of decision making. Decisions by public accountants are to serve the public interest. Such service is performed through adherence to the principles of the profession, by following appropriate rules, and by using sound judgment. Ideally this judgment will be shaped by technical knowledge and practical insight into the key features of a given situation. This judgment should also employ complex intellectual and moral analysis that shows sensitivity to moral issues and a capacity to resolve ethical dilemmas.

It is natural for an accounting ethics textbook to focus on decision making and emphasize the principles and rules of accounting practice. To say that an accountant must demonstrate both technical proficiency and ethical sensibility as marks of competence seems normal enough, as well. The conceptual framework of financial accounting, accounting standards (including standards for auditors), and professional codes of conduct support accountants in the important roles they play in business and society. The principles, rules, and codes set the patterns for the accountant's production and communication of financial knowledge (and for the auditor's review of that process). Most importantly from an ethical viewpoint, these documents state the guidelines for evaluating accounting decisions and measuring the competency of those who make them.

In previous chapters, we discussed a decision scenario: a moral agent addresses an ethical problem, defines this problem, and seeks a practical solution through analysis and decision making. We have imagined the moral agent as an accountant whose situation poses a problem (or problems) that has both a technical accounting component and a moral issue (a conflict of values in a business setting, a dilemma). In this situation the accountant/moral agent is supposed to demonstrate technical proficiency by solving the accounting problem through an application of the appropriate accounting definitions, principles and rules. The accountant should also show ethical sensibility – by recognizing the moral issue, weighing decision alternatives, and making action-choices that are ethical. Finally, the accountant/moral agent must justify the action taken by giving reasonable arguments which make use of appropriate accounting standards and ethical judgment.

The view that accounting is a principles-driven, rule-oriented practice with an emphasis on decision making allowed us to highlight utilitarian and deontological features that were embedded in accounting practice. We left open the choice of which moral tradition to emphasize – to follow moral rules or to create happy results. We did not direct anyone to adopt either utilitarian values or deontological principles as their dominant ethical perspective. (Keep both traditions as part of your "toolkit" – as important resources for practical decision making.)

We now extend discussion beyond these two traditions, to treat aspects of ethics that do not focus only on decision making and applying accounting standards to business circumstances. Our reason for this: utilitarian and deontological conversations about practical decisions – analysis, judgment, and choices – have a tendency to over-emphasize action. These discussions invariably draw attention to what the moral agent *does*, but they neglect who the moral agent *is*. Furthermore, with so much attention given to the circumstances of decision making, questions about the place of moral values in the person's life and the quality of conduct over the long term are dismissed. But we will now introduce a new agenda: the issue of personal character and the intellectual and moral resources which the person brings into decision circumstances.

In effect, we now shift from concentrating on "the accountant's ethic of duty" to "the accountant's ethic of virtue" (to use the Doucets' language). We will not, however, forget issues of duty. The two traditions of moral philosophy, utilitarianism and deontology, do indeed provide rich resources for exploring how accounting standards and professional principles impose moral obligations on the accountant. It does make sense to speak of accountants' decision making as bringing principles and rules into service for stakeholders and the public interest. Yet it is also important to expand the agenda for ethics conversations beyond the issues of duty and compliance to rules. A third moral tradition, virtue ethics, will support our exploration of the accountant's character and the challenge of long-term behavior. It should help us see that accounting ethics is not limited just to principles, rules, and making decisions. Ethics has a central concern to understand the moral agent, as well as the nature of decision making and taking moral action.

In the 1980s, a few accounting educators began to spend classroom time on ethics instruction and the moral development of the next generation of accountants. Their ethics courses focused mostly on the students' technical knowledge of accounting standards and the development of analytic skills and judgment through classroom exercises. Students learned how to address particular business circumstances and to make decisions in view of the prescribed standards of their future profession. The education priority in these classrooms focused on teaching moral reasoning; using principles and rules to address moral dilemmas and solve ethical problems. It is interesting to note, however, that in this same period some philosophers began criticizing their colleagues for this very emphasis. These critics thought philosophy gave too much attention to deliberating on correct actions, concentrating on principles, following rules of behavior – all those efforts to match judgments with appropriate standards. Many philosophers, argued the critics, were too much concerned for principles, rules, and compliance. These critics, among them the "new" virtue ethicists, claimed that fellow philosophers had overlooked the significance of personal character – the inner dispositions and character traits of the moral agent. They had failed to see that right actions were not only linked to external principles and rules and the "performance of duty". Action flows out of character – shaped by the person's motives and intention – the virtue ethicists claimed. Right actions come from personal "goodness," the "virtues" of the individual, and the realization of intellectual and moral traits through intention-directed behavior. In the best of conditions, such character-shaped actions emerge from people who are flourishing, expressing their humanity in lives well lived.

This "turn to character and virtue" was nothing new in the field of philosophy. In fact, its intellectual "father" is the ancient Greek philosopher Aristotle and his classic publication *Nicomachean Ethics*. Keeping these ancient roots in mind, our discussion will blend modern elements with the ancient in our own conversation about character and ethics. With the help of Aristotle and his modern student, Alasdair MacIntyre, we will show how thinking about personal character and virtue is crucial for describing the ethical dimensions of accounting practice (Aristotle, 1985; MacIntyre, 1984).

Thus far in the book, we have proceeded as if ethics focused primarily on the answer to the question: "What should I do (in this particular situation)?" And to answer that question, we turned to moral principles and rules and considered the consequences of action-choices. Virtue ethics, by contrast, poses different questions as the fundamental concern of ethics: "How should I live? What kind of person should I be? How do I live well?" And the answer to these questions is: "I ought to live a life where I flourish, a life of excellence, a life of reason and happiness, a self-satisfying life."

In the moral tradition of virtue ethics, the human being is conceived as a person who lives within a community and must develop character traits that enable him to thrive as a human being in that community. Aristotle, for example, thought the Greek lived and thrived – flourished – only as a citizen within the polis, the Greek city-state. It was possible to "live well" only if the person were able to develop character traits that supported the performance of his civic roles and guided him through his vocational activities within the city-state. To flourish, "to live well" and be happy, the person needed to acquire mental and moral dispositions; that is, establish stable and reliable traits of character and structure his inner life with "virtues". These intellectual and moral dispositions would become fixed parts of the person's mental capabilities, embedded as part of the person's orientation to the world, lodged into his mind as distinct capacities strong enough to shape his motives for action. Together with the faculty of reason, the virtues would direct the person's activities in his civic and vocational responsibilities. By cultivating virtues and the formation of character wherein virtues were embodied – ready to hand to be realized in decision making about particular actions – the person's conduct emerges to enhance community life (as well as express his own well-being.)

The virtues, learned through experience, reflection, and habit formation, constitute the goodness of the person. In effect, they are the fundamental resources for ethical decisions and moral action, for living and moving through city life. The person's virtues come into play through the politician's dialogue and within the craftsman/artisan's creation of a sculpture or a drama. These qualities of character show themselves as the sea captain leads his crew through a hazardous voyage and in the soldier's combat skills and support of his comrades in battle. The evaluation of the moral worth of an action involves assessing the virtues that have been brought to bear on actions, asking whether the particular virtues expressed were appropriate in a situation. But more important than the moral assessment of a single decision or any action-choice in isolation are the questions concerning the virtuous character of the person. How might the virtues show themselves in one action after another, in the long-term conduct and patterns of life-long behavior in the community? What kind of person is this? Does his goodness show through his actions? As he moves through life, what virtues does he demonstrate time and time again?

Virtue, Character, and the Good Life

To describe what is needed in order for a person to flourish within a society and what is necessary in order to thrive as one human being among others, attention is focused on personal character. As social beings that have rational capacities, we also need specific character traits, inner dispositions, to guide our conduct and shape our actions within the community. In addition, our virtues make it possible to balance our reason with our desires and non-rational inclinations; in this way, we can find emotional satisfaction in the things we do. As the basic components of a life-well lived, the individual needs "virtues".

Virtues enhance the goodness of a person and express that goodness in his or her actions. These inner dispositions – such as courage, honesty, benevolence – are acquired through experience and self-reflection on personal behavior. They are also gained through observation and dialogue focusing on models, the exemplars of admirable action. Virtues are learned and become embedded in a person's character, set in the mind as resources to be brought to bear in motivating and directing actions. Virtues shape the person's intention to express goodness in his personal activities: to keep a promise, to support a friend in need, to be compassionate when confronted with someone who suffers.

Virtues are intrinsically valuable: it is good to possess courage and have integrity, to be predisposed to loyalty and trustworthiness. Some virtues support the person himself: having the discipline to complete a job, the intuitive grasp of a physical task, insight into a natural process. Virtues are also useful for serving others; having the patience to hear a complaint and the determination to solve the problem that frustrates the speaker, being hospitable to the lonely stranger, showing calm when others are agitated and distressed. Whether oriented to personal needs or for the service of others, virtues are fixed and reliable aspects of character. They remain available to put into play over and again whenever circumstances call for them. Generosity shows itself in one relationship after another; determination serves many tasks; "calmness endures through many a storm".

For the moral tradition of virtue ethics, the goodness of the person – his or her possessing virtues and thus having the capacity to ground personal motivations and intentions in specific qualities of character – has primacy over decision making itself. In this ethical reasoning: the concern about how to be a virtuous person has a higher priority than the issue of acting correctly or doing the best thing in a given circumstance. Asking about the person's virtues is more important than consideration of external principles or the rules governing specific behaviors. This is more significant than deliberating on the possible consequences of one's own actions. While it is good, even necessary, to ask: "What shall I do (in this situation)?" It is better, first, to wonder: "What good qualities, what admirable traits, do I need in order to be a good person?" This is *because virtues acquired by the person and embedded within his/her character are necessary for making decisions about correct actions. It is the virtues that are the essential components of the life that flourishes.* Correct actions that are determined by moral principles and the good results of actions – each has less moral value than do the cultivation of virtues and the virtue-inspired conduct through which people flourish (Oakley & Cocking, 2001).

Virtue Ethics: A Decision Scenario

The decision-making pattern of virtue ethics is quite different from the scenario we have presented for the ethics of duty. In that earlier scenario utilitarian and/or deontological questions and answers were examined: "What should I do: create utility or follow my moral duty?" By contrast, we now ask the primary questions of virtue ethics: "What kind of person should I be?" and "How can I live well?" We now "hear" the response: "Be a person who flourishes, thrives and is well satisfied within the community." This question and response pattern addresses the key concerns of the moral tradition of virtue ethics. Consider the following scenario.

A person engages in decision making and takes one action or another – possibly a process with due deliberation and measured judgment – but it could just as easily be a decision that is spontaneous. Imagine that this experience leads to a bit of success through the action, resulting in the person living well in the moment; the decision enables the person to thrive through the exercise of reason and judgment. In virtue ethics language: the decision tests the impact of one character trait or another (potentially: the traits are "virtues in the making"). If the person's action-choice affords a measure of intellectual and emotional satisfaction, this sets into motion a process of habit formation that may result in the establishment of a personal virtue. He or she will gain an inner disposition as an acquired dimension of that person's character. This moment of successful, self-satisfying living confirms that the blending of reason, emotion, personal knowledge and inner disposition has revealed a pattern for decision making and behavior worthy of future repetition. Over time, repetition of decisions that make use of this newly established personal virtue (in conjunction with reason and practical judgment) will result in the formation of a stable, fixed character trait. If the trait shapes personal motives and directs action, it will then become habitual – a moral virtue embedded in his character. This character trait, a virtue, will express goodness within the person and will itself become important in future decisions about specific actions and a key feature of the person's long-term conduct.

In this habit-formation process of moral development, a virtue (indeed, several virtues) will embed itself as part of the person's structure of character and become internalized as a "regulative ideal" (Oakley & Cocking, 2001) for addressing future decisions. Facing questions about what to do in a new situation, "the virtue as a regulative ideal" will function as a standard of excellence, driving personal motivation and shaping the intentions to be realized in the next action-choice. In effect, the virtue will adjust the person's motives and intention for action, with the expectation that the action will represent excellence, a fineness of quality in accordance with the regulative ideal.

These virtues, acquired through experience and habit formation and put into play in practical decision making, are marks of essential goodness within the personal character of an individual: They are intrinsically good qualities to be admired in and of themselves. They are also significant resources for living well and achieving good things through action – in effect, they "do good" as the person lives well.

This acquisition, possession and expression of character virtues in making decisions about action mark a crucial ethical process in virtue ethics thinking. To complete a picture of this process, the virtue-oriented philosophers elaborate on the concept of practical wisdom, or practical judgment. This intellectual trait coordinates the interplay of reason, emotion, and the virtues whenever a situation calls for deliberation about action. Practical wisdom (in Greek, *phronesis*) is the intellectual trait, the complex skill set of perception, insight, motivation that constitutes the person's ability to assess the key features of a decision situation. In such a situation, practical wisdom makes it possible for a person to deliberate and act virtuously – for that moment to be the occasion for demonstrating the virtues in action. Deliberation about a situation, the exercise of practical wisdom, includes the identification of the issues that are posed (problem-definition) by a given action. It concerns the values at stake in the decision and the interests (desires and needs) of the parties involved. The exercise of practical wisdom calls for insight to predict how the involved parties might react or be affected by the decision alternatives. Practical wisdom deals with possible actions that express or contribute to a life well-lived. It asks: "Do these decisions support a flourishing life for the moral agent and for those affected by the decision?" Practical reasoning seeks to address the real needs of those affected; it conveys the goodness of the moral agent and supports the well-being of others.

Practical wisdom presupposes self-awareness about the make-up of one's own character. It focuses on the particular virtues possessed by the individual and the distinct regulative ideals that motivate and direct the action he or she may take. It is through practical wisdom that the virtues are expressed through particular actions, with effective judgment bringing into play the virtues that are appropriate to the concrete features of the situation. Deliberation may pose these types of questions: Is this a time when courage and loyalty should come to the fore? Is this a moment when I should express my independence from some other person or group or should I in this circumstance offer preferential treatment to a person who deserves it? Practical wisdom must guide the person through such options.

Practical wisdom holds together the demands of reason and the press of emotions. Practical wisdom disciplines the moral agent, constraining him not only to act virtuously by expressing both reason and emotion as invaluable components of a flourishing life – but also to appreciate the results of the action or be satisfied by the virtue-directed act itself. Virtuous action and its appreciation mark a life that flourishes. Such a blend of reason and emotion will lead to "doing good" amidst a life that is well-lived. In brief: practical wisdom holds together reason, emotion, and virtue in a balanced fashion. It is through such a balance that the intrinsic goodness of the virtues, the exercise of reason, and the disciplining of emotion can express the qualities of a well-lived moment. It will then be the case (and with many such moments shaped by the effective use of practical wisdom) that a lengthy pattern of virtuous conduct (reasonable and emotionally satisfying action, time and time again) will mark the life well lived.

PRACTICAL WISDOM

The capacity to "direct virtues toward excellent performance within a given situation" is described (in virtue ethics terms) as the function of "practical wisdom" (practical judgment). Practical judgment (in Greek, *phronesis*) is an intellectual capacity to assess the salient features of a situation, make judgments about human behaviors and relationships, and consider how to exercise a particular virtue (or virtues) in the context of a life that flourishes – to thrive and live well. Practical judgment in its ethical dimension is the moral effort to carry out or realize an intention to act virtuously – first, to be motivated and then to act in an appropriately ethical manner. This moral capacity is a comprehensive ability that integrates technical knowledge, awareness of the significant features of a given situation, and realistic insight into the nature of human behavior. Practical wisdom grasps human ends and how people may flourish (what people need in order to live well). Such reasoning is the capacity to bring appropriate virtues to bear in "doing the right thing at the right time," to thrive through practical action.

Virtue Ethics and Accounting Practice

The ancient philosophers identified both intellectual and moral virtues. For example, Aristotle spoke of theoretical wisdom, intuitive intelligence, and scientific/empirical knowledge and, of course, practical wisdom as crucial intellectual virtues for lives that flourished. He also listed the moral virtues of courage, justice, temperance (moderation), and friendship – along with numerous other virtues. In particular, Aristotle considered both groups of virtues – intellectual and moral – as vital for the flourishing of life within the Greek city-state, a unique society with distinctive institutions and specific social ideals. While Aristotle's particular listing of Greek virtues may not be all that important for a contemporary treatment of accounting ethics, his making a direct link between a particular community and those virtues acquired and put into action by the members of that community is, in fact, quite significant for our purposes (Aristotle, 1985).

Earlier we illustrated how elements of utilitarian and deontological thought are present in accounting practice – whenever decision making gives high priority to principles and rules and to judgments that honor the spirit, as well as the letter, of current accounting standards. As we shifted our focus to speak of "character and virtue" in this section, we expanded our ethics discussion. We do not intend, however, to set aside accounting principles and rules. We continue to think of accounting as a principles-driven and rules-oriented enterprise.

Think again of Aristotle's insight: the values of a particular community and the goal to thrive in that community are directly tied to the expression of distinct virtues. It is Aristotle's modern student, Alasdair MacIntyre, who helps us understand the particular role of intellectual and moral virtues in accounting. In effect, we can construe accounting as a community whose "accountant-citizens" exercise their virtues in order that they and the community might flourish.

To make the leap from Aristotle's view of virtues within the city-state to modern accountants who demonstrate their competency by performing their duties, we turn to MacIntyre. His insight focuses on the idea that virtues function to support the purposes of a particular "practice". For MacIntyre, a practice is a cooperative enterprise whose particular purposes are achieved through the "virtues in action" of its member-practitioners. These members are the people who voluntarily commit themselves to achieve the goals of the enterprise. For MacIntyre, a practice is a socially constructed enterprise in which people express their particular dispositions of character, their intellectual and moral virtues, as they act to achieve the goals of the practice. As an arena of purposeful activity (a "domain of ethics"), the practice supports the intellectual and moral capabilities of practitioners. The practice provides the "social space" for the deliberation and analytical activity of its members (in Aristotle's language, the exercise of their practical wisdom) so that they can express their virtues and produce their "internal goods" in fulfilling the purposes of their practice. (MacIntyre, 1984, pp. 187–191).

As an example of the internal goods of specific practices, MacIntyre cites the unique "analytical skill, strategic imagination, and competitive intensity" that demonstrate excellence in the practice of chess. He also treats the internal goods expressed by the modern portrait painter – in the act of painting and in portrait's naturalistic expression of a distinctive quality of life. These "internal goods" of chess and portraiture are crucial to the achievement of the purposes of the two practices. The intellectual skills of analysis and imagination – the player's virtues – motivate particular chess moves, help him to execute his strategy and display the emotive force of his competitive energy as crucial features in fulfilling the purposes of the game/ practice of chess. The artist's perception, physical coordination, and technical knowledge of his materials are blended through practical judgment to produce on the canvas a portrait that communicates a unique image of the human spirit. In the language of virtue and the life well lived: the internal goods of the activity of painting and the product of that activity (the portrait itself) express the goodness of the artist's virtues, the virtues' realization in the practice of portraiture, and the flourishing of a life through artistic expression.

It is quite difficult to describe accurately the precise relationship between the virtues possessed by the chess player and the artist and the processes each uses to bring their intellectual and moral dispositions into play on the chess board or canvas. Yet as MacIntyre suggests: the products of the game and the portrait are created through activities that "come out" (emerge) from the virtues of the player and the artist through deliberation and judgment. The skillful chess move and the successful game strategy, as well as the sequence of brushstrokes that results in an image that evokes the humanity of its subject can rightly be understood as marks of excellence. They are internal goods, crucial features of their respective practices; these virtue-directed activities realize the purposes of the practices (and the humanity of the practitioners themselves!).

Given this understanding of a practice, where the purposes of a cooperative enterprise are achieved and its guiding ideals realized as practitioners exercise their virtues (their intellectual and moral traits of character), we can now connect the virtue ethicists' concern for character and virtue with the earlier treatment of accounting principles and rules. We see the relationship between the accountant's duty and his application of the contemporary standards of accounting in particular accounting decisions.

Consider accounting as a practice with its stated mission of communicating high-quality financial information to stakeholders. The ideal of accounting is the production and communication of financial information of high quality, useful for stakeholders' business decision making. As the expression of its highest values, the accounting community shares this mission statement among its membership as a "guiding ideal" that is intended to draw its members into a shared rationality of purpose and conduct. The practice then structures itself and strives to achieve its purposes through the activities of its membership. The standards-setting and regulatory institutions of the practice project its principles through a conceptual framework, codes of professional conduct, and regulatory statements. These standards support and specific regulating institutions monitor accountants' activities. The organizations set rules for appropriate role models for accountants, and they govern specific activities and decision procedures within accounting practice. These institutions with their projected principles and rules create "an infrastructure" to support accountants' effort to achieve the purposes of their practice. The institutions and the principles/rules establish the "cooperative arena" in which the accountant's virtuous activities are to be performed.

Given this context of purpose, ideals, regulatory agencies, principles, and rules, the individual accountant does not operate in a vacuum as he or she aspires to personal goals of pursuing excellence. The accountant is not alone in expressing virtues, seeking to live well or flourish (Dobson, 2007). Like the ancient Greeks, building character and exercising their virtuosity within their city-states, modern accountants acquire specific virtues appropriate for their practice as they train to become accountants (by forming appropriate habits that manifest technical and ethical competence). These learned virtues become the intellectual "skill sets" and moral resources for fulfilling the purposes of accounting. Expressing their virtues through accounting actions, accountants manifest "internal goods." These internal goods which embody the intellectual and moral traits make possible the production of financial statements with high-quality information. They also support the issuance of audit opinions based on appropriate methods of gathering evidence and manifesting sound judgment (judgment that is both technically proficient and ethically sensible). In brief: the accountant acts virtuously in the context of a mission-oriented practice, guided by its ideals and making use of its institutional support-structure. At best, the virtuous accountant works within a nurturing community, with personal aspirations and virtuous actions in synch with the mission of the practice. The accountant makes use of the infrastructure of ideals, principles and rules to give expression to his inner dispositions and to exercise practical wisdom in connection with specific accounting decisions. The internalized (intellectual and moral) virtues of the accountant, his regulative ideals, shape the accounting activity to achieve the fundamental purpose of accounting practice – the virtuous ideal of communicating high-quality financial information.

VIRTUE ETHICS LANGUAGE AND ACCOUNTING PRACTICE

In the specialized language of virtue ethics, the accountant's virtues are called forth by specific "demands of the world" to be realized by action in "a field of virtue" or "domain for virtue". In this arena, practical wisdom (analysis and deliberation) exhibits awareness of the salient features of the decision circumstances – including the appropriate human needs to be met – and this sound moral reasoning "directs the aim of the virtue" toward excellence in the practical actions that are taken. In MacIntyre's language, the internal goods of the practice are expressed in realizing the essential purpose of accounting practice.

Accounting: The Ideals of Accounting Practice and the Accountants' Virtues

Accounting ethics scholars currently discuss accountants' virtues in relation to the stated ideals and principles of accounting practice. The scholars use the language of virtue ethics to describe the acquisition of virtues through experience, reflection and habit formation. The learning process supports the development of a character that is structured by stable and reliable virtues. These virtues become "ready to hand" for shaping motivation in accounting decision making. These ethicists present lists of accounting virtues, sketch out their features, and explain why particular intellectual and moral traits are important, even necessary, for the accountant's performance (Mintz, 1996; Cheffers & Pakaluk, 2005).

It should be no surprise that most of the virtues are repeated from list to list: integrity, honesty, trustworthiness and faithfulness, passion for seeking and stating the truth, impartiality and objectivity, technical and moral "competence," and even courage and justice. The scholars also point out exemplary behaviors by accountants and point to admirable role models within the history of accounting practice. These scholars share a common understanding of the basic meanings of the various terms. What is more, if you were to take one scholar's list of accountant's virtues as the distinctive markers for exemplary roles and admirable behavior within accounting practice, it is unlikely that their items would differ much from the exemplary roles and admired behaviors suggested by another scholar's virtue list (Doucet & Doucet, 2004; Libby & Thorne, 2004).

The authors of this textbook would also include these virtues on their own "list". This is because there is a strong connection between the stated ideals and principles that are projected as the standards of accounting (and auditing) – the guiding ideals of the practice – and the character traits that become the internalized "regulative ideals" of practicing accountant. The scholars have described account-ants' virtues as the inner dispositions of character that correspond to the external ideals and standards that support the over-riding purposes of financial accounting (and auditing).

Earlier in the chapter, we showed how utilitarian and deontological patterns of reasoning were useful for understanding aspects of accounting practice. This final section has confirmed that the virtue ethics tradition can also help us to understand accountants' ethical capabilities – especially on how their ethical sensibilities and ability to make ethical decisions emerge from their character, from their virtuous habits. This use of the language of the virtue ethics tradition to describe character and virtue within the accountant makes a clear, practical connection to the stated ideals of accounting – for both the inner virtues and the external standards must "come into play" to achieve the purposes of accounting practice. As the Doucets would say (with the authors): the accountant does indeed have both an ethics of duty and an ethics of virtues.

CHAPTER REVIEW QUESTIONS

1. (LO3) According to utilitarianism, what criterion is used to decide whether a particular action is correct or good?

2. (LO3) Explain the difference between a categorical imperative and a hypothetical imperative. Give an example of each type of imperative from the accounting standards or the codes of conduct.

3. (LO3) Within deontology, what is the criterion for evaluating an action? (What makes an action "of moral worth"?)

4. (LO3) According to deontology, what are the distinctive marks of a human being? Why are these traits or characteristics of an individual so important for decision making?

5. (LO5) Explain why virtues are important for accounting practice.

6. (LO6) Explain what practical wisdom or practical judgment is. What role does it play in linking virtues to particular actions?

7. (LO 5) Make your own list of the virtues that an accountant needs to achieve the purposes of accounting practice. Be sure to include both intellectual and moral virtues in this list.

CASES

8. Estimating a Future Expense[1]

The cost associated with mothballing a nuclear power plant at the end of its useful life, approximately 20 years in the future, will be paid by the utility company when the plant is obsolete at the end of the 20 year period. When should the expense be recognized for this expenditure? Current utility users receive the benefit of this plant. Do accounting rules require them to pay the cost in terms of increased utility rates by including the expense of the future mothballing in their rates, or should the expense be delayed for 20 years, until the cash is actually paid out?

Required:

a. According to the philosophical guidelines of utilitarianism, the accountant should produce financial statements of high quality so the reports are useful to all stakeholders. How should an accountant apply the principles of utilitarianism to decide how this expense should be recorded?

b. If you choose to act in a manner consistent with the principles of deontology which requires the accountant to "do the right thing for the right reason", what is the right thing to do? What is the right reason for your decision?

c. To record an expense, the accountant must be able to estimate the amount of the expenditure. Will it be difficult to estimate an expense to be paid 20 years in the future?

d. If you choose to recognize the expense after 20 years, what categorical imperative does this support?

e. If you choose to recognize the expense over the 20 years when the power plant will be used to generate electricity, what categorical imperative does this support?

9. Allowance for Sales Returns

Arctic Cat Manufacturing is preparing its year-end financial statements in late December. Audrey Brooks, the controller of Arctic Cat, has heard that the unusually dry winter has prompted a large number of returns of snowmobiles to the company. She wants to take a conservative approach and reduce sales revenue by an estimate of future returns. Her supervisor, Sharon Johnson, prefers to record sales at the highest level, possibly arguing that it is too early in the winter to predict the rate of returns.

Required:

a. According to the philosophical guidelines of utilitarianism, the accountant should produce financial statements of high quality so the reports are useful to all stakeholders. Assume that Brooks estimates the returns to be $10 million, while Johnson's estimate is $1 million. How should an accountant apply the principles of utilitarianism to decide which estimate is correct?

b. How will the accountant demonstrate his or her technical competence and ethical awareness in this situation?

10. Accelerating Sales Revenue

In order to increase revenue at the end of the year, Publishers, Inc., a distributor of books and magazines, offers its customers the opportunity to purchase books and magazines at a 35% discount, if they increase their purchases by 25% over the prior month. Marcia Quincy, the controller, complains to the financial vice president, Andy Banes, that recording revenue in this fashion will hurt the company in the future; plus it may result in a great deal of work when the excess stock is returned. Andy replies that this policy is the only way the company can increase its net income to obtain a short-term loan at the bank. Andy adds: "What difference does it make if we encourage our customers to purchase inventory items a little early, even if they return them? The sales will come in the future. Besides, by the time they return the inventory, we'll have the loan and it won't make a difference if net income is lower next year."

Required:

a. Answer Andy's question, "What difference does it make?" Based on your knowledge of the current accounting standards, does it make a difference if the sales are recorded this year or next? Is either method acceptable in this circumstance? If you choose to act in a manner consistent with the principles of deontology which requires the accountant to "do the right thing for the right reason," what is the right thing to do? What is the right reason for your decision?

b. Evaluate the bank's ability to make a rational decision regarding the short-term loan if you recognize revenue this year or the following year. In which instance is the bank likely to make a better decision?

11. Revenue Recognition for Installment Sales

Jane Wagner and Justin Stine are reviewing the accounting rules for recording an installment sale. Wagner and Stine work in the plastics division of their company, which has been under pressure to improve earnings. Their division has just made a large installment sale, and they want to record it in a fashion that makes the division look better. The total revenue generated as a result of the installment sale is $100 million, to be paid in five yearly installments of $20 million. Normally the division does not use installment sales to generate income, but in this instance they believed it was justified given the size of the sale and the potential benefit to the division. Wagner says that they should recognize all the revenue in year one, because this will help the division meet its sales quota and assure that management receives favorable evaluations and salary increases. Stine doesn't believe it appropriate to recognize all the revenue in year one for installment sales. He argues that they should recognize gross profit as the cash is received. Wagner says: "We can get by with recording all the revenue in the first year and setting up a note receivable for the balance due. Management will think we are acting correctly because they will not recognize that an installment sale is different from other types of sales. Besides, this is just a 'normal' sale with credit terms of five years, and not much different than those sales with the normal credit terms of 60 days."

Required:

    a. According to the philosophical guidelines of utilitarianism, the accountant should produce financial statements of high quality so the reports are useful to all stakeholders. How should an accountant apply the principles of utilitarianism to decide how the installment sale is recorded?

    b. If you choose to act in a manner consistent with the principles of deontology which requires the accountant to "do the right thing for the right reason", what is the right thing to do? What is the right reason for your decision?

    c. Identify a categorical imperative that might apply in this situation.

    d. If you choose to recognize revenue in year 1, what categorical imperative does this support?

    e. How will the accountant demonstrate his or her technical competence and ethical awareness in this situation?

12. Obsolete Inventory

John Harris and Susan Ernest are discussing the inventory obsolescence policy for Smith Communications, a manufacturer of satellite dishes used for communication purposes. Since changes in technology make inventory parts obsolete very quickly, obsolescent inventory is a major problem. Harris has a suggestion for reducing the dollar amounts on the obsolete information report, and he is discussing this idea with Ernest, his supervisor. Last year the auditors ran a computerized report of all inventory items having no activity in the last twelve months. Several thousand dollars of inventory appeared on this report. This year, expecting that the auditors will run a similar report, Harris has suggested to Ernest that they make it appear that all inventory items are still being used by transferring parts from one location to another. Harris says: "The auditors will never catch this transfer. They are not smart enough to consider the way we moved this inventory. They will simply run their computer reports, and if the report tells them that the part number was used in the past twelve months, they will not consider how it was used. It is important for us to start this process about six months before year-end and to complete it a couple of months before the auditors arrive. I think it will work just fine. We used to get auditors that would think, but now they are so fascinated by computers that they sometimes fail to realize what they're doing."

Required:

a. According to the philosophical guidelines of utilitarianism, the accountant should produce financial statements of high quality so the reports are useful to all stakeholders. How should an accountant apply the principles of utilitarianism to decide how obsolete inventory is reported?

b. If you choose to act in a manner consistent with the principles of deontology which requires the accountant to "do the right thing for the right reason", what is the right thing to do? What is the right reason for your decision?

c. Identify an "if–then" accounting standard related to inventory that might be useful for an accountant in this situation. How does referring to this "if–then" standard help the accountant make a decision about the correct way to report obsolete inventory?

d. How will the accountant demonstrate his or her technical competence and ethical awareness in this situation?

13. Contingent Liability for Toxic Waste Cleanup

Jeff Clairmont, the controller for Johnson Chemicals, has just received a notice from the Environmental Protection Agency (EPA) regarding the cleanup of the Mendota Heights Toxic Disposal Site. The cleanup is scheduled to begin in 2014 and to last for five years. Estimated costs of the cleanup are $558 million. Johnson Chemicals will be charged a share of the cleanup to represent their dumping activity over the past fifty years. Currently, this is estimated to be $48 million at a minimum, and it may go much higher. The chief financial officer, Jennifer Ordahl, has suggested ignoring the potential liability until the actual charges are received in a bill from the EPA. At most, Jennifer suggests using footnote disclosure to indicate the potential liability.

Required:

a. According to the philosophical guidelines of utilitarianism, the accountant should produce financial statements of high quality so the reports are useful to all stakeholders. How should an accountant apply the principles of utilitarianism to decide how this contingent liability should be recorded?

b. Identify several alternatives available to the company, based on your knowledge of the current accounting standards. Do accounting rules specify the decision to be made in this situation? Is there room for interpretation in the implementation of the accounting standards? Identify an "if–then" accounting standard related to contingent liabilities that might be useful for an accountant in this situation. How does referring to this "if–then" standard help the accountant make a decision about the correct way to report this liability?

c. If you choose to act in a manner consistent with the principles of deontology which requires the accountant to "do the right thing for the right reason," what is the right thing to do? What is the right reason for your decision?

d. How will the accountant demonstrate his or her technical competence and ethical awareness in this situation?

14. Expense Recognition

As accounting supervisor, your job is to review the year-end adjusting entries and approve them before they are posted to the trial balance. You are watching the revenue and expense entries carefully this year because your bonus will be based on net income. You realize that the higher the net income, the bigger your bonus will be, so you are anxious to process as many revenue transactions as possible. Your normal pattern is to process transactions involving revenue the same day they are received and transactions to recognize expense within a week. Bill Anderson, the controller of the company (and your boss), has asked you to process all entries in a timely fashion at the end of the year, so the financial statements will be accurate. You wonder if you should change your personal policy to comply with his request, even though it will reduce your bonus.

Required:

a. According to the philosophical guidelines of utilitarianism, the accountant should produce financial statements of high quality so the reports are useful to all stakeholders. How should an accountant apply the principles of utilitarianism to decide how year-end adjusting entries are recorded?

b. If the accountant records revenue entries on a timely basis and delays recording expense entries does the accountant follow accrual accounting requirements?

c. Consider the profit and loss statement and the balance sheet of this company. Explain how the definitions of financial statement elements from the conceptual framework could be used to help the accountant decide whether to record revenue and expense transactions in a timely fashion. How might "if–then" rules be helpful for determining whether revenue and expenses should be recognized?

d. How will the accountant demonstrate his or her technical competence and ethical awareness in this situation?

15. Tax Return Preparation by the Big Four Accounting Firms

According to a recent article in *The Wall Street Journal*, the Big Four audit firms earn approximately 20% of their total revenue from tax preparation. The article reported that the Big Four accounting firms used temporary workers and part-time employees to prepare tax returns in the current tax season, sometimes setting up separate "compliance centers" staffed by temporary employees and shipping returns to these central locations for processing. The temporary workers are paid as little as $10 per hour, but the clients are billed at the rate for Big Four employees, as much as $100 per hour or more. Most firms hide their use of temporary employees, because they believe their clients are "indifferent" about who prepares their return as long as it is signed by a partner or manager of a Big Four firm. The head of the tax division for one of the firms says that they see no reason to advise a client that a temporary employee filled out their tax return: "It doesn't seem relevant." This leads clients to believe they are receiving the services of accountants with "elite credentials" whenever they pay the premium fee charged by the Big Four accounting firms. A tax client of one of the firms, when informed of this practice, said that he is generally satisfied with the work the firm has done. He had known that the tax partner signing the return didn't actually prepare it. "But in all honesty, they should tell the clients" about mailing their tax data to temporary employees in other cities. Another client, when learning of this practice, said: "That's not a very ethical thing to do. They should have told me."

Required:

    a. Is it unethical for Big Four accounting firms to hire part-time and temporary workers to prepare tax returns? What is the ethical dilemma described in this case?

    b. Do you believe that all clients are indifferent about who prepares their returns as long as a Big Four manager or partner signs the return?

    c. Why are Big Four firms engaging in this practice? Do they really believe that the client doesn't care?

    d. What parties should be considered in making this decision? Who benefits? Who is harmed?

    e. Is the virtue of integrity at stake in the Big Four decision?

NOTE

    1. This case will be presented in several chapters with different questions for each chapter. This will illustrate how each of the tools can be used to help the accountant make a decision that reflects both technical proficiency and ethical awareness.

REFERENCES

Aristotle (1985) *Nicomachean Ethics*, translated by T. Irwin. Indianapolis, IN: Hackett Publishing Company.

Cheffers, M. & Pakaluk, M. (2005) *A New Approach to Understanding Accounting Ethics: Principles, Professionalism, Pride*. Manchaug, MA: Allen Davis Press.

Dobson, J. (2007) Applying virtue ethics to business: The agent-based approach. *Journal of Business Ethics and Organization Studies*, 12(2): 1–4.

Doucet, M. & Doucet, T. (2004) Ethics of virtue and ethics of duty: Defining the norms of the profession. *Research on Professional Responsibility and Ethics in Accounting*, 9: 147–168.

Kant, I. (1981) *Grounding for the Metaphysics of Morals*, translated by James W. Ellington. Indianapolis, IN: Hackett Publishing Company.

Libby, T. & Thorne, L. (2004) The identification and categorization of auditors' virtue. *Business Ethics Quarterly*, 14(3): 479–498.

MacIntrye, A. (1984) *After Virtue: A Moral Theory*, 2nd edn. Notre Dame, IN: Notre Dame University Press.

Mintz, S. (1996) The role of virtue in accounting education. *Accounting Education*, 1(1): 67–91.

Oakley, J. & Cocking, D. (2001) *Virtue Ethics and Professional Roles*. Cambridge, England: Cambridge University Press.

CHAPTER SIX

Professional Ethics as a Resource for Decision Making

LEARNING OBJECTIVES

By the end of this chapter you should be able to:

1. Understand the nature of a profession and describe accounting as a profession.
2. Explain why professions exist and how professional ethics is a defining characteristic of any profession.
3. Describe what professional ethics entails and how professional ethics influences decision making.
4. Understand the nature of codes of ethics and how they function.
5. Describe codes of ethics for accounting.
6. Understand how professional ethics and codes of ethics in accounting may be used in accounting practice.

ACCOUNTING AS PROFESSIONAL PRACTICE

Reminder: Accounting is a practice; accountants produce business knowledge and communicate it to stakeholders, who use this knowledge to make business decisions.

Reminder: Accountants should exercise a dual competency: technical proficiency – knowledge of accounting standards and capacity to apply them in practice – and ethical sensibility – capacity to recognize moral issues, resolve ethical dilemmas, and demonstrate the motivation and commitment to do the right thing; that is, act ethically.

> *Reminder:* Accountants may on the one hand use accounting standards and principles as resources for decision making, and on the other hand they may be informed by their own moral values and beliefs. Thus, accounting ethics decisions may draw on both institutional and personal resources.

ACCOUNTING AND PROFESSIONAL ETHICS

In the previous chapters, we have outlined the nature of accounting and how it includes both a technical and an ethical dimension. We have emphasized how accountants may draw on various sources of competence for decision-making purposes. First, we illustrated how accounting standards inform the accountant on how accounting information ought to be prepared in order to present high-quality information to users of financial information. Because those users of information may be seen as stakeholders of the accountant's decisions and actions, we also shed light on how moral philosophy may serve as a resource for decision making. Moral competence may enable the accountant to make decisions informed by assessments of how various choices influence relevant stakeholders and whether or not these choices violate important moral principles.

This chapter brings these two dimensions of accounting together at the institutional level. Accounting is not just a vocation carried out by individuals who are trained to prepare financial statements and who are employed by companies or firms that need their distinctive knowledge and skill to perform such services. Accounting is also *a profession*. This means that accountants are a group of individuals who voluntarily bind themselves to one another to be held accountable to professional standards – principles, rules, and codes of ethics. In brief: the accounting profession is an institution that administers (or "manages") both the technical and ethical features of accounting practice.

In this chapter, we briefly describe accounting as a profession, with particular emphasis on the professional ethics of accounting. We treat the nature of a profession, and then describe what it means to say that accounting is a professional practice. We then show how professional ethics can serve as a resource for making accounting decisions. Third, we discuss the use of codes of ethics in professional practice and outline the IFAC Code of Ethics for accountants. Finally, we discuss how such a code of ethics may support the decision making of accountants.

PROFESSIONAL ETHICS AS A RESOURCE TO MAKE ACCOUNTING DECISIONS

Let us consider this chapter's topic in light of the decision model that we use in this book. The contents of the chapter reflect the last component in the section that elaborates on the *Problem-Solving Resources*, which is represented in column two of Figure 6.1. In this chapter we discuss how professional ethics may be a resource for accountants who face ethical problems. We will explore how professional ethics may both promote the ethical awareness of the accountant and aid the accountant's attempts to resolve ethical issues. In this exploration, we will look at concrete elements in the professional ethics of accountants and auditors. To achieve this goal, we must

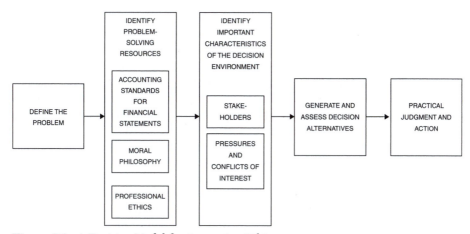

Figure 6.1   A Decision Model for Accounting Ethics

understand the rules related to the preparation of financial statements. In Chapter Four and Chapter Five, we shed light on how accounting standards and moral philosophy can serve as resources for addressing the technical and the ethical dimensions of the problems accountants face. In this chapter, we see how professional ethics bridges those two dimensions by complying with the standards for preparing high-quality financial reports.

ACCOUNTING AS A PROFESSION

In ordinary language, we often refer to someone as a professional just to indicate that the person is highly qualified for a specific task or does a job well. A more precise meaning of the concept "professional" is tied to being part of a distinct type of organization that provides an important public service, a "profession". This term denotes particular kinds of vocations that have special features and are practiced under distinctive conditions. Among the common professions are medicine, law, nursing, psychological counseling, and accounting and auditing.

A profession is a social community that administers a distinctive occupation organized to serve a society. Typically, the profession has a monopoly on administering that occupation, to oversee its practice and those who perform its tasks. A profession should be seen as a *community* comprised of those who are qualified (and certified) to work within that community. The members of a profession have an educational background – knowledge and skills – that allows them to practice the occupation. The fact that the occupation is *administered* by the profession through its agencies and institutions means that its members and their activities are to be guided by particular standards, rules and codes. These professional bodies grant rewards for following these standards and mete out penalties (or sanctions) when serious violations of these standards occur. The penalties, for example, mean that the professional body can prohibit individual members from performing their distinctive tasks, practicing their unique occupation, if these members violate professional standards and fail to serve the public interest. The profession is *organized for a society*; this means that the profession administers the benefits associated with its members' ability to offer specific services to the general society (for instance, give legal advice, perform surgery or practice dentistry). This management of the profession is achieved by mandating and enforcing a knowledge-oriented and skillful self-discipline within the profession. In other words, the general society delegates the task of carrying out specific functions (for instance, auditing) to the profession, and this professional body ensures that the special practice of performing these functions (preparing a financial statement or auditing it) is carried out in a manner that serves the needs and desires of the society that allows the profession to exist. To say that professions typically are *monopolies* means that the professional occupation (with its special functions and distinctive tasks) cannot be practiced by just anybody. These tasks, the duties of the special occupation, are to be performed only by members of the profession, those who are qualified and certified by the professional body itself. Given this limitation, professions are self-protective against possible competitors. Most importantly, the members of the profession have the great responsibility to carry out their practice in a manner that justifies the monopoly status of the profession. They are obligated to fulfill the roles assigned to them within the profession, so that the general society can be served.

Professions consist of numerous individuals who have volunteered their services to an occupation or practice. These individuals have professional rights and duties because of their membership in the profession. Professionals are granted privileges and have restraints and limitations. A professional member is allowed to do things that others, non-professionals, cannot do. For instance, surgeons may cut into other people's bodies, and auditors may inspect the confidential information of company-clients. At the same time, however, being a professional means acceptance of constraints and limitations – there are things prohibited to professionals that others may do. For instance, a surgeon may not freely engage in a romantic relationship with a patient; an auditor may not talk openly about the interesting things he or she has found within the financial records of a client. In addition, there are actions taken by a professional – even mandated – that are contrary to the norms and values of common morality that are honored by those who are outside a given profession. For instance, we accept that defense attorneys do everything in their power to defend a violent criminal, even when their efforts may seem repugnant to an ordinary citizen. Yet it is socially unacceptable for a private person to do such a thing. In a word: there are standards of behavior for professionals, and professionals are held accountable to those standards by the administrative functions and management roles of the profession itself. Professionals are bound to the specific discipline of their occupation, and they will be held accountable if they violate the standards of their own profession. Yet given these constraints and obligations, the day-to-day practice of professionals permits a great deal of autonomous behavior, a wide scope of judgment and personal decision making. In this context, it is not common that professional bodies need to sanction or penalize their individual members, and the supervisory functions of professional bodies over their members are seldom used.

Because professions have monopoly status in their society, the administration of their members' activities is best understood as a type of management for the sake of a social responsibility. Professionals perform important social functions; they play an invaluable role in the general society. Because of this, professions are held to be responsible primarily to the general society itself; professions serve the public interest. By extension, individual members of the profession are liable to that society for the manner in which they carry out their professional duties and play their distinctive roles. For this social responsibility professional bodies develop systems for self-regulation with the aim of legitimizing their own functions in the eyes of the public. Professions support their own members as they serve the needs and expectations of society.

This system of self-regulation includes standards-setting organizations which develop professional standards and codes of ethics. There are also institutions that permit the profession to discipline its members whenever professional standards are violated or codes of conduct ignored. By means of these agencies, standards and enforcement procedures, the profession disciplines its members and holds them accountable to the constraints and limitations of the profession. Professional bodies hold their members to public service. To the extent that many professionals act in ways that violate such standards, it may threaten the legitimacy of the profession, violating the public's trust, and this may undermine the profession's very existence. In the wake of the big accounting scandals of the 2000s and the demise of the auditing firm Arthur Andersen, the auditing profession in the United States of America found itself in such a situation. The scandals undermined public trust and called into question the monopoly status of the accounting profession, with its privileges and responsibilities to serve public needs. Given the threat of accounting scandals that may erode public trust, professions are very concerned about maintaining the respect and goodwill of their stakeholders and the general society. To counter potential threats to their privileged status and to act in responsible fashion, professions continually develop and update their standards and codes and strive to meet social expectations and retain public trust.

PROFESSIONS

A profession is a community within a broader society that administers an occupation organized for that society. Typically, the profession has a monopoly for administering that occupation, for managing its members. Professional bodies govern the professional practice of its members. They do this by developing professional standards and codes of ethics, monitoring the roles and behavior of its members as they perform their duties, and by sanctioning those professionals who violate the standards.

Accounting (and auditing) is a profession that shares the characteristics outlined in the definition above. The degree of professionalization – and thereby of regulation – differs among countries, but generally, accountants are regulated by accounting regulatory bodies. This chapter focuses on professional ethics, and we limit our presentation of professional ethics to the standards and codes developed by the International Ethics Standards Board for Accountants (IESBA), which is part of the International Federation of Accountants (IFAC).[1] In the following, we will outline the code of ethics developed by IESBA and discuss its use for accountant decision making.

PROFESSIONAL ETHICS

As indicated above, each profession not only has a particular competence or qualification base at its core, but it also has a particular ethos. It develops a professional ethic for its membership. This ethic communicates a distinctive mode of appropriate behaviors for serving the general public. The purpose of professional ethics is at least fourfold. First, professional ethics contributes to raising the awareness of professionals about the ethical dimensions of their practice. The existence of a professional ethic is important because it communicates to professionals that there are important ethical issues related to their practice, alerting members to particularly significant ethical problems. Second, professional ethics typically encompasses codes of ethics and other tools for decision-making purposes. This demonstrates that professional ethics, through its explicit principles and rules, is to serve as a decision-making aid for accountants in concrete situations. Ideally, the toolbox of professional ethics should help accountants to identify moral issues, resolve dilemmas, and act appropriately whenever they encounter ethical problems in accounting situations. Third, professional ethics serves as a significant means of legitimization for the profession vis-à-vis society. The fact that the profession is bound to specific ethical standards of behavior and character may promote public trust that the members of a profession will be held accountable for their actions. Fourth, professional ethics encourages the profession to hold its membership accountable in the event that professional standards of conduct are violated. Society can expect the professionals to exercise self-discipline or face penalties administered by the professional body itself. Thus, professional ethics marks the existence of a social contract that binds the members of the profession to function on behalf of the general society.

Professional ethics, then, advocates standards of conduct for the members of a profession. Such standards are typically codified and compiled in codes of ethics or ethical guidelines. Yet in addition to the written documents that make explicit the ethics of the profession in concrete terms, it should be noted that professions also develop implicit expectations of ethical behavior; there are professional norms and standards that shape actual practice yet are not written down as rules or stated in codes of conduct. This type of tacit knowledge (i.e., knowledge that professionals "just know" without necessarily having read it somewhere) is an important dimension of every type of professional ethics. Generally, however, professions aim to codify and make explicit their ethical expectations for their membership as public information for the stakeholders of that profession.

PROFESSIONAL ETHICS

Professional ethics outlines standards of conduct that are expected for the members of a profession. The standards of conduct are usually codified in ethical guidelines or codes of conduct. Professions may hold their members accountable if they violate the rules or ignore the ethical principles of the profession.

For decision-making purposes, the value of professional ethics is that it supports accountants in making better – and more ethical – decisions. Accountants and auditors are likely to face ethical problems in their professional practice, and professional ethics can help accountants both to identify ethical problems in accounting and to deal with them. In Chapter Three, we defined an ethical problem as a problem where multiple values are at stake for different stakeholders. Professional ethics can help the accountant in several different ways to face such problems. First, professional ethics typically indicates the types of problems professionals are likely to face. We might say that professional ethics points out common pitfalls of professional practice. Second, professional ethics typically presents appropriate solutions to such problems and provides practical guidance in the face of ethical issues. The level of specificity of such solutions may vary – from principles that serve as overarching indicators of goals for which accountants ought to strive to specific action rules that prescribe what should be done in specific circumstances.

Accountants have at least four distinct challenges posed by ethical issues that arise in professional practice. First, there is the challenge of identifying that one is, in fact, faced by an ethical problem. This necessitates moral sensitivity on the part of the accountant, since he or she needs to realize that a situation presents an ethical issue. Second, the accountant faces the problem of systematically reflecting on the ethically relevant dimensions of the problem. As discussed in Chapters Three and Five, this requires a suitable vocabulary and ethical sensibilities that enable the accountant to emphasize the relevant aspects of the problem and assess them in light of particular ethical standards. Third, the accountant faces the challenge of making a judgment (i.e., to generate alternatives, assess them, and decide what to do). Finally, there is the challenge of actually taking what one believes to be the right course of action. There may be many obstacles to acting in line with one's judgment, and the next three chapters will explore in depth several features characteristic of the decision environment that may discourage the accountant from doing the right thing.

Professional ethics can support accountants in facing these four challenges. As discussed above, codes of ethics typically aid the professional in identifying and addressing the common ethical issues of the practice. Such help guides the accountant's judgment process to address the ethical issues he or she faces. Furthermore, professional ethics also indicate actions to take (or avoid) which may promote (or hinder) his or her ability to act on his professional judgment. For instance, codes of ethics for auditors prevent auditors from taking on family members as clients. These explicit standards help the auditor to avoid a situation where objectivity will be threatened and thus facilitate the auditor's ability to rely on his or her own professional judgment to act in the appropriate manner.

Some principles are commonly advocated in the various versions of professional ethics (i.e., across many different professional fields). This is because various societies expect many of the same things when it comes to the conduct of their professionals, including professional integrity, competence, objectivity and confidentiality in the relationship between the client and the professional. In Chapter Three, we introduced two of these useful principles for detecting ethical problems – the principle of equal treatment and the public principle. Both principles are advocated by professional codes in many societies.

The principle of equal treatment is intended to shape a profession's approach toward the individuals and groups that it serves (clients, patients, or customers).

Most, if not all, professions have equal treatment as a fundamental principle. This is typically captured in principles for objectivity, absence of bias, and fairness. In accounting, accountants are expected to prepare financial statements similarly for all types of entities, and to provide similar information to all stakeholders (to show no favoritism or bias in communicating financial information to any given stakeholder). In accounting there are few exceptions to this. An example of the equal treatment principle is presented in the professional codes for auditors, which state that confidentiality is universal (i.e., applicable in all situations), except for situations where the SEC or entities with similar regulatory powers subpoena auditors to disclose confidential information.

The public principle is another ethical expectation common to many professions, although it is often expressed implicitly rather than as explicit statements in the codes of conduct. As emphasized above, professional ethics plays an important role in the legitimization of the profession in society. That is, professions depend on the trust and acceptance of third-party spectators, whether or not they are actually current clients or customers of the profession. This means that the type of rationality expressed in the public principle – "act in a way that you would be comfortable evincing to a third-party spectator" – is an important part of the self-regulation of professions. In many codes of ethics, one can find principles or guidelines that reflect such rationality. For instance, one of the fundamental principles of the IFAC code of ethics and the AICPA Code of Professional Conduct for accountants is that accountants and auditors should act in ways that do not discredit the profession. This is codified in the guidelines in several different forms.

One of the main aspects of professional ethics is that it applies to situations where individuals act in their professional roles; that is, professional ethics is role-based ethics. The accountant agrees to take on the professional role of an accountant and thereby becomes subject to the expectations for that role. This does not mean that the accountant should act like a "robot" – there are important personal dimensions of any role and professional judgment is a critical aspect of decision making within any role. There are also changing role expectations over time, and this implies that social expectations will vary in their influence over professional roles and judgment.

In Figure 6.2, we see the threefold influence on how individuals carry out their professional roles. On the one hand, they are influenced by the professional standards and norms that are part of the professional role. Professional ethics is an important part of this professional responsibility, which is role-mediated; that is, specific responsibilities come with particular roles. At the same time, professionals are subject to standards of common morality. Because of this, the professional standards of a profession may sometimes be criticized in the general society, and these criticisms may ultimately lead to changes in the profession's standards and ethics. Finally, professionals also experience an individualized sense of personal responsibility, which may sometimes make it hard for them to act in accordance with professional responsibilities. A common example is the professional responsibility of doctors and surgeons at birth clinics to participate in abortions. There are several cases of doctors who choose for personal reasons to abstain from carrying out this part of their professional roles, and there are also instances of doctors who are not willing to refer their patients for abortions.

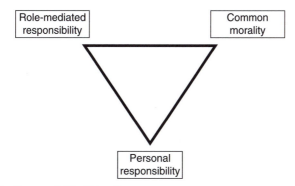

Figure 6.2   The Responsibility Triangle

Source: Ims, K.J. (2006) Take it personally. In Zsolnai, L. & Ims, K.J. (eds) *Business Within Limits: Deep Ecology and Buddhist Economics*, p. 222. Oxford/Bern: Peter Lang Academic Publishers.

There is, then, sometimes tension between the professional ethics of the individual and the personal and societal pressures that also influence professional attitudes, personal choices, and specific behavior. These pressures may, in some instances, discourage the individual from acting in accordance with standards of professional ethics. For this reason, professionals need to reflect on whether or not the standards and ethics of their profession are in line with their personal values, since it may not be possible for a person to remain active in a professional role that generates serious conflicts between professional expectations and personal values.

As mentioned above, a profession's ethics may be communicated to its members in many ways. It can be part of the profession's educational process; it can be communicated through mentors and various forms of socialization; it can be stated in codes of ethics and the key policy documents of the profession. Codes of conduct are usually considered the most important pillar of professional ethics, and we focus on the content of several codes in the remainder of this chapter.

CODES OF ETHICS AS TOOLS FOR DECISION MAKING

Ethical guidelines and codes of ethics are important tools of professional ethics. All professions have codes of conduct. In addition, many firms and organizations also have their own such codes and guidelines for behavior. Typically, these documents are part of a larger "toolbox" of ethics resources available within organizations, which may also create "ethics hotlines" for advice from experts or senior employees, form ethics committees, and hold ethics courses and seminars for employees or professional members.

The terms, "ethical guidelines," "codes of ethics," and "codes of conduct" are often used interchangeably, and for the purposes of this book, we use them as synonyms. Usually, codes of ethics are more extensive statements than are an organization's ethical guidelines, and codes of ethics often include value and mission statements. We will not, however, focus on such differences. Ethical guidelines and codes of ethics each state the fundamental principles that should guide behavior in professional practice. Typically, codes include both broad principles and more detailed guidelines or rules for behavior.

CODES OF ETHICS

Codes of ethics state the fundamental principles that should guide behavior in professional practice. Typically, the codes include both broad principles and more detailed guidelines for behavior.

Codes of ethics work in at least three ways. On an overarching level, they work as regulatory mechanisms that can be used to regulate the behavior of professionals. To the extent that sanctions are attached to the codes, such as banning members who violate codes, these threats and penalties can be a powerful influence on behavior. Moreover, codes of ethics have an important function of expressing social norms for professionals, and thus can make it socially costly for professionals to act in violation of those norms. Often some explicit statements in the codes of ethics become unnecessary because their contents become "part of the DNA" of the profession or the organization. For instance, auditors arguably do not need to read the code of ethics for auditors in order to be reminded that they are supposed to be independent or to maintain confidentiality. This expectation becomes a part of the social fabric of the auditing community, and individual auditors are governed by this implicit norm. Codes of ethics influence the beliefs and values of professionals so that these norms become "taken-for granted". In a word, they become institutionalized as a part of the professional DNA of the individual.

THE CODE OF ETHICS FOR PROFESSIONAL ACCOUNTANTS

The International Federation of Accountants (IFAC) is the global organization for the international accountancy profession. An important part of IFAC is the international standard-setting boards, among them the International Ethics Standards Board for Accountants (IESBA). IESBA develops and publishes the code of ethics for professional accountants, as well as other publications and documents pertaining to the professional ethics of accountants. The code of ethics is the cornerstone of the official professional ethics of the international accounting profession. IESBA is an independent standard-setting body, and its code of ethics is designed to be internationally appropriate. This means that the code is not limited to particular sociocultural ethics or values but rather is intended to communicate the shared values and principles that characterize the ethos of accountancy across nations and cultures.

IFAC AND IESBA

The International Federation of Accountants (IFAC): The global organization for the accountancy profession dedicated to serving the public interest. IFAC issues tools, guidance, and resources to support member bodies and their members who are professional accountants in business or employed in small and medium-size practices.

The International Ethics Standards Board for Accountants (IESBA): An independent standard-setting body that serves the public interest by setting high-quality ethical standards for professional accountants and by facilitating the convergence of international and national ethical standards, including auditor independence requirements, through the development of a robust, internationally appropriate code of ethics.

The IESBA Code of ethics is a comprehensive document that includes codes of ethics for professional accountants, with a separate section of ethics for auditors. The code distinguishes between ethics for accountants in public practice and for accountants in business. This distinction is linked to our earlier discussion about roles and role-based ethics. Accountants in business have a different role than accountants in public practice, and they answer to a different group of stakeholders (we develop this idea further in Chapter Seven). Accountants employed by business organizations may carry out various accounting tasks for their businesses, some of which may be for internal purposes only, such as cost accounting. This implies that the ethical ramifications of the decisions made by these accountants are generally not an explicit concern of the general society (even though some of the business decisions made on the basis of the company's accountant may have significant consequences for society). By contrast, accountants in public practice carry out tasks that are specifically intended to address the interests of the general public, and the primary accountability of auditors is to society at large (rather than to their company-clients). For this reason, the ethical standards of these two groups of accountants are different.

The code of ethics has three main parts. The first part outlines the fundamental principles of the code of ethics. The second part applies those principles to professional accountants in public practice. The third part applies the principles to professional accountants in business. The code is outlined as follows. First, the principles and corresponding standards are presented. Thereafter, potential threats to the principles are indicated. Finally, safeguards that may reduce or eliminate the threats are discussed. The general structure of the code suggests a threefold approach to accounting-ethical decision making:

1. Identify threats to compliance with the fundamental principles.
2. Evaluate the significance of the threats identified.
3. Apply safeguards, when necessary, to eliminate the threats or to reduce them to an acceptable level.

To the last point on safeguards, the following is added: "Safeguards are necessary when the professional accountant determines that the threats are not at a level at which a reasonable and informed third party would be likely to conclude, weighing all the specific facts and circumstances available to the professional accountant at that time, that compliance with the fundamental principles is not compromised." Here, we see clearly how the public principle is integrated into the code, with the emphasis on the view of an "informed third party". It follows from this that one does not only apply safeguards in order to reduce the threat to actual decision making but also for purposes of appearance. That is, some safeguards are applied in order to express to the public that measures are taken. This relates to the issue of ensuring that the legitimacy of the profession is not threatened and public trust is retained.

In the following, we take a closer look at the fundamental principles before we explore the code's approach to threats and safeguards.

The Fundamental Principles

There are five fundamental principles in the code of ethics, and these are pillars upon which the code is built. A professional accountant shall comply with the following fundamental principles:

1. Integrity
2. Objectivity
3. Professional competence and due care
4. Confidentiality
5. Professional behavior.[2]

We discuss each of the principles in the following paragraphs.

The definition of *integrity* is to be straightforward and honest in all professional and business relationships. Honesty and transparency are important virtues in all professional practice. Acting with integrity means staying true to the values of the profession and not attempting to mislead the client.

Objectivity means not allowing bias, conflict of interest or undue influence of others to override professional or business judgments. The call for objectivity is where the principle of equal treatment is most clearly manifested in the code of ethics for accountants. Objective decision making means acting in a manner that does not unduly prioritize some stakeholders over others unless there is a valid reason to do so.

Professional competence and due care means maintaining professional knowledge and skill at the level required to ensure that a client or employer receives competent professional services based on current developments in practice, legislation, and techniques. This principle advocates acting diligently and in accordance with applicable technical and professional standards. A cornerstone of any professional relationship is the expectation that the professional will act in line with the best available knowledge and practice of the profession. No patient would want a surgeon who conducted 1950s surgery in 2013, and no client will accept an accountant who prepares financial statements on the basis of outdated knowledge. Thus, keeping up to date on new accounting standards and relevant knowledge is an ethical responsibility for the accountant. In this discussion of competence and due care, we see how the technical and ethical responsibilities of the accountant overlap.

Accountants should respect the *confidentiality* of information[3] acquired as a result of professional and business relationships and not disclose any such information to third parties without proper and specific authority (unless there is a legal or professional right or duty to disclose). Nor should the accountant use the information for personal advantage for himself or for third parties. The duty to maintain confidentiality is very strict, but there are exceptions in cases where the client releases the accountant from confidentiality or in cases where regulatory bodies subpoena the accountant in order to disclose confidential information.

Professional behavior is expected of accountants. This means complying with relevant laws and regulations and avoiding any action that discredits the profession. This principle directly relates to the conduct of the accountant, and has a compliance dimension as well as a reputational dimension. First, it deals with the responsibility for acting in accordance with the laws and regulations that govern accountancy. Second, it deals with acting in a manner that is compatible with maintaining the reputation and legitimacy of the accountancy profession in the eyes of the general public. This principle can be seen as an overarching principle that overlaps with the other principles, in the sense that it relates to the overall conduct of the accountant and the degree to which he or she complies with the relevant expectations of the profession.

Threats and Safeguards

The IESBA code of ethics also outlines threats to the fundamental principles and lists safeguards that can be applied in order to eliminate or reduce such threats. The code of ethics distinguishes between five different types of threats which are common in that professional practice of accountants:

1. Self-interest threats
2. Self-review threats
3. Advocacy threats
4. Familiarity threats
5. Intimidation threats.

Self-interest threats refer to threats that a financial or other interest will inappropriately influence the professional accountant's judgment or behavior. If the accountant's professional judgments advance his or her own interests, it will, in effect, become more difficult to be unbiased and objective. This refers not only to conscious but also to spontaneous decision making, for biases also have a strong influence on the unconscious assessments and the more spontaneous decisions of individuals. For this reason, professionals are discouraged from having private interests related to their professional assignments. For instance, auditors may not own stock in the companies they audit. (More discussion will be given to the distinction between conscious (deliberative) decisions and more spontaneous (heuristic) decisions in Chapter Nine.)

Self-review threats refer to threats that a professional accountant will not appropriately evaluate the results of a previous judgment made or service performed by the professional accountant, or by another individual within the professional accountant's firm – a prior judgment on which the accountant may be tempted to rely in a decision process that is aspect of a current service. This reliance on a prior judgment may become a serious hindrance to uncovering errors made in previous decisions. This type of threat is quite significant, especially when the earlier decisions are made by the accountant himself or by colleagues. Generally, earlier decisions by persons who are close to the accountant are assessed favorably by that accountant. There is also a bias towards believing that decisions previously made within the accountant's firm are correct, when they may, in fact, be wrong.

Advocacy threats refer to threats that a professional accountant will promote a client's or employer's position to the point that the professional accountant's objectivity is compromised. There is a risk that professionals may – consciously or unconsciously – become advocates for clients, in the sense that they may see the interests of the client as being important also to themselves. This may lead to unduly favorable treatment of the client.

Familiarity threats refer to threats that with a long or close relationship with a client or employer, a professional accountant will be too sympathetic to that client's interests or too accepting of their work. A problem in any client relationship is that the bond between the professional and the client may become strong enough to persuade the professional to treat the client in an inappropriate, favorable, way. This may be a threat to the principle of equal treatment and, more fundamentally, to the general principle of objectivity.

Intimidation threats refer to threats that a professional accountant will be deterred from acting objectively because of actual or perceived pressures, including attempts to exercise undue influence over the professional accountant. This type of threat includes direct attempts to make accountants act differently than they otherwise would, as well as various types of more indirect situational pressures to act in ways contrary to how the accountant would without these pressures. Examples are time pressure and various forms of implicit social pressure. We discuss different types of pressure on decision making in more detail in Chapter Seven.

The different types of threats may overlap. For instance, the familiarity and the advocacy threats are fairly similar, and many situations may be characterized by both. Similarly, intimidation threats may often be intimidating solely because they are relevant to the self-interest of the accountant. An explicit attempt at pressure may be: "Prepare the financial statements in this way, or you'll lose your job." A more subtle attempt at pressure may be: "In this organization, we reward team players – those who help us reach our goals." As we can see, there may be overlap between self-interest threats and intimidation threats.

Given these threats against sound professional practice, there is a need for measures that protect the individual professional as well as the profession at large against the threats. As a practical, solution-oriented part of the professional ethics of accountants, the code of ethics also outlines concrete safeguards that the individual accountant may apply to counteract potential threats.

Safeguards are actions or other measures that may eliminate threats or reduce them to an acceptable level. According to the code of ethics, they fall into two broad categories:

1. Safeguards created by the profession, legislation, or regulation.
2. Safeguards in the work environment.

This implies that threats to the fundamental principles in professional practice may be addressed at the level of the profession (i.e., that the professional body develops and distributes measures that may aid individual professionals and firms in their decision making and behavior). In addition, the firms themselves may develop measures to safeguard against such threats, and these safeguards may be both necessary and effective to ensure professional behavior that complies with the code of ethics.

According to the code, safeguards created by the profession, legislation, or regulation include:

- Educational, training, and experience requirements for entry into the profession.
- Continuing professional development requirements.
- Corporate governance regulations.
- Professional standards.
- Professional or regulatory monitoring and disciplinary procedures.
- External review by a legally empowered third party of the reports, returns, communications or information produced by a professional accountant.

The code also outlines safeguards that may increase the likelihood that the accountant is able to identify or deter unethical behavior. Such safeguards (which may be created by the accounting profession, legislation, regulation, or an employing organization) include:

- Effective, well-publicized complaint systems operated by the employing organization, the profession or a regulator, which enable colleagues, employers and members of the public to draw attention to unprofessional or unethical behavior.
- An explicitly stated duty to report breaches of ethical requirements.

In addition, firms may themselves have a number of codes, rules, and structures in place. These guidelines may support the professional accountant in safeguarding against threats and go beyond the general safeguards of a profession to focus specifically on ethical issues of relevance to the individual firm. An example of this type of safeguard is when an auditing firm has rules about whether and when one of its auditors should be removed from a client relationship to avoid the threats of familiarity or advocacy.

Considered in their entirety, these threats and safeguards illustrate where ethical issues in accounting may emerge, as well as institutional and individual strategies for addressing those threats.

USING PROFESSIONAL ETHICS IN DECISION MAKING IN ACCOUNTING

In the previous sections, we have outlined the content of the professional ethics "toolbox" and discussed the various purposes it might have. In this book, however, the main question is how professional ethics may be used in accounting practice in order to support the accountant in practical decision making whenever ethical issues appear. In this section, we discuss a case in order to illustrate how professional ethics, in the form of suggestions on a decision process, can aid a moral agent (an accountant) in addressing a significant ethical issue.

The IESBA code of ethics also indicates a decision procedure for using the code when faced by an ethical issue. In the first chapter of the code, this is described as follows:

"A professional accountant may be required to resolve a conflict in complying with the fundamental principles. When initiating either a formal or informal conflict resolution process, the following factors, either individually or together with other factors, may be relevant to the resolution process:

- relevant facts
- ethical issues involved
- fundamental principles related to the matter in question
- established internal procedures, and
- alternative courses of action.

"Having considered the relevant factors, a professional accountant shall determine the appropriate course of action, weighing the consequences of each possible course of action. If the matter remains unresolved, the professional accountant may wish to consult with other appropriate persons within the firm or employing organization for help in obtaining resolution."

It is interesting to note that the procedure suggested in the code combines three schools of moral philosophy that were discussed in Chapter Five. First, the code itself has a principled approach to morality, which is related to the deontological perspective. Second, the procedure suggests that the accountant should weigh the consequences of all possible courses of action, which is related to the logic of utilitarianism. Finally, the procedure suggests that accountants should consult with experienced and wise decision makers in particularly challenging cases, which is in line with the learning from experience (one's own and that of a mentor) that characterizes virtue ethics. In this way, the code of ethics is arguably informed by several of the most prominent schools of thought in moral philosophy.

In the following, we attempt to shed light on how the fundamental principles as well as the safeguards intended to protect the principles against various threats, may be applied by means of the procedure suggested in the code of ethics. Let us consider the following case.

CASE: AUDITOR–CLIENT CONFIDENTIALITY

Anne Sorenson, an auditor for KPMG, is working on the audit of Amgen, Inc. Amgen is a biotechnology company based in Thousand Oaks, California. The audit has been fairly routine so far, but today Anne overheard a very exciting piece of information. Amgen has just completed a series of tests with mice related to the *ob* gene and leptin, the protein produced by the gene. During these tests, obese mice lost about 40% of their body weight after only a month of daily injections of leptin. With trials on humans ready to begin within a year, the promise of a cure for obesity seems hopeful.

That evening, Anne is talking to her parents over the phone. She is so excited about this finding that she tells her parents about the potential cure for obesity. After getting off the phone, and as Anne is telling her roommate about her interesting day, she realizes that she is divulging confidential client information. Her roommate, a stockbroker at Merrill Lynch, is excited about the information and wants to recommend that all her investment customers purchase Amgen stock before the information is public and the stock price goes up. Anne wonders about what she has just done.

The problem in this case is fundamentally related to the professional role of Anne Sorenson as an auditor and the particular responsibility that follows from that role. If we use the procedure above, our first question is: What are the relevant facts of the case? Briefly summarized, we may say that (1) Anne Sorenson is an auditor for KPMG; (2) in her role as an auditor for Amgen, she learned of the *ob* gene, which she would likely not have learned about had it not been for her role as Amgen's auditor; (3) she disclosed this information to her roommate, who is a stockbroker, as well as to her parents.

The next question to ask is: what are the ethical issues involved? First and foremost, there is clearly an ethical issue with regard to her professional role, since she has disclosed client information to outsiders who should not have that information. Furthermore, we might add that since acting on inside information is illegal, she has facilitated illegal action on the part of her roommate, the stockbroker (and perhaps to a lesser extent with regard to her parents). Perhaps it is likely that the stockbroker will act on this information, with potential negative consequences for herself, and, in that case, Anne will have played a part in creating an ethical issue for her roommate. In part, the ethical issue is based on a violation of principles, and in part it is based on an assessment of (potential) negative consequences.

The third question to ask is: what are the fundamental principles related to the issue? Here, the principle of confidentiality is clearly violated. By disclosing the information, Anne is violating her responsibility for maintaining client confidentiality. It should be noted here that Anne is in a private setting when she discloses the information, and perhaps that is the reason she acted this way. In a situation where she is not in her "professional mindset," she divulges information perhaps without thinking that this is problematic. But her professional responsibility with regard to confidentiality transcends the particular roles she plays in her private life. Confidentiality is as important in private settings as in professional settings.

In addition to violating the principle of confidentiality, Anne is not acting in line with professional behavior, as she does not act in accordance with her professional responsibility, and she also acts in a way that may discredit her profession. One may argue that she is acting in violation of the principle of professional competence, since she does not demonstrate the professional competence and awareness that is adequate to ensure that her client receives high-quality professional services (which would include maintaining confidentiality). It is, however, not clear that she violates the principles of integrity and objectivity, since she is not being biased or unduly influenced, nor in any way being dishonest. Rather, this is a case of unprofessional behavior.

The fourth question to ask is: what internal procedures are in place? The case does not tell us this, but we can assume that KPMG has both procedures aimed at preventing auditors from disclosing confidential client information and procedures that should be followed if an auditor does disclose such information.

The final question to ask is: what are the alternative courses of action available to Anne? In some sense, the damage is already done. Anne has disclosed the information and cannot "take it back." Yet this may be a situation where Anne can reduce the negative consequences of violating the principle of confidentiality. Anne has not publically disclosed the information. Rather, she has privately told family and a friend about the information, and we can assume that these people have Anne's interests in mind. There is arguably a difference between disclosing the information to her parents and to her roommate – for two reasons. First, her parents are her closest family, and will likely not do anything to harm Anne, but we know less about her relationship with her roommate. Second, there is a difference between the parents and the roommate with regard to their roles, since the roommate is a stockbroker (and the parents are not). If Anne were to tell her parents about her mistake and ask them to keep the information to themselves, we can assume that they would do so. Her roommate, by contrast, may weigh the pros and cons of using the information and may even be willing to sacrifice her friendship to Anne for the sake of the financial gain that may result from acting on the inside information. Even so, there is the possibility that she would be willing to keep the information to herself and not act on it, in order to save Anne's professional life.

From a consequentialist perspective, then, it seems that Anne telling the roommate is more ethically problematic than her telling her parents. Both are equally wrong when considered in relation to the fundamental principles of the code of ethics, but with regard to the likely consequences, the two acts seem quite different.

With regard to Anne's alternatives, we can at least envision the following: (1) disclose her violation to KPMG and to Amgen, in order to allow them to try to minimize the harm from the breach of confidentiality; (2) try to persuade her roommate and her parents to keep the information to themselves; (3) do nothing. Each alternative can be assessed according to the fundamental principles, and in addition one may conduct a general ethical assessment by using the theories of moral philosophy presented in Chapter Five.

In Chapter Nine, we will discuss how to generate and assess relevant alternatives, so we will not go into this topic in depth here. We can, however, briefly comment on the three alternative courses of action outlined in this case. Doing nothing does not seem to be a particularly responsible action, either with regard to the principled approach or with regard to a consequentialist perspective. This would mean not trying to minimize the potential harm made by disclosing the information, and this course of action could make the problem worse. With regard to the two other alternatives, one might suggest that the first option – admitting the violation to KPMG and Amgen – seems most appropriate from a principled, deontological perspective. This would be honest and straightforward and in line with the principle of integrity. Yet, the second option – trying to persuade her parents and her roommate to keep the information to themselves – is perhaps more suitable when seen through a consequentialist lens. This option could lead her to eliminate the negative consequences, even though she has already violated the relevant principle. From a professional ethics perspective, then, option 1 is likely the most appropriate, but when professional responsibilities are disregarded, option 2 might be equally fruitful.

The case and the decision procedure sketched above illustrates the threefold components of principles, threats and safeguards in professional ethics. The procedure outlined here follows the guidelines in the IESBA code of ethics, but one could envision other approaches that might similarly address the relationship between principles, threats and safeguards. In Chapter Eight, we will revisit the issue of how to manage and judge ethical issues in accounting, based on both professional and personal values and responsibilities.

SUMMARY

In this chapter, we have explored professional ethics as a resource for the decision making of professional accountants. As illustrated in our decision model, we see professional ethics as one of the three main sources of knowledge that can be applied by professional accountants in the face of ethical problems.

The professional ethics of accounting is codified in the IESBA code of ethics, which is published by the International Federation of Accountants (IFAC). The code of ethics is based on a set of fundamental principles – integrity, objectivity, professional competence and due care, confidentiality, and professional behavior. The professional ethics of accounting is oriented towards protecting and promoting these principles. The code includes an outline of common threats to the principles, as well as various safeguards that can be applied in order to reduce or eliminate such threats. The identification of threats to the fundamental principles and the development of strategies or approaches that safeguard against such threats are important aspects of the professional ethics of accountants. Professional ethics used properly can be a valuable source of technical and ethical knowledge for accountants that are facing ethical issues.

In the following chapters, we move from the resources that support accountants' decision-making processes to shed light on factors in the decision environment that may influence the accountants' decisions. To do this, we give more insight into environmental and situational factors that may be the source of threats against the fundamental ethical principles of accounting.

REVIEW QUESTIONS

1. (LO1) What is a profession?
2. (LO1) What does it mean that accounting is a profession?
3. (LO2) Explain the role of professional ethics for professions.
4. (LO3) What is the difference between professional ethics and ethics in general?
5. (LO3) Which tools do professional ethics typically include?
6. (LO4) Explain what a code of ethics is.
7. (LO4) How can codes of ethics be used in decision making?
8. (LO5) What are the fundamental principles of the IESBA code of ethics for accountants, and what does each of them mean?
9. (LO6) What do we mean by threats and safeguards in professional ethics?

CASES

10. Tenet Healthcare Corporation and KPMG

In 2006, the Securities and Exchange Commission (SEC) charged three KPMG auditors with altering audit work papers. The work papers were changed after the fact to make it appear as if KPMG had properly performed the audit. Modifications included adding comments to work papers, backdating documents, and creating audit documentation after the fact. The investigation showed that the audit team spent more than 500 hours altering more than 350 working papers. Auditing standards require an auditor to complete the work of the audit before the audit opinion is issued. Critical areas on Tenet's financial statements had not been completed before the opinion was issued, and the information in the critical areas proved to be important to the accuracy of the financial statements. KPMG changed the audit work papers to make it appear that they had done the work during the audit and had decided that changes to the financial statements were not needed.[4]

Required:

a. Describe the technical proficiency and ethical sensibility required of the auditor in this case. Did the auditor meet these requirements?

b. Identify specific sections of the code of conduct that apply in this situation.

c. Why did the auditor think it would be better to have made the wrong decision about whether a critical area required changes in the financial statements rather than decide to issue the audit opinion without finishing the audit work? Are both decisions violations of the standards?

11. Ernst & Young Hong Kong

Police raided the accounting offices of Ernst & Young in Hong Kong in 2009 to gather evidence about the audit work done in related to Akai Holdings Ltd, an electronics maker. Akai filed for bankruptcy in 2000 with $1.8 billion of debt on its books, the largest bankruptcy filing in the city at that time. The raid had been made due to a request from the bankruptcy trustee, Borrelli Walsh. Walsh stated that the accounting firm had been negligent in the performance of the audit and the negligence had led to substantial losses for Akai. Walsh alleged that information in the work papers had been forged during the audit process. Edmund Dung, the manager on the audit engagement was fired by Ernst & Young after being suspected of forgery in preparing audit work papers. Ernst & Young settled Walsh's claim against the audit firm for a "substantial" amount of money.[5]

Required:

    a. Discuss the accounting and ethical problem if an auditor prepares forged audit documents.

    b. What principles in the AICPA and the international code of conduct were violated by the forgery?

    c. What rules in the AICPA and the international code of conduct were violated by the forgery?

    d. Was the bankruptcy trustee right to file a suit against the accounting firm for negligence in the audit? Was the audit firm justified in firing Dung?

12. Ernst & Young Violations of Independence Rules

The Securities and Exchange Commission charged Ernst & Young with ethics code violations for engaging in lucrative business deals with an audit client.[6] Ernst & Young had entered into a marketing arrangement with PeopleSoft to sell and install PeopleSoft software. Under the agreement, Ernst & Young agreed to pay royalties to PeopleSoft of 15–30% for each software sale, with a minimum guaranteed payment of $300,000. During the time of this agreement, Ernst & Young served as the auditor for PeopleSoft. According to the SEC: "An auditor can't be in business to jointly generate revenues with an audit client without impairing independence." Ernst & Young vigorously contested the charges, saying that its work for PeopleSoft "was entirely appropriate and permissible under the profession's rules. It did not affect our client, its shareholders, or the investing public, nor is the SEC claiming any error in our audits or our client's financial statements as a result of them."

Required:

    a. Evaluate the statement made by Ernst & Young that they did nothing wrong because no one was harmed. Is the statement true? Is it an appropriate defense against a claim of lack of independence?

    b. Discuss the accounting and ethical issues of this situation. What might outsiders think of this arrangement? What might the competitors of PeopleSoft think?

13. Stein Bagger and Ernst & Young Denmark

At a banquet in November 2008, Ernst & Young honored IT Factory, a Danish software company, for its exceptional growth. One thousand guests were at the banquet, including the tax minister from Denmark and leading business people, to recognize the efforts of the software company. Stein Bagger, the chief executive of IT Factory, was not in the audience to pick up the award for "Entrepreneur of the Year". Instead he was in Dubai, trying to avoid investigators who were searching for him after discovering the biggest accounting fraud in Denmark in decades in his company.

Most of the business recorded in the financial statements for IT Factory was fake. Mr. Bagger set up fictitious firms to get money from banks and then used those fake companies to falsify large orders for software and service. He bought services from himself, using other people's money.

The chief investigator of the fraud says that it amounted to about $185 million. Although this sum is small in comparison to many of the recent accounting frauds, it was enough to cover Mr. Bagger's lavish lifestyle of sports cars and vacations in the French Riviera.

KPMG audited the financial statements for IT Factory from 2005 to 2007. Deloitte had audited the books for the previous two years. From 2003 to 2007, the company reported that its revenue grew 69 times and profits rose 288 times, to $22 million. In 2008, the company expected to quadruple its profit. At least 95% of IT Factory's business was fictitious. The auditors failed to report that the financial statements were materially misstated during this time.

Mr. Svensson, the head of a competing Danish software company, sent email warnings that IT Factory did not have enough customers to explain its explosive growth. IBM in Denmark received one of the emails from Mr. Svensson but still gave IT Factory the award for "Best Partner" in the software business line. The head of IBM Denmark described IT Factory as "creative and visionary".

Dorte Toft, a freelance journalist, wrote a blog challenging Mr. Bagger's extraordinary growth figures. She said that Mr. Bagger went to great lengths to maintain his deceptions. He had claimed to have a PhD from San Francisco Technical University. She questioned this, since there was no such school. Mr. Bagger hired Vicki Lang, an American artist living in Copenhagen, to pose as an official from San Francisco State University (a university that does exist). Mr. Bagger told Ms. Lang to explain that his nonexistent university had been merged into San Francisco State and to confirm that he had a PhD in international business. Ms. Lang thought that his request was a little strange, but she was happy to have a job.

Speaking to a Danish newspaper, Mr. Bagger said that he felt guilty for what he had done. He said, "I can understand that some people feel I let them down". Ernst & Young has withdrawn his award for "Entrepreneur of the Year" stating that they were deceived by Stein Bagger.[7]

Required:

    a. Describe the technical proficiency and ethical sensibility required of the auditors in this case. Did the auditors of the firm (KPMG and Deloitte) meet these requirements?

    b. Identify specific sections of the code of conduct that apply in this situation.

    c. Why did IBM choose to ignore the information from the competitor of Stein Bagger regarding the level of growth in the company? Were the competitors harmed by Bagger's actions?

    d. Was Bagger correct in his assessment that he let people down?

14. Anglo-Irish Bank, Ireland

In 2008, Anglo-Irish Bank was Ireland's third largest bank. It has since been nationalized during the financial crisis and subsequently merged into the Irish Bank Resolution Corporation. The entity was given an entirely new name, in part in order to avoid associations with the wrongdoings of the former management group of Anglo-Irish Bank.

In 2008, the Central Bank of Ireland conducted a routine inspection of Anglo-Irish Bank and realized that the bank had substantially understated its account for "loans to directors". Chairman Sean FitzPatrick and board member Lars Bradshaw had taken out loans each year from 2000 to 2008 to buy shares in the bank. In all of these years, FitzPatrick transferred the loans to another bank just before year-end audits, so that the account for "loans to directors" was understated yearly. The loans were as much as €87 million in 2008, but the transfer of the loans meant that the account for loans to directors appeared as being only €40 million. The loans themselves were not necessarily problematic (however, few, if any, bank officials seemed to be aware of the loans), but the understatement meant that FitzPatrick had conducted accounting fraud.

In 2007, FitzPatrick's shares were worth approximately €80 million. However, following the revelation of the director loans – as well as the toll of the financial crisis – Anglo-Irish stock fell by 98% until 2009, when FitzPatrick's shares were worth approximately €1.5 million.

FitzPatrick, Bradshaw, and CEO David Drumm all resigned in December 2008. In the 2009 Annual Report, Anglo-Irish stated that the actual magnitude of its loans to directors was €155.8 million at the end of 2009. In addition, the bank expected losses on the director loans (as a consequence of the dramatic stock price drop) of as much as 70% of their total value (approximately €110 million).

The chief executive of the financial regulator criticized external auditor Ernst & Young for not having identified the hidden loans. The head of Anglo-Irish Bank's internal auditing, Walter Tyrrell, claimed that only FitzPatrick and Bradshaw knew about the loans. The internal audit procedure in the bank was to randomly select loans for inspection. None of the director loans were selected.

The Irish government injected €3 billion into the company in 2009 and thus became its biggest shareholder. In July 2011, Anglo-Irish Bank eventually became part of the Irish Bank Resolution Corporation.

Required:

    a. What is the problem both from an accounting and an ethical point of view?

    b. Describe the technical proficiency and ethical sensibility required of the auditors in this case. Did the auditors of the firm meet these requirements?

    c. Identify specific sections of the code of conduct that apply in this situation.

    d. If the loans were not illegal, why was the bank so hesitant to report them? Why did stock market react so strongly to the loan information?

15. Berkshire Hathaway Inc.

Berkshire Hathaway Inc. (BHI) is an American holding company where Warren Buffett is CEO and chairman. Recently, the BHI executive David Sokol – who was widely considered to be the most likely successor to Buffett as CEO and chairman – handed in his letter of resignation. He claimed his decision was based on the desire "to build wealth for his family and philanthropic activities".

Soon after the resignation, it became known that Mr. Sokol had failed to disclose important information to Mr. Buffett and BHI about his stock purchase in Lubrizol – a chemical company whose acquisition by Berkshire Hathaway he had engineered. Mr. Sokol purchased the stock in Lubrizol while he was engineering the acquisition. When Berkshire Hathaway reached a deal in March 2011 to acquire Lubrizol for $9 billion, Mr. Sokol's personal stake rose in value by roughly $3 million. Mr. Sokol's purchase of stock was in violation of BHI's code of ethics, where it is clearly stated that employees should not invest in companies that "*may be* involved in a significant transaction with Berkshire". The acquisition of companies is a core activity for Berkshire Hathaway.

Legally, there is no rule mandating that executives disclose their holdings in targets for acquisition or merger. This means that Mr. Sokol may not have broken the law; nor is he an accountant bound by accounting standards and codes. However, BHI has a strict ethics code, and Warren Buffett has on many occasions expressed its essence with statements like: "*If it's questionable whether some action is too close to the line, just assume it is outside and forget about it.*" Mr. Buffett also famously expressed: "*Lose money for the firm, and I will be understanding. Lose a shred of reputation for the firm, and I will be ruthless.*" Ultimately, then, it was the company's code of ethics that led to Mr. Sokol's downfall – not legislation or accounting rules.[8]

Required:

    a. Describe the ethical problem in this case and give an account of why Mr. Sokol's behavior is a problem from an ethical point of view.

b. What were Mr. Sokol's alternatives after having purchased the stock? For each of the alternatives, describe how key stakeholders would benefit or be harmed.

c. Berkshire Hathaway asked its Audit Committee to investigate the case and publish a report to the public on its facts and how Mr. Sokol's actions violated BHI's code of ethics. This was explicitly requested by Mr. Buffett. Berkshire Hathaway had three alternatives upon becoming aware of Mr. Sokol's actions: (1) do nothing, (2) investigate the case and not disclose the information to the public, (3) investigate the case and disclose the information to the public. From an accounting ethics perspective, do you think Mr. Buffett chose the right alternative? Discuss all three alternatives and evaluate whether they are appropriate choices from an ethics point of view.

16. Ernst & Young and Confidential Client Information

James Gansman, an Ernst & Young partner, met a friend Donna Murdoch at Ashleymadison.com, a website for people in search of extramarital affairs. At the time Gansman advised companies involved in mergers how to combine workforces. Gansman began sharing confidential information with Murdoch about upcoming mergers of Ernst & Young clients.

Murdoch did not have the money to invest in stock so she might benefit from this information, but she met another man on Ashleymadison.com, Richard Hansen, who was willing to lend her money to purchase stock for the companies about to merge. Eventually Gansman also contributed part of his bonus so she could purchase stock in the merging companies. Between November 2005 and September 2007, Murdoch traded on at least 18 Ernst & Young deals, making about $400,000 from the transactions. Early in 2007, Murdoch's name began to appear on SEC watch lists for suspicious trading around mergers.

Gansman was convicted of six counts of securities fraud. He never made a cent from the transactions, but is expected to spend three to five years in prison for his crimes.[9]

Required:

a. What is the problem both from an accounting and an ethical point of view?

b. Describe the technical proficiency and ethical sensibility required of Gansman in this case. Did he meet these requirements?

c. Identify specific sections of the code of conduct that apply in this situation.

d. If Gansman did not benefit financially from the transactions, why should he be held accountable?

e. Why is insider trading an ethical problem for the professional accountant?

17. Enron's Code of Conduct

What would you think of a corporate code of conduct that said it would "rip your face off"? Andrew Fastow, the chief financial officer of Enron, had a Lucite cube on his desk saying that when Enron said it was going to "rip your face off" it would indeed "rip your face off".

The culture at Enron brought amazing growth. Kenneth Lay and Jeffrey Skilling had taken a natural-gas pipeline company and turned it into a global trading giant. Enron executives were well paid. Investors and analysts loved the company. International banks were happy to finance Enron investments.

Enron used special purpose entities to remove assets that were not performing well off the balance sheet of the company. Off-balance sheet partnerships were also created to generate income from the assets removed from the balance sheet. This allowed Enron to have the best of two worlds. The company could recognize revenue from transactions from assets that were not on their books and could avoid the debt costs associated with generating the revenue by keeping the debt on the partnerships' books. Companies look good when they can generate revenue without using assets to do so. But, the debt on the partnerships' books was guaranteed by Enron. When the partnerships were unable to repay the debt, the debt reverted to the books of Enron.

By the time Enron filed for bankruptcy in December 2001, 6,000 employees had lost their jobs. Many of them had lost their entire retirement savings. Almost $100 billion of shareholder value was destroyed as Enron stock fell to pennies a share. As a result of the fraud, several company executives were sent to prison and one of the largest auditing firms in the world, Arthur Andersen, closed after losing its right to conduct audits for public companies in the US.[10]

Required:

    a. Describe the decisions that an accountant might make that would be consistent with the company motto of "ripping the face off" of its customers.

    b. Would these decisions reflect technical competency or ethical awareness?

NOTES

1. In the United States, the Code of Professional Conduct is written by the AICPA. Detailed information about this code is given in Chapter Nine.

2. The principles of the AICPA Code of Conduct are: (1) responsibility, (2) the public interest, (3) integrity, (4) objectivity and independence, (5) due care, and (6) scope and nature of services. Additional information is given in Chapter Nine.

3. In the AICPA Code of Conduct, the requirement to maintain confidentiality is found in Rule 301, not in the principles section of the code.

4. SEC Press Release 2006-45, "SEC Charges three former KPMG auditors for altering audit working papers," Washington, DC, March 30, 2006.

5. Jeffrey Ng, "Hong Kong Police raid Ernst & Young," *The Wall Street Journal*, October 1, 2009; James Pomfret, "Police raid E&Y's HK office in Akai enquiry," *Reuters*, September 30, 2009.

6. Michael Schroeder & Scot J. Paltrow, "SEC says Ernst & Young violated independence rules in past audits," *The Wall Street Journal*, May 21, 2002.

7. A. Higgins, "For Denmark's Entrepreneur of Year, something was rotten," *The Wall Street Journal*, December 17, 2008.

8. Berkshire Hathaway Inc. News Release, "Trading in Lubrizol Corporation shares by David L. Sokol," April 26, 2011; Andrew Ross Sorkin, "Buffett lets the facts bury Sokol," *The New York Times*, May 2, 2011.

9. Dennis K. Berman, "Insider affair: An SEC trial of the heart," *The Wall Street Journal*, July 28, 2009.

10. A.K. Kranhold Raghaven & A. Burrionuevo, "How Enron bosses created a culture of pushing limits," *The Wall Street Journal*, August 26, 2002; M. Pacelle, "Enron Report gives details of deals that masked debt," *The Wall Street Journal*, September 23, 2002.

CHAPTER SEVEN

Stakeholders in Accounting Ethics: Pressures and Conflicts of Interest

ACCOUNTING AND STAKEHOLDERS

Reminder: Accountants produce business knowledge and communicate it to stakeholders, who use this knowledge to make business decisions.

Reminder: Accountants can draw on several resources in order to make ethically sound decisions – accounting standards and principles, theories of moral philosophy, and professional codes of conduct may inform the accountant in the decision-making process.

Reminder: Accountants are influenced by various factors in the decision-making environment, and these factors need to be considered by the accountant so that decisions are not unduly influenced by these pressures.

ACCOUNTING AND STAKEHOLDERS

In the preceding chapters, we have outlined resources for decision making in accounting ethics. The resources discussed in those chapters – standards and principles for the preparation of financial statements, theories of moral philosophy and standards of professional ethics – may aid the accountant in searching for ideal solutions to the technical and ethical challenges faced in accounting practice. In this chapter, we turn our attention toward obstacles that stand in the way of making ideal decisions. In the real world, there are numerous factors that can hinder a professional from making sound professional decisions and acting on good judgment. An important skill for a professional accountant is the ability to recognize characteristics of the decision environment that may threaten his or her ability (1) to make good judgments and (2) to act in accordance with those judgments.

Thus far, we have conceived of the world outside of the accountant as if it were an "audience," in the sense that many members of society receive the accounting information prepared by the accountant. In many cases, we have indicated that there are particular individuals, groups or organizations that may have an interest in influencing the decisions of the accountant. In this chapter, we explore how such types of influence may come into play – where they come from, how they work and how the accountant may resist such influences.

We have frequently spoken about "stakeholders". For the purposes of accounting, it makes sense to make a distinction between two aspects of being a stakeholder. Throughout the book we have referred to all "users (and potential users) of accounting information" as stakeholders. Anyone who is likely to use accounting information should be thought of as a stakeholder of the accountant's communication. As we have argued, to communicate with these diverse stakeholders the accountant should be unbiased in the preparation of accounting information. To be impartial is an important principle of the professional codes for accountants and auditors. Anyone who makes an effort to read and comprehend accounting information should have the opportunity to acquire impartial and objective information as it is conveyed by the accountant.

In this chapter, we expand the notion of a stakeholder to allow us to explore further the ethical dimension of the accountant's choices and behavior. We will shed light on the stakeholder concept as it has been developed in stakeholder theory. This implies seeing stakeholders as *individuals or groups who can affect, or be affected by, the decisions of the accountant*. We will discuss how stakeholders are important for the accountant's decision making both because they may influence the decision-making process and because stakeholders may be influenced positively or negatively by the decisions of the accountant. In this discussion, we treat the role of stakeholders both from an instrumental (or strategic) perspective and from a moral perspective. We will discuss the role of stakeholders in applying pressure to the accountant during the decision-making process and show how stakeholders may create conflicts of interest that may threaten the accountant's judgment.

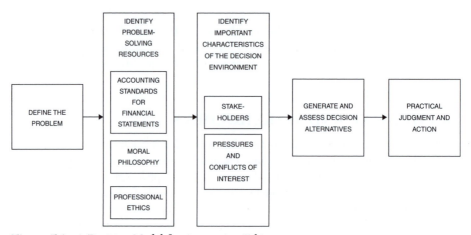

Figure 7.1 A Decision Model for Accounting Ethics

Let us consider the topic of this chapter in light of the decision model used in this book (reproduced in Figure 7.1). This chapter deals with the third column of the model – *Identify Important Characteristics of the Decision Environment*. In the chapter we treat both of the themes included in column three of the decision model – *Stakeholders* and *Pressures and Conflicts of Interest*.

The chapter continues as follows. First, we place the chapter theme within the decision-making model. Second, we explore the concept of a stakeholder, both from an instrumental and from a moral point of view. Third, we discuss characteristics of stakeholders that are important from a decision-making perspective. Next, we illuminate how stakeholders may exert various forms of pressure on the accountant's decision-making process. Finally, we discuss how conflicts of interest may arise in accounting practice and the role of stakeholders in creating these conflicts.

STAKEHOLDERS AND THEIR INFLUENCE ON ACCOUNTING DECISIONS

In Chapter Two and Chapter Three, we demonstrated how ethical problems in accounting are the basis of the book's approach to accounting ethics. We defined ethical problems as problems where multiple values are at stake for multiple stakeholders. This implies that ethical problems involve decisions where different action alternatives may have a variety of influences on the accountant and the stakeholders who affect or are affected by the accountant's decision. The fact that in any given ethical problem multiple values may be at stake for a variety of stakeholders gives rise to the following questions. First, which values are at stake? Second, for whom are those values at stake? The first question deals with the ethical content of decisions – how the decision is relevant for the well-being or the interests of others. The second question is concerned with the identity of the "others" – the parties who ought to be taken into account in a given decision – and with the consideration of the extent to which their interests may influence the choices that are made.

In the field of business and economics, the emphasis on stakeholders is fairly novel. In the recent past, we considered the interests of the shareholder to be of primary concern, but in the past two decades the discourse about stakeholders has been integrated into the core of business literature. In 1970, Milton Friedman published the landmark piece, "The social responsibility of business is to increase its profits," in which he argued that shareholders are the only group that should be taken into account in decision making in business. This had long been the dominant position in business. It should be noted, however, that Friedman did not dismiss the idea that it might be rational for businesses to take the interests of others (employees, communities, customers) into account, since this may be an effective strategy to promote the performance of the company and thereby serve the interests of the shareholders. Despite this view, Friedman did not consider it an ethical issue to address the interests of parties other than the shareholders of the company.

Now, decades after Friedman's article, the concept of the stakeholder has become commonplace in business, following the publication of Edward Freeman's *Strategic Management: A Stakeholder Perspective* (1984). In this book, Freeman disagreed with Milton Friedman's one-sided emphasis on shareholders. Freeman argued that stakeholders of a company – customers, employees, suppliers, governments, and others – may have rights to make claims against that company. Not the least of these stakeholders are those on whom harm is inflicted, in the form of so-called negative externalities. These aggrieved stakeholders have legitimate claims against the company which has harmed them. The prototypical example that is used to illustrate this viewpoint focuses on people who live along a river that is contaminated by emissions from a factory. The moral intuition of most people is that the people living along the river have a legitimate claim on the company, a claim that emissions should either be managed in a better way, or the people be compensated for the harm caused by the factory. Such a stakeholder perspective presumes that businesses have responsibilities toward others and not only to their own shareholders – even when legislation does not specify this.

Since Freeman published his work on stakeholders, the idea that companies have responsibilities to a wider group of stakeholders has become part of mainstream economic thought. In addition, the individual decisions of people in organizations should also be addressed in a stakeholder perspective; that is, the decision maker should take into account how his or her decisions influence stakeholders both inside and outside the organization. In this chapter, we take this perspective on stakeholders as we treat accounting decisions. The decisions made by the accountant clearly have implications for stakeholders in the narrow sense; that is, for users of accounting information. Accountants are responsible for providing relevant and faithfully representative information to these stakeholders. The accountant's decisions can also influence individuals or groups in other ways – especially if the accountant fails to produce high-quality information. For instance, consider the manifold negative effects for the employees of Enron and Arthur Andersen that resulted from the accounting fraud and the inadequate practice of that company and audit firm.

This book employs a stakeholder perspective on ethical decision making in accounting. We argue that the accountant should (1) address the question of which stakeholders are influenced by the accountant's decisions and how they are influenced, and (2) address the questions of how stakeholders may attempt to influence the decisions the accountant is about to make, whether or not such an influence is acceptable and whether it necessary to resist that particular stakeholder influence.

This approach implies that a stakeholder perspective on accounting relates to both the instrumental and the moral dimensions of stakeholder influence. That is, it is important for the accountant to be aware of key stakeholders, both because they are important for the accountant's ability to make sound decisions and because the stakeholder may be influenced either negatively or positively by these decisions. The ethicality of the decisions are at stake in these matters. A stakeholder analysis may thus be seen as "killing two birds with one stone," for sound stakeholder analysis may prevent the accountant from causing undue harm to particular stakeholders and may also protect the accountant's decision-making process against inappropriate stakeholder pressure.

STAKEHOLDERS

A stakeholder is any individual, group, or entity that may influence, or be influenced by, the accounting decision. Stakeholders are important both for instrumental (or strategic) and for moral purposes. It is important for the accountant to be aware of key stakeholders, because they are important to his or her ability to make sound decisions, and because they may be negatively or positively influenced by these decisions. These matters are crucial for the ethical quality of the accountant's decision.

This way of thinking about stakeholders presupposes seeing stakeholders as a broad group. It includes current stakeholders, in the sense of individuals or groups who are either affected by the decisions already made by the accountant, or who are exerting pressure on the accountant as choices are considered. It also includes potential stakeholders; this means the individuals or groups who could be affected by a decision the accountant is about to make.

CHARACTERISTICS OF STAKEHOLDERS

In this description of stakeholders, the defining characteristic of a stakeholder is that the stakeholder either (1) is affected by or (2) may affect the accountant's decisions. This means that many people or groups may be considered as stakeholders for any given decision. But how can the accountant distinguish between the different types of stakeholders? Are not some of them more important or more relevant than others within a situation? The resources (of time and energy) available to the accountant for the consideration of stakeholders of a particular decision are bound to be limited. This means that the accountant will have to set priorities among stakeholders. He must address the interests of those who are most powerfully influenced by his decisions (or most negatively affected) and seek to determine which of the stakeholders may attempt to assert inappropriate pressure on his decision making.

A framework for determining stakeholder priorities was developed by Mitchell, Agle, and Wood (1997), who highlighted the key characteristics of stakeholders, and

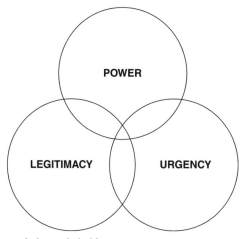

Figure 7.2   A Framework for Stakeholder Prioritization

Source: Mitchell, R.K., Agle, B.R. & Wood, D.J. (1997) Toward a theory of stakeholder identification and salience: Defining the principle of who and what really counts. *Academy of Management Review*, 22(4): 853–886.

suggest how they might be used systematically to evaluate stakeholders and assess their potential influence. According to these scholars, the three most important stakeholder characteristics are *power, legitimacy, and urgency*. By classifying stakeholders with respect to these three characteristics, it is possible to identify stakeholders according to whether they are powerful, have legitimate interests in a situation, or have urgent interests that ought to be considered.

Figure 7.2 below shows a Venn diagram of these three characteristics, where we see that eight groups of stakeholders can be distinguished. The two extremes are, respectively, (1) stakeholders who are characterized by all three factors, which is illustrated by the intersection of all three circles, and (2) stakeholders who are not characterized by any of the factors; that is, they are not powerful and do not have legitimate or urgent claims. These stakeholders are visually placed in the area outside all three circles. The remaining six groups are stakeholders which are either characterized by one of the three factors (for instance, stakeholders who have urgent claims, but are neither powerful nor legitimate, and thus are placed in the part of the "urgency" circle that does not overlap with the two other circles), or by two of the three factors (for instance, stakeholders who are powerful and have urgent claims, but are not legitimate, and thus are placed in the intersection of the circles for power and urgency).

Let us consider each of the three characteristics in order to shed light on what they mean and how the accountant should think about them. Of the three concepts, *power* is arguably the most intuitively familiar concept. A simple definition of power is that it refers to someone's ability to make other people do something they would not otherwise have done. Power relates to one's ability to influence others. According to Mitchell, Agel, and Wood (1997), "a party to a relationship has power, to the extent that it has or can gain access to coercive, utilitarian, or normative means to impose its will within the relationship". In the accounting context, a stakeholder is powerful if he or she is able to influence the accountant's decision either by force (coercive power), by catering to the accountant's interests (utilitarian power), or by setting a standard or norm that makes the accountant act differently (normative power). The first type of power (coercive) is direct and explicit, while the two other forms are more implicit and indirect, and thus may be harder to recognize than the former more direct and explicit forms of power.

The second characteristic in the framework is *legitimacy*. This is a concept that is less readily understandable on the basis of our everyday language. According to Mitchell, Agel, and Wood (1997), legitimacy is "a generalized perception or assumption that the actions of an entity are desirable, proper, or appropriate within some socially constructed system of norms, values, beliefs and definitions". Simply put, legitimacy deals with whether or not a given individual's claim with regard to his interests in a case is relevant and grounded in beliefs and values that are accepted by society. For instance, if a person has been wrongfully quoted in a newspaper, and he contacts the newspaper's editor to get the error corrected, most people would agree that his claim is legitimate. We can agree on (1) that he is in fact misquoted, (2) that this is unacceptable, and (3) that the newspaper should make an effort to correct or compensate for the person for the wrongdoing. This shows how legitimacy is a characteristic that has to do with values held in a society and the beliefs regarding whether those values are violated. Legitimacy deals with whether or not there is a shared understanding that a given stakeholder's interests should be taken into account.

The third characteristic of the framework is *urgency*. When we talk about something being urgent, this can mean one of two things: that it is time-sensitive (i.e., that time is of the essence) or that it is particularly critical for the stakeholder. (It may also be both time-sensitive and critical.) Thus, urgent claims can be claims of a time-sensitive nature, or claims that are critical for the stakeholder. As we see, the question of urgency does not relate to the stakeholder per se, but to the interests of the stakeholder. It could, for example, be the case that a supplier is awaiting outstanding payment for goods that have been delivered and has a loan payment that is due tomorrow. In this case, it is urgent that the supplier is paid, so that he will not fail to complete the loan payment. In this case, time is of the essence because if the money does not arrive tomorrow, it does not make a difference if it arrives in two, three, or four days – by then it will already be too late.

As illustrated in Figure 7.2, we may distinguish between different configurations of these three characteristics: powerful stakeholders with urgent claims, legitimate stakeholders without power, and so on. These distinctions and analysis of stakeholder characteristics can be used to determine, in a given case, which stakeholders' interests should be taken into account. The degree to which the stakeholder has these three characteristics determines the *salience* of the stakeholder (i.e., the importance of the stakeholder) and how pressing it is that the interests of that particular stakeholder be taken into account.

As the description of the three characteristics suggests, power is arguably a characteristic that is very relevant when it comes to making an instrumental or strategic assessment of a stakeholder. Whether or not a given stakeholder can influence

STAKEHOLDER CHARACTERISTICS AND SALIENCE

Stakeholders have three important characteristics – power, legitimacy, and urgency. Power refers to the ability to influence, either by coercive, utilitarian or normative means. Legitimacy refers to the perception of being appropriate within a shared set of norms and values. Urgency refers to whether or not the stakeholder has time-sensitive claims or claims that are of a particularly critical nature. The salience of the stakeholder depends on these three characteristics.

(or harm) you is an essential aspect in the decision of whether or not to address the interests of that stakeholder. By contrast, the opposite of power is powerlessness, which means that there is a moral dimension of power, as well. In many traditions of moral philosophy, whether someone is powerless (i.e., vulnerable) is an important characteristic to consider with regard to how they should be treated. This means that power is also an ethical issue.

Legitimacy and urgency are clearly relevant to an ethical assessment. Legitimacy deals with whether or not the interests of the stakeholder are reasonable and are grounded in shared conceptions of what is appropriate; legitimacy relates to the question of *what is ethically relevant.* This question is fundamental to ethical decision making, since the distinction between the ethically relevant and the ethically irrelevant is a necessary feature of moral judgments (Rest, 1994). Urgency also has important ethical implications – both with regard to the issue of time-sensitive claims and to claims that are critical to the stakeholder. The utilitarian philosopher John Stuart Mill (1962) argued that consequences that have high *intensity* for the individual are especially important in an ethical assessment (Rachels & Rachels, 2009). By intensity, Mill refers to consequences that have a great impact, which typically will be the case for urgent claims – especially those that are critical for the stakeholder.

Using the framework outlined here: it is possible to make systematic distinctions between stakeholders that can help us make better decisions. In order to see how the framework might be used in practice, let us return to the case of the auditor Anne Sorenson, which we discussed in Chapter Six on professional ethics.

CLASSIFYING STAKEHOLDERS IN PRACTICE

There are many different ways that one might use the stakeholder framework of power, legitimacy and urgency – from an intuitive, "rule-of-thumb" approach, to a structured and detailed analysis. A key question in the use of the framework is whether we should consider the three characteristics as "either–or" characteristics (i.e., either you are powerful or you are not, and so on), or if we should think of them as degrees (from very powerful to nearly powerless). For instance, one could classify stakeholders as having high, moderate or low power, and so on; such a classification will allow a more nuanced discussion of stakeholder characteristics and their implications for the accountant.

Let us review the Anne Sorenson case by using this framework. This will shed light on how such considerations can be made in practice. The case is reprinted in the box below as it was presented in Chapter Six.

CASE: AUDITOR–CLIENT CONFIDENTIALITY

Anne Sorenson, an auditor for KPMG, is working on the audit of Amgen, Inc. Amgen is a biotechnology company based in Thousand Oaks, California. The audit has been fairly routine, but today Anne overheard a very exciting piece of information. Amgen has just completed a series of tests on mice related to the *ob* gene and leptin, the protein produced by the gene. During these tests, obese mice lost about 40% of their body weight after only a month of daily injections of leptin. With trials on humans ready to begin within the year, the promise of a cure for obesity seems hopeful.

That evening, Anne talks to her parents over the phone. She is so excited about this finding that she tells her parents about the potential cure for obesity. After getting off the phone, Anne also tells her roommate about her interesting day, but then she realizes that she is divulging confidential client information. Her roommate, a stockbroker at Merrill Lynch, is excited about the information and wants to recommend that all her investment customers purchase Amgen stock before the information is made public and the stock price goes up. Anne wonders about what she has just done.

The first step of a stakeholder analysis is to ask the two questions related to the ethical problem: what is at stake and for whom? We should first make an overview of the relevant stakeholders, as well as of their interests. Who are the persons or groups who have something at stake in the situation and what are their interests?

In the case of Anne Sorenson, there are some stakeholders who are "present" in the story. Anne is herself a stakeholder, and her interest – at least after the fact of disclosing the information – is to correct the wrongdoing, and in doing so, prevent her own firing and save her professional reputation, which may be at stake in her disclosure of confidential information. Her employer KPMG is a stakeholder, since the company's reputation and its relationship to the client are also at stake. The company's interest is to maintain both.

Anne's roommate is a stakeholder – not only because she can influence Anne's destiny by acting on the information, but also because she can be harmed if it becomes known that she has acted on inside information. Her interests are mixed. It is in her interest to give sound investment advice, but at the same time, it is also in her interest to act in a manner that protects her professional credibility. By extension, the roommate's employer, Merrill Lynch, is a stakeholder, since the company may be harmed by her potential illegal investments (on the basis of inside information). Anne's parents are stakeholders in a similar way as Anne's roommate. Their primary interest, however, is probably to ensure that Anne is not harmed. This means that they are not a threat to Anne's interests in the same way that the roommate may be.

The company Amgen and its shareholders are also stakeholders, since their interests can be harmed by the disclosure of the confidential information. The company wants the information to be kept secret until the company makes the information public. Furthermore, regulatory bodies are relevant stakeholders in this story, since their role is to regulate in a manner that discourages actors in financial markets from dealing with inside information.

In addition, there are some stakeholders who are peripheral, like the potential users of the cure for obesity. Their interest is to get the product available, but it is unlikely that this situation will change the likelihood of this happening. The potential investors who can make use of the roommate's inside information can also be seen as stakeholders; their primary interest is to make successful investments.

With this review of stakeholders, we can assess all stakeholders in light of the Mitchell *et al.* framework for stakeholder prioritization. This implies assessing the degree to which the stakeholders are powerful, have legitimate claims and have urgent claims. In the following, we do this assessment by using a "high, moderate, low" classification for the three characteristics of each stakeholder.

Anne had considerable power before disclosing the confidential information, but she is arguably less powerful after the fact. She still has a chance to persuade her parents and her roommate to keep the information to themselves, and she may be successful at doing so. There is, however, considerable uncertainty in this situation, which suggests that Anne has but a moderate level of power. As long as Anne does not inform her employer, KPMG is not able to influence the situation because the firm does not know about situation. For all practical purposes, KPMG has low power.

Anne's parents and the roommate both have high power, in the sense that they have the opportunity to act in a way that will harm Anne, if they wish to do so. Their intentions are unknown to us, but, generally, we would expect the parents not to act on this opportunity, while it is hard to predict what the roommate will do. Merrill Lynch, the roommate's employer, has low power, since the company is uninformed. The same goes for regulatory institutions, potential shareholders, and Amgen, each of whom needs to be informed before they can take any action. It is important, therefore, to distinguish between *actual power in the situation*, which depends on having knowledge that enables you to act, and *latent power to influence the situation*, which means that you have power to influence if and when you gain critical information about the situation. In such a perspective, we would argue that the regulatory institutions, for instance, have high latent power, but in the current situation, they have no power because they do not have the critical information about the situation.

With regard to legitimacy, Anne has low legitimacy, since the entire situation is created as a consequence of her unprofessional conduct. One may debate whether this threatens the legitimacy of her employer as well. Perhaps this suggests that in the current situation, KPMG has moderate legitimacy. Anne's parents and her roommate have high legitimacy at the current time; however, any intention they may have to act on the inside information would undermine their legitimacy completely (i.e., low legitimacy). Several stakeholders have highly legitimate claims against Anne and the other actors in the case (even without their being aware that they have such claims): Amgen, Merrill Lynch, shareholders, and potential shareholders, as well as regulatory bodies, have highly legitimate interests in the situation.

There are degrees of urgency with regard to the stakeholders' interests. It is highly urgent for Anne that she manages to resolve the situation. This is urgent both in the sense of time being an issue, and because it is critical for her ability to maintain her career as an auditor. Nothing appears to be urgent for the parents (at least based on the

Table 7.1 Stakeholder Characteristics in the Anne Sorenson Case

Stakeholder	Power	Legitimacy	Urgency
Anne Sorenson	Moderate	Low	High
KPMG	Low	Moderate	High
Parents	High	High	Low
Roommate	High	High	Moderate
Merrill Lynch	Low	High	High
Amgen and its shareholders	Low	High	Moderate
Regulatory institutions	Low	High	Low
Potential investors	Low	High	Low

information in the case), while there is an issue of time for the roommate, since she needs to act quickly if she intends to act on the inside information before the company makes it public. Given this, we can see her situation as being of moderate urgency. It is urgent for KPMG and Merrill Lynch that their reputations not be harmed by their own employees who disclose confidential information or act on inside information. Thus, we may argue that both have high urgency. It is at least moderately urgent for Amgen and its shareholders that the information is not made public before they choose to do so (perhaps even highly urgent, depending on what their plans are, and how they are influenced by the premature disclosure of the information). For regulatory institutions, this is not an urgent case, even though it may become important to them later to investigate such a case. For potential investors, this is a situation of low urgency, since they do not depend on this specific investment.

In the preceding paragraphs, we have made a simple analysis of the situation on the basis of the three characteristics. We summarize it visually in Table 7.1.

The table depicts stakeholder characteristics and provides a point of departure for making decisions in light of this assessment. In this case, the table includes the auditor herself, Anne Sorenson, even though she is the actor from whose perspective we analyze the case. It is likely that she will consider her own interests when safeguarding against the potential negative consequences of her own mistaken disclosure. From a strategic point of view, the roommate is the most dangerous stakeholder, since she has the power to act and an urgent reason to do so. From a moral point of view, however, Amgen and its shareholders, as well as KPMG and (potentially) Merrill Lynch, have much at stake in the situation, even though they have not acted to create the situation. A simple ethical assessment would suggest that their interests are highly important in the situation.

In and of itself, a stakeholder classification of this type does not solve the problem. But in an action-oriented perspective, it can help the accountant make sense of a situation. In light of our decision model, this type of analysis can help do two things. First, it allows the accountant to assess potential threats in the decision environment, in the form of powerful stakeholders who may attempt to attain their own objectives by applying pressure on the accountant. Second, it allows the accountant to distinguish between ethically relevant consequences and risks for each stakeholder who has interests in the situation. Thereby, the accountant may get a better grasp of what is at stake in the situation from an ethical point of view, and understand this in relation to the ideals that were discussed in Chapters Four, Five, and Six (standards for preparing financial statements, theories of moral philosophy, and standards of professional ethics).

In the following section, we address the specific issue of pressure in the decision environment. The section discusses how the accountant may be influenced by actors or circumstances that characterize the decision environment and how awareness of this problem may safeguard against undue influence from those pressures.

PRESSURES ON THE ACCOUNTANT IN THE DECISION-MAKING PROCESS

In the discussion of the stakeholder characteristics above, we have argued that powerful actors may apply pressure on accountants and auditors in order to influence the decisions they make. The accountant may be aware of this pressure, or the pressure may be applied by the stakeholder in such a manner that the accountant does not fully understand just how he is being influenced. In addition to these direct attempts at influence, there are pressures in the decision environment that are not necessarily applied by actors. For instance, time pressure may play an important role in the accountant's decision process. There are numerous deadlines in accounting practice, and it is well established that time pressure influences decision making (Svenson & Maule, 1993). In addition, other external pressures may influence the decision-making process, such as social pressure or pressure that follows from job design or the job environment (e.g., see Trevino, 1986).

In the context of this chapter, the issue of pressure is central. As outlined in Chapter Six, the code of professional ethics for accountants suggests that the accountant should act in ways that make it less likely that undue influence can be exerted either directly or indirectly. For instance, if an auditor sees a potential conflict of interest in taking on a client – because the client is a neighbor of the auditor – the auditor should attempt to avoid the conflict of interest. He might suggest that another auditor at the auditing firm take on the client. Pressure is not inevitable; the professional accountant usually has opportunities to limit the impact of relevant pressures, and should do so whenever possible.

In cases where pressure is more implicit, this can be more difficult to do. For instance, time pressure may be hard to avoid, and it is likely that the accountant is susceptible to making poor judgments under heavy time pressure (Svenson & Maule, 1993). Other types of pressure in the organizational environment can also influence the accountant's or auditor's judgment. For instance, Bazerman, Morgan, and Loewenstein (1997) argue that the pressure for generating revenue on individual auditors leads them to make biased judgments that serve the interests of clients. That is, auditor independence may be threatened by implicit pressure for the audit firm to maintain good relationships with clients. Such a pressure is more difficult for the individual professional to manage, and this bias can often operate at an entirely unconscious level.

Various forms of social pressure may also be exerted on the individual accountant, in the form of implicit norms in the community of accountants or in the organizational

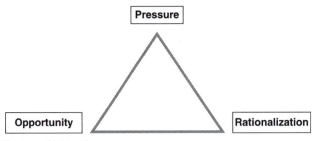

Figure 7.3   The Fraud Triangle

Source: Wells, J.T. (2008) *Principles of Fraud Examination*. New York: Wiley.

culture. For example, if there is a culture of never questioning your superiors, it will be much harder for the accountant to withstand pressure from managers to make questionable adjustments to the financial statements.

For the individual accountant to avoid falling victim to these forms of pressure, it is necessary that he or she be oriented toward recognizing pressure in the decision environment. This involves recognizing how the interests of powerful stakeholders may be a threat to decision making and recognizing other features of the environment that may influence decisions. One framework that can promote such awareness is the fraud triangle.

The Fraud Triangle: Pressure, Opportunity and, Rationalization

In Chapter Four, we presented the fraud triangle, which suggests that when fraud occurs three conditions are often present: (1) there is pressure on the decision maker (i.e., the accountant), (2) the opportunity to conduct fraud exists, and (3) the person engaging in the fraud has the ability to rationalize the behavior (cf. Wells, 2008). This is illustrated in Figure 7.3.

The fraud triangle has important implications for the accountant. For one thing, by thinking about the types of opportunity the accountant has for committing fraud and deliberate violations of rules and regulations, the accountant may anticipate situations in which he or she may become the target of pressure. Furthermore, by using the kind of interest mapping we have done in the Anne Sorenson case, he may also anticipate which stakeholders will try to influence him. This anticipation can make it easier to safeguard against attempts at undue influence. Finally, by being aware of the possibility for rationalization, the accountant can critically examine his own reasons and justifications for acting, so that he does not blindly become victim of the pressures from others.

CONFLICTS OF INTEREST

In the section on pressure, we discussed types of pressure that may create bias in the accountant's decision making. A prominent determinant of such pressures is conflict of interest. In the code of professional ethics for accountants (Chapter Six), avoiding conflicts of interest is an important topic, as it is one of the gravest threats to professional integrity – both because it may influence actual decision making and even because of the appearance that it may do so. Nevertheless, decision makers often face conflicts of interest which may harm not only their interests and those of the firm, but may also have a considerable negative impact on stakeholders.

According to the IFAC Code of Ethics, there are two different forms of conflict of interest for accountants:

1. The professional accountant undertakes a professional activity related to a particular matter for two or more parties whose interests with respect to that matter are in conflict.

2. The interests of the professional accountant with respect to a particular matter and the interests of a party for whom the professional accountant undertakes a professional activity related to that matter are in conflict.

The conflict can either be between the interests of two stakeholders both of whom are represented by the accountant, or between the interest of the accountant and the interest of one or more stakeholders.

Moore *et al.* (2005) argue that there are several psychological processes that make conflicts of interest damaging. First, conflicts of interest affect the accountant's judgment by pressuring his perception to be more selective; that is, he may unconsciously overlook or disregard information that goes against his interest or the client's interest. Second, escalation of commitment may lead accountants or auditors who have already acted in a biased manner to continue to do so – even without consciously choosing to do so. Finally, human beings have a poor ability to judge accurately their own susceptibility for being biased and this may permit them to enter into relationships that will influence their decision making in inappropriate ways, even when they believe that this will not happen. We overestimate our own integrity and ability to make sound judgments; therefore we fall victim to conflicts of interest, with their negative influence on decision making.

In Figure 7.4, we illustrate a simple stakeholder model that may illustrate how conflicts of interest create imbalances in professional relationships, to the detriment

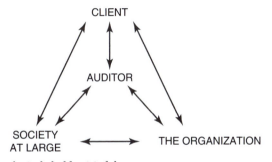

Figure 7.4   A Simple Stakeholder Model

of stakeholders and with harm to the quality of accounting information and the audit opinion.

Figure 7.4 illustrates the key relationships of an auditor, in order to exemplify the impact of conflicts of interest. The auditor has at least three distinct professional responsibilities. First, he is employed by the audit firm and is responsible for performing his professional tasks properly and effectively. Second, he has clients for whom he has a responsibility to provide sound audit services. Finally, and most importantly, he has a social responsibility toward society at large, since the auditor represents the interests of society, which needs assurance that the financial information communicated by companies is high-quality information that is relevant and faithfully representative.

In the event that one or more of these stakeholders aim to influence the decisions of the auditor, it is likely to impact other stakeholders negatively. We refer to such attempts at influence – which can be overt and direct or covert and indirect – as *secondary transactions*. The auditor's primary transactions are the following: the auditor works on behalf of the firm and is compensated by salary; the auditor provides audit services to the client as he is given access to relevant data (and that the client pays audit fees to the auditing firm); and the auditor ensures that society at large receives high-quality financial information given that society grants professional autonomy to the community of auditors to engage in this activity.

Secondary transactions refer to all exchanges between the parties that are not part of the primary transaction. These may be financial benefits, which in their most problematic form constitute bribery or corruption. One can also argue that the auditing firm may use its bonus system selectively to promote behavior that is in line with maintaining relationships to key clients (cf. Bazerman *et al.*, 1997). An even more subtle – and therefore more interesting – form of secondary transactions includes several other forms of benefits that can be exchanged between stakeholders. For example, these may include access to social spheres (golf clubs, social networks) or various types of social reinforcement (reward and punishment) inside the organization. Access to resources and opportunities for promotion are additional types of benefits that can serve as secondary transactions that may subtly influence the accountant's decision making. In Figure 7.5, secondary transactions are illustrated by the dashed arrows, which indicate that the strengthening of one relationship within the stakeholder network may adversely affect other stakeholders external to the secondary transaction.

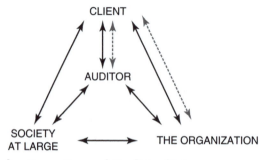

Figure 7.5   Secondary Transactions and Conflicts of Interest

For the reasons discussed above, accountants should be very concerned to assess critically whether they are engaged in relationships where conflicts of interest may arise. This relates not only to situations where conflicts of interest are explicit and evident, such as the case of an auditor taking on his brother's company as a client, but it also concerns instances where the accountant engages in professional or social interactions that are likely to lead to bias (conscious or unconscious), as a result of the benefits he may reap (or the potential costs he may avoid).

SUMMARY

In this chapter, we have shed light on important characteristics of the accountant's decision environment. The purpose of the chapter has been to explore how such factors in the environment may influence the accountant's decision-making process, as well as how the accountant should attempt to manage these challenges.

The main factor to consider in the accountant's decision environment is the role of stakeholders. This involves understanding how stakeholders may influence the accountant's decision-making process, as well as understanding how the stakeholders may be affected by the accountant's decisions and actions. Stakeholder influence has both an instrumental (or strategic) dimension and an ethical dimension. Mapping stakeholders and their interests can help the accountant understand what is at stake and for whom. It may also enable the accountant to distinguish between the various stakeholders and their interests on the basis of relevant characteristics.

The accountant can distinguish between stakeholders and create a basis for prioritizing between their interests by conducting a three-part analysis. This involves investigating the degree of power (or powerlessness) of the stakeholders, which determines the extent to which they may influence the accountant (strategic), or are vulnerable to the impact of the accountant's decisions (moral). Furthermore, it involves investigating the degree of legitimacy and urgency of stakeholders' interests, which can be the basis of distinguishing ethically relevant interests from more irrelevant ones.

Stakeholders' influence on the accountant constitutes one type of influence on the accountant's decision process. In a second type of influence, the accountant may be influenced by various forms of pressure in the decision environment. Time pressure is an important factor that may threaten the accountant's ability to exercise sound judgment. This may render the accountant susceptible to other forms of inappropriate influence. In addition, financial pressures of the competitive market or social pressures by the culture of the audit firm (pressures from superiors or peers) may exert considerable influence on the accountant, and there may be subtle, even unconscious, biases that can distort decision making. Such pressures can be difficult to resist.

Finally, conflicts of interest are an important source of influence on the accountant's decision-making process. In their professional roles, accountants and auditors may find themselves in situations where they are consciously or unconsciously biased in their judgments. This may especially arise in cases where the primary transaction (i.e., the task performance of the accountant in doing his job, whether it is preparing financial statements, making audit judgments, and so on) is undermined by secondary transactions in the form of payments, favors, or other personal benefits that the accountant may gain by acting as other parties want him or her to act, rather than according to sound judgment.

An important part of a sound ethical decision-making process for accountants is to address characteristics of the decision environment that may interfere with the accountant's decisions. By addressing the factors discussed in this chapter, the accountant may become aware of, and thus be enabled to manage, potential hindrances to complying with the technical and ethical standards of accounting practice.

CHAPTER REVIEW QUESTIONS

1. (LO1) What is a stakeholder?
2. (LO1) How do we understand the concept of a stakeholder in an accounting context?
3. (LO2) How are stakeholders important for decision making in accounting ethics?
4. (LO3) What are the most important characteristics of stakeholders?
5. (LO3) Why and how is stakeholders' power important for accountants?
6. (LO3) What does it mean that a stakeholder is legitimate?
7. (LO3) Explain what it means that a stakeholder has an urgent claim.
8. (LO4) How can stakeholders exert pressure on accountants in the decision process?
9. (LO5) What types of pressure may influence the decision making of accountants?
10. (LO6) What is a conflict of interest?

CASES

11. Year-End Adjusting Entries
Eduardo Garcia has just been hired as the controller for Toro Enterprises. To become familiar with the company, he is reviewing the financial statements for 2013. The previous controller completed the year-end financial statements before he left and mailed them to the holder of the long-term bonds as required by the debt covenants. Eduardo is dismayed to find several errors in the financial statements. The previous controller, George Wilson, prepared several adjusting entries on January 10, 2014. The explanations for these entries were "to avoid default on the debt covenant". George had recognized revenue on a large order received on December 28 but shipped on January 3, and had reduced depreciation expense by $2,300,000. Both of these items were designed to increase earnings per share to the required amount.

Required:
   a. What is the accounting and ethical problem for Eduardo? What pressure does Eduardo face?

b. Based on your knowledge of accounting standards, what is the appropriate accounting treatment for these items?

c. Identify the stakeholders affected by the errors in the financial statements presented to the bondholders. Who benefits? Who is harmed? Is there a conflict of interest between the stakeholders?

d. What alternatives are available to Eduardo? Is it worse to admit to the bondholders that your predecessor made a mistake than to hide it?

e. What would you do? Why?

12. Parmalat

Parmalat, a company based in Parma, Italy, sells dairy products around the world. The company employs 36,000 employees in 30 countries. On December 24, 2003, Parmalat filed for bankruptcy protection in Italy and a few days later the court in Parma, Italy, declared Parmalat insolvent. Parmalat's stock traded on the Milan stock exchange and its debt instruments were sold in the United States.

On December 9, 2003, Calisto Tanzi, Parmalat's chairman and chief executive officer, and Stefano Tanzi, a senior Parmalat executive, met with representatives of a New York City private equity firm regarding a possible buyout of Parmalat. The Tanzis were interested in a buyout of Parmalat due to liquidity problems at the company. A representative of the equity firm questioned how the company could have a liquidity problem when they had a large amount of cash on their balance sheet. Stefano Tanzi stated that the cash was not there and that the company had only €500 million in cash. And furthermore, Parmalat's debt was actually €10 billion, much higher than the €2.1 billion the balance sheet showed. The final audit disclosed debt of $18 billion, almost $16 billion of which had never been reported.

Parmalat had entered into fraudulent transactions to hide the financial position of the company. The fraud perpetrated at Parmalat was simple. Parmalat forged documents on a scanner, ran the documents through a fax machine to make them look authentic, forged signatures from old documents and simply copied them on the new agreements. Parmalat entered into fraudulent transactions four times a year to inflate the financial statements when the quarterly results were due. At times the inflated results were unreasonable, including the report that claimed a unit of Parmalat sold enough milk to Cuba for each person to drink 55 gallons of milk a year.

Cash Fraud

The fraud started to unravel in early December 2003, when the Bank of America Corp. informed Parmalat that an account supposedly held by Bonlat containing $4.8 billion did not exist. The money was supposedly held in an account at the Bank of America in New York City. The bank account and the assets did not exist. The confirmation returned from the account had been forged. Executives at Parmalat have described this account as a fraud. The account, in the name of Bonlat, was created in 1998 with Grant Thornton's assistance to hide fraudulent transactions from the Deloitte auditors.

Long-term Debt Fraud

In 2003, Parmalat understated the long-term debt on its financial statements by at least €7.9 billion. The same year, Parmalat, being an Italian company listed on the US stock exchange, marketed $100 million of notes payable to US investors. The securities appeared to be issued by a company with less debt and a higher level of assets than was actually the case. Parmalat also told US investors that it had used its excess cash balance to repurchase debt securities worth €2.9 billion. The company had not repurchased these securities and they remained outstanding. Parmalat removed the debt from the financial statements, stating that they did not have to record the debt because they owned it. Outsiders could not understand why they did not simply cancel the debt, if it had been purchased; but, of course, cancellation was impossible because the debt was still outstanding.

The SEC charged Parmalat with securities fraud, stating that from 1998 to 2002, Parmalat sold nearly $1.5 billion in notes and bonds to US investors and "grossly and intentionally" misstated their financial statements to misrepresent the risk associated with the notes and bonds.

Misappropriation of Assets

From 1997 to 2003, Parmalat transferred at least €800 million to the family's tourism business run by the daughter of Mr. Tanzi, the owner. More money is believed to have been transferred to Parmalat's soccer team, run by Mr. Tanzi's son, Stefano. The Tanzi family company, La Coloniale SpA, owns 51% of the stock of Parmalat.

The Auditors

Grant Thornton and Deloitte & Touche, the auditors for Parmalat, were fired in 2003. PricewaterhouseCoopers was hired to investigate the fraud. They issued a report in January 2004 indicating that Parmalat had debt of $18 billion, roughly $16 billion of which had not been previously reported. The net income reported by Parmalat was five times the actual earnings. The Parmalat prosecutors allege that Adolfo Mamoli and Giuseppe Rovelli, partners at Deloitte's Italian firm, contributed to Parmalat's collapse by certifying that the financial statements had no material misstatements despite clear and systematic evidence of fraud.

The Parmalat fraud is the largest fraud to occur in Europe. The fraud surprised many people. Until 2003, Parmalat received a clean audit opinion from its auditor, borrowed money from many international banks, and issued bonds with the assistance of investment bankers on Wall Street. One might ask how so many outsiders missed the signs of Parmalat's deception.[1]

Required:

    a. Discuss the accounting and ethical issues of this situation.

    b. Who are the stakeholders?

    c. Consider the conflicts of interests and the pressure on Parmalat. Was anyone harmed or did anybody benefit by the possible choices?

13. Backdating Stock Options

A stock option gives the owner the right to buy shares of stock at a future date for a fixed price. The fixed price is often set at the market price of the stock on the date of the grant, because the accounting standards do not require the company to recognize compensation expense if the option price is equal to the market price on the date of the grant. The owners of the stock option benefit from the option when the stock price increases above the price at the date of the grant.

Companies that issue *backdated stock options* backdate the date of the stock option grant to an earlier date when the stock price was lower. In this way, the value of the stock option is higher because the individual will receive the difference between the price at the grant date and the market value price when the stock is sold. Stock options that are backdated to an earlier date when the stock price is lower are referred to as options that are "instantly in the money". This means that they have value immediately and the recipient does not have to wait until the stock price increases before having something of value.

Backdating stock options is not illegal if the company recognizes compensation expense for the difference between the market price on the day the stock option is granted and the market price on the day the stock option is backdated. The company should also disclose the fact that the grants were made at the market price on the date the option was backdated. Failing to recognize compensation expense and to disclose that the stock options were not issued at the market price on the day of the grant for backdated stock options does violate securities laws

The Securities and Exchange Commission investigated 140 firms in 2006 and 2007 for potential problems with backdated stock options and filed civil charges against 24 companies and 66 individuals for offenses related to backdated stock options. At least 15 people have been convicted of criminal charges. When companies with backdated stock options correct their financial statements, the statements are restated with millions of dollars of compensation expense added to the income statement.

The largest backdated stock option restatement: Broadcom, a computer chip manufacturer in California, reported the largest restatement due to improperly backdating stock options. Broadcom recorded $2.24 billion in extra expenses. The most offensive backdated stock option scenario: stock prices dropped after the terrorist attacks on the World Trade Center and the Pentagon in the United States on September 11, 2001. Dozens of companies granted stock options to top executives when the stock price for the company was at a 60 year low. But in fact the stock grants were made weeks later and backdated to the date when the stock price hit its low. The companies backdated stock options to the week of the terrorist attacks when the stock market had its worst week in 60 years and pretended that the stocks options were granted on the favorable dates.[2]

Required:

    a. Discuss the accounting and ethical issues of this situation.

    b. Who are the stakeholders?

    c. Consider the conflicts of interest and the pressure on companies to issue stock options. Is anyone harmed or benefited by the possible choices?

14. Internal Controls for Cash Disbursements

According to an article in the newspaper, stealing $2.3 million from the Dakota Bank was simple. Joe Kramer, who lost the money gambling, was the bank's only full-time employee. Kramer said he began gambling to make the payments on a $50,000 loan to a friend, because the friend was unable to pay the loan. In a one year period, Kramer made 15 trips to Las Vegas, gambling to cover the $50,000 loan. Kramer, waiting for sentencing on a federal charge of looting, was fired from the bank one week before the institution was declared insolvent and closed its doors.

Required:

    a. Who are the stakeholders in this case?

    b. In the absence of effective internal control, what factors might have influenced Kramer not to embezzle?

    c. What internal controls might have prevented Kramer's theft?

    d. Joe Kramer lives in a town with fewer than 500 people. Would you be suspicious, in a town of this size, if the manager of the bank went to Las Vegas more than once a month? As a customer of the bank, what might you do to ensure that the manager was acting properly?

15. Accounts Receivable Write-Offs

John Simpson, the controller for Marshall Steel, is reviewing the accounts receivable aging schedule for the 2014 financial statements. One of his clients, Evans Manufacturing, has recently made several management changes and completed a restructuring of its long-term debt. In the past year, *The Wall Street Journal* has carried several stories regarding its financial difficulties. At the end of 2014, Evans Manufacturing has an outstanding balance of $2,600,000 on its account, a portion of which is more than 120 days past due. Management has assured Simpson that they will pay the balance owed as soon as they get their debt restructured. Based on this assurance, Simpson has decided not to write off the account at year-end and not to provide an allowance for a write-off in 2015. In January 2015, Simpson notices a report in *The Wall Street Journal* that Evans Manufacturing has filed for bankruptcy. From past experience Simpson knows that in bankruptcy situations he will collect less than 10% of the balance owed, so an adjustment probably should be made to the 2014 financial statements that have not yet been issued. Because this write-off will have a major impact on his financial statements, Simpson wants to ignore it until 2015, but he is not sure whether he can justify hiding this information from outsiders.

Required:

    a. What is the ethical dilemma described in this situation? The accounting problem?

    b. Identify the stakeholders in this decision. Who benefits? Who is harmed?

    c. What alternatives are available to John? Discuss and evaluate them.

    d. Would there be any temptation for John to ignore this new information about bankruptcy?

    e. What would you do? Explain your decision.

16. Warranty Expense

Cooperman, Inc., a pharmaceutical company, has a salary arrangement for 2014 that grants the financial vice president and several other executives $500,000 bonuses if net income increases by at least $100,000,000 in 2014. Noting that the current financial statements report an increase of $93,000,000 in net income, vice president Dick Bailey asks Elizabeth Watkins, the controller, to reduce the estimate of warranty expense by $10,000,000.

Required:

    a. What is the ethical dilemma in this situation?

    b. Relying on your knowledge of accounting standards to answer this question: what should Elizabeth do?

    c. Who is harmed if the estimate is lowered? Who benefits?

    d. What would you do? Do you have a choice about what to do if your supervisor tells you to reduce the warranty expense? (Do specific virtues come into conflict in this case?)

17. Samsung Group

The Samsung Group, with corporate headquarters in Seoul, South Korea, is the world's largest company by revenue with yearly revenue of $173.4 billion in 2008. The Samsung Group includes several business units including Samsung Electronics, the world's largest electronics company, Samsung Heavy Industries, the world's second largest shipbuilder, and Samsung C & T, a major global construction company. Since 2005 Samsung has been the world's most popular consumer electronics brand. It is the best known South Korean brand in the world. South Korea has been referred to as the "Republic of Samsung".

    In 2008, Kun-Hee Lee, the chairman of Samsung, was found guilty of tax evasion and given a suspended prison term. Mr. Lee paid a $110 million fine and back taxes equal to the fine. The judge in the case determined that his crime was not serious enough to send him to prison. The news broadcast of the decision by the judge came at the end of a six month investigation of the company. The news coverage and the announcement of the verdict was viewed as a prolonged, national shaming of the company, its executives, and the Lee family, the founders of the company.

    This fraud was brought to the attention of the justice department when a whistle-blower from Samsung alleged that the company had created secret bank accounts for paying bribes to influential South Koreans. The judge found no evidence of bribery but indicted Mr. Lee for using secret accounts to hide $4.5 billion in assets he inherited from his father, who founded the Samsung Company. This money had escaped taxation. Prosecutors had asked for a prison term for Mr. Lee, but the justice system in South Korea often allows the company to punish its executives rather than the courts even when the official decision is made in the courts.

South Koreans have complicated feelings towards Samsung. The company accounts for about 15% of the gross domestic product for the country. Many South Koreans feel that the company is too big and powerful, but fear that exposing the company to legal action could lead to a breakup of the company, and this would allow foreign investors to own parts of the company. Justice in South Korea must balance the demands of society for accountability against the possible harm to the Korean economy. This means that judges in South Korea often make decisions that are consistent with the broader sentiments in South Korean society rather than decisions based on a rule of law. In this case, Samsung, rather than the courts, took the most significant action resulting from the indictment – the chairman of the company resigned after the indictment was issued.[3]

Required:

Consider society as one of the stakeholders in this decision.

   a. What are the consequences of a justice system that balances the demand for accountability with the possible harm to the economy?

   b. How does an accountant make a technically proficient and ethically sensible decision when these consequences are a factor?

   c. In this setting, what are the conflicts of interest between stakeholders and how are they resolved?

   d. Can you think of decisions made by regulators in your country that reflect an emphasis on society as the major stakeholder in the decision?

18. Iraqi Food Contracts

American food companies are under investigation for possible fraud in connection with contracts to supply food to the US Army in Iraq. The inquiry is considering whether the companies set excessively high prices for food sold to a Kuwaiti firm called Public Warehousing Co., the Army's main food contractor for the war zone. Public Warehousing has revenue of about $3.6 billion per year, employs more than 20,000 people, and receives more than $1 billion per year to supply food to troops in Iraq and Kuwait.

Investigators have two questions regarding the contracts with Public Warehousing: (1) are the rebates received from various supplies by Public Warehousing proper; and (2) does Public Warehousing make exclusive arrangements with some suppliers, ignoring the competitive pricing that may be possible if prices from competing suppliers are considered?

Military contracts typically pay suppliers the cost of the goods they purchase plus a profit margin (referred to as a cost plus profit contract). Public

Warehousing's role is to negotiate the lowest prices. Both the supplier of the goods and Public Warehousing have an incentive to inflate the cost of the goods, because they could share the profit. Federal law prohibits government contractors from obtaining money due to false or fraudulent reasons.

Sara Lee, one of the US suppliers of meat and bakery products, paid Public Warehousing 5% of the purchase price as a rebate. This agreement was negotiated by Paul Simmons, a Sara Lee executive in charge of military sales. Simmons previously served as chief warrant officer for the Army. Sultan Center, the primary Kuwaiti supplier, paid a 10% refund to Public Warehousing on all orders received from the military. Sultan Center is owned by a Kuwaiti family that is one of the largest shareholders of Public Warehousing.

David Staples, a top procurement officer at the Army, once worked for Sara Lee's Jimmy Dean sausage unit. The records show that Mr. Staples required Army food contractors to purchase products from certain suppliers rather than allowing the contractors to shop around. Sara Lee is the favored supplier for chicken, turkey, ham, and sausage. All the beef purchased for US troops in Iraq and Kuwait comes from Quantum Foods, a meatpacker from Illinois. Quantum is represented by a former Army employee, Emily Prior. Until 2002 Ms. Prior had held Mr. Staples' job in the Army.[4]

Required:

a. Identify stakeholders in this situation. Who benefits; who is harmed?

b. What is the accounting and ethical problem discussed in this case?

c. How are conflicts of interest between stakeholders relevant to the case? What pressures does an accountant face negotiating the supplies contracts or paying for the contracts?

NOTES

1. SEC Litigation Release No. 18803, July 28, 2004; SEC Litigation Release No 18527, December 30, 2003; H. Sender, D. Reilly & M. Schroeder, "Parmalat investors missed red flags," *The Wall Street Journal*, January 7, 2004; A. Galloni, D. Reilly & C. Mollenkamp, "Skimmed off: Parmalat inquiry finds basic ruses at heart of scandal," *The Wall Street Journal*, December 31, 2003; Alessandra Galloni, "Scope of Parmalat's woes emerges," *The Wall Street Journal*, January 27, 2004; Alessandra Galloni & David Reilly, "Auditor raised Parmalat red flag," *The Wall Street Journal*, March 29, 2004; SEC Litigation Release No. 18527, December 30, 2003; A. Galloni, & D. Reilly. "Two Italian partners at Deloitte may face charges over Parmalat," *The Wall Street Journal*, May 13, 2005.

2. M. Maremont "Backdating likely more widespread," *The Wall Street Journal*, August 18, 2009; M. Maremont, C. Forelle & J. Bandler, "Companies say backdating used in days after 9/11," *The Wall Street Journal*, March 7, 2007; C. Forelle & J. Bandler, "Broadcom co-founder Nicholas faces much of backdating onus," *The Wall Street Journal*, January 24, 2007.

3. E. Ramstad, "Former Samsung chairman found guilty," *The Wall Street Journal*, July 17, 2008; E. Ramstad, " Samsung chairman charged with tax evasion," *The Wall Street Journal*, April 18, 2008; Samsung Group, Wikipedia, http://en.wikipedia.org/wiki/Samsung_Group, March 11, 2010.

4. G.R. Simpson, "Food companies face U.S. probe over Iraq deals," *The Wall Street Journal*, October 17, 2007.

REFERENCES

Bazerman, M.H., K. Morgan & G.F. Loewenstein. (1997) The impossibility of auditor independence. *MIT Sloan Management Review*, 38(4).

Freeman, R.E. (1984) *Strategic Management: A Stakeholder Perspective*. Boston: Pitman.

Friedman, M. (1970) The social responsibility of business is to increase its profits. *The New York Times Magazine*, September 13: 122–126.

Mill, John Stuart (1962) *Utilitarianism, On Liberty, Essay on Bentham*, edited by Mary Warnock. New York: A Meridian Book, The New American Library.

Mitchell, R.K., Agle, B.R. & Wood, D.J. (1997) Toward a theory of stakeholder identification and salience: Defining the principle of who and what really counts. *Academy of Management Review*, 22(4): 853–886.

Moore, D.A., Tetlock, P.E., Tanlu, L. & Bazerman, M.H. (2006) Conflicts of interest and the case of auditor independence: Moral seduction and strategic issue cycling. *Academy of Management Review*, 31(1): 10–29.

Rachels, J. & Rachels, S. (2009) *The Elements of Moral Philosophy*, 6th edn. Boston: McGraw-Hill.

Rest, J.R. (1994) Background. Theory and research. In Rest, J.R. & Narváez, D.F. (eds) *Moral Development in the Professions: Psychology and Applied Ethics*. Hillsdale, NJ: Lawrence Erlbaum Associates.

Svenson, O. & Maule, A.J. (1993) *Time Pressure and Stress in Human Decision Making*. Dordrecht: Springer.

Trevino, L.K. (1986) Ethical decision making in organizations: A person–situation interactionist model. *Academy of Management Review*, 11(3): 601–617.

Wells, J.T. (2008) *Principles of Fraud Examination*. New York: Wiley.

CHAPTER EIGHT

Generating and Assessing Decision Alternatives: Practical Wisdom and Action

LEARNING OBJECTIVES

By the end of this chapter you should be able to:

1. Understand the process of proposing specific solutions to accounting ethics problems.
2. Understand problem-definition in accounting ethics situations.
3. Explain the process of posing and evaluating possible solutions to accounting ethics problems.
4. Explain the process of evaluating decision alternatives in light of accounting standards and through reasoned moral inquiry.
5. Describe pressures and conflicts of interest that influence decisions and taking action.
6. Understand the importance and the difficulty of moving from judgments and choices to action within the decision process.
7. Understand the application of practical wisdom in assessing decision alternatives.

DEFINING ACCOUNTING ETHICS PROBLEMS AND RESOURCES FOR DECISION MAKING

Reminder: Situations in accounting ethics often pose both an accounting problem and an ethical problem.

Reminder: Defining a problem includes recognizing the gap between the ideal for a circumstance and identifying the limitations, restrictions, and distractions in a current situation.

Reminder: The conceptual framework of accounting, accounting standards, and professional codes of conduct are key resources for defining accounting ethics problems and shaping the decision process to solve these problems.

Reminder: The accountant's inquiry and analysis during the decision process can make use of the resources of moral philosophy. Decision making is enhanced by selected features of moral philosophy – the concepts, questions, and answers of philosophical ethics as they become relevant to the specialized tasks of accounting.

Reminder: Focusing on the moral tradition of virtue ethics: the accountant as a moral agent engages in a decision process with a character shaped by intellectual and moral virtues. The accountant's virtues are expressed in moral reasoning and through ethical actions.

INTRODUCTION

The contents of Chapter Eight continue treatment of the decision model. The issues discussed in the chapter fit within the last two boxes in the decision model reproduced in Figure 8.1, labeled *Generate and Assess Decision Alternatives* and *Practical Judgment and Action.* The chapter treats several cases where an accountant must define accounting and ethical problems in a given situation, identify and describe their main features, and engage in a decision process to solve the problems. Primary

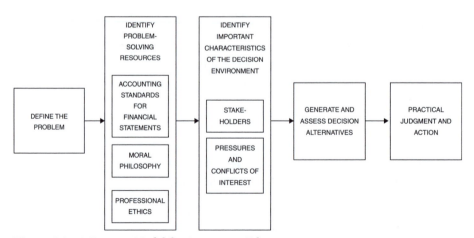

Figure 8.1   A Decision Model for Accounting Ethics

attention is given to the process of posing alternatives to address the accounting issue and resolve the moral dilemma within the situation. These possible solutions to the accounting and ethical problems are evaluated and action-choices are suggested. The decisions and suggestions for the course of action are assessed. This evaluation takes into account the several resources that express the values and norms of contemporary accounting practice (the conceptual framework, accounting standards, and codes of conduct). The assessment will also consider the concepts and patterns of inquiry of moral philosophy. Special attention is given to the concept of practical wisdom and the judgments made as the accountants' virtues are brought to bear in circumstances where principles and rules of accounting practice are applied. Practical wisdom concerns how virtues are expressed whenever principles and rules are employed to deal with stakeholders' conflicts of interests and cope with various pressures in business situations.

REFLECTIONS ON OUR DECISION MODEL

As we developed the chapters of this book, we have made repeated references to our own decision model. This repetition highlights specific ideas and key values in our accounting theory and approach to accounting ethics. First, we claim that accounting situations often pose both an accounting problem and an ethical problem; thus we can emphasize the importance of turning toward the resources of accounting standards and moral philosophy in order to address these two types of problems. At the most basic level, we affirm the ethical obligation of the accountant to adhere to accounting standards (including the conceptual framework and the principles expressed in professional codes of conduct). Such compliance is the accountant's ethics of duty, as we have labeled it. The values and norms of contemporary accounting practice ought to shape the decision processes of every accountant. As professionals, accountants "adhere to the principles and follow the rules," as we have argued.

We give comparable importance to the use of reasoned argument and the resources of moral philosophy. The accountant as moral agent ought to engage in reasoning that makes use of the concepts, concerns and patterns of argumentation (inquiry, analysis, decision making, and explanation) that are associated with philosophical ethics. The traditions of moral philosophy are best seen as rich resources for the specialized tasks of accounting ethics decision making. In short, the intellectual and moral resources of philosophical ethics enable us to consider accounting as a domain of "applied ethics" (as we have earlier argued). Let us take all these features together. When accounting situations are rightly perceived as having two dimensions, the dual competency of accounting can be achieved through using the resources of accounting standards and moral philosophy. The competent accountant – that is, the professional who is technically proficient and ethically sensible – can identify and define moral issues and resolve these problems and dilemmas whenever they are encountered in accounting situations.

The earlier chapters have also gone beyond decision scenarios to highlight another key feature of ethics inquiry, the topic we called, "the ethics of virtue". The main concerns of this topic include the development and realization of character traits, virtues, as crucial components of personal and professional life that the accountant brings to bear in moral awareness, decision making, and action-choices. The intellectual and moral virtues embedded in the accountant's character, we have argued, are themselves significant resources for the accountant's practice. With this in mind, our discussion of accounting ethics cases advocates using the concepts and patterns of reasoning of the virtue ethics tradition. As we have seen, a number of accounting ethics scholars turn to this tradition of moral philosophy. In addition to Mary and Thomas Doucet, whose work we cited in Chapter Five, Steven Mintz and Roselyn Morris, Mark Cheffers and Michael Pakaluk, and Linda Thorne highlight the significance of the accountants' (and auditors') virtues as necessary components in their decision making (Doucet & Doucet, 2004; Mintz, 1996; Mintz & Morris, 2011; Thorne, 1998; Cheffers & Pakaluk, 2011).

The structure of our decision model includes a comprehensive list of resources that are available for decision making. These intellectual and moral elements are crucial for identifying moral problems within accounting situations, for analyzing the key features of these issues, resolving the dilemmas, and taking ethical action. The following treatment of accounting ethics cases and professionals' decision making brings these key elements together: (1) the demands of a dual competence on the part of accountants, (2) moral reasoning that presupposes the existence of technical and ethical problems in accounting ethics situations, (3) the accessibility of the rich resources of professional standards and moral philosophy, and (4) the existence of intellectual and moral virtues within the individual characters of working accountants. In particular, the chapter concentrates on the task of generating and assessing decision alternatives (after moral issues are identified and defined).

YEAR-END ADJUSTING PROCESS, ADJUSTING ENTRIES, BAD DEBT EXPENSE ESTIMATES

The following cases give examples of accounting and ethical problems involving adjusting entries and processes of matching expenses and revenues. The decision process includes identifying the accounting problem and the ethical problem(s). You are asked to focus on the main features of the problems and to propose alternatives and decide on appropriate solutions to the problems. The inquiry and analysis includes evaluating decision alternatives. You should make use of the resources provided by the accounting standards and the traditions of moral philosophy.

Case 1: Performance-Based Bonuses

John Feagin and Beth Larson, accountants at Smith Manufacturing, are discussing the year-end adjusting process. Beth has just had lunch with the president of the company, Lindsay Norton, and Lindsay suggested that Beth could be a good friend by doing her part to increase net income for the current year. Lindsay has just purchased a new house, and she is relying on her bonus payment to furnish the home. If Beth could make sure that net income increased by at least 10% this year, Lindsay would receive a substantial bonus. Lindsay suggested that Beth aggressively accrue revenues at year-end and delay recording as many expenses as possible. Beth is confused by this request and asks John for advice.

    a. Discuss the accounting and ethical issues of this situation. Who are the stakeholders? Consider the conflicts of interest and the pressure on Beth. Is anyone harmed or benefited by the possible choices?

    b. What alternatives are available to Beth? What advice should John offer?

    c. What does Beth stand to gain by complying with Lindsay's request? What does she stand to lose?

    d. What advice would you give Beth? How would you explain your position to John?

Case 2: Recording Expense Entries

The controller for Anderson Electric, Ron Foss, is reviewing the year-end adjusting entries prepared by the accounting staff for approval before they are posted to the general ledger. Angela Bennett, the company president, has suggested that the December accrual for wage expense be delayed until January, because the company needs to report a higher net income for the year. The December 31 financial statements will be reviewed for a loan by the bank. The company has a better chance of getting the loan if its net income is higher, and the loan will have a lower interest rate if the company appears to be healthy. Ron is unsure whether he should comply with the president's request. It doesn't seem to Ron that it is terribly important whether the expense is recorded in December or January. He wonders about the relevant accounting standards. Ron also knows that the company needs the loan to continue paying the salaries next year, so he does not want to do anything to jeopardize his own salary.

    a. What is the ethical dilemma described in this problem?

    b. Based on your knowledge of the accounting standards, what is the answer to this dilemma?

    c. Identify the interested parties involved in the decision. Who benefits? Who is harmed?

    d. List several alternatives available to Ron.

    e. What would you do? Explain your answer.

Case 3: Bad Debt Expense

Andrew Olson, controller for Phoenix International, has a new employment contract for 2014. The company has experienced rapid growth in the last year and management negotiated a bonus arrangement for its top executives. Andrew is excited about the new arrangement: if net income increases 10% over the prior year, he is entitled to a substantial bonus. In anticipation of the bonus, he is about to purchase a new boat on an installment plan. He has the check written for the down payment on the boat and plans to mail it today. He is confident that he can use the bad debt expense account to show that income increased by 10% this year. This account is just an estimate, and because he knows the increase in net income is currently above 6%, he should be able to manipulate the bad debt expense estimate to increase net income to the 10% level. If he lowers the estimate slightly, he is guaranteed his bonus and his new boat.

a. What is the accounting issue involved in this problem?

b. Should Andrew lower his estimate to permit payment of the bonus? Why or why not?

c. Who are the stakeholders in this situation? Who benefits? Who is harmed?

d. What would you do if you were in this situation? Defend your answer.

e. If Andrew does not lower his estimate, how might he explain his decision to the other executives (who might also lose their bonuses)?

f. If Andrew does lower his estimate, how can he justify his decision?

Case 4: Operating Loans

John Haug, controller of Tenant Company, is reviewing the year-end financial statements with Tom Henry, the company president. The financial statements currently report a net income of $10,563,480 before adjusting entries. Tom is applying for a bank loan to build a new manufacturing facility and would like to report a net income of at least $12,750,000. Tom suggests accruing several large sales based on orders received, even though the goods will not be shipped at year-end. He says, "If we record sales revenue for these two large orders, our net income should be more than $12,750,000. We will never notice the loss of these sales next year, because when we build the new manufacturing facility our sales revenue will dramatically increase."

a. What is the accounting problem described in this case? Is there an ethical problem?

b. Based on your knowledge of the accounting standards, can you resolve this dilemma?

c. What alternatives are available to John?

d. What would you do? Would your answer change if you knew the financial statements would not be audited, so it would be unlikely that your "error" would be caught?

e. Would your answer change if you knew that Tom's bonus depended on increasing net income to $12,750,000? Why?

f. Would you change your mind if you knew the president would fire you if you did not increase net income to his goal of $12,750,000? Is your answer ethical?

Case 5: Bad Debt Expense

Steve Olson and Sally Bosh, accountants at the sportswear division of Hanes Clothing, are discussing the bad debt expense allowance to be recorded at December 31, 2013. In 2012 they based their estimate on 2% of net credit sales. The actual percentage written off in 2013 was 2.5%. Sally suggests that they increase the percentage to 4% for 2014. She says, "Even though I expect the bad debt write-offs to be about the same in 2013, I am a little concerned about our net income. With our current figures, our income has increased by 18%. That's a great increase, but probably not something we can match in 2014. If we report an increase of 18% in net income this year, the corporate office and the market analysts will expect us to achieve an 18% or higher growth rate in 2014. It might be simpler if we just increase our bad debt expense to 4% to keep our net income at a 10% increase. That way, we'll look good this year, but won't raise unreasonable expectations from the corporate office and will still be able to meet the expectations of analysts."

    a. Explain why increasing the allowance for doubtful account percentage reduces net income.

    b. Should Sally be concerned with the growth rate for the sportswear division when estimating the allowance for doubtful accounts? Is this improper? Explain your answer.

    c. Does the estimate of bad debt expense pose an ethical dilemma for Steve and Sally? If so, state the dilemma and give your reasons.

    d. Identify the interested parties involved in this decision. Who benefits? Who is harmed?

    e. Does reliance on the accounting standards resolve this dilemma? Explain your answer.

    f. What alternatives are available to Sally?

    g. What would you do? Why?

Evaluation of Decision Alternatives: Cases 1–5

In general terms, each of the five cases above presents the accounting problem of accruing expenses and revenues to serve the primary purpose of financial accounting to communicate high-quality information to potential users and to do this in accordance with the principles and rules of contemporary accounting standards. Notice that in each case there are pressures of time and deadlines and pressures exerted by one stakeholder or another to increase or decrease the net income, in effect to "manage the earnings" of the company. The basic resource that is necessary for resisting these pressures is a solid grasp of the fundamental principle and the specific techniques of the accrual method. Knowledge of the concepts and the processes of moral reasoning is also important.

    The accrual principle requires the accountant to recognize revenues as the goods have been shipped or the services provided and to recognize expense when the company has received the benefits of the good or service. This means that revenues and expenses should be recorded in the appropriate period.

    In the first case, "Performance-Based Bonuses," Beth has been asked to "accrue revenues aggressively" but "delay recording" some expenses in the year-end adjustment process. Considered as an action to take, this is a prospective decision. In this situation, the accounting problem has to do with whether the basic principle of the accrual method is achieved by pursuing this alternative. To address the problem, Beth must ask: "When is the appropriate period for recognizing revenues and the related expenses? Is it appropriate to recognize revenue in one period but to delay recognition of the related expenses to another period?" According to the accounting standards, Beth should answer: "It is *not appropriate* to recognize the revenue, for example, from a sales order in one period while delaying recognition of the expenses related to that sale." Of course, she might remind herself (and even say to Lindsay?) that one recognizes revenue when an order is shipped, without waiting for receipt of the customer's payment, for this does meet the accounting standards. *But delay in recognizing the expenses is not ethical.*

Both John and Beth, as professional accountants, should understand their "ethic of duty" to follow the contemporary accounting standards. Yet despite the clear accounting standard, Lindsay as president of the company is exerting real pressure on Beth. This pressure is a key feature of the situation: Beth confronts a significant dilemma. As a powerful stakeholder, Lindsay has appealed to Beth's "friendship" and suggested that Beth's virtue of expressing "loyalty" ought to come into play in this situation. The dilemma is created because Beth has a duty to her profession, an obligation to honor and advance the principles and rules of professional accounting. This duty challenges Beth's expression of loyalty to Lindsay. Explicitly, recognizing the revenues and expenses in proper fashion serves the purpose of providing high-quality information to various groups of stakeholders – current stockholders, potential investors, lenders. Beth's overriding duty, beyond her loyalty to the company president, her "friendship," is to provide a faithful and relevant representation of the financial status of the company to these "outside" stakeholders.

Beth might well appeal to the "public principle" in explaining her decision to John (and any of the stakeholders in this case). By this we mean that Beth show a willingness to explain her decision to every party who is interested in the outcome of the situation. What is more, Beth's performance of her duty honors the public trust and will likely build up respect for the accounting profession.

In the second case, "Recording Expense Entries," the accounting problem also has to do with the appropriate application of the accrual method, this time with the proper recognition of wage expense. Ron, the accountant, should know that wage expense should be recognized in the period in which the labor service is done; that is, when the company has received the benefit of the service. In addition to the pressure exerted by the company president, Angela, Ron – worrying about his own salary – is distracting himself from meeting his professional obligation to follow the standards of accounting. He is, in effect, one of the stakeholders in the situation. Yet even given the emotional power of this personal conflict of interest, it should still not outweigh Ron's ethic of duty. An accountant is supposed to serve other stakeholders, not advance his or her own interests. The financial and emotional impact on Ron himself must be dismissed as he evaluates his decision alternatives.

Failure to record wage expense properly may cause real harm to the bank; the loan officer will not have the high-quality information that is necessary for determining the risk of advancing a loan to Anderson Electric. The officer will not be able decide on the correct rate of interest to charge because he or she will not know the actual risk.

The alternative of delaying the wage expense until January is manipulative and deceptive. In utilitarian terms, it will not lead to "happy results" and will not maximize utility for the stakeholders. In deontological terms, the financial statements will not "tell the truth" about the financial status of the company. In the language of virtue ethics: Ron's advice does not embody the virtue of honesty; his failure to resist Angela's pressure demonstrates a lack of integrity and courage. He has subordinated his own decision making to some other person.

What is more, Ron has put his complex intellectual skills and technical knowledge (his intellectual "virtues") into the service of an unworthy goal, the protection of his own company's interest at the expense of another institution that does not deserve such treatment. (Thus he violates the ethical principle of fair treatment.) Finally, Ron might ask himself: "Would I be happy to have my decision examined in a newspaper account or as the subject of a TV news item?" (the public principle).

The third case, "Bad Debt Expense," brings a new twist – the responsibility to make "the best estimate" in an accounting situation. In this case, Andrew, the controller, anticipates a bonus and the purchase of a new boat with that bonus. The bonus is linked to an increase of net income by 10% over the previous year. He reasons that if he lowers his estimate of the bad debt expense account, this will have the impact of increasing net earnings for the year, thus making him eligible for his bonus.

Because from one year to the next, it is difficult to guess how high the estimate of bad debt expense should be, Andrew seems to think that his slight adjustment (to lower the estimate) will not harm anyone and since there is no precise rule in the accounting standards for such a practice, that he is doing nothing wrong. In his mind, there seems to be neither an accounting problem nor any particular ethical problem. The other stakeholders that he considers are the executives who will also gain a bonus if the net income is increased by 10% over the previous year.

But is Andrew reasoning correctly according to the accounting standards and meeting his own ethical responsibilities? The accounting problem centers on what are acceptable practices for making estimates regarding the bad debt expense. While the standards do not prescribe a precise formula for such a decision, a number of things are normally considered. Sometimes a company estimates bad debt expenses as a percentage of the total credit sales, looking at the accounts receivable written off during previous years (usually two, three, or four years) as a check on the realism of the estimate. In another method, typically accounts receivable are considered overdue after a period of time, 20 or 30 days, for example. The company then determines different categories of late payments, starting with the "due date," and then counting the total days that the accounts receivable are late; for example, 1–30, 31–60, 61–90, and so on. This method presupposes that one can determine the number and the value of accounts receivable for specific periods of time. For either method, one might also consider an assessment of market conditions and any policies the company may have in place to extend credit to customers, however risky they might be. (What these have in common is that they have nothing directly to do with a goal increasing net income, but are focused on determining a pattern of payment.) What is more, because estimates are usually accompanied by explanatory footnotes in the financial statements, Andrew may well point to market conditions or changes in policy with regard to extending credit to specific classes of customers to support his rationale for changing the estimate.

Yet whatever the acceptable alternatives for computing the estimate and expressing the footnote, one must ask with regard to Andrew's ethical problem in this situation: "Who benefits and who gains if the bad debt expense estimate 'triggers' or fails to trigger the conditions for bonuses?" If the estimate triggers bonus payments, the company is liable for the payments to its executives. These moneys, in effect, reduce net income and possibly deprive stockholders of dividends or reduce revenue available for other company purposes. From another angle, the net income that results from manipulating the bad debt expense estimate is a form of "managed earnings," suggesting that management policies of production and marketing (for example) have prompted the company growth, when in reality the increase in net income is a type of "accounting trick".

If we focus on Andrew's explanation to justify his decision – either to lower or to hold the bad debt estimate steady with previous years – we can identify the executives as a stakeholder group (that may or may not receive the bonuses linked to increased net income). Andrew's explanation, however, should take other important stakeholder groups into account. The "public principle" behind an explanation makes it possible to assess whether Andrew's decision constitutes "fair treatment" for these groups (whatever its impact on the executive group.) Finally (to complicate the issue!), it may be argued that if the lower estimate is very slight (in relation to total credit sales, or compared with actual write-offs in previous reporting periods), the overall impact on net income is not a material consideration so the ethical issue is of little importance.

In our fourth case, "Operating Loans," the decision is whether or not to increase net income by recognizing the revenue from two large orders as adjusting entries at year-end. This is considered a prospective action, even though the goods will not be shipped at year-end. The increased net income will likely enhance the possibility of a bank loan (or ensure a loan at a lower rate of interest than probable if net income is lower). Is this action permissible under contemporary accounting standards? Is there an ethical problem in recording the sales revenue in this manner?

What is the accounting problem in the situation? There is a straightforward answer: revenue should be recognized when the order is shipped. Because the goods are not yet shipped, revenue should not be recognized in the year-end adjusting process. The ethical problem is also straightforward: a failure to follow accounting standards is unethical, a failure to meet the accountant's ethics of duty as the obligation to meet professional standards. By not communicating high-quality information to stakeholders (the bank), the bankers will not be able to confirm the past performance of the company or predict future performance. This will hinder the bank's decision on whether or not to grant a loan and make it difficult for them to determine an interest rate appropriate to the risk.

Of course, if the net increase were linked to a bonus payment or if you were threatened with the loss of your job in such a situation, these are significant pressures that could distract you from doing your professional duty. Nevertheless, following the accounting standard is a sound moral principle, an imperative (in deontological language). It may be argued that the utilitarian standard of utility is more difficult to apply here, as it may be difficult to balance the personal consequences of losing a bonus or being fired with the benefits of providing high-quality information to various, but anonymous stakeholders. But it is also clear that the situation calls for the expression of the virtues of honesty and integrity, courage to stand against pressures, and a commitment to "tell the truth" in your accounting practice. As we see: the resources of moral philosophy can play a role in evaluating the decision alternatives of this case.

The fifth case, "Bad Debt Expense," returns to the issue of making a best estimate on a bad debt allowance, but the decision has a unique twist. Steve and Sally wonder whether the company's net earnings may be too *high*! They are concerned that higher net income may inflate expectations for future performance and that this may be harmful (in some way) to the company. To offset this worry, they consider increasing the estimate for bad debt (so that net income will be somewhat reduced).

Again, the accounting problem is that the standards do not specify exactly how estimates are to be made. We see that the company has used a method based on a percentage of credit sales, with a review of the actual write-off in one previous year. Steve and Sally consider raising the estimate from the previous write-off of 2.5% to 4%, even though Sally does not expect the actual write-off to increase.

As with the previous example, the normal patterns of making estimates look at credit sales, delays in payment, and actual customer behavior. To bring a concern for net income into this process does not fit this pattern, but does it constitute an ethical problem, let us say, a manipulation or deception that causes harm to someone or is it an example of failing to perform a professional duty? Insofar as the decision will reduce the quality of information that is communicated to stakeholders, the accountant's ethic of duty is violated. What is more, present stockholders will be harmed by the artificially lowered net earnings; potential investors will not have a faithful and relevant representation of the company performance (the distorted picture will not confirm previous performance or predict the company's financial future). It may well be that Sally and Steve are more worried that the high expectations will create "on the job" pressures for themselves and fellow employees than they are concerned to carry out their jobs as professional accountants. They are distracted from serving the interests of outside stakeholders and honoring the public trust.

A VIOLATION OF ACCOUNTING STANDARDS? BUT NOT AN ETHICAL PROBLEM?

Case 6: Matching Expenses to Revenue

Andrea's new accounting supervisor, Kathryn Baldwin, is very demanding and wants everything done perfectly. She reviews the supplies account for St. John's College and wants to know why Andrea is expensing the computers purchased this year. She says, "Don't you know that computers should be depreciated over three years? Your behavior is unethical. You should never expense equipment that can be used for more than one year. Didn't you learn anything in school? The only way a company can prepare an accurate income statement is to match expenses with revenues. If you take all the expense for the computers in year one, but use these computers for three years, you are not matching revenues and expenses. I can't believe you would engage in this type of unethical behavior."

    a. Is there an accounting problem? Is there an ethical problem?

    b. How should Andrea respond?

    c. Is Andrea acting unethically? Should she change her procedure for expensing computers?

    d. How should Andrea explain her decision to Kathryn?

The selection of this case addresses a concern generated by the authors' classroom experience and their previous use of ethics textbooks. In the books and classroom, accounting problems and ethical problems are almost always "packaged" and labeled in the cases. In real life, accounting situations do not come pre-packaged with labels that point to the accounting and ethical problems embedded in the circumstance. And while it is common for real life situations with confusing technical accounting issues also to have moral issues, this is not always the case.

Consider Kathryn's comments about what Andrea has done (a retrospective attitude) with regard to technical accounting rules and her remark about Andrea's supposedly unethical behavior. First ask: "Is Kathryn correct about the appropriate accounting standard with regard to equipment purchases where the equipment will be used for three years (or more)?" If Kathryn is correct, then Andrea has made a mistake by not depreciating the computers. She should not have taken all the computer expense in year one. But now ask a second question: "Is Andrea's accounting decision unethical?" Of course, we might answer (as we have in discussing previous cases) that failure to apply the appropriate accounting standard in itself violates an ethics of duty. This, however, is not a satisfactory remark for this situation. Recall the discussion in Chapter Two regarding the expectation that accountants demonstrate a dual competency, where technical knowledge and ethical sensibility are both crucial. From that discussion, you will remember that ignorance of technical requirements or lack of technical proficiency is not necessarily a failure of ethics. It is possible to be virtuous but also to be technically incompetent. (Thus Kathryn's scathing remark: "Didn't you learn anything in school?")

Consider this case in prospective terms: assuming that Andrea realizes her accounting mistake, should she now revise the financial statements by depreciating the computers? More pointedly, will Andrea in some fashion be unethical if knowing the appropriate accounting standard, she now does not change the statements? To address these questions, you might ask: "Are there any stakeholders who are harmed by either expensing the computers or depreciating them?" Quite likely, no stakeholders are harmed. (The school is not likely to be owned by stockholders or to be evaluated by outsiders for investment purposes, so its net earnings are not that important. No school officials are going to be evaluated, promoted or paid bonuses in relation to this accounting decision; no bank loans are at stake.)

From another angle, the school management will, of course, be concerned about the market value of its property, plant, and equipment, but since there is no cash flow associated with the accounting decision to recognize computer expense or depreciate the computers (no tuition fees at stake), no harm is done by Andrea's decision. Is Andrea acting unethically by expensing the computers if she chooses not to depreciate them in a financial restatement? Because no harm is done to stakeholders, no cash flow is impacted, and there is no conceivable loss of goodwill or reputation to the institution that can be linked to this decision, there is no ethical issue at stake. Andrea is not acting unethically, even though she is not following the accounting standards.

INTERNAL CONTROLS AND EMBEZZLEMENT

Case 7: The Christian Thief

A large Christian church in the Midwest held three worship services each Sunday. Its voluntary offering was collected and counted by three ushers at the first two services. The ushers listed the checks and the loose cash on a slip and put the list and offering in the church safe. The third offering, however, was counted by the congregational treasurer, who then calculated the total for three services, prepared the deposit slip and placed the offering in a bank drop box on Sunday afternoon. This process went on for about five years.

In response to suggestions by an "audit review committee," the practice was examined, and it was determined that the treasurer had embezzled as much as $25–50,000 over the period, simply by removing loose cash and manipulating the deposit amounts accordingly. The head pastor decided to fire the treasurer but not to publicize the theft or prosecute the treasurer through the courts. (The pastor stated that the publicity would anger parishioners and affect the congregation's future offerings.) The assistant pastor disagreed with the pastor's decision. He wanted to play the role of "whistle-blower". He argued that the treasurer should be prosecuted and the case publicly discussed, claiming that the trial and publicity would deter a future crime and eventually sway public opinion that the church had taken proper steps to overcome its earlier mistakes. In effect, there would be a wave of sympathy and goodwill expressed for the congregational decision.

a. What is the accounting problem?

b. What is the ethical problem associated directly to the theft?

c. What conflicts of interest are expressed in the disagreement between the pastors?

d. If you were an accountant, what advice might you give to the pastors?

This case demonstrates the accounting problem of internal controls and a failure to make use of an independent auditor during the five year period. The church treasurer took advantage because there was no "segregation of duties" in the collection, counting, and depositing of the Sunday offering. The paperwork that listed the earlier services' offering was left available to the dishonest treasurer who could then manipulate the totals without being caught. (This is to say nothing of the poor practice whereby the treasurer counted the third service offering by himself, with no one else checking the amount or witnessing the handling of the loose currency.)

In terms of the elements of the "fraud triangle," discussed in Chapter Four, the treasurer had ample *opportunity* to engage in fraud – both to misuse (steal) the congregation's resources and to manipulate the Sunday morning reporting system and the procedure for preparing the bank deposit slips. In addition, the temptation to remove loose currency likely became a strong *pressure* that was exaggerated because Sunday after Sunday the treasurer did not have to worry about being caught. Finally, the treasurer-thief might have *rationalized* his behavior by thinking that the amount each week was rather small and the loss did not do significant damage to the church or its projects.

The disagreement between the pastors over how to treat the theft and deal with the thief expresses differing views about the *power* and *legitimacy* of stakeholders (an issue treated in Chapter Six). The pastors regard the congregational membership as a significant stakeholder group, with a legitimate stake in the fate of its weekly offering moneys. Despite their legitimate stake, the membership was rendered powerless to prevent the theft because of the lack of internal controls. Both pastors recognize the members' current power in their ability to give or withhold future offerings. This ability means that the aggregate influence of the membership continues to represent a strong financial power (and future choices to exercise such power may well be translated into pressures to influence congregational policy and effect the pastors' own positions of authority).

Quite likely both pastors realize these things, but they differ in assessing how the members may respond to news of the theft and the propriety of the thief's punishment. (Is it severe enough? Is he being treated better than he deserves?) The pastors likely differ on how publicity may affect the reputation of the congregation or the membership's respect for the "management–pastoral" team. In this case, will anger at the theft, the thief, or the pastor-manager's failure undermine the willingness of members to contribute money to the congregation? Will compassion and a spirit of forgiveness prevail? Or will practical concerns for the financial well-being of the congregation predominate? (In effect, will the intellectual or the moral virtues of the aggregate membership influence the level of their future participation in the church?)

TO BRIBE OR NOT TO BRIBE: THAT IS THE QUESTION

Case 8: Corrupt Practices and Bribery

Liebold Manufacturing is an American company that builds small-engine machinery for lawn-care, woodland management, and low-acreage farming. It owns a factory in Burmathai, an emerging nation. The managers of this plant want to expand to a new site. Their project is being delayed because local government officials and some building contractors have solicited bribes, threatening further delays and have even threatened to block the project altogether.

In this region, it has become common practice to deal with such matters by hiring consultant firms which will handle the construction contracts and municipal permits. In effect, the consultants "negotiate" the bribes and pay them without the direct knowledge of the manufacturing company. The bribe moneys are included in the general payment made by the manufacturer to the consulting firm.

John Lundal, the factory manager in Burmathai, and his chief accountant, Ted Owens, are discussing their complicated situation. John says, "Payment of bribes is a normal business practice in Burmathai. This plant expansion is vital to our business here. If we do not expand (pay the bribes that are necessary), we will no longer be able to compete in this local market." Ted counters, "It is against American law to pay bribes." (According to American law, The Foreign Corrupt Practices Act of 1977, payment of a bribe by an American company is an illegal business practice, even if it is done in a foreign nation.) Ted continues, "We cannot show such transactions in our financial reports. It would be unethical for me to hide the bribery transactions in the financial statements. Do not ask me to do this."

John responds, "You cannot be serious. We cannot let some American law or American accounting rules prevent us from doing business in Burmathai. We have a right to pursue our own business interests and we must 'play by the local rules' (where everyone accepts bribery as a normal business practice). Isn't this a social contract idea? Ted, do you want to keep your job?"

a. What is the accounting problem? The ethical problem(s)?

b. John, the manager, is a key stakeholder. Is his power great in this situation? Is he a legitimate authority over Ted; is his business view of this matter also legitimate?

c. Does Ted have a right to resist paying bribes, even if the project is blocked, appealing to accounting standards and professional codes of conduct?

d. Discuss the ethical aspects of turning to the consulting firm as a "bribe negotiator". This common practice means, in effect, that the manufacturing company condones the pattern of bribery and is aware that its money is being used to pay off contractors and officials.

There are powerful pressures at play in this situation – Liebold Manufacturing is struggling to compete in the Burmathai market, Ted's job is at stake, legal issues play a role, paying bribes will lead to falsifying financial statements and business records. In this context, it is important to "define the problem" by identifying the accounting issue(s) and determining the nature of the ethical dilemma.

The American Foreign Corrupt Practices Act does not directly cite accountants, nor do accounting standards specify that "accountants are not to pay or receive bribes," but keep in mind the primary purpose of accounting. The accountant is supposed to produce and communicate high-quality information – faithfully representative and relevant – to stakeholders. Professional codes of conduct advise the accountant to avoid behavior that undermines public trust in the profession. These expectations demonstrate an ethical problem in the circumstance, and Ted's professional responsibilities call him to an "ethics of duty". He should not be involved in the falsification of financial statements (for the purpose of hiding bribe moneys).

Imagine, for the moment, that Ted did comply with his boss' instructions and got involved with the bribery payments by hiding the transactions in the financial statements. How could he justify his actions publicly? Could he report to his board of directors, stockholders, potential investors that he had written the bribe payments into one expense account or another? Would Ted find it acceptable if a TV report were to describe the company's action? By invoking this "public principle," we can see there is something wrong here!

Yet consider the powerful pressure of Liebold Manufacturing's desire to compete in the Burmathai market. Could that purpose be achieved by hiring a local consulting firm to handle the contract negotiations and permit arrangements to move the expansion project forward? With this practice, neither John, the manager, nor Ted, the accountant, would have direct knowledge of the bribery payments, and Liebold Manufacturing's financial statements could be prepared by recognizing the various expenses related to the consulting fees (without specifying bribery payments). Might this be an acceptable alternative, for it is a common practice in some markets (even though almost every nation has legislation directed against bribery and other forms of business corruption)? In effect, John and Ted "turn a blind eye" as the consulting firm takes the necessary measures for pushing the project forward (including the payment of bribes). Without direct knowledge (and without documentation!), neither John nor Ted will be breaking the American law or ignoring specific accounting standards or violating principles of a professional code.

Such an approach, however, seems to be entering a morally "gray" area. This would especially be the case if John asked Ted to work with the consulting firm on the expense invoices they submit to Liebold Manufacturing. In effect, Ted would be giving them "expert" accounting advice on how to keep the bribe payments secret. In utilitarian terms, active participation in a practice founded on bribe payments would be difficult to justify as an acceptable means for creating happiness for the citizens of Burmathai, manufacturing companies and other stakeholders. In deontological terms, it would be difficult for Ted to state a moral principle that would be reasonable, and he might be hard pressed to advocate the Liebold practice of working with such a consulting arrangement as an admirable "universal" practice that could be recommended to others. In virtue ethics language, would "turning a blind eye" really advance the virtue of honesty or express personal integrity? Would not "truth telling" be undermined in this practice?

In yet another angle, we could focus on Ted's own commitment as an employee to the business goals of Liebold Manufacturing. In this light, Ted might advise John to delay the project, to "muddle along," and continue to struggle in the Burmathai market: "Maybe things will change with regard to the practice of bribery. Burmathai has its own anti-bribery laws, there are social reformers who publicly denounce bribery and the business environment may be changing. Maybe even we could publicize our own frustration and speak out against those officials and contractors who were blocking a business project that really would benefit Burmathai's society by creating more jobs, fostering economic growth, and expanding the tax base. We do not have to sit by idly and accept the normalcy of corruption."

A final set of remarks: our discussion of this case is weighted against the acceptance of the practice of bribery, of course. Yet, in the language of Chapters Two and Six, Ted, John, and Liebold Manufacturing may be forced to pay a high cost for making ethical decisions, following the American law, and adhering to the spirit, if not the letter, of accounting standards and codes. The company may be forced out of the Burmathai market; John might be removed by his American supervisors for not acting in the company interests by using a consulting firm; Ted's advice to wait or for Liebold to criticize Burmathai society may be deemed too "political" or too much beyond the scope of ordinary business activity by the board of directors or the American management.

Case 9: Cash Salary Payments at Joe's Taco Shop

Joe employs 50 full- and part-time workers at his taco shop. Forty employees are full-time and he pays their salaries by transferring the money to their bank accounts. He makes retirement fund payments, healthcare payments, workman's compensation payments, and tax payments to the government for these employees. Several of his part-time workers ask that he do the same for their wages, but he wants to pay the part-time workers in cash. This means that he does not have to withhold income tax from their salaries or make payments to the government for their retirement and healthcare benefits. Both Joe and the employees benefit by this approach. Joe avoids paying for health insurance and retirement benefits (about 35% of the wage expense). The employees benefit because they can choose not to pay income tax on the cash payments. The employees receiving cash payments may also be illegal immigrants working in the country without permission.

Joe's accountant is unsure whether he should follow Joe's orders. They would be violating employment laws, making distinctions between full- and part-time workers, and possibly limiting some part-time workers' insurance, health, and pension benefits in the future. But Joe insists, arguing that his restaurant's competitors follow these practices and he is faced with strong financial competition. He also states that many workers favor this arrangement. According to employment laws the employer is required to withhold money for tax liabilities and submit a report to the taxing authorities. The employee fills out his or her final tax return and pays the outstanding tax bill. The employees receiving cash payments can choose whether to report their income on state and federal tax forms, but most will not to avoid possible trouble with immigration authorities.

    a. Discuss the accounting and ethical issues of this situation.

    b. Who are the stakeholders?

    c. Consider the conflicts of interests and the pressure on Joe and his accountant. Is anyone harmed or benefited by the possible choices?

    d. What should Joe and his accountant do?

    e. Does it make an ethical difference if the actions of the accountant and Joe are contrary to employment laws?

    f. What would you do in this situation?

    g. If Joe and his accountant decide to break laws, would you report them to the proper authorities? Would you be a "whistle-blower"? Defend your answer.

This case is constructed from a series of conversations between the authors and a student who worked in a Southern California taco shop. The student/worker expressed much frustration about the different categories of workers at the taco shop, the payment arrangements and the owner's withholding of various payments from the employees' wages. The student was acutely aware of "on the job" pressures arising from his employer's efforts to stay in business in a highly competitive market. We also had the experience of discussing this case with first-year university students in California. This discussion exploded into angry denunciations of "illegal immigrants," confrontations where one student yelled at another, "That is what is wrong with your kind of people," suggesting ethnic and racial tensions, and the discussion transformed itself into a heated debate about immigration policy, exploitation of youthful workers, and the right of state and federal governments to extract payments that may or may not be paid out years later for retirement and healthcare benefits.

Like the Liebold Manufacturing "bribery" case, the circumstances of Joe's Taco are quite complex, and awareness of the social setting and local business environment is critical for grasping the its main features. The successful marketing of fast food depends on the strategic placement of restaurant outlets and advertising, including "word of mouth". Profitability and competiveness is directly linked to business efficiency – in particular, reducing the wholesale expense of food products and skillfully managing labor costs. (It helps to make a tasty taco, too!)

In the American setting, the employer withholds a portion of the worker's salary to forward to state and federal tax authorities. These moneys count against the worker's tax liability and also are placed in their personal account within the government retirement fund, the Social Security program. Usually the company has a group health plan for which full-time workers are eligible and the employer makes payments to the insurance company. Workman's compensation for financial protection in case of injury is to be withheld from all workers' wages and is to be forwarded by the employer to the appropriate government state and federal agencies. At the end of the year each worker is also to "self-report" on his income to the state and federal tax authorities (with the possibility that the workers' reports may not match the amounts forwarded by employers). In this context, Joe's employment-wage decisions will be influenced by his perception of how his competitors may be paying their workers and handling insurance, workman's compensation, retirement, and tax-withholding payments.

There are key legal issues to consider. One must ask about the employer's legal requirements for full-time and part-time workers. Normally the distinction is based on the number of hours worked each week by the laborer, with 40 hours usually considered a full-time schedule. Next the employer must consider which payments are required by law for each class of workers. State and local taxes, Social Security (federal retirement and healthcare), workman's compensation are required for all employees. Privately funded health insurance is optional – some employers do not offer insurance to any workers, some only to full-time workers; most often part-time workers are not covered by employer-based insurance programs.

The principal legal issue has to do with the employer's obligation to make payments for all workers: Social Security, state and federal taxes, workman's compensation. Any decision not to make payments for part-time workers violates state and federal laws. The accountant, then, must ask whether his professional duty includes obedience to these same state and federal laws.

Let us proceed as we did in the Liebold Manufacturing "bribery" case. If Joe decides to break the law and not forward the proper payments to government agencies for those part-time workers whom he pays in cash ("under the table"), the accountant has the accounting problem of how to recognize those cash transactions. How does the accountant prepare the financial statements if the transactions are not recorded as wage expense (to prevent any interested government stakeholder from seeing wage payments where no withholding moneys were taken)? He might, for example, set aside some of the sales revenue – not putting it on the books at all. This understates net income (and one could not tell that Joe's cash payments "flowed out" to the part-time workers). In another accounting decision, he might record the wage payments in as an operating expense (let us say, "miscellaneous expense," which does not classify its items, or "selling expense," costs incurred by salesmen or marketing campaigns).

Yet, we ask: aren't these decisions questionable in terms of ethics? Isn't the accountant's effort to hide Joe' illegal action also deceptive and manipulative for the outside stakeholder? The financial statements do not faithfully represent the financial status of Joe's Taco. Even if the impact on the net income of Joe's Taco is minimal, don't the falsified entries verge on fraud? From another angle: can a virtuous accountant, who knows the technical standards of the profession and has character traits of honesty and integrity, and who believes himself to be intellectually and morally bound "to tell the truth," engage in this type of accounting activity?

Even with these things in mind, we can ask many other questions that will complicate the issues. Are young, part-time workers harmed very much if their retirement payments and income taxes are not withheld and they have those moneys for current-day use? Shouldn't the worker have the right to forgo workman's compensation as an insurance benefit he or she may not need, since taco preparation and serving are not dangerous tasks? If some of these part-time workers are, in fact, non-residents who work without proper government papers, are they not performing worthwhile labor in society? Their presence in the country should not be ended if some tax authority, examining wage and withholding documents, were to inform an immigration agency that it suspected that Joe's workers were "illegal immigrants". And think of the public benefit of inexpensive tacos!

As Joe's accountant, what would you do? Let us say that you refuse to prepare financial statements to hide the cash payments to the part-time workers. Would you risk your job on this decision? Would you "whistle-blow" and inform government authorities about Joe's cost-cutting efforts? Or, by contrast, would you try to convince Joe to pay everyone – full- and part-time workers – "above the table" and to make all the required payments to the government agencies (and seek other means to cut costs and remain competitive, possibly advertising Joe's Taco as a place of enlightened labor practices!)?

We authors confess that we ourselves have been unable to reach consensus on resolving the accounting and ethical problems in this situation. A major factor in our disagreements is a perception that Joe's approach to part-time workers is common in the fast-food industry and to alter it is to be at a significant competitive disadvantage, and little real harm is done to the young workers. (In fact, there are benefits to a higher "take-home pay" in the form of unreported cash.) We share the ambivalence about the long-term healthcare and pension programs of the US and speculate that young workers who do not make payments early in their work careers are not much harmed by that action alone. We debate the social benefits and potential harm of having a large corps of undocumented workers, and we are suspicious about the sharing of tax and insurance information among government agencies. All in all, then, we dare not speak authoritatively on Joe's Taco. We will not tell anyone what to do!

REFLECTIONS ON CASE ANALYSIS: PRACTICAL WISDOM AND DELIBERATIVE JUDGMENT

We have generated and evaluated decision alternatives in the previous case analyses. The discussion of these cases and those in Chapters Four and Six demonstrated the many key elements of our decision model; but the decision processes did not follow some specified blueprint or fit into a lock-step pattern for resolving accounting and ethical problems. We made numerous *judgments* as we applied accounting standards – the principles and rules of contemporary practice – to the various cases. As we engaged in moral inquiry, we considered selected features of moral philosophy to use in decision making and to evaluate our action-choices. Instead of a blueprint or pattern, the decision process demonstrated a *deliberative* form of analysis. This analysis expressed skillful judgment grounded in technical knowledge of accounting and awareness of moral philosophy, plus a capacity for reflection and insight into the particular features of each case. Decisions and action-choices were to emerge from a reasonable assessment of the distinctive aspects of each given situation.

The moral tradition of virtue ethics treats this deliberative judgment and disposition of reflection and insight as a special type of practical knowledge called "practical wisdom". Earlier we commented on this form of knowledge/judgment (Chapters Three and Five), and we now expand on that discussion.

PRACTICAL WISDOM

In the virtue ethics tradition, practical wisdom is the capacity to bring an appropriate virtue or virtues to bear in a situation which contains a moral issue or dilemma. The realization of the virtue should fit the specific circumstances, that is, be appropriate for the distinctive aspects of the situation. Expanding on this idea, practical wisdom is a type of judgment expressed in moral inquiry and decision making. Such insight assesses human motivations and individual behavior and is used to support the selection of alternatives that demonstrate self-conscious, knowledgeable ethical actions.

Practical wisdom is a concept that emphasizes that moral inquiry should support ethical action. In classical terms, this is not a form of "theoretical knowledge". It is judgment put to use to do "the right thing at the right time"; in virtue ethics language, to act virtuously, "live well and flourish" in the specific role you play in the community and in the choices you face in the day-to-day circumstances you face. Practical wisdom is an "intellectual virtue" that shows itself in sound judgments in the concrete, practical activities of daily life (and professional tasks). In particular, practical wisdom shapes the reflection on a situation and provides the necessary insight to bring the appropriate virtue to address a moral problem or resolve a dilemma (honesty, courage, integrity, generosity).

As we understand this form of knowledge and judgment, it is the intellectual ability to embody principled behavior in a circumstance and to apply the appropriate rule of practice to an accounting situation. The accountant is to bring the technical knowledge of accounting standards into a case and also to act according to the principles expressed in the professional code. Guided by practical wisdom, he or she demonstrates both technical and ethical competence, fitting action-choices correctly to the specific features of the situation.

Virtue ethicists have long argued that the intellectual ability to express the appropriate virtue in a situation is a learned skill. To "direct" or "aim" the virtue (like an archer aims the arrow) to do right things (and flourish) is a judgmental capacity that depends on time and experience. A person gains such wisdom through the long practice of facing moral issues (dilemmas) and working through concrete decision processes to resolve them. Just as the virtues themselves are formed within one's character through experience and habit formation (Chapter Five), so also is practical wisdom honed as a skill through time and experience. Practical wisdom as the skill of making judgments is *learned by doing*.

With these things in mind, we can now think back on the cases we have already considered. In effect, we can also affirm the teaching practice of case analysis itself! In case studies, the student is drawn into situations and spends time gaining experience in defining problems, identifying important features of a situation, generating and evaluating decision alternatives, and making action-choices. Aided by their teachers and peers, the students' analysis and choices are evaluated and their capacity for reflection and gaining insight in the particularities of an accounting situation can be "tested" (and hopefully enhanced).

Even beginning with the "attendance list" case of Chapter Two, the authors' own treatments of the cases now allow for a review in light of the concept of practice wisdom. We can ask: "Is obedience to the class list requirement an ethical duty?" "How shall I best demonstrate loyalty to my classmates – either by signing for them when they are absent or by fulfilling the lecturer's rule and maintaining classroom order?" "If I whistle-blow, will I maintain the social contract of the class or is there simply no consensus to obey the rule, anyway?"

Consider the year-end adjustment cases. We can pose questions about the appropriate accounting rules, the principles of professional codes, the relevance of specific accountant virtues: "What is the correct pattern for accruing revenues and expenses, according to accounting standards?" "Should I support my boss's request (loyalty to her) or do my duty (follow the current accounting standards)?" "Should I manipulate the earnings record of my own company or must I consider first the bank's interest and need for having high-quality financial information in order to process a loan request?"

In the discussion of expensing or depreciating the college's computers, is it significant that depreciation expense does not generate cash flow or that no stock-holders are affected by the "accounting mistake"? In the Liebold Manufacturing "bribery" case, is it relevant that the building project is not in the United States or that hiring a consulting firm to avoid direct knowledge of bribe payments is commonplace in Burmathai?" (Keep in mind that practical wisdom presumes specific awareness of key details within each unique situation.)

Can we claim that an accountant's experience of one year-end adjustment dilemma may teach him or her what to do in another comparable circumstance the next year? Might resisting one inappropriate request for personal friendship and loyalty make a similar request less of a distraction for an ethical decision when it arises sometime later in the accountant's career? In effect, does the accountant actually "build character" or "gain in practical wisdom" by successfully resolving ethical dilemmas or repeatedly applying the appropriate accounting standard – despite the presence of stakeholder pressures, time constraints, and moral problems? The authors believe this to be the case.

HUMAN MOTIVATION AND BEHAVIOR: INCENTIVES AND SUPPORT FOR ETHICAL ACTION

For further elaboration of the concept of practical wisdom, we can turn to the longer cases on the theft of church offering money and the complexities of Joe's Taco. In the authors' treatment of these two cases, most time was given to the ethical dilemmas, rather than the specific features of the accounting problems (internal controls, in the church case, and producing high-quality financial statements in the case of Joe's Taco). In the following discussion, however, we focus on questions of whether the proposed decision alternatives and action-choices represent reasonable assessments of ordinary human motivations and the willingness of stakeholders to "pay the costs" of acting ethically. Does the disagreement between the pastors about how to deal with the treasurer-thief and the various alternatives to Joe's paying cash "under the table" for part-time workers express reasonable views of how people might act in these individual circumstances?

In our understanding, practical wisdom includes making realistic judgments about human nature and the ways people try to cope with moral pressures, mistakes and fraud, and the uncertainties of linking past behaviors with future decisions and their outcome. In the church case, for example, could it have been anticipated that the "loose system" of counting the offerings might lead to temptation and the possibility of an ongoing pattern of theft and deception? Or would it be more realistic to believe that a conscientious Christian volunteer would not consider such a theft, even given temptation and the low probability of being caught? Looking at the pastors' disagreement, might parish members seriously alter their money-giving pattern, simply because they are upset at the theft or because they disagree with how the thief is punished? Might they put pressure on the manager-pastors for failing to protect the offering? By contrast, are not other considerations – the ethical teachings of the church, a theology of forgiveness and compassion, high priorities on current programs and mission of the organization – going to play a much greater role in the members' decision making than their attitudes about the theft and the thief or desires to "punish the pastors"? The exercise of practical wisdom calls for us to make realistic assessment of how Christian members might act, but what constitutes "realism" in this situation?

Looking realistically at Joe's Taco, we might find it easy to think that Joe would try to cut costs and save money by paying his part-time workers "under the table" and not withhold moneys for tax, workman's compensation, or retirement benefits. Yet is it reasonable to believe that the part-time workers might think they are much harmed by the practice – since they are likely to be young and probably do not think much about their own retirement in the distant future? It may be more realistic to imagine the part-timers' concern for workman's compensation and possible loss of financial protection in case of injury. Is it actually realistic to base a decision on the possibility that some federal agency will trigger a move to deport those part-time workers who entered the country without proper papers? Or to give weight to some hypothetical chance that the Social Security benefits of the distant future may be lost to many – so why worry about the withholding payments now?

Does practical wisdom direct us to consider that workplace tension may arise between full- and part-time workers somehow linked to cash payments "under the table"? Would any particular worker think it worthwhile somehow to "blow the whistle" on Joe (as a "political" effort to speak out against employing "illegals")?

And, anyway, maybe the full-time employees whose wages and withholding, insurance and future benefits are not threatened by Joe's decision are not – in a realistic assessment – stakeholders in this case, after all.

It should be apparent that the above questions which have been posed do not suggest blueprint or prescribed patterns for the pastors' or Joe's decisions. Nor would even the answers to these questions necessarily point toward clear-cut action-choices that would satisfy all the issues within the situations. Yet awareness of the crucial function of practical knowledge, specifically, practical wisdom, in these cases should demonstrate that professional accounting decision making and thoughtful moral reasoning goes far beyond simplistic blueprints or "cookie-cutter"/"paint by numbers" decision processes.

CHAPTER REVIEW QUESTIONS

1. (LO4) What is the accounting standard for recognizing revenue for a sale of goods?

2. (LO4) Is the payment of a bribe unethical for an accountant? "Hiding" the payment in the financial statements?

3. (LO5) What pressure may arise (to manipulate the financial statements) whenever bonus payments are linked to yearly earnings?

4. (LO3) As you consider an estimate for bad debt expense, is it appropriate to take into account its impact on company earnings? Why or why not?

5. (LO1) What are retrospective and prospective actions?

6. (LO7) In your own words, what is practical wisdom in relation to an accounting situation where there is a moral issue or dilemma?

7. (LO7) Practical wisdom is an intellectual ability. What does this ability have to do with moral virtues or assessing ethical alternatives?

8. (LO5) What pressures may arise at year-end with regard to adjusting entries and company earnings?

9. (LO4) Can it be unethical to understate a company's earnings? What pressures may lead to this decision?

10. (LO4) Give an example where an accountant's loyalty to company management might conflict with his or her "ethics of duty".

11. (LO6) In the Joe's Taco case, explain why an accountant might know his professional duty, but hesitate to do it. (Think of conflict of interest, assessing possible consequences of action, "social contract" issues.)

CASES

12. Travel and Entertainment Expense for a Not-for-profit Company
A recent article in a newspaper described several questionable business practices in a not-for-profit insurance company. An audit had documented questionable spending for executives' travel and annual board retreats at a resort. The chief executive of the insurance company said that steps had been taken to correct the

deficiencies noted in the audit. He apologized for several actions, including a business trip to Hawaii when he billed the insurance company $800 for a helicopter ride. The executive defended the board's annual retreats as educational, but he agreed that the expenditures for cocktails, golf, and golf lessons for board members and their families might not have been reasonable expenditures for a not-for-profit insurance company.

Required:

a. Discuss the accounting and ethical issues of this situation. Who are the stakeholders? Consider the conflicts of interest and the pressure on the chief executive. Is anyone harmed or does anyone benefit by the possible choices?

b. Would these expenses have been questioned if the insurance company operated as a for-profit enterprise? What are the key distinctions in the two types of insurance companies that may affect the way expenses might be treated?

c. During the interview a reporter asked the executive if it was fair that his company was held to different standards than the standards for for-profit insurance companies. What issue is the reporter raising? If you were a chief executive officer in this position, what might you say to the reporter? Do you think standards for these two types of companies should differ?

d. We have stated that accountants need both technical and ethical competence. Discuss how this is important in this particular case.

13. Business Expenditures for a Not-for-profit Company

Dan Green has been working on the audit of a not-for-profit residential treatment facility for mentally disturbed teenagers. Dan is an employee of one of the Big Four audit firms. He is a second year auditor, and this particular engagement is the first audit where he is in charge of the fieldwork. He is currently reviewing the working papers of the assistant working with him, in preparation for the manager's visit next week. The audit has gone well, and the audit team is currently reviewing invoices for expense items related to the audit of the income statement. Dan has just uncovered several invoices that are puzzling to him, including an invoice for yacht insurance, several invoices for lavish entertainment expenses, including cigars and food in connection with a conference in Chicago; invoices for expensive clothing purchased as gifts for the directors of the organization; and invoices for oriental rugs for the house provided to the director of the facility. Since there is no body of water large enough to support a yacht within hundreds of kilometers of the facility, Dan feels he must question the accounting staff about this expenditure. According to the controller, the yacht is moored off the coast of California and is used by the director to entertain friends.

Required:

a. Discuss the accounting and ethical issues of this situation.

b. Who are the stakeholders?

    c. Consider the conflicts of interest and the pressure on Dan. Is anyone harmed or does anybody benefit by the possible choices?

14. Sonali, Requests for Financing

Surya P. "Pat" Patangay, a small gold-jewelry seller in Oceanside, California, easily defrauded Wells Fargo & Co. out of $14.5 million.[1] Patangay says his ruse worked because of lax auditing standards at Ernst & Young. To obtain loans, he fabricated documents showing sales revenue of $70 million per year, but yearly sales never totaled more than $1.5 million. The auditors relied on copies of documents rather than originals, sent confirmations to 50 post office boxes of bogus customers, and, during an inventory count, failed to uncover fake gold.

In the mid-1980s, Patangay founded Sonali Corporation, a company importing ornate 22 karat gold, a purer gold than that usually sold in the USA. He sold the gold to American jewelers. Because jewelers did not pay for the gold until it was sold, and the foreign gold suppliers required cash on delivery of the gold, Patangay arranged financing with US banks to cover the gold purchase. The financing from a bank covered the delay between his payments to suppliers and the jewelers' payments.

When Patangay first approached the bank for a small-business loan, they asked for financial records. Patangay had no financial records, so he created them in his office, starting with original documents and making fictitious documents using a copy machine. (For example, he took a receipt for a $10,000 sale and changed it to a $100,000 transaction.) Using this deception, he received an unsecured loan for $250,000.

Such techniques enabled Patangay to deceive auditors during their on-site visits. He reports that he showed Ernst & Young auditors "some real documents, nothing important. The receivables, payables, invoices, my bank statements, I made them up."[2] His bank statement scam, for example, created an illusion that millions of dollars were flowing through his company bank account. This involved altering original statements in a manner that should have been detected by the auditors. These "client-prepared documents" successfully fooled Ernst & Young. In this and other aspects of the audit, the accountants "never insisted on originals. If they had, I would have failed the audit."

In another matter, auditors did not notice the bogus list of 50 customers who supposedly owed money to the company because auditors failed to notice that the accounts receivable listing did not include street addresses. These letters were forwarded to 50 post office addresses Patangay himself rented, thus enabling him to pose as those customers and falsify confirmation responses.

When auditors examined gold and jewelry in Sonali's vault and safe-deposit boxes, the stock included lengthy spools of gold-plated costume chain. The auditors asked to take a sample chain for valuing, but Patangay suggested that they be satisfied with a pre-cut piece (of genuine gold that he had prepared) rather than cut the chain. The auditors complied with his request. Patangay, now facing legal punishment, does not blame the auditors for his troubles: "But their audit procedures have big flaws that people can take advantage of."[3]

Required:

    a. Discuss the accounting and ethical issues of this situation.

    b. Who are the stakeholders?

    c. Consider the conflicts of interest and the pressure on Patangay. Is anyone harmed or benefited by the possible choices? Would the bank have been harmed if Patangay had been able to repay the loan?

    d. Do you think the auditors should be penalized for their errors?

15. Satyam Computer Services

In 2009, R. Ramalinga Raju, the founder and chairman of Satyam Computer Services based in Hyderabad, India, resigned from his position, stating that he had overstated profits for several years, overstated the amount of money owed to the company in debt repayment, overstated its cash balance by $1 billion and understated its liabilities. Satyam (the name means truth in Sanskrit) provides information technology services for many of the world's largest companies and employs 40,000 people in 49 offices around the world. Satyam stock was sold on stock exchanges in India and the US, and the company was audited by PWC.

Indian prosecutors allege that Mr. Raju created 13,000 fictitious employees and directed the salary payments for these employees to accounts owned by businesses he controlled. The fictitious salaries amounted to $4 million per month. The money was used to purchase land around Hyderabad. Mr. Raju thought that land development would be a more profitable business than information services, so he decided to divert money from the computer service company to the land company owned by his family.

Two partners of PWC were arrested and charged with criminal conspiracy and cheating in connection with the fraud investigation at Satyam Computer Services. Mr. Raju, his brother B. Rama Raju, and Srinivas Vadlamani, the former chief financial officer, were arrested on charges of forgery, cheating, and breach of trust.

Satyam was purchased by Tech Mahindra (a company listed on the stock exchange in the UK and Germany) in 2009 and now operates under the name Mahindra Satyam.[4]

Required:

    a. Discuss the accounting and ethical issues of this situation.

    b. Who are the stakeholders?

    c. Consider the conflicts of interest and the pressures on Mr. Raju. Is anyone harmed or does anybody benefit by the possible choices?

16. Madoff

Bernie Madoff entered into the simplest fraud of all – he simply made up the numbers. Mr. Madoff operated a well-known investment fund. According to the latest statements sent to investors, the fund had a net worth of $64.8 billion. In fact, Mr. Madoff had not entered into any trades in the past 13 years, and the investment fund had only $1 billion in assets.

The fraud depended on a combination of loyal employees and family, falsified client statements and financial trading documents, and investors who felt privileged to be his clients. The investors were so happy with the steady return generated by the fund that they rarely withdrew money from the investment fund.

The fraud began to unravel in December 2008, when Mr. Madoff admitted to his sons that his investment fund was a big lie. The fraud wiped out life fortunes making wealthy investors poor and causing numerous charities and foundations to close. The fraud affected large and small investors from elderly retirees in Florida to actor Kevin Bacon and Nobel Peace Prize winner Elie Wiesel.

On March 12, 2009, Mr. Madoff pleaded guilty to charges that he ran a massive Ponzi scheme where investors lost billions of dollars. On March 13, 2009, the 70-year-old Mr. Madoff was sent to jail. During the court proceedings, the judge had asked Mr. Madoff how he set up the Ponzi scheme. He said that at the beginning of the fraud, he felt compelled to give institutional investors strong returns despite the weak stock market and the national recession. He stated, "When I began the Ponzi scheme I believed it would end shortly and I would be able to extricate myself and my clients from the scheme. However, this proved difficult and ultimately impossible."

Mr. Madoff's fund was described as a Ponzi scheme because he took money from investors, but he did nothing with the money. The investors received statements showing that the fund was generating healthy returns on the investments. Ponzi schemes typically end after a few years because the later investments are insufficient to cover the withdrawals on the earlier investments. But Mr. Madoff's Ponzi scheme did not end quickly because investors rarely withdrew money from the fund. They were pleased with the returns generated by the funds, so the money was not withdrawn to be invested in an alternative fund.

Mr. Madoff's investment fund was audited by Friehling & Horowitz, CPAs. David Friehling was arrested and charged with securities fraud, aiding and abetting investment adviser fraud, and filing false audit reports to the Securities and Exchange Commission. Mr. Friehling faces a maximum of 105 years in prison. The criminal complaint against Mr. Friehling stated that he didn't verify the existence of assets that Mr. Madoff reported or the security trades that Mr. Madoff said he made. Mr. Friehling also failed to examine the bank account through which billions of dollars of client funds flowed. Mr. Friehling was the sole auditor at Friehling & Horowitz. He had audited Mr. Madoff's financial statements since 1991.

In addition to the criminal complaint against the auditor, the SEC also filed a civil complaint against Mr. Friehling. The civil complaint alleged that Mr. Friehling and his family had investment accounts at the Madoff firm worth more than $14 million. This is a blatant conflict of interest and violates the auditing rule requiring an auditor to be independent from the clients he audits. He and his family have withdrawn at least $5.5 million from the fund since 2002, according to the SEC.

There were numerous red flags for this company. Several outsiders had speculated that the results reported on the Madoff investment fund were not real. The SEC received six warnings about Mr. Madoff's business over 16 years. The SEC conducted three examinations and two enforcement investigations into the company, but no action was taken as a result of the investigations. Outsiders reported that the accounting firm auditing Mr. Madoff's fund had only three employees, one of whom was 78 and lived in Florida, and one of whom was a secretary. The firm operated in a 13 foot by 18 foot office. Observers wondered how an accounting firm of that size could audit an investment firm the size of Mr. Madoff's firm.

Clients in Europe also suffered losses when Mr. Madoff's investment fund was disclosed as a sham. European banks, funds, and individuals lost billions of euros in the collapse of Mr. Madoff's fund. The clients of Banco Santander SA, Europe's second largest bank by market value, lost €2.33 billion when the Ponzi fund collapsed. Swiss Bank Union Bancaire Privee lost $1.25 billion. Many wealthy families in Spain were brought into Mr. Madoff's investment fund through Emilio Botin, the chairman of Banco Santander. Sometimes banks recommended the funds to its customers and lent money to the investor to finance the investment. In this way, even banks who did not invest in the fund suffered losses when the fund was declared to be a Ponzi fund with few assets.[5]

Required:

    a. Discuss the accounting and ethical issues of this situation.

    b. Who are the stakeholders?

    c. Consider the conflicts of interest and the pressure on Madoff. Is anyone harmed or benefited by the possible choices?

    d. Why was the auditing arrangement so important for hiding the fraud?

17. AIJ Japan

In June 2012, Japanese police arrested the president, Kazuhiko Asakawa, of asset management company AIJ for selling investment funds knowing that the performance figures for the fund were fictitious. AIJ Investment Advisors had 94 clients with pension funds invested with the firm. In March of 2012, Japan's Securities and Exchange Surveillance Commission (SESC) inspected the investment records of the firm after a disclosure by company executives that they could not account for most of the pension money they managed. The SESC alleged that Asakawa had lost $1.3 billion of the client's money and had been hiding losses for the investment firm for 10 years. At the same time as company executives were hiding the losses of the firms, they prepared false performance records to obtain new clients to invest pension funds with the firm.

The fraud at AIJ has been referred to as the "Japanese Madoff". Japanese credit-rating company Rating & Investment Information Inc. (R&I) reported as early as 2009 that AIJ had "unnaturally stable returns" over a 10 year period even though the overall market reported a downward trend. "People in the industry had wondered about the company – they'd always thought something was shady," reported Nagamori, an R&I employee.

Prosecutors have asked for a prison sentence of 15 years for Asakawa. He has admitted his guilt on charges of fraud and violation of the financial instruments and exchange law. Eleven of seventeen pension funds have been forced to consider disbanding due to the loss of their funds.[6]

Required:

a. Assume that you are the accountant preparing the falsified performance reports as ordered by Asakawa. What accounting and ethical problems do you face in this situation?

b. Who are the stakeholders?

c. Consider the conflicts of interest and the pressures you face. Discuss them.

NOTES

1. Jeff D. Opdyke, "Fraud perpetrator points finger at auditors for lax standards," *The Wall Street Journal*, March 1, 2002.

2. Opdyke, "Fraud perpetrator points finger at auditors for lax standards," *The Wall Street Journal*, March 1, 2002.

3. Opdyke, "Fraud perpetrator points finger at auditors for lax standards," *The Wall Street Journal*, March 1, 2002.

4. R. Guha, "Satyam Computer to hire over 4,000 staff," *The Wall Street Journal*, February 18, 2010; R. Guha, "Wider fraud is seen at India's Satyam," *The Wall Street Journal*, November 26, 2009; J. Range, "Pricewaterhouse partners arrested in Satyam probe," *The Wall Street Journal*, January 25, 2009; N. Sheth, J. Range & G. Anand, "Corporate scandal shakes India," *The Wall Street Journal*, January 8, 2009.

5. T. Catan, & C. Bryan-Low, "European clients were cultivated within social networks by word of mouth," *The Wall Street Journal*, December 16, 2008; A. Lucchetti & T. Lauricella, "Investors were told they had a total of $64.8 billion," *The Wall Street Journal*, March 10, 2009; R. Frank, A. Efrati, A. Lucchetti & C. Bray, "Madoff jailed after admitting epic scam," *The Wall Street Journal*, March 13, 2009; I. Dugan, "Madoff didn't buy securities for years," *The Wall Street Journal*, February 21, 2009; A. Efrati, "Accountant arrested for sham audits," *The Wall Street Journal*, March 19, 2009; K. Scannell, "SEC botched inquiries into Madoff scheme," *The Wall Street Journal*, September 3, 2009.

6. "Prosecutors seek 15 years in prison for AIJ chief charged with fraud," *Kyodo News*, July 2, 2013; Alsuko Kana Inagaki & Phred Dvorak, "WSJ: Newsletter warned of 'Japanese Madoff' in 2009," *Wall Street Journal*, February 24, 2012; Hiroyuki Kachi, "Employees of AIJ arrested in Japan," *Wall Street Journal*, June 20, 2012.

REFERENCES

Cheffers, M. & Pakaluk, M. (2011) *Accounting Ethics and the Near Collapse of the World's Financial System*. Sutton, MA: Allen David Press.

Doucet, M. & Doucet, T. (2004) Ethics of virtue and ethics of duty: Defining the norms of the profession. *Research on Professional Responsibility and Ethics in Accounting*, 9: 147–168.

Mintz, S. (1996) The role of virtue in accounting education. *Accounting Education*, 1(1): 67–91.

Mintz, S. & Morris, R. (2011) *Ethical Obligations and Decision Making in Accounting*, 2nd edn. New York: McGraw-Hill.

Thorne, L. (1998) The role of virtue in auditors' ethical decision making: An integration of cognitive development and virtue ethics perspectives. *Research on Accounting Ethics*, 4: 291–308.

PART III

ACCOUNTING IN SOCIETY

Auditing Ethics

By the end of this chapter you should be able to:

1. Understand the role and responsibilities of the independent auditor.
2. Explain the important values, standards, and virtues in auditing as described in the professional codes of conduct in the profession and their role in shaping the ethics of auditing.
3. Explain the role of heuristics and biases in determining auditor decisions.
4. Understand the auditor's role related to ethics in the areas of financial statement disclosure and earnings management.
5. Explain the role of the auditor in the corporate governance process.

THE ROLE AND RESPONSIBILITIES OF THE AUDITOR

An auditor is hired by the shareholders of the company (usually through the audit committee) to conduct an audit. During the audit process, the auditor gathers evidence about whether the financial statements of the company are prepared in accordance with the applicable financial reporting framework (the accounting standards). At the end of the audit process, an audit opinion is issued with the auditor's statement that the financial statements have been prepared by the company in accordance with the applicable financial reporting framework or that they have not complied with this reporting requirement. Outsiders use audited financial statements and the auditor's word (the opinion) as a primary source of information about the company. Stakeholders rely on the information to make decisions related to the company so if auditors fail to perform their professional responsibility, outsiders receive bad information and may make bad choices. Bad choices related to a company include: granting a company a loan when you would not have done so if the "true" financial picture had been known; buying stock in a company when you would not have bought the stock if the "true" financial picture had been known; or failing to sell stock when you would have had the "true" financial picture been known. All these consequences affect the cash flow of the individuals involved. For this reason, it is important that the decisions made by the auditor demonstrate both the technical proficiency and the ethical sensibility that outsiders expect.

Technical proficiency for auditors involves knowledge about the accounting standards and knowledge about the auditing standards. We have spoken about the rules accountants must follow related to the accounting standards in previous chapters. In this chapter we will focus on the technical rules in the auditing standards that guide the auditor in performing on audit.

The auditing standards specify the technical rules auditors must follow when they conduct an audit. There are two main sets of auditing standards in the world. The international auditing standards are written by the International Auditing and Assurance Standards Board (IAASB, 2013), a part of the International Federation of Accounting (IFAC). The US auditing standards for public companies are written by the Public Company Accounting Oversight Board (PCAOB, 2013). The standards from the IAASB and the PCAOB are listed in the Appendix to this chapter. An auditor would demonstrate technical proficiency during an audit by following the auditing standards. Let's consider how the auditor would demonstrate ethical awareness during an audit.

VALUES, STANDARDS, AND VIRTUES IN THE PROFESSIONAL CODES OF CONDUCT

Ethical awareness by the auditor begins by following the professional codes of conduct. Chapter Six discussed professional ethics codes as a resource for decision making. There are two professional codes of conduct that apply to auditors today: the American Institute of Certified Public Accountants (AICPA) Code of Professional Conduct sets the ethics standards for the accounting profession in the USA, and the Code of Ethics for Professional Accountants written by the International Ethics Standards Board for Accountants (IESBA) sets the ethics standard for the accounting profession outside the United States. Let us look at each of these ethics codes briefly.

The AICPA code of professional conduct is composed of two sections, a section that describes the basic conceptual framework of the profession's rules and regulations, and another section that expresses the particular rules that govern the professional practice of the accountant. Most of these rules apply to every member of the profession, but some rules are restricted to members in public practice only.

The AICPA code of professional conduct requires the accountant to comply with the following principles:

- **The Public Interest**   A member should accept the obligation to act in a way that will serve the public interest, honor the public trust, and demonstrate commitment to professionalism.
- **Integrity**   To maintain and broaden public confidence, members should perform all professional responsibilities with the highest sense of integrity.

- **Objectivity and Independence**   A member should maintain objectivity and be free of conflicts of interest in discharging professional responsibilities. A member in public practice should be independent in fact and appearance when providing auditing and other attestation services.
- **Due Care**   A member should observe the profession's technical and ethical standards, strive continually to improve competence and the quality of services, and discharge professional responsibility to the best of the member's ability.
- **Scope and Nature of Services**   A member in public practice should observe the Principles of the Code of Professional Conduct in determining the scope and nature of services to be provided.

The rules of conduct are found in Sections 100–500 of the code. They are described below.

The AICPA Rules of Professional Conduct

Section 100. Independence, Integrity, and Objectivity

Rule 101.   **Independence.** A member in public practice shall be independent in the performance of professional services as required by standards promulgated by bodies designated by Council.

Rule 102.   **Integrity and Objectivity.** In the performance of any professional service, a member shall maintain objectivity and integrity, shall be free of conflicts of interest, and shall not knowingly misrepresent facts or subordinate his or her judgment to others.

Section 200. General Standards

Rule 201.   **General Standards.** A member shall comply with the following standards and with any interpretations thereof by bodies designated by Council.

   (a) *Professional Competence.* Undertake only those professional services that the member or the member's firm can reasonably expect to be completed with professional competence.

   (b) *Due Professional Care.* Exercise due professional care in the performance of professional services.

   (c) *Planning and Supervision.* Adequately plan and supervise the performance of professional services.

   (d) *Sufficient Relevant Data.* Obtain sufficient relevant data to afford a reasonable basis for conclusions or recommendations in relation to any professional services performed.

Rule 202.   **Compliance with Standards.** A member who performs auditing, review, compilation, management consulting, tax, or other professional services shall comply with standards promulgated by bodies designated by Council.

Rule 203.   **Accounting principles.** A member shall not (1) express an opinion or state affirmatively that the financial statements or other financial data of any entity are presented in conformity with generally accepted accounting principles or (2) state that he or she is not aware of any material modifications that should be made to such statements or data in order for them to be in conformity with generally accepted accounting principles promulgated by bodies designated by Council to establish such principles that has a material effect on the statements or data taken as a whole. If, however, the statements or data contain such a departure and the member can demonstrate that due to unusual circumstances the financial statements or data would otherwise have been misleading, the member can comply with the rule by describing the departure, its approximate effects, if practicable, and the reasons why compliance with the principle would result in a misleading statement.

Section 300. Responsibilities to Clients

Rule 301.   **Confidential Client Information.** A member in public practice shall not disclose any confidential client information without the specific consent of the client.

The rule shall not construed (1) to relieve a member of his or her professional obligations under rules 202 and 203, (2) to affect in any way the member's obligation to comply with a validly issued and enforceable subpoena or summons, or to prohibit a member's compliance with applicable laws and government regulations, (3) to prohibit review of a member's professional practice under AICPA or state CPA society or Board of Accountancy authorization, or (4) to preclude a member from initiating a complaint with, or responding to any inquiry made by, the professional ethics division or trial board of the Institute or a duly constitute investigative or disciplinary body of a state CPA society or Board of Accountancy.

Rule 302.   **Contingent Fees.** A member in public practice shall not:

(1) Perform for a contingent fee any professional services for, or receive such a fee from a client for whom the member of the member's firm performs,

    (a) an audit or review of a financial statements; or

    (b) a compilation of a financial statement when the member expects, or reasonably might expect, that a third party will use the financial statement and the member's compilation report does not disclose a lack of independence; or

    (c) an examination of prospective financial information; or

(2) Prepare an original or amended tax return or claim for a tax refund for a contingent fee for any client.

Section 500. Other Responsibilities and Practices

Rule 501. **Acts Discreditable.** A member shall not commit an act discreditable to the profession.

Rule 502. **Advertising and Other Forms of Solicitation.** A member in public practice shall not seek to obtain clients by advertising or other forms of solicitation in a manner that is false, misleading, or deceptive. Solicitation by the use of coercion, over-reaching, or harassing conduct is prohibited.

Rule 505. **Form of Organization and Name.** A member may practice public accounting only in a form of organization permitted by law or regulation whose characteristics conform to resolutions of Council.

A member shall not practice public accounting under a firm name that is misleading. Names of one of more past owners may be included in the firm name of a successor organization.

A firm may not designate itself as "Members of the American Institute of Certified Public Accountants" unless all of its CPA owners are members of the Institute.

The international code of ethics is written by the International Ethics Standards Board for Accountants. This board is a subcommittee of the International Federation of Accountants (IFAC). The International Code has three parts. Part A provides the fundamental principles of professional ethics for professional accountants and provides a conceptual framework that professional accountants should use in making decisions involving audit practice. Parts B and C describe how the conceptual framework applies in certain situations. Part B applies to professional accountants in public practice. Part C applies to professional accountants in business. Part A of the code of ethics for professional accountants requires the accountant to comply with the following principles:

- **Integrity** To be straightforward and honest in all professional and business relationships.
- **Objectivity** To not allow bias, conflict of interest or undue influence of others to override professional or business judgments.
- **Professional Competence and Due Care** To maintain professional knowledge and skill at the level required to ensure that a client or employer receives competent professional services based on current developments in practice, legislation, and techniques and act diligently and in accordance with applicable technical and professional standards.
- **Confidentiality** To respect the confidentiality of information acquired as a result of professional and business relationships.
- **Professional Behavior** To comply with relevant laws and regulations and avoid any action that discredits the profession.

The rules for practicing accountants in public practice and in business are found in sections 200 and 300 of the code. These sections are summarized below.

Professional Accountants in Public Practice

Section 200.   **Introduction.** Identifies self-interest, self-review, advocacy, familiarity and intimidation as threats to complying with the fundamental principles.

Section 210.   **Professional Appointment.** Requires the auditors to only accept clients that allow them to comply with the fundamental principles and to provide only those services they are competent to perform.

Section 220.   **Conflicts of Interest.** Avoid threats to objectivity or conflicts of interest.

Section 230.   **Second Opinions.** Think twice about providing them; the other accountant knows more about the situation than you do.

Section 240.   **Fees and Other Types of Remuneration.** Quote whatever fee you want for services provided, but do not quote a fee so low that it is difficult to perform the engagement in accordance with the standards. In certain situations referral fees may be permitted, contingent fees are usually not.

Section 250.   **Marketing Professional Services.** When marketing your services, the professional accountant shall not make exaggerated claims for services offered, qualifications possessed or experience gained, or make disparaging references to the work of others.

Section 260.   **Gifts and Hospitality.** When received from a client, the nature, value and intent of the offer should be considered. The gift or hospitality should be considered as trivial and inconsequential to be accepted.

Section 270.   **Custody of Client Assets.** The accountant should not assume custody of client money or other assets, unless permitted to do so by law. If permitted the accountant should keep the assets separate and use them only for the purpose to which they were intended.

Section 280.   **Objectivity, All Services.** The accountant shall determine whether there are threats to objectivity for all services provided. A family or close personal or business relationship may threaten objectivity. An accountant providing assurance services must be independent in mind and appearance to express an opinion; section 290 provides more details.

Section 290.   **Independence – Other Assurance Engagements.** In the case of audit engagements, it is in the public interest that members of audit teams, firms, and network firms shall be independent of audit clients.
Independence comprises:
Independence of mind. The state of mind that permits expression of a conclusion without being affected by influences that

compromise professional judgment, allowing the individual to act with integrity and exercise objectivity and professional skepticism. Independence in appearance. The avoidance of facts and circumstances that are so significant that a reasonable and informed third party would be likely to conclude that a firm's or a member of the audit team's integrity, objectivity, or professional skepticism has been compromised.

Professional Accountants in Business

Section 300.   **Introduction.** A professional accountant in business shall not knowingly engage in any business or activity that impairs integrity, objectivity or the good reputation of the profession. Threats come from self-interest, self-review, advocacy, familiarity, and intimidation.

Section 310.   **Potential Conflicts.** The accountant's responsibilities to their employer may conflict with the obligations of the accountant to comply with the fundamental principles. The responsibility to the fundamental principles is more important than the responsibility to the employer.

Section 320.   **Preparation and Reporting of Information.** Information shall be prepared fairly, honestly, and in accordance with relevant professional standards.

Section 330.   **Acting with Sufficient Expertise.** The accountant shall only undertake tasks for which the accountant has sufficient training or experience.

Section 340.   **Financial Interests.** Accountants should avoid financial interests that may create threats to compliance with the fundamental principles. This includes holding a direct or indirect financial interest in the employer's organization and the value of the interest is affected by the decisions of the accountant.

Section 350.   **Inducements.** Try to avoid receiving or giving gifts, hospitality, preferential treatment, and inappropriate appeals to friendship or loyalty.

Let us consider two of the principles used in both codes to see how they result in rules for auditors. Both codes have a principle of due care. The principle of due care states that auditors should observe the technical and ethical standards of the profession and discharge their professional responsibilities. Rule 201 and 301 of the AICPA code provide specific rules related to the principle of due care. Rule 201 requires the auditor to follow the standards related to undertaking only those jobs where the auditor has the level of professional competence needed to perform the job, to exercise due professional care while performing the job, to adequately plan and supervise the audit, and to obtain sufficient relevant evidence to provide a reasonable basis for an opinion. Rule 301 requires auditors to keep the information received from the client during the audit confidential. Section 210 and 230 of the international code also provide specific rules related to the principle of due care. Section 210 requires auditors to only accept clients where they can comply with the fundamental principles and to provide only the services they are competent to perform. Section 230 requires auditors to think twice about providing second opinions because the first auditor knows more about the situation than the new auditor. The professional codes provide these rules as specific ways the auditor can exercise due care in an audit.

Objectivity is another principle where rules for auditors arise from the principle. The principle of objectivity says that the auditor should not allow bias, conflict of interest or undue influence to affect the decisions of the auditor. In the AICPA code, Rule 203 and 501 provide specific rules related to the principle of objectivity. Rule 203 says that the auditor should not express an opinion that the financial statements are not materially misstated if they are. Rule 501 says that the auditor should not commit an act discreditable to the profession. Section 200 and 220 of the international code also provide specific rules related to the objectivity principle. Rule 200 says that the auditor should recognize that self-interest, self-review, advocacy, familiarity, and intimidation are threats to following the fundamental principles. Rule 220 says that the auditor should avoid threats to objectivity and conflicts of interest. As these examples have illustrated, the principles in the codes are expressed as specific rules in both codes of professional conduct.

As you can see by reviewing these two codes, they have many similarities. The concept sections of the codes share the principles of integrity, objectivity, and due care. The AICPA code adds public interest and the scope and nature of services to its principles section, while the IFAC code includes confidentiality, professional behavior, and professional competence. You can also see that the two codes share many of the same rules: for example, the requirement that auditors perform their professional responsibilities with both independence in mind and independence in appearance, the requirement that auditors only accept clients if they have the competence to perform the services, the prohibition against contingent fees for work done and against exaggerating the potential benefits of the services offered. These codes of conduct discuss the virtues that auditor should possess, and they also establish rules of conduct that auditors should follow. For example, auditors should possess the virtue of objectivity. They should not allow bias, conflicts of interest, or undue influence on the part of others to override what they know to be the correct decisions (according to the accounting standards). They should abide by the rules of conduct related to the requirement for acting as an independent auditor – an auditor who has no direct financial interest in the company under audit and an auditor who acts with integrity and objectivity and exercises professional skepticism in the performance of audit tasks.

AUDIT JUDGMENT

Decision making in the auditing setting falls under a category of decision making referred to as "decision making under conditions of uncertainty". What we know about decision making in this setting has been described by several scholars. In 1974, Tversky and Kahneman published an article titled "Judgment under uncertainty: Heuristics and biases" (*Science*, vol. 185). Some of the ideas presented in this early paper were elaborated in a book written by Kahneman in 2011 called *Thinking, Fast and Slow*.

These are excellent resources if you are interested in learning more about this topic after reading the material in this chapter.

It is, of course, appropriate to claim that auditors engage in "decision making under conditions of uncertainty" when they perform an audit. The aspect of uncertainty is what makes auditing decisions so difficult. The auditor is always assessing the likelihood that the financial statements are misstated as he or she reviews the evidence. Audits are conducted by using an audit risk model where the risk of saying the financial statements are not misstated when they are misstated is equal to the risk that material misstatements are present in the financial statements times the risk that the auditor fails to catch the material misstatement. Each of these decisions is made under conditions of uncertainty. The auditor never knows whether his decision is correct; this is because the auditor never looks at all the data related to the financial statements, but audits only a sample of the data. Even when the audit opinion is issued, the auditor accepts some risk that the opinion is incorrect. This risk is typically 5–10% in an audit. So, when the auditor says that the financial statements are not materially misstated, an assumption is made that he or she is wrong 5–10% of the time. Given such considerations, the audit process can accurately be understood as a series of decisions made under conditions of uncertainty; that is, where the auditor never knows *with certainty* that he or she is making the right decision.

System 1 and System 2 Thinking

Consider the following picture.

Looking at this picture allows you to experience your mind in automatic mode. As you look at the cat, you experience the joint act of seeing and a process of intuitive thinking. As surely and quickly as you can see that the cat is white and furry, you can respond to think, possibly, that this cat might be a good pet to have in the house. What you see might push you to immediately think into the future. If you like cats, you can imagine having a cat like this someday. If you do not like cats or if you are allergic to them, you might plan to stay away from such an animal. A premonition of the kinds of things the cat might do next may come into your mind automatically and without effort. You did not intend to decide whether this was a nice cat or to anticipate what you might do in the future if you came across such a cat or if you owned such a cat. These thoughts just "pop into your head". Your reactions to the picture were not ideas you consciously worked out or achieved, they just occurred to you. These responses to the picture of the cat are examples of "fast thinking".

Now consider this problem:

$$13 \times 47$$

You know that this is a multiplication problem and that you could solve it with a calculator or pen and pencil. But without spending time on solving the problem, you would not be sure of the correct answer because the correct answer does not come automatically to mind. As you work out how to solve this problem, you go through a series of events. You retrieve from memory the program for multiplication that you learned in school and then you implement the program. Making the computation is a conscious effort where it is important that you keep track of where you are and contemplate where you are going, plus keep any intermediate results fixed in your memory. This process is mental work, requiring effort, deliberate action to solve the problem, and an orderly approach to arrive at the correct answer. This is an example of "slow thinking".

For many years psychologists have been interested in these two ways of thinking. Various terms have been used to describe the two methods. Kahneman (2011) refers to these ways of thinking as System 1 thinking and System 2 thinking.

- System 1 thinking operates automatically and quickly, with little or no effort and no sense of voluntary control. We call this the "automatic" or "intuitive" system.
- System 2 thinking allocates attention to the effortful mental activities that demand it, including complex computations. We call this the "deliberative" system. (Kahneman, 2011, pp. 20–21)

In our role as professional auditors, we should most often employ System 2 processes; that is, be self-consciously deliberative in our decision making. We make audit decisions through deliberation (or "after" deliberate reasoning). We make self-conscious choices and deliberate decisions about what to think and what to do as we face a situation within our auditing tasks – for example, as we wonder whether accounts receivable may be materially misstated. System 2 thinking should be the dominant mode of the auditor's decision process. But as we reflect on the ordinary circumstances of decision making, we can see that deliberative reasoning may not always prevail in the audit process because there is a certain power in our automatic responses to situations, an appeal for intuition to be given high priority.

Automatic and intuitive thinking (System 1) and deliberative reasoning (System 2) are both active when we are awake. System 1 runs automatically and often System 2 runs at a "low effort" mode where only a portion of its capability is being used. System 1 continually generates responses to situations, prompting suggestions for System 2, including impressions, intuitions, intentions, and feelings. If all goes smoothly in response to an ordinary situation, System 2 adopts the suggestions of System 1. The spontaneous impressions and intuitions of this mode of thinking are consciously adopted by deliberate thinking and become the established beliefs of the decision maker.

If the use of the automatic system runs into trouble, the individual calls on deliberative reasoning (System 2) to provide a more self-conscious process of analyzing the details and features of a situation to assess the circumstance and solve any important problem it may pose. If intuition and an automatic response to a situation (System 1) do not prompt a ready answer to the individual's question or seem a satisfactory response to a circumstance, he or she calls on System 2 thinking to address the situation and to resolve the problem it poses. This is what happened when you were asked to determine the answer to the "13 × 47" multiplication problem. Deliberative reasoning (System 2) thought is activated when the mind detects an event that violates the model of the world or upsets the pattern anticipated by System 1 thought. The event is a surprise that activates deliberative reasoning to assess the significance of this unanticipated occurrence. The event is surprising because the model of the world maintained by System 1 does not foresee the surprising event. In such a case, System 2 is asked to search its memory or to engage in a process for some kind of "story" that makes sense of the surprise event. In addition to helping a person "make sense" of events, System 2, deliberative reasoning has the job of continuously monitoring behavior. Self-conscious thought, for example, keeps you polite even if you are angry and cautious as you drive at night through in the mountains. In short, most decisions you make originate in automatic or intuitive responses to situations (System 1). System 2, deliberative reasoning only gets involved in a decision process when something in the situation is surprising, not easily assessed, or some problem emerges for which there is no automatic answer available.

In ideal circumstances, System 1 and System 2 thinking processes divide the work of decision making to minimize effort and maximize performance. System 1 does its work of responding to a situation at a minimum of effort. System 2 only gets involved when System 1 encounters something in a situation with new and surprising features that were unanticipated, and hence perplexing. In such cases, automatic or intuitive responses are not satisfactory and self-conscious thought becomes necessary. System 1 is quite good at what it does, in rapidly responding to ordinary, familiar circumstances, but it does have biases. It is likely to make errors in those situations where surprise events take place and in circumstances that complicate the expectations of the decision maker. As we consider the audit process in this chapter, we will explore some of the potential errors made by System 1 thinking, circumstances where automatic or intuitive response might cause problems and lead to faulty decision making. We discuss this topic under the category of audit ethics because too frequent reliance on System 1 thinking leads to biased reasoning and poor decisions. Because the professional codes of conduct for auditors forbid them from making biased decisions, knowledge about potential sources of bias in the process of decision making is a critical first step in avoiding such errors in judgment in the audit task.

So, what is the common form of bias generated by System 1 thinking? Sometimes an intuitive or automatic response to a situation misinterprets a situation. It may not grasp the importance of a key event; it may fail to address a significant problem that is posed. System 1 thinking does not make use of an orderly, sequential logic; it may not grasp or appreciate statistical analysis. System 1, an intuitive approach, does not keep track of decision alternatives. It may not even generate alternate choices or may forget those it rapidly rejected. The self-conscious projection and assessment of action-alternatives are tasks of System 2 reasoning. These activities of reflection and memory take willful effort and directed attention. But if – for some reasons – the individual is too busy or too "lazy" to employ such deliberative thinking and this leads to poor decision making, a person's intuition may tempt him or her to believe almost anything. Automatic responses may seem so satisfying. Another complicating factor with reliance on System 1 thinking is that an individual cannot easily set it aside. The appeal of intuition can be quite powerful.

If a person relies on an intuitive approach (System 1) when he should use deliberative reasoning with its self-conscious reflection, memory, and anticipation of results, he or she may be too easily satisfied by an automatic assessment of a situation. He or she may be tempted to accept a too simplistic answer to the question posed in the situation or misunderstand an issue entirely. In an audit situation, the individual may not see what is most important – which financial elements are most significant; which previous accounting decisions may be flawed. Because System 1 responses are automatically made by the person, they may "just skim the surface of a situation" and the individual may fail to perceive the main features of the situation or to address the actual problems that are posed. In this context, it is crucial to recognize situations where surprising events may occur and mistakes may be likely. In those situations the auditor should employ System 2, deliberative reasoning in making decisions. The purpose of this chapter is to help us recognize situations where System 1 thinking may generate the wrong decision, and encourage us to take the effort to use self-conscious, deliberative processes in thinking through the auditing tasks in these situations.

We must be warned: even when the auditor realizes that System 2 thought is required in a situation, System 1 thinking is automatic and intuitive responses take place quite quickly in a given situation – often as soon as we are introduced to information. Because automatic and intuitive responses are often appealing and powerful in their influence (and not easily cast aside), it takes self-conscious effort on the part of the auditor to overcome these responses. It takes serious willpower and discipline to reject the often simplistic assessments, answers, and decisions conveyed by intuition and "fast thinking". This self-conscious effort to resist the appeal of intuition is necessary, so that deliberative reasoning can adequately assess auditing situations and successfully address the critical questions they pose. If we do not overcome a temptation to be satisfied by our intuition, we will be "stuck" with these inadequate, "automatic" responses. Our decisions will contain serious mistakes.

Eight biases are briefly discussed in the following section to suggest some of the ethical problems associated with making biased judgments during the audit process. Knowledge regarding these biases will allow the auditor to reject the intuitive responses provided by System 1 thinking and direct him or her to engage in System 2 deliberation.

The Heuristics and Biases Generated by System 1 Thinking

The biases relevant in the audit setting include the following:

- Confirmation bias
- Halo effect

- What you see is all there is (WYSIATI)
- Substituting questions
- Affect
- Law of small numbers
- Anchoring
- Representativeness.

Let's look at these biases in some detail so you will recognize them when they occur in the audit decision-making process.

The *confirmation bias* can be understood by considering the following questions:

Are the financial statements materially misstated?

Are the financial statements not materially misstated?

These two questions may generate different examples of the client's behavior. In the first instance, the decision maker searches for *confirming* evidence that the financial statements are misstated. Examples come to mind of information gathered during the audit process that might suggest a material misstatement in the financial statements. In the second instance, the decision maker searches for confirmatory evidence that the financial statements are not misstated. In this situation, examples come to mind of information gathered during the audit process that suggest that the financial statements are not materially misstated; that they are correct. The confirmatory bias favors an uncritical acceptance of the suggestions made by System 1 thinking.

Consider the audit process. Is it the auditor's job to gather evidence to show that the financial statements prepared by management are correct or that they are incorrect (not materially misstated or materially misstated)? Let us see how the evidence collection process works.

At the beginning of each audit, the client hands the auditor a set of financial statements. These financial statements contain management's assertions (i.e., existence, completeness, valuation) regarding the financial statements. To evaluate management's assertions regarding the financial statements, the auditor identifies relevant assertions for significant accounts and then gathers evidence to determine if these assertions contain misstatements. Should the auditor be looking for confirmatory evidence of the negative fact (the financial statements are materially misstated) or confirmatory evidence of the positive fact (the financial statements are not materially misstated)? In the audit process we do a little of each type of inquiry.

We identify fraud risk factors to gather evidence about how the financial statements might be misstated (this is confirmatory evidence for the hypothesis that the financial statements are misstated). The auditing standards require us to perform the audit with professional skepticism (a questioning mind and a critical attitude). If we audit with professional skepticism, we should search for confirmatory evidence that the financial statements are materially misstated. But we also begin the audit with the financial statements numbers that the client has prepared, rather than our own estimate of the numbers. Perhaps the best place to consider how beginning with client numbers may lead us toward "confirming that the client numbers are correct" thinking is to consider how we audit estimates.

Consider the allowance for doubtful accounts receivable as a type of estimate that is often found on the balance sheet of a company. The relevant assertions for accounts receivable are existence and valuation. The auditor would consider evidence related to the allowance to assess the accuracy of the valuation assertion of accounts receivable. Accounts receivable should be valued at the amount of cash that the company expects to collect the following year on the outstanding accounts receivable balance at year-end. This estimate is a guess. It is audited by using analytical procedures. The auditor compares the current year balance to the prior year balance to see if it is reasonable (if a similar percentage of accounts receivable were written off in the prior year). The auditor should also consider the impact of changes in economic conditions on the likelihood of customer repayment and ask whether the sales policies have changed so that credit is now being extended to riskier or less risky customers. The auditor does not begin the review of this allowance with the belief that "the allowance for uncollectible accounts receivable is misstated". Instead, the auditor begins with the general idea that this allowance is an estimate and the auditor must determine if this estimate appears reasonable. Perhaps approaching an audit from a perspective where the auditor "assumed the financial statements were misstated and searched for the misstatements" would place the auditor in a better position to find misstatements than to "assume the financial statements are correct and find evidence to support this".

The *halo effect* is something that we have all experienced. This is the tendency to like (or dislike) many things about a person or situation, even those things that you have not experienced first hand. The halo effect is one way that System 1 represents the world as being more simple and coherent than it really is. Consider two descriptions of controllers at one of your audit clients. What do you think of Scott and Chris?

Scott: intelligent – hardworking – stubborn – critical

Chris: critical – stubborn – hardworking – intelligent

If we consider the traits in the sequences that are given, most of us would likely rather work with Scott than Chris. Presenting Scott's first two traits in this order changes the evaluation of his last two traits. Stubbornness is seen as a good trait in a person who is intelligent and hardworking. You expect intelligent and hardworking people to have a critical ability to evaluate information. By contrast, given the sequence of traits presented for Chris, he might be considered a critical and stubborn person who is hardworking and intelligent and a person who might be trouble for the auditor because he may criticize the actions of the auditor and refuse to answer the auditor's questions.

Typically we observe the personality characteristics of the clients with whom we work in a given sequence over which we have no control. The sequence is crucial because it influences the way in which we perceive the person – despite the "randomness" of its presentation – because the earlier impressions are often given greater weight than later impressions. Sometimes the influence of earlier information is so powerful that the later impressions are virtually ignored.

Now, consider the impact of the halo effect applied to two audit clients. Consider two descriptions of audit clients. What do you think of each client?

ABC Corporation: profitable – expanding – high debt-to-equity ratio – risk-taking

DEF Corporation: risk-taking – high debt-to-equity ratio – expanding – profitable

Which client would you rather audit? It looks like the DEF Corporation is probably riskier to audit than the ABC Corporation. A high debt-to-equity ratio and evidence of an attitude of risk-taking is to be expected for a company that is both profitable and expanding (ABC Corporation). By contrast, expanding a company even if it is profitable may not be such a good thing if that company is risk-taking but already has a high debt-to-equity ratio (DEF Corporation).

Consider now how you obtained your information for these two clients. Might you have gained these impressions in random fashion from reading about the company, talking to executives in the company, and reviewing last year's working papers? Is there any logical reason to evaluate company DEF differently from ABC based on the information we have (without taking into account the order in which we learned their traits)? If the sequence of the presentation of traits has prejudiced my attitude toward a person or a company, how do I avoid this bias? As a decision maker one possible way to avoid this bias is to treat each piece of information as independent and thus to disregard the manner in which I gained the information. If I think in this "independent" way, I do not evaluate a high debt-to-equity ratio in the context of a profitable and expanding company; I evaluate the high debt-to-equity ratio by itself. To get the most information out of different sources of evidence and to evaluate that information properly (and guard against bias), you should always try to consider sources as independent of each other.

The bias of *what you see is all there is* (WYSIATI) means that the individual jumps to conclusions based on limited evidence created by System 1. System 1 is an associative machine. To make a decision, it works only with the information at hand. System 1 creates the best story it can with the information it already has, but this mode of thinking does not allow for information that it does not have. The amount and quality of the information that System 1 has is relevant, to be sure, but the information that is missing may be crucial to a thoughtful decision. When information is missing, System 1 thinking jumps to conclusions; it functions in a partial vacuum. Consider this statement: "MNO Corporation is well run and profitable." Would you like to do business with this company? Your answer of "yes" may be premature when you consider the next piece of information presented to you. What if the sentence continues, "and is absolutely ruthless in all business dealings"?

Think now about the question that you did not ask when you made your decision about whether you would like to do business with the company. You did not ask, "What information do I still need in order to decide whether I want to do business with the company?" System 1 got to work on its own based on the first description of the company. Well run is good. Well run and profitable is very good. The best story that System 1 can prepare from the two adjectives describing the company is that doing business with such a company would be good. If new information comes in, the story could be revised, but it is a good story as it stands. System 1 likes coherent stories and if a person is busy or lazy, he or she may employ System 2 thinking merely to accept the intuitive explanations offered by System 1 without further consideration. He or she accepts System 1 conclusions as if they are well-established results. System 2 is capable of a more careful systematic approach to decision making, but the individual will not make the conscious effort to analyze the situation unless System 1 thinking has been unable to find a satisfactory meaning in the situation or "prepare a coherent story" about what is taking place.

So, what does it take for System 1 thinking to construct meaning in a situation and to tell its story? System 1 needs information that is consistent, but this information need not necessarily be complete. In fact, knowing just a little makes it easier to construct a good story than knowing a great deal. System 1, intuitive thinking, finds it easy to jump to conclusions based on limited information as long as the information is consistent. Such automatic or intuitive thinking does not concern itself with either the quality or quantity of the information it processes; it only needs the information to be consistent to suggest a straightforward coherence.

How might this bias affect the audit process? A major assumption we make about the company we audit is that the past predicts the future. We begin the analytical review process during the planning stage of the audit by comparing the current financial statement numbers to the prior year financial statement numbers. If there has been little change in the numbers, then we assume that everything is fine. In this case, for many of the income statement numbers, analytical review evidence is all the evidence that we gather. And this evidence is evidence only of consistency, not evidence of anything else. Because our System 1 thinking finds consistent evidence to be satisfactory, we are happy not to look for any other evidence, even if the evidence that we have reviewed is incomplete.

Consider how the bias of "what you see is all there is" might be present in our assessment of internal controls. Internal controls are mechanisms put in place by management to prevent or detect misstatements in the financial statements. The auditor must document his or her understanding of internal controls to perform an audit. The auditor decides to test internal controls only if he or she thinks that internal controls are working (they might be effective in preventing or detecting misstatement). The only internal controls the auditors can test are documented controls. The auditor can review signatures on documents indicating, for example, that a review of the documentation was done before the transaction was processed. The auditor can also review independent reconciliations done by employees indicating that someone reviewed the transaction information that someone else generated. When the auditor decides to test a control, the only evidence the auditor gets is evidence about whether the control is working. The auditor does not get any evidence about whether the account balance or class of transaction related to the transaction is correct. Evidence that the control is working is only evidence of that (what you see is all there is). It is not evidence that the financial statements are not misstated.

System 1 can also be understood as the mechanism the person uses to first assess the potential danger the individual faces. It constantly monitors what is going on and generates assessments of the situation without intention and with little or no effort. These basic assessments turn into fixed judgments when they are substituted for more complex decision making and conscious reflection and problem solving for difficult questions. System 1 also allows you to rapidly substitute one judgment for another. Consider the mental shotgun.

Whenever your eyes are open, System 1 is continuously assessing the space around you. Through this process, you develop a mental picture of all the objects in your space; where they are, their identity, and their shape. This process is automatic, so it happens without any intention on the part of the individual. Other, more deliberative computations are undertaken only when necessary. For example, you do not maintain a continuous assessment of whether or not your favorite politician will win the next election. These assessments are voluntary but likely spontaneous; they happen only when you need the information. Yet a person's control over intended assessments is not perfect. We often assess more information than we need or want. This has been referred to as the *mental shotgun*. With a shotgun, it is impossible to shoot at a single point. The pellets from the shell scatter in a wide area around the target. System 1, in other words, does much more – in scattershot fashion – than the deliberative effort of System 2 would do in the situation. And System 2 thinking does not take place unless the individual self-consciously chooses to think in this way.

Would it be a problem if an auditor responds only to the simplistic assessments of a System 1 approach or answers only the easier questions generated in this mode of thinking? Let us consider how this might happen.

During an audit, the auditor asks many questions and gathers evidence to find answers. The auditor does not have the option of leaving key questions unanswered about the elements of the financial statement. In this context, however, System 1 thinking is prone to pose many questions and answers that may not be directly related to the financial statements or may be unimportant for the audit process. Yet System 1 may try to address these many trivial matters. The normal state of your mind is that you have opinions and feelings about many things that flood into your consciousness. You like or dislike the people that you work with in management before you know much about them. You may believe your audit client is doing well before you have analyzed their performance this year. Whether or not you state these assessments, or even admit them to yourself, they may have a strong impact on your decision making. Given that you may have answers to questions the nature of which you have not yet clearly defined and assessments and attitudes you cannot really explain, your System 1 mode of thinking may lead to biased decision making.

So, how do we generate opinions about complex matters where we know very little and situations in which we encounter new, unanticipated events? If System 1 cannot easily interpret what is going on or find an answer to the hard questions that the situation may pose, it will substitute a simplistic interpretation and generate an easier question to answer. This is referred to as *substitution*. Substitution is a decision "heuristic". A heuristic as defined by Kahneman (2011, p. 98) is a "simple procedure that helps find adequate, although often imperfect, answers to difficult questions".

In some circumstances, substituting one question for another can be a reasonable decision. Gerd Gigerenzer (2008; 2010) has written several books that

Table 9.1   Questions arising in the audit setting

Real Question	Heuristic Question
What is the risk that my audit client has engaged in fraud?	Do I think the audit client is honest or dishonest?
How likely is it that my client will be in business the following year?	Can I assume my client will stay in business because he is in business now?
How likely is it that my audit client has bribed foreign officials?	How do I feel about companies bribing foreign officials to allow them to do business in a country?
How far should the auditor go to keep the audit client happy?	Is my client happy today?

emphasize the benefits of heuristic decision making in professions, including heuristic decision making for emergency room doctors as an example. Yet the type of decision making to which we have referred in this previous section is not a matter of heuristic decision making consciously chosen by the individual. It is, rather, decision making that occurs automatically as an expression of the mental "shotgun" approach, the spontaneous or automatic response to a situation. When heuristic decision making is not consciously chosen by the individual, but is an automatic decision made by System 1, then its results are likely not to be adequate for the professional auditor. Consider Table 9.1, which lists questions that might arise in the audit setting and should be addressed by the audit (the real questions) and the heuristic questions associated with them that may spontaneously arise in System 1 thinking and distract the auditor.

The heuristic question represents a question supplied by System 1 which may be answered immediately and easily. But does it really address the real question that should be answered in the audit setting, a problem that is likely to require careful reasoning on the part of the auditor? For adequate decision making, the heuristic questions need to be fitted to the real question and the answers to those questions must fit the audit needs, that is, be answers for the "real questions" of the situation. The weakness of System 1 thinking is that it does not consider whether the answer to its question is appropriate for some carefully considered question that addresses the needs of the audit. System 1 thinking merely generates questions and answers with little regard for a conscious deliberative process. If, then, the auditor is too busy or too lazy to employ deliberative analysis to pose real questions that address audit needs and to generate thoughtful alternatives and carefully reasoned decisions, then the reliance on System 1 intuition results in mistaken judgments and faulty decisions.

The *affect* heuristic says that people make decisions about the world based on their likes and dislikes. Your emotional attitude about how easy a client is to work with or how well dressed the controllers and CFO appear to be drive your assessments about the level of risk at the audit client. Although System 2 is capable of more logical thinking than judging a client by the way its executives dress, it does not function as a monitor on the decision maker's own emotions about many other things. In another aspect, a System 2 search for information does not examine the intentions that underlie beliefs but only whether a particular belief is consistent with the existing beliefs.

Judging the level of risk of a client as low when its executives are well dressed is consistent with whether some original "model" of the way the world is can be reaffirmed by the belief that is prompted by the situation. If, for example, the auditor believes that the client is easy to work with, he may continue in this attitude, despite particular client actions that would logically suggest otherwise.

Kahneman lists several characteristics of System 1 thinking in his book. Relevant characteristics for audit decision making are listed below. System 1 makes the following assessments:

- Generates impressions, feelings, and inclinations, and when endorsed by System 2 these become beliefs, attitudes, and intentions;
- Operates automatically and quickly, with little or no effort;
- Distinguishes the surprising from the normal;
- Infers and invents causes and intentions;
- Neglects ambiguity and suppresses doubt;
- Is biased to believe and confirm;
- Focuses on existing evidence and ignores absent evidence;
- Computes more than intended; and
- Sometimes substitutes an easier question for a difficult one. (Kahneman, 2011, p. 105)

As you can see from this list, several of these assessments could lead the auditor to be more confident than he or she should be, because the assessments are not based on the evidence available to the auditor. The tendency to generate feelings and turn them into beliefs is not a good trait for an auditor. The practice of inferring causes and intentions or inventing them does not lead to good audit decision making. The neglect of particular ambiguities and dismissal of doubt (a failure of professional skepticism) can lead the auditor to evaluate the evidence as sufficient when it is not. The inclination to believe the audit client and to seek automatic confirmation of the client's assertions is not helpful in conducting a professional audit. Outsiders relying on the independence of the auditor would not be happy with this audit approach. In another matter, an auditor who focuses only on the existing evidence and does not consider the missing evidence is not doing a good job of evaluating the necessary evidence for a comprehensive audit. Finally, inferring results that cannot be supported by evidence and substituting easier questions for the more difficult, yet vital, ones can never lead the auditor to an accurate opinion in the audit process.

Let us consider the heuristic of the law of small numbers and how it might result in biased decision making in the audit process. This heuristic is a restatement from probability theory of the "law of large numbers". The law of large numbers asserts that the average value of the results obtained from a large sample size should be close to the "true" expected value of the population. So it may seem reasonable on the surface that if this theory applies to large samples, why would it not apply to small samples? But "there is no law of small numbers" at all!

The auditing standards often permit an auditor to make decisions based on his or her professional judgment. Two examples that permit this type of judgment are when an auditor determines the materiality level for a company and when the auditor calculates the sample size for an internal control or substantive test. For this guidance to be reasonable, it should be possible to show that the auditors' professional judgment is reliable in making such decisions. For such reliability, one of the following conditions must be present: (1) the auditor must understand statistical theory related to probability, (2) decision making must be structured so the auditor is forced to engage in System 2 thinking, or (3) the intuitive thinking done by the auditor has been developed (let us say, by practical education and work experience) so their intuitive (System 1) thinking somehow generates correct decisions. Let's look at each of these situations briefly.

What does it mean to say that the auditor should understand statistical theory related to probability, and how did the auditor develop this skill? All the decisions related to the likelihood of something occurring (material misstatement, fraud, going concern, inventory obsolescence, for instance) are probability decisions. So, the auditor should understand probability theory, particularly the effect of base rates on the likelihood of an event happening. For some reason, accounting education has not focused on this type of expertise so auditors have not been taught how to evaluate the likelihood of events occurring. So, this option has not been taken by the profession in terms of improving the professional judgment of the auditor.

Next let us consider how to engage System 2 in the decision process. Remember, the intuitive judgments made by System 1 tend to be overly confident and extreme. Consider this approach to estimating the likelihood that sales revenue is misstated:

1. What sales revenue would you have predicted for this company for the current year if you knew nothing about the company? (This is the baseline prediction that you would make if you had no information.)

2. What would you estimate sales revenue to be for this company? (This is your intuitive judgment.)

3. What is the correlation between your intuitive judgment and your first prediction? The correlation between two factors is the proportion of shared factors among their determinants. The correlation is always a number between 0 and 1.

4. If the correlation is 0.30, move 30% of the distance from your baseline prediction toward your intuitive judgment. This gets you to a prediction that is influenced by your intuitive judgment, but is more moderate.

Let us consider an example of how this might work before we move on to the last factor that might be used to influence professional judgment.

Consider the example of auditing ABC Corporation. The auditor has a general idea of how the economy has done in the last year. Based on this knowledge, the auditor might believe that sales revenue has increased by about 10% in the past year over the prior year's sales revenue. Based on this estimate for all companies, this is the baseline estimate for any company for which the auditor conducts an audit. So, the answer to question 1 is 10% growth in sales revenue. A company with sales revenue of $100,000,000 is expected to have a net income of $110,000,000 in the current year.

The auditor's estimate of sales revenue for the ABC Corporation is higher than the average. The auditor expects to see sales revenue of $140,000,000 in the current year. This is the answer to question 2, the intuitive judgment of the auditor.

Now consider the determinants of the two numbers. Clearly, both numbers are affected by general economic conditions in the country, the level of expansion in production facilities, interest rates for long-term debt, the political system in the country, and the supply of money. But the audit client may be affected by issues that are not shared by all businesses: industry changes, technological advances, supply problems, increased competition in the industry, the extent of international operations, and the impact of foreign currency changes on financial statements to list but a few. So you might ask: how many common factors does your intuitive estimate share with the baseline estimate of growth? In this example, let's say only 40%. This is the answer to question 3. Now we adjust our estimate in step 4 by taking 40% of the difference between my original prediction and the baseline amount (40% of $30,000,000 is $12,000,000); adding this amount to the baseline gives me an estimate of $122,000,000. This estimate still reflects an intuitive judgment about this particular company, but this estimate is not as extreme as a System 1 assessment would be.

Finally, consider the intuitive judgment of the auditor. If the professional judgment of the auditor follows the belief that the law of large numbers for random sampling applies equally well to small samples, then the professional judgment of that auditor is flawed. The strong bias in believing that small samples closely resemble the large populations from which they are drawn is consistent with the type of processing we expect with System 1; it exaggerates the coherence and consistency of the evidence that is presented to us. To this point then, professional judgment does not yet appear to have made a very good decision choice. The auditor needs to introduce System 2 thinking into the decision process. This takes conscious effort on the part of the auditor.

The *anchoring heuristic* is relevant to the auditor because of the way an audit is done. The anchoring heuristic assumes that the estimate that an individual makes for a number stays close to the original number. The final number chosen by the individual has become "anchored" in the first number that the individual has seen. One of our favorite fraud cases involves a company called Sonali, a gold importer from Oceanside, California. Sonali's financial statements were almost completely fictitious, including reported revenue of $70 million when actual revenue was $1.5 million. Because the auditor worked with the financial statements prepared by management as the starting point for the audit, his or her estimate of revenue was anchored on the $70 million figure reported by the company. The auditor did not consider that revenue was actually only 2% of the amount reported by management and that 98% of the revenue was fictitious. In all probability, there are not many auditors who would expect such a large misstatement in sales revenue.

Think about how negotiations work. If you want to negotiate a salary increase with your employer, you start with a higher number than you will settle for, knowing that during the negotiation process your target salary will be reduced. The person who makes the first move has the opportunity to anchor the negotiation at the top of the expected range. So, if you want an increase of $20,000, you start with $25,000, not $5,000, knowing that you will receive a raise closer to your target if you anchor the decision on $25,000, not $5,000. It is difficult to imagine any other way to perform an audit than to start with the financial statements prepared by the client, but the auditor must recognize the effect that anchoring might have on your decisions, particularly for accounts that are estimates (e.g., bad debt expense). One suggestion to get around the anchoring effect is to consider what your estimate would have been if the anchor were not present. The conscious decision to develop an independent estimate may prompt System 2 thinking and this may allow you to avoid anchoring on the number provided by the client.

Sometimes people make predictions about others based on how well those people seem to represent the stereotypes of the group with which they are associated. This bias is referred to as the heuristic of *representativeness*. Judging the likelihood of something having certain traits by its supposedly being representative of the ascribed traits of a particular group may lead to the correct answer, but if the stereotype of the group's traits is false (and stereotypes generally are), the right prediction will not be made.

Consider the following example. One year near the end of the audit, the CEO of the company came into the auditor's office at the company to apologize to the auditor. CEOs do not often apologize to auditors. Explaining the reason for the apology, the CEO reminded the auditor of one large storage room in the warehouse that the client had not counted when it did the annual inventory count. Because the client had not counted the room, the auditor was delayed from her test counts. The CEO continued, stating that the client employee had not done the counting of the room because he knew a woman was in charge of the inventory counts for the audit firm, and he believed that she would not notice that the room was not counted. The CEO assured the auditor that the employee was suspended for three days without pay because of his behavior. Consider the error in evaluating a female auditor from a Big Four firm according to some likelihood that she might represent the employee's faulty stereotype of women's abilities. In most cases, judging a person in terms of how they may fit a stereotypical representation of a given group will lead you to a faulty assessment (as the employee got to consider during his three day suspension).

Be careful about the stereotypes you bring to the audit engagement. Make sure that the decisions you make during the audit process are based on evidence, not on your impressions of the company or the employees of the company. Making decisions based on stereotypes is hard to defend when you are asked to justify your decision, either to your supervisor or to the regulators.

The Ethics of Financial Statement Disclosure and Earnings Management

There are three common types of financial statement disclosure: (1) footnotes to the financial statements, (2) the management, discussion, and analysis section of the audit report, and (3) press releases made by the audit client. The footnotes are audited by the auditor which means that the auditor gathers evidence to support the information in the footnotes. The management, discussion, and analysis section of the audit report is just reviewed by the auditor, but not audited. This means that the auditor reads the management, discussion, and analysis written by management to make sure that it does not state information contrary to the audited material in the annual report. The auditor does not gather evidence to support the information in this report. Companies often disclose their quarterly earnings and their annual results in a press release to the public. This information may also be posted to their website for readers to review. Auditors do not audit press releases, although they may review the information at the request of their client before it is released to the public.

There is one other source of disclosure although we do not think of it as financial statement disclosure. When the company issues an audit report, this annual report contains the financial statements and the footnotes, the audit opinion, the management, discussion, and analysis statement, and information about the company. The information about the company is often twice as long as the financial statements, footnotes, opinion, and management, discussion, and analysis section. Annual reports are often 150 or more pages. The audited material may be less than 50 pages of this report and it is typically in the back portion of the audit report following the company information and management's assessment of how well they did last year. The auditor would typically review this information to see that it does not contradict anything in the financial statements.

What are the ethical issues associated with financial statement disclosure? How might an auditor demonstrate ethical awareness in reviewing the disclosures made in the audit report? The starting point for disclosure is to assume that the client will not disclose anything that the client is not required to disclose. Gathering information has a cost to it. It is almost always a good assumption to start from the position that nothing extra is disclosed. Of course, that does not mean that everything that should be disclosed is disclosed, so the auditor gathers evidence to support the disclosure in the footnotes and makes sure that all required disclosures are made. The disclosure should also be written in a format that is understandable to the reader. Things that a company must disclose that make the company appear less appealing to the outside stakeholders might be written in a way that obscures the meaning of the disclosure. The management, discussion, and analysis section of the annual report is also likely to be written by management to be more positive than evidence would support. It is the auditor's job to make sure that this section does not contradict or misconstrue the information in the footnotes and the financial statements.

Consider an example of footnote disclosure and management, discussion, and analysis disclosure for Amazon. Amazon is a company founded in 1995 that markets its products solely through retail websites. Amazon originally sold books and electronic items but has expanded its business into all areas of consumer goods. Amazon refers to its website as the store with the world's biggest selection. Amazon reported sales revenue of $61,093 million and a net loss of $39 million in 2012. Footnote 1 – "Description of Business and Accounting Policies" – describes the company's determination of the cost of sales (cost of goods sold).

Cost of sales consists of the purchase price of consumer products and digital content where we are the seller of record, inbound and outbound shipping charges, and packaging supplies. Shipping charges to receive products from our suppliers are included in our inventory, and recognized as cost of sales upon sale of products to our customers. Payment processing are related transaction costs, including those associated with seller transactions, and classified in "Fulfillment" on our consolidated statements of operations. (Amazon Annual Report, 2012, p. 48)

The auditor will audit the information in this footnote. This means that he or she will examine evidence to determine that the cost of the inventory sold by the company has been determined in the manner described by the client. Amazon states that they determine the cost of inventory sold by taking the purchase price of the inventory and adding the cost of shipping charges to receive the goods from the suppliers and shipping costs to mail the goods to the customers, plus the cost of packaging materials to mail the package. The auditor can determine whether Amazon follows its stated policy by reviewing the entries in the inventory records. The auditor also must determine if Amazon followed its stated procedures that these are in accordance with the accounting standards. In the decision-making process associated with an audit, the review of this form of disclosure involves two steps: (1) does the client follow the procedures that they describe in the footnote; (2) are the procedures in accordance with the accounting standards? Auditing this disclosure is primarily a matter of demonstrating technical proficiency.

Consider now the comment in the "Management, Discussion, and Analysis" section of the annual report, keeping the same issue in mind. The disclosure in this section of the report is only reviewed by the auditor and not audited.

We expect our net cost of shipping to continue to increase to the extent our customers accept and use our shipping offers at an increasing rate, our product mix shifts to the electronics and other general merchandise category, we reduce shipping rates, we use more expensive shipping methods, and we offer additional services. We seek to mitigate cost of shipping over time in part through achieving higher sales volumes, optimizing placement of fulfillment centers, negotiating better terms with our suppliers, and achieving better operating efficiencies. We believe that offering low prices to our customers is fundamental to our future success, and one way we offer lower prices is through shipping offers. (Amazon Annual Report 2012, p. 25)

It is a good thing that the auditor only has to review this information. There is no evidence that supports anything in this statement because this statement forecasts the future. So how does the auditor review this statement? Technical proficiency does not help us here. This statement must be reviewed based on whether it is reasonable and whether it provides information contrary to the information reported in the financial statements and the footnotes. Shipping cost was $2,437 million in 2011 and $2,854 million in 2012 (Amazon Annual Report 2012, p. 25). Shipping cost increased in the past year, so it is reasonable to expect it to continue to increase. If the management of Amazon were trying to tell me that they expected shipping cost to decrease, this would be more difficult to believe; this seems unlikely. There are some statements in this section written by management that I do not understand: (1) they say that they expect shipping costs to increase and one of the reasons is because "we reduce shipping rates"; (2) they also say that they expect to reduce shipping costs over time by "achieving higher sales volumes". I don't know why higher sales volumes reduce shipping costs, unless the shipping services give them a discount for volume. The auditor could have asked management these two questions when reviewing the management, discussion, and analysis section of the annual report. Any forecasting done by management should be reviewed by the auditor with a critical eye and an awareness of ethical issues associated with disclosure. The crucial question the auditor must ask when reviewing the management, discussion, and analysis section of the annual report is whether outsiders receive information that is contrary to the information reported in the financial statements and its footnotes.

What is "earnings management"? Companies "manage earnings" to meet earnings targets, receive bonuses, get loans, meet analysts' forecasts, and maintain growth in earnings per share. There are ways to manage earnings within the choices permitted by the accounting standards, but when we speak of earnings management today, we are often thinking about the manipulation of reported earnings, disclosing earnings in ways that are not permitted by the accounting standards. When we use the term "earnings management," this means something bad, an inappropriate form of financial disclosure. Given the current usage of the term, it is the auditor's job to prevent earnings management. In this context, the auditor should be ethically aware when auditing the footnotes of the company and reviewing the management, discussion, and analysis section of the audit report to make sure that outsiders receive high-quality information from the annual report (disclosures that provide relevant information and information that describes the economic reality of the transaction).

The Auditor's Role in the Corporate Governance Process

What is the corporate governance process? We consider the auditor, the audit committee, the board of directors, and executives of the company to play a key role in managing the company for the benefit of the owners of the company. The auditor plays a unique role in this process because he or she has been hired by the audit committee to issue an opinion on whether management has prepared the financial statements in accordance with the accounting standards. Outsiders are willing to rely on the word of the auditor because the auditor is independent from the company and has no reason not to tell the truth. But if the auditor fails to do his or her job by not exercising technical proficiency or demonstrating ethical awareness during the audit process, the auditor does not protect the interests of outsiders. If the auditor fails to fulfill his or her role, no one else steps in to do the job so outsiders receive low-quality information to use in decision making.

APPENDIX

International Auditing Standards

- ISA 200, Overall Objectives of the Independent Auditor and the Conduct of an Audit in Accordance with International Standards on Auditing
- ISA 210, Agreeing the Terms of Audit Engagements
- ISA 220, Quality Control for an Audit of Financial Statements
- ISA 230, Audit Documentation
- ISA 240, The Auditor's Responsibilities Relating to Fraud in an Audit of Financial Statements
- ISA 250, Consideration of Laws and Regulations in an Audit of Financial Statements
- ISA 260, Communication with Those Charged with Governance
- ISA 265, Communicating Deficiencies in Internal Control to Those Charged with Governance and Management
- ISA 300, Planning an Audit of Financial Statements
- ISA 315, Identifying and Assessing the Risks of Material Misstatement through Understanding the Entity and Its Environment
- ISA 320, Materiality in Planning and Performing an Audit
- ISA 330, The Auditor's Responses to Assessed Risks
- ISA 402, Audit Considerations Relating to an Entity Using a Service Organization
- ISA 450, Evaluation of Misstatements Identified during the Audit
- ISA 500, Audit Evidence
- ISA 501, Audit Evidence-Specific Considerations for Selected Items
- ISA 505, External Confirmations
- ISA 510, Initial Audit Engagements – Opening Balances
- ISA 520, Analytical Procedures
- ISA 530, Audit Sampling
- ISA 540, Auditing Accounting Estimates, Including Fair Value Accounting Estimates, and Related Disclosures
- ISA 550, Related Parties
- ISA 560, Subsequent Events
- ISA 570, Going Concern
- ISA 580, Written Representations
- ISA 600, Special Considerations-Audits of Group Financial Statements (Including the Work of Component Auditors)
- ISA 610, Using the Work of Internal Auditors
- ISA 620, Using the Work of an Auditor's Expert

- ISA 700, Forming an Opinion and Reporting on Financial Statements
- ISA 705, Modifications to the Opinion in the Independent Auditor's Report
- ISA 706, Emphasis of Matter Paragraphs and Other Matter Paragraphs in the Independent Auditor's Report
- ISA 710, Comparative Information-Corresponding Figures and Comparative Financial Statements
- ISA 720, The Auditor's Responsibilities Relating to Other Information in Documents Containing Audited Financial Statements
- ISA 800, Special Considerations-Audits of Financial Statements Prepared in Accordance with Special Purpose Frameworks
- ISA 805, Special Considerations-Audits of Single Financial Statements and Specific Elements, Accounts or Items of a Financial Statement
- ISA 810, Engagements to Report on Summary Financial Statements.

PCAOB Auditing Standards

- AS No. 1: References in Auditors' Reports to the Standards of the PCAOB
- AS No. 3: Audit Documentation
- AS No. 4: Reporting on Whether a Previously Reported Material Weakness Continues to Exist
- AS No. 5: An Audit of Internal Control Over Financial Reporting That Is Integrated with An Audit of Financial Statements
- AS No. 6: Evaluating Consistency of Financial Statements
- AS No. 7: Engagement Quality Review
- AS No. 8: Audit Risk
- AS No. 9: Audit Planning
- AS No. 10: Supervision of the Audit Engagement
- AS No. 11: Consideration of Materiality in Planning and Performing an Audit
- AS No. 12: Identifying and Assessing Risks of Material Misstatement
- AS No. 13: The Auditor's Responses to the Risks of Material Misstatement
- AS No. 14: Evaluating Audit Results
- AS No. 15: Audit Evidence
- AS No. 16: Communications with Audit Committees
- AU 110 Responsibilities and Functions of the Independent Auditor
- AU 150 Generally Accepted Auditing Standards
- AU 161 The Relationship of Generally Accepted Auditing Standards to Quality Control Standards
- AU 201 Nature of the General Standards
- AU 210 Training and Proficiency of the Independent Auditor
- AU 220 Independence

- AU 230 Due Professional Care in the Performance of Work
- AU 315 Communications Between Predecessor and Successor Auditors
- AU 316 Consideration of Fraud in a Financial Statement Audit
- AU 317 Illegal Acts by Clients
- AU 322 The Auditor's Consideration of the Internal Audit Function in an Audit of Financial Statements
- AU 324 Service Organizations
- AU 325 Communications About Control Deficiencies in an Audit of Financial Statements
- AU 328 Auditing Fair Value Measurements and Disclosures
- AU 329 Substantive Analytical Procedures
- AU 330 The Confirmation Process
- AU 331 Inventories
- AU 332 Auditing Derivative Instruments, Hedging Activities, and Investments in Securities
- AU 333 Management Representations
- AU 334 Related Parties
- AU 336 Using the Work of a Specialist
- AU 337 Inquiry of a Client's Lawyer Concerning Litigation, Claims, and Assessments
- AU 341 The Auditor's Consideration of an Entity's Ability to Continue as a Going Concern
- AU 342 Auditing Accounting Estimates
- AU 350 Audit Sampling
- AU 390 Consideration of Omitted Procedures After the Report Date
- AU 410 Adherence to Generally Accepted Accounting Principles
- AU 411 The Meaning of Present Fairly in Conformity With Generally Accepted Accounting Principles
- AU 435 Segment Information
- AU 504 Association With Financial Statements
- AU 508 Reports on Audited Financial Statements
- AU 530 Dating of the Independent Auditor's Report
- AU 532 Restricting the Use of an Auditor's Report
- AU 534 Reporting on Financial Statements Prepared for Use in Other Countries
- AU 543 Part of Audit Performed by Other Independent Auditors
- AU 544 Lack of Conformity With Generally Accepted Accounting Principles
- AU 550 Other Information in Documents Containing Audited Financial Statements
- AU 551 Reporting on Information Accompanying the Basic Financial Statements in Auditor-Submitted Documents
- AU 552 Reporting on Condensed Financial Statements and Selected Financial Data
- AU 558 Required Supplementary Information
- AU 560 Subsequent Events

- AU 561 Subsequent Discovery of Facts Existing at the Date of the Auditor's Report
- AU 622 Engagements to Apply Agreed-Upon Procedures to Specified Elements, Accounts, or Items of a Financial Statement
- AU 623 Special Reports
- AU 625 Reports on the Application of Accounting Principles
- AU 634 Letters for Underwriters and Certain Other Requesting Parties
- AU 711 Filings Under Federal Securities Statutes
- AU 722 Interim Financial Information
- AU 801 Compliance Auditing Considerations in Audits of Governmental Entities and Recipients of Governmental Financial Assistance
- AU 901 Public Warehouses – Controls and Auditing Procedures for Goods Held.

CHAPTER REVIEW QUESTIONS

1. (LO1) Describe the role of the auditor. Explain why this job is important to outsiders.

2. (LO2) What purpose do the professional codes of conduct serve for the profession? Is it important that a profession has a code of conduct?

3. (LO3) What role do heuristics play in the judgment of an auditor? If System 1 thinking is automatic, how does the auditor prevent him or herself from making decisions based on heuristic rules?

4. (LO4) Disclosure seems to be more important today than it was ten years ago. Is this an example of "out of control regulators" or a realistic assessment of the importance of disclosure to outsiders?

5. (LO3) Describe the danger of attaching too much importance to internal control evidence. How does the auditor avoid this bias?

6. (LO5) What role does the auditor serve in the corporate governance process? Is this role important?

CASES

7. PWC Japan

Kanebo, a cosmetics company in Japan, reported fictitious revenue of more than $2 billion from 1999 through 2003. This accounting fraud is the largest fraud reported in Japan. The Tokyo stock exchange requires firms to be de-listed after filing financial statements with a negative net worth for more than three years. If Kanebo had correctly reported its net worth, it would have been negative for the five years from 1999 to 2003.

In 2006, the Japanese financial regulator imposed a two-month suspension on Chuo Aoyama PricewaterhouseCoopers over its part in the accounting fraud at Kanebo. PWC International said that it would work with Chuo Aoyama to improve its practices, but at the same time granted a new firm, Aarata, the right to be an affiliated PWC office. Many of the Chuo Aoyama accountants transferred to the new PWC affiliate firm. Four months later, Chuo Aoyama reopened with a name change to Misuzu. Misuzu was forced to close in 2007 as a result of their involvement in the accounting fraud in Nikko Cordial.[1] This means that PWC, the largest accounting firm in the world, has a smaller role than the other Big Four auditors in auditing companies in the third largest economy in the world.

Required:

  a. Audit firms are organized as networks of partnerships (or professional service corporations) not as corporations. This means that the partners have little influence over the work done by the foreign affiliates, but face a loss of professional reputation when accounting fraud related to the foreign affiliates is reported in the business press. Is this fair?

8. Ernst & Young and Medicis Pharmaceutical

In 2012, Ernst & Young paid a $2 million fine to the Public Company Accounting Oversight Board (PCAOB), the auditing regulatory authority in the US, to settle a claim that they violated auditing standards in the audit of Medicis Pharmaceutical for 2005, 2006, and 2007. The PCAOB found that the auditors failed to properly evaluate the sales return reserve account on the financial statements. Ernst & Young allowed Medicis to use replacement cost rather than sales price to estimate the dollar amount of the sales return reserve.

Medicis sells pharmaceutical products that are date stamped with an expiration date. The return policy for the company allows the customer to return the drugs that have expired for a full refund of the sales price. According to the accounting standards, a company selling a product with a right of return can recognize revenue from the transactions at the point of sale if it is able to estimate the amount of future returns. If the company can estimate the amount of the returns, it must reduce sales revenue and cost of sales in the income statement to reflect the estimated returns. Medicis did not comply with accounting standards. The company calculated the amount of the sales return reserve at the replacement cost and not at the sales price. Ernst & Young knew or should have known that the sales return reserve did not comply with accounting standards.

The PCAOB also faulted Ernst & Young for the disclosures that the auditor permitted Medicis to make in the company's financial statements. The accounting standards require a company to disclose all significant accounting policies in the financial statements, particularly accounting policies related to the recognition of revenue. This disclosure is typically made in Footnote 1 in the financial statements prepared by the company. Ernst & Young allowed Medicis to issue financial statements without disclosing the revenue recognition policy related to the calculation of the sales return reserve.[2]

Required:

   a. Discuss the accounting and ethical problems that Ernst & Young faced.

   b. Did the auditor know that the sales return reserve calculated by the client was not in accordance with the accounting standards?

   c. Would the auditor have been aware that the disclosure made by the client in footnote 1 about the revenue recognition policy was not in accordance with the accounting standards?

   d. Evaluate the quality of information outsiders received.

9. PWC and Satyam India

In 2011, PWC International India paid a $1.5 million fine to settle a claim that the audit firm failed to follow PCAOB auditing standards in the audit of Satyam Computer Services. This fine is in addition to the $6 million fine that the Securities and Exchange Commission levied against the international auditing firm.

In auditing the financial statements of Satyam, PWC allowed Satyam to mail the confirmation requests to the banks to verify the cash balances and used as evidence the completed confirmation forms received from the company. Auditing standards require the auditor to control the mailing of confirmation requests and to receive the confirmation replies at the audit firm. Failure to correctly apply auditing procedures to confirm the cash balance allowed Satyam to inflate their cash balance by $1 billion. As a result of this disciplinary action, PWC India will not be able to accept new audit engagements for US issuers of stock until an independent review shows that it has modified its audit procedures.[3]

Required:

   a. Describe the technical proficiency and ethical awareness required of the auditor in this case. Did the auditor meet these requirements?

   b. Identify specific sections of the auditing standards and the codes of conduct that apply in this situation.

   c. How does this decision against PWC International affect PWC in the rest of the world? Are professional service organizations harmed when one group of the organization fails to meet professional standards?

10. Ahold and KPMG

Two KPMG auditors, Kevin Hall and Rosemary Meyer, were accused of improper professional conduct in the audit of the financial statements of US Foodservice, a distribution company. US Foodservice inflated the revenue reported by the company by recognizing income from fictitious promotional allowances or recognizing the promotional allowance early. The two KPMG auditors identified valuation, existence, and completeness of the promotional income and receivable as a significant audit area. During the audit, they found numerous cases where the company recognized promotional income when they should not have. In vouching vendor payments received by the company, the auditor discovered that the company had recognized significant unearned prepayments of promotional allowances as income. The working papers show that the auditors identified the revenue recognition attached to these prepayments as audit adjustments, but the adjustments were subsequently removed by liquid white-out. The very existence of the prepayments in the vendor payment file contradicted management's claim that they did not have any vendor prepayments and the auditors failed to investigate this discrepancy. The auditor ignored most of the contradictory evidence in the work papers, relying on management representations to confirm previous management representations. The SEC found that Hall and Meyer failed to comply with generally accepted auditing standards by: (1) failing to exercise due professional care; (2) failing to maintain an attitude of professional skepticism; (3) failing to obtain sufficient competent evidence; and (4) substituting management representations for competent evidence.[4]

Required:

    a. Describe the technical proficiency and ethical sensibility required of the auditors in this case. Did the auditor meet these requirements?

    b. Identify specific sections of the auditing standards and the codes of conduct that apply in this situation.

    c. Why did the auditors choose to ignore the evidence and instead believe management?

    d. What should the auditors have done in this situation?

11. Parmalat and Deloitte & Touche

Parmalat's audits used Deloitte auditors in at least 30 countries, including Italy, the United States, Canada, Mexico, Brazil, and the Netherlands. The auditors in the other countries frequently let the Italian auditors make the final decisions related to the audit since they signed the audit report. Investors around the world relied on the audit report issued by Deloitte & Touche on the Parmalat financial statements. Parmalat filed for bankruptcy in December 2003. The financial statements of the company had hidden a fraud that ran for ten years with €14 billion removed from the company during that time, some into the hands of top executives, and some to finance an overly ambitious expansion policy in South America.

    The fraud was compared to a Ponzi scheme where Parmalat managers used billions of dollars borrowed from investors around the world to cover up losses from their expansion in South America. When the company covered up the losses in the company, they were able to continue to borrow money. When they were no longer able to borrow money, the company collapsed. At the time of the collapse, Parmalat's assets were overstated by €4 billion and its debt was understated by at least €7.9 billion.[5]

Required:

    a. Describe the technical proficiency and ethical sensibility required of the auditors in this case. Did the auditor meet these requirements?

   b. Identify specific sections of the auditing standards and the codes of conduct that apply in this situation.

   c. Various offices of Deloitte & Touche are attempting to limit their liability, putting the responsibility for the failed audit on Deloitte & Touche Italy. Should auditors be able to limit their liability on the work done on an audit if they were not the primary auditor?

12. General Electric

In September 2002, the SEC opened an informal investigation into the retirement packages offered by General Electric (GE) to former CEO Jack Welch, who retired in 2001.[6] The compensation package, negotiated in 1996, became public information as a result of divorce proceedings between Welch and his wife, Jane. Her divorce filings report an "extraordinary" lifestyle, largely paid for by GE funds, even after Jack's retirement in 2001.[7]

The divorce filing reported that GE paid for country club memberships, family phones and computers in five homes; flowers; wine and maid service; sports tickets to the Red Sox, Yankees, and Knicks games; Wimbledon tickets; opera tickets; and, in addition, expenses for autos, many of the costs of a GE-owned apartment in New York City (valued at $80,000 per month), and the use of GE-owned jets valued at $291,865 per month.

SEC regulations require companies to disclose such benefit contracts, but do not specify the nature of the disclosure. SEC regulations require companies to disclose the compensation paid to the five highest-paid executives, but do not require companies to disclose the amount paid to retired executives. GE said that the board had approved Welch's retirement package in 1996. The company included a copy of the agreement in its 1996 proxy filing. The contract, according to the GE report, states that Welch will have access for the remainder of his life to company services provided to him prior to retirement, "including access to company aircraft, cars, office, apartments and financial-planning services" plus reimbursement for "reasonable" travel and living expenses.[8]

The SEC requested information from GE regarding the disclosure to shareholders and the public for the executive perks given to Welch. Welch has insisted that all benefits were disclosed, but he has also said that he will give up most of the perks and begin paying GE $2–2.5 million per year for the use of the company apartment and company planes. Welch said he would give up the perks, even though he thought they were reasonable at the time of negotiation, to avoid misperception in the current environment of corporate scandal.

Required:

   a. Discuss the accounting and ethical issues of this situation.

   b. Who are the stakeholders?

   c. What was the auditor's responsibility for this disclosure?

   d. Consider the conflicts of interest and the pressure on General Electric.

   e. Is anyone harmed or does anyone benefit by the possible choices?

13. Ernst & Young
Refer to the description of the Ernst & Young independence problem with PeopleSoft in Chapter 6. What heuristic might Ernst & Young have used to allow it to think that selling Peoplesoft software and auditing Peoplesoft would not cause a violation of the Code of Professional Conduct? Explain why Ernst & Young was wrong to apply this heuristic in this setting.

14. Halo Effect Heuristic
Explain how the heuristic referred to as the halo effect allows outsiders to assume that an audit done by Ernst & Young US is the same as an audit done by Ernst & Young International. Is this heuristic helpful to either outsiders or the audit firm?

15. Medicis and the Anchoring Heuristic
Refer to the facts in the Medicis problem on page 264. Explain how the anchoring heuristic may have allowed Ernst & Young to accept Medicis' use of replacement cost instead of sales price to value the sales return reserve. Would it have been difficult for Ernst & Young to force Medicis to change how it determined the reserve?

16. Satyam and the Representativeness Heuristic
Problem 9 described the cash confirmation process at Satyam. How did PWC's acceptance of Satyam to mail the confirmation requests and forward the answers to PWC represent the decision heuristic of representativeness? Was this decision reasonable?

17. Ahold and Heuristic Judgment
Refer to the facts described in problem 10. Why would auditors ignore conflicting evidence in the audit work papers? Is there a heuristic that explains how auditors might have made this decision?

NOTES

1. "Former Chuo Aoyama forced to call it quits," *The Asahi Shimbun*, February 21, 2007; "PWC can bite the bullet, like it did in Japan," *Business Today*, February 2, 2013; "Japanese firm admits $1.37 billion accounting fraud," *Global Ethics*, April 18, 2005.

2. PCAOB News Release, "PCAOB announces settled disciplinary order for audit failures against Ernst & Young and four of its partners," Washington, DC, February 8, 2012; PCAOB Release No. 105-2012-001, "In the matter of Ernst & Young LLP, Jeffrey S. Anderson, CPA, Ronald Butler, Jr., CPA, Thomas A. Christie, CPA, and Robert H. Thibault, CPA," February 8, 2012.

3. PCAOB News Release, "PCAOB announces settled disciplinary order against PricewaterhouseCoopers International Firms in India for audit violations related to Satyam," Washington, DC, April 5, 2011.

4. SEC, "In the matter of Kevin Hall, CPA, and Rosemary Meyer, CPA," Administrative Proceeding, File No. 3-12208, February 16, 2006.

5. David Reilly & Alessandra Galloni, "Facing lawsuit, Parmalat auditor stresses its disunity," *The Wall Street Journal*, April 28, 2005; US Securities and Exchange

Commission, "SEC alleges additional violations by Parmalat Finanziaria, SpA, and simultaneously settle civil action," Litigation Release No. 18803, July 28, 2004.

6. "SEC investigates package that GE offered to Welch," *The Wall Street Journal*, September 16, 2002.

7. Matt Murray, JoAnn Lublin & Rachel Emma Silverman, "Welch's lavish retirement package angers General Electric investors", *The Wall Street Journal*, September 9, 2002.

8. Murray, Lublin & Silverman, "Welch's lavish retirement package angers General Electric investors", *The Wall Street Journal*, September 9, 2002.

REFERENCES

Gigerenzer, G. (2008) *Gut Feelings: Short Cuts to Better Decision Making*. London: Penguin Books.

Gigerenzer, G. (2010) *Rationality for Mortals: How People Cope with Uncertainty*. London: Oxford University Press.

International Auditing and Assurance Standards Board (IAASB) (2013) *2013 Handbook of International Quality Control, Auditing, Review, Other Assurance, and Related Services Pronouncements: Volume I and Volume II*. International Federation of Accountants.

Kahneman, D. (2011) *Thinking, Fast and Slow*. London: Penguin Books.

Public Company Accounting Oversight Board (PCAOB) (2013) *Auditing Standards, 2013*. http://pcaob.org/standards/auditing/pages/auditing_standard_1.aspx (accessed December 7, 2013).

CHAPTER TEN

The Accountant in Society: Deciding for Ethical Action

LEARNING OBJECTIVES

By the end of this chapter you should be able to:

1. Explain the ideas of technical proficiency and ethical sensibility.
2. Describe the various resources for addressing accounting and ethical problems within business situations.
3. Describe a decision process for addressing an ethical issue within an accounting institution.
4. Explain the following statement: An ethical action in accounting suggests that the accountant has intellectual and moral virtues and has engaged in a thoughtful, deliberative process of decision making.
5. Understand the key features of a profession in modern society.
6. Explain why a modern society might grant professional status to accounting.
7. Explain why an ethical accountant is important for "the marketplace".
8. Explain why audit firms should remain independent from their clients and why such independence is difficult to maintain.
9. Describe key features of social contract theory.
10. Describe some of the goals of Corporate Social Responsibility (CSR).

THE ACCOUNTANT AS MORAL AGENT

Reminder: Accounting is a discursive practice.

Reminder: The accountant is obligated to provide high-quality financial information to stakeholders.

Reminder: To do this requires a dual competency – technical proficiency and ethical sensibility.

Reminder: There are many resources available to resolve accounting problems and ethical problems.

Reminder: The needs and expectations of the general society are the foundation for the practice of accounting within a profession. The accounting profession calls for an ethics of duty and an ethics of virtue on the part of its members.

CHAPTER THEMES

The chapter has three main themes: (1) the role of the individual accountant as decision maker; (2) the accountant as a member of a profession which serves the public interest; and (3) the accountant and accounting organizations as citizens and institutional participants in the market and the wider society.

THE INDIVIDUAL ACCOUNTANT: MAKING ETHICAL DECISIONS

As we have repeated over and again: the accountant is supposed to prepare financial information in high-quality reports for various stakeholders. Our earlier discussions focused on the accountant's decision making as the vital process for addressing any accounting problems posed by this financial reporting and any moral issues that were encountered.

This decision process, considered as crucial within what we called "a discursive practice," should result in high-quality information. (In Chapter One, we construed a high-quality financial statement as one of "the internal goods" necessary for meeting the goals of accounting practice.) We can consider these accounting reports (financial statements) – the cumulative results of many accounting decisions – as a "public good". These accounting decisions and resulting financial statements play a vital role in modern societies, especially for the marketplace, where resources are allocated, goods and commodities produced and distributed, and capital is moved. The public good produced by accountants is high-quality information, financial knowledge upon which numerous stakeholders make their business and regulatory decisions.

The central topic of this book is the crucial ethical obligation placed on accountants. This duty binds them to show their intellectual and moral "high character" (their moral deliberation and virtues) as they perform their distinctive tasks. We have spoken of the accountant's ethics of duty and virtue as a demand for practical competency – an expectation of technical proficiency and skill in making ethical judgments. We have also provided examples and case studies so that you can demonstrate the accounting skills of technical awareness and ethical problem solving.

We emphasized the individual accountant's decision process. We also considered the ethical dimensions of the effort to produce high-quality financial reports that could be useful for stakeholders. Our decision model calls attention to a "toolkit" of intellectual and moral resources to aid decision making. This toolkit includes: (1) accounting standards and guidelines for preparing financial statements, (2) professional codes of conduct, and (3) the traditions of moral philosophy. We presented examples of moral reasoning and illustrations of virtuous action and asked you to use these resources to address cases and resolve accounting and moral dilemmas.

In addition to accounting and philosophical resources that are "external" to the individual, we treated the "internal" personalized aspects of cognitive and moral development. These discussions include the exercises and experiences of habit formation through which virtues become embedded as intellectual and moral character traits. These inner resources support the accountant's recognition of ethical dilemmas and help in the deliberative process of identifying moral issues and resolving dilemmas. These cognitive and moral resources enable the individual to generate and assess decision alternatives, make moral judgments and take ethical actions (to be committed to act ethically). This discussion of external and internal resources, character formation, and deliberative reasoning is oriented to accounting practice and practical decision making. The intended use of this book – with its decision model, treatment of moral dilemmas and review of cases – is centered on the support of ethical practice. The accountant's decision process is to result in knowledge-based and ethical action. The study of accounting ethics should help you make accounting judgments and act in ethical ways as a professional.

THE SOCIAL CONTEXT FOR THE ACCOUNTANT'S DECISION MAKING: THE ETHICAL DOMAIN

The previous chapters discussed the individual accountant's decision process. We treated the accountant's duty to solve accounting problems and to recognize moral issues in situations. We addressed accounting dilemmas with moral deliberation and the exercise of practical wisdom. While addressing technical matters and ethical concerns, we argued, the accountant acts as a moral agent (as decision maker) to realize virtues, express them in the decision process, and take ethical actions appropriate to the given situation.

Our description did not portray the accountant as an isolated individual, separated from various social contexts. We treated the accountant in an organizational and institutional context, in various social settings. For example, we described accounting as a discursive practice, that is, as a cooperative enterprise that calls for individuals to realize their intellectual and moral virtues to achieve the goals of the practice. These goals are achieved through the "internal goods" of communicating financial knowledge of a company's economic position and performance. To use both technical and ethical terms: in this cooperative practice, accountants are obligated to produce high-quality financial statements, and auditors must attest to the relevance and faithful representativeness of the reports the accountants prepare. (See Chapter One.)

To further illustrate the accountant's social context, accounting practice is described in professional terms. The regulative ideals and ethical constraints that shape accounting practice are communicated as the shared values of the accounting community. These values are also stated in the explicit statements of professional codes of conduct. The codes express professional standards of expertise. These are the goals of a self-regulated discipline. The codes define professional identity, prescribe professional roles, and guide specific accounting actions. These standards of expertise and patterns of disciplined behavior are vital for serving the expectations and needs of society. The social need for high-quality financial information prompts the granting of professional status to the practice of accounting (Cowton, 2008).

As we have seen, accounting practice presupposes a complex social context filled with groups and organizations. The company accountant and the auditor provide financial information about business entities which range in size from small private companies to huge corporations owned by many shareholders and employing thousands of workers. Company accountants answer to management teams; external audit firms are hired by the companies' boards of directors. Accountants work in these companies and in the audit firms. The accountants and auditors prepare and review financial statements for use by groups of stakeholders, some who invest or loan money to the companies and others who regulate them through legislation and government agencies. The company accountant, the auditor in a firm, and their professional counterparts in regulatory agencies all play vital roles in modern society. The stakeholders who provide capital (investors and lenders) need dependable, high-quality information in order to make decisions about whether to support particular business and their activities. Without clear and accurate financial information, interested investors and lenders will not risk their capital to support a given company's production of goods and services for the market. By producing high-quality financial information, accountants support numerous groups, organizations and individuals. In a word: accountants are enmeshed in society and engaged in activities that are crucial for the movement of capital in the market. This social (business) arena is the ethical domain in which accountants display their dual competence – technical proficiency, to be sure, but especially ethical sensibility.

When we speak of accountants making decisions, we refer to their exercise of professional judgment, a knowledge-based and ethically sensible practical wisdom. This judgment operates within the social context of economies where companies produce goods and provide services to a mass market of customers and clients. These companies are themselves dependent on the movement of capital from investors, lenders and from those same customers and clients. The accountant prepares financial statements for manufacturing concerns that are organized for production and marketing and for corporations that offer financial and other services.

Through the disclosure of a company's financial information, the needs of the market (and the wider society) are served by the communication of data and accounting analysis of key features of financial performance. This is done so that investors and lending institutions can decide whether or not to provide capital to that business. To carry out this key market function of preparing and attesting to the reliability of financial statements, accountants and auditors engage in a cooperative enterprise (the practice of accounting), work within companies and audit firms and act as members of the accounting profession. They function as integral members of organizations and institutions; they play key roles in a complex environment of capital markets, businesses, professional, and regulatory bodies.

Considering the social dimension in which accountants work, we also emphasize the crucial ethical obligations of this task. We call attention to the requirement that the accountant disclose financial information and communicate accounting knowledge that does not misrepresent a company's current financial position or past performance. The accountant must resist any and all pressures that interfere with this duty. The pressures and distractions to the accountant are often many and powerful. Some are exerted by circumstances (time deadlines, demands for efficiency and cost reduction, bonus arrangements linked to earnings, analysts' forecasts and concern for stock prices). Other pressures are generated by stakeholder groups – management, boards of directors, stockholders, and even the auditor's own firm. Still other pressures arise when particular individuals attempt to distract the accountant (company managers and employees, professional colleagues, analysts).

In this social context of diverse organizations and individuals, standing against powerful pressures and serious distractions, accountants "must do their job". They cannot subordinate their judgments to anyone else. The accountant must communicate high-quality information to stakeholders in order to achieve the fundamental goals of accounting practice and maintain the well-being of the accounting profession and thus honor the public's trust. He or she must make rational, free, and autonomous decisions (to borrow from Kant's language.) As a number of accounting ethics scholars assert: accountants are to "tell the truth" in their disclosures. In their "ethics of truth telling and disclosure" accountants are to paint "a true picture of a company" in the financial statements and public reports (Duska, Duska & Ragatz, 2011, pp. 13–17). Christopher J. Cowton, a British scholar, refers to the accounting profession as a "moral community" in which the accountant shares a common culture with fellow professionals. This profession binds itself to a high standard of ethics to serve the public. Enjoying social and economic power, accounting professionals ought to exercise a "principles-based integrity" in their professional roles and duties (Cowton, 2008).

Approaching issues of professional identity and social responsibility as Christopher Cowton does, Michael Pakaluk and Mark Cheffers cite the accountant's personal responsibility and call for principles-directed behavior. To uphold the high ideals of their profession, accountants should "practice habits of integrity and truthfulness" in all areas of their lives, "take responsibility for their own actions," and recognize that the profession "provides for truthfulness and conditions of trust in a modern market economy." (Pakaluk & Cheffers, 2011, pp. 196, 397, 402–3) Ethicists Steven M. Mintz and Roselyn E. Morris identify ethical reasoning as a key component of professional judgment and call for its exercise to serve public needs and interests (Mintz & Morris, 2011). To provide decision-useful knowledge, to tell the truth in disclosure, to uphold the high ideals of a profession, to provide truthfulness and conditions of trust, to use ethical reasoning and exercise professional judgment – these mark the high social expectations for accounting professionals to realize their virtues in practice, that is, to be "excellent and virtuous." For our own part, we discussed the ethics of duty and the ethics of virtue to shape decision making and support ethical discourse and practice.

THE MORAL STRUCTURE OF ACCOUNTING: ECONOMIC EVENTS AND ACCOUNTING DISCOURSE

These expressions of "ethical advice" to accountants reveal a common appreciation of the accountant's task to communicate "faithfully representative" and "relevant" information about economic activity. Key features of this accounting discourse can be discussed in terms of a "moral structure" that frames efforts to understand "what is going on" whenever particular people or groups engage in economic activity. This structure of accounting discourse presumes that economic events impact the material world and the outcome of economic activity has significant meaning for different people from those who first take the economic actions (engaging, for example, in financial transactions). C. Edward Arrington, an American scholar, describes this structure of event and language (his description is labeled a "moral ontology of accounting"). Arrington argues that "giving an account" of an economic action involves (1) describing the event in its human origin, (2) assessing its impact on the material world, and (3) addressing its meaning for those whose "life-world" is affected by that activity (Arrington, 2007). The ethics of such a discourse, argues Arrington, is grounded in an obligation (1) to communicate an objective understanding of the economic activity, (2) to share an understanding of how the event impacts the world (i.e., stands in relationship to other economic events and to human actors, an "inter-subjective understanding"), and (3) to acknowledge that this communication of economic information has a "private" meaning for stakeholders who make use of it. These stakeholder-participants in accounting discourse have an opportunity to use the information they grasp by their "subjective understanding". The stakeholders' use of financial information will be shaped by their unique talents, resources and purposes. With this sketch of accounting disclosure, Arrington tells us that the first obligation of accounting discourse is to present an intelligible description of an economic event, which assumes that economic activity shapes the material world and will be understood by stakeholders from their own personal perspectives and used for their own purposes. "[G]iving accounts is, at its origins, an activity in which economic events become intelligible – intelligible to *someone* in the context of *their* world as living in community *with particular others*" (Arrington, 2007, p. 8).

We can now establish a link between the ethical advice given by those accounting ethicists and Arrington's sketch of a moral structure for accounting discourse. By calling for truthful presentation, a principles-based integrity, and an ethics of duty and virtue, we see that Arrington's concern for an intelligible disclosure of economic events – his assertion that the accountant must try to "describe what is going on" – is itself an ethical demand. Arrington calls for the accountant to "make sense" of economic events so that the meaning of these human actions can be established for the "agents" who originated the economic actions, who made things or made things happen, and who can therefore be held morally accountable by others for these actions. This meaning can be grasped and further "constructed" by those whose lives are influenced by the economic events (Hines, 1988). Furthermore, it can be assumed that all stakeholders to whom accounting discourse is addressed have their own purposes for using the accounting information they receive. The accountant is held morally responsible for producing intelligible accounts. And what is more, in Arrington's view: when the accountant "constructs" an interpretation of "what is going on," this interpretation will then constitute the intellectual foundation from which a moral assessment of the economic activity (and the discourse itself) can proceed. In other words, given access to the knowledge of what has happened (conveyed through the accountant's reports), any stakeholder can evaluate its rightness or wrongness, or its conformity or non-conformity to any stated or implicit ethical standards.

This advice given by ethicists to "tell the truth," when coupled with the identification of a moral structure of accounting that underlies its discourse, permits us to emphasize the accountant's ethical obligation, the key social responsibility of accounting, to disclose clear, accurate, and reliable information. The three-fold claim that accounting discourse is (1) grounded in the facts of economic activity, (2) that it should convey how the economic events shape the material world, and (3) it should be conveyed in a language that enables stakeholders to grasp the relevance of this information for their own lives is a sweeping and powerful demand. As the previous chapters have shown: accounting standards for this discourse demand the technical, as well as the ethical, competence of the accountant. And as we have seen, many intellectual and moral resources are available to support appropriate disclosure of economic events.

Most importantly for this chapter: we can evaluate accounting discourse and the accounting profession. We will assess their importance for the market and general society in terms of this moral structure of disclosure. We can consider the ethics of accounting and not only the ethics of accountants. That is, we can go beyond a concern for individual decision making to consider the role of accounting as an institution in society, and we will address the challenges to ethical accounting practice in the contemporary business environment. We have colleagues in this endeavor. The agenda to examine accounting in society is pursued by many scholars who contribute to the academic journals, *Accounting, Organizations and Society* and *Critical Perspectives on Accounting*. These topics are a central concern of an excellent accounting ethics textbook by Ken McPhail and Diane Walters (McPhail & Walters, 2009).

THE PERCEPTION THAT ACCOUNTING IS ONLY A TECHNICAL CRAFT, BUT NOT AN ETHICAL PRACTICE

Chapter One began by considering the present state of accounting in society and various calls for reform. We cited business scandals and the public outcry for ethical behavior and acknowledged a quarter-century of reform efforts in accounting. Our textbook, we asserted, represents our own response to accounting reform, marking our particular concern for accounting education, as well as our own dissatisfaction with the limited attention that is given to ethics in business school curricula and academic research.

Despite the professional concerns expressed about accounting education in the past two decades, and even with the curricular expansions to include more ethics training, we thought there was significant need to place more emphasis on the ethical dimensions of accounting. We also discussed ethical elements that were already embedded (and too little noticed) in accounting practice and discourse about accounting. We argued that current reforms were dominated by technical matters, expressed in rules, oversight procedures and compliance matters. We did not, however, consider this to be an adequate reform. In brief: the book points to a continuing tendency on the part of many scholars, teachers and practitioners to regard accounting as basically a technical craft. But accounting is a moral enterprise, too.

Once again, in this chapter, we criticize this narrowly technical perception of accounting in society, especially as this attitude continues to influence accounting education. In 2004, Paul Williams connected the recent business scandals to a failure of academics to teach the language, "the vocabulary," of ethics. Williams criticized the neglect of ethics in the education of business and accounting students. Because of this failure, he argued, practicing accountants were ill-equipped to recognize and resolve ethical dilemmas. They found it difficult to speak of ethics at all – even in the face of large-scale fraud and manifest harm to the public (Williams, 2004).

Several University of North Texas scholars have also elaborated this perspective and explain its power by referencing what is called the Old Institutional Economics Theory. This theoretical analysis argues that the foundational values of modern economics have gained power, "hegemony," over other key social institutions. This corporatist, economic hegemony has permeated higher education, rendering accounting (along with many other disciplines) as a "technical discipline". In this education, which has been "commodified," accountants are trained as "disciplined specialists" to provide "objective, technical information" to managers who "plan, control and make decisions". In effect, accountants are trained not to see themselves as independent "moral agents".

The Texas scholars deplore this state of affairs: they call for major reforms in accounting education (we agree!). As fledgling members of the accounting profession, soon to engage in accounting practice, the students should learn that "accounting is a moral discipline" not a "technical discipline that is neutral and objective". This education should enhance their identity as "learned citizens" and ethically sensitive professionals (Mayper *et al.*, 2000). In contemporary language, the students need "an educational intervention" to provide them with "a vocabulary of ethics" and "moral skills." This intervention is critical so that accountants will equipped to recognize the moral implications of accounting practice and the social responsibilities of their professional lives (Mayper, Pavur, & Merino, 2005, pp. 40–1).

The social power of economic institutions and their corporate-economic values is so pervasive that it can "mask the moral aspects" of the accounting discipline. A "technicist" education developed under this hegemony can "suppress students' moral reasoning and independent thought" (intellectual and moral qualities that every learned citizen and every accountant needs!) (Mayper, Pavur & Merino, 2005, pp. 34, 36) Accountants have a moral structure of discourse, where telling the truth about "what is going on" in the human construction of economic events and their meaningful communication to others is a high ethical priority. Given this, one can only support such an "educational intervention" intended to foster independent thinking and moral sensitivity. In fact, we have written an accounting ethics textbook to contribute to such an intervention!

PROFESSIONALISM IN SOCIAL CONTEXT

Accounting discourse is shaped by "a moral structure" intended to foster intelligible communication about economic events to represent the financial positions and performances of business entities. Accounting information is supposed to be meaningful so it can be useful to stakeholders for their own purpose-driven, self-interested decision making. We have identified numerous resources that support this moral discourse of accounting by providing technical and ethical "tools" for the accountant's use. We argued that *The Conceptual Framework*'s goal of high-quality accounting information and adherence to the principles and standards of accounting practice are mandated by the accountant's ethics of duty. The task of faithfully representing relevant accounting knowledge prompts the accountant to bring distinctive intellectual and moral virtues into the communication process (the ethics of virtue). In brief: accountants must demonstrate – in their decision making and communication of financial information – a dual competence of technical proficiency and ethical sensibility.

In contemporary society the "institutional logic" of the accounting profession projects these ideals for accounting discourse and practice (Suddaby, Gendron & Lam, 2009). The distinctive goals and principles, "rules, values, and virtues," of accounting become part of the shared culture, a common understanding of roles and duties shared by members of professional associations (Melé, 2005).

The accounting profession is charged with the responsibility for communicating financial information to serve the needs of citizens and organizations in society and thereby to serve "the public interest". Historically the accounting profession is one of the institutions developed to regulate the market and guard against the excesses of untrammeled self-interests by market participants. Accountants through their professional organizations establish principles, set rules and support an internal cultural of technical and ethical expectations. Some expectations are explicitly stated in professional codes of conduct and policy statements, but a substantial portion of the professional values and norms are communicated informally through the extended conversation of the profession's membership (its community of discourse). In this way, ideals are shaped into an implicit value system shared by the membership.

Public acceptance of the accounting profession as an institution that regulates the excesses of the market imposes a powerful social expectation of *professional independence*. This norm is also nurtured within the profession itself. The accounting profession is to be *independent*, and the accountant/professional should be autonomous in professional judgment and resistant to social pressures that can distort accounting discourse. The accounting profession as institution is supposed to remain independent from the corporations, businesses, providers of capital and customer/clients that are the key players in the market economy. An independent accounting profession serves the essential market function of providing reliable financial information – objective, impartial, unbiased economic knowledge – but in doing their work, professionals should not be tied to the interests or preferences of the market participants who may use that accounting information. Neither the profession as institution nor its individual members should allow the commercial interests of any particular stakeholder (including the interests of the accountant's own firm) to influence the preparation of financial statements or their attestation by an independent audit.

The profession is to remain independent of market participants and wary of key commercial values that seem to drive much of market activity. The profession is not a government agency; it stands at some distance from the government's legal and bureaucratic structures to regulate market activity. To maintain separation from government, like the effort to remain independent of market players, often takes strenuous effort and watchful attention. This is because professions are granted legal and social privileges by the government so that they can perform public service. In addition, the profession shares oversight of the market with government agencies. For example, the US government mandates features of the accountant's reporting responsibility (yearly reports for public companies, the Sarbanes–Oxley legislation requiring that management sign off on financial statements). The government also infringes on firm–client relationships through judicial decrees that public interest supersedes the interests of client and firm (*US v. Arthur Young*, 465 U.S. 805, 1984) and by legislation (in Australia, 1999 and 2001) that accounting rules must consider companies' access to capital in international financial markets (Kaidonis, 2008). But as an ideal, the accounting profession both guards its separation from market stakeholders and appreciates that it does not function as a bureaucratic government agency.

The professional codes of the AICPA and the IFAC express important principles regarding auditor impartiality and objectivity whenever accountants prepare and verify financial reports. For example, the AICPA Code of Conduct's principle of objectivity "imposes an obligation to be impartial, intellectually honest and to be free of conflicts of interest" (AICPA Code of Conduct, Section 55, Article IV.01). Accountants are expected to be objective and are counseled against relationships that threaten to impair objectivity. The American and international codes include lists of particular relationships to avoid, including not to conduct audits where the firms or individual accountants have financial interests in client companies, provide tax services for the companies or when a company is engaged in litigation against one of the other clients of the firm. The codes even direct auditors not to conduct audits where they have relatives who work in a client company.

Concerned to maintain the reputation of the profession and "to honor the public trust," the professional codes not only counsel public accountants to maintain "independence in fact" but also "independence in appearance." In the spirit of the American code (and strengthening its impact for compliance), the Sarbanes–Oxley legislation makes it unlawful for an auditor to offer specific non-audit services to clients during the period during which the firm conducts those clients' audits. (Sarbanes–Oxley 201, cited in Duska, Duska & Ragatz, 2011, Appendix A, pp. 221–2)

THE ACCOUNTANT AND THE PROFESSION IN THE MARKET AND SOCIETY

The public has long trusted professional accountants to prepare impartial financial statements and conduct objective audits. This expectation conveyed by legislation, court rulings and judicial decisions is also projected as the professional ideal by codes of conduct and the shared culture of the membership of professional bodies. Yet even with this ideal, several recent developments in accounting firms, the large number of audit scandals among business frauds, and the many signs of public misgiving about accounting professionalism raise significant questions about accounting in the contemporary United States and around the world. We will discuss some of these developments in several cases where audit firms failed to maintain independence from their audit clients.

Auditor Independence

PeopleSoft and Ernst & Young

In 2002, the Securities and Exchange Commission (US) charged Ernst & Young with ethics code violations for its partnership with PeopleSoft in a software program during a period in which the firm conducted audits on PeopleSoft. The SEC charged the firm with misconduct in 1995–1999: In this period the tax division of Ernst &Young had an agreement to develop and market a software program for payroll and tax withholding issues. Royalties from the arrangement were forwarded to PeopleSoft. This arrangement, charged the SEC, violated ethics code principles on auditor independence. In 2004 the SEC penalized the firm $1.7 million, forcing it to return fees plus interest to PeopleSoft shareholders; the SEC also barred the firm from taking on new audit clients for six months. The SEC judge's administrative ruling called the arrangement "reckless, highly unreasonable and negligent," thus signaling the importance of the principle of independence. Commenting when Ernst & Young accepted the penalty, an official in the SEC's enforcement division said, "Auditor independence is critically important to investors. When auditor independence rules are violated, it undermines investor confidence" (USAToday.com, May 16, 2004).

US Foodservice, Inc., a subsidiary of Royal Ahold

As part of an aggressive strategy of business expansion, Royal Ahold, a large grocery and food service company, acquired numerous businesses in Asia and the Americas in the late 1990s and early 2000s. In this period, Ahold acquired US Foodservice (USF), and USF, like many other Ahold acquisitions, faced strong pressures to increase earnings. The company used a marketing strategy of "promotional allowances" for large vender purchases. The vendors were expected to pay large rebates for the huge inventories USF purchased. These payments, labeled "prepayments," were improperly recognized in the company's financial statements for 2001 and 2002. (Rebates should be recorded as reductions in costs of goods sold and recognized when goods are sold, but they were booked immediately to increase 2002 earnings. The inventory was not sold in 2002, so the rebates on the unsold portion should have been recorded in the year of the sale.)

A number of vendors pleaded guilty to falsifying audit confirmation letters as the company misrepresented the payments in its financial statements. The SEC filed a civil suit against Ahold, the parent company of USF, and several Ahold managers were charged with securities fraud by the SEC. (The managers settled the case, but two of the managers were later found guilty of fraud in a Dutch court.) USF agreed to pay $30 million to settle civil charges connected with a portion of the rebates linked to sales to the US government. In addition, two KPMG auditors, Kevin Hall and Rosemary Meyer, were investigated by the SEC for improper professional conduct in their audit and review of USF for the years 1999 and 2000.

The SEC investigation claimed that Hall and Meyer had discovered that USF had recognized substantial unearned "prepayments" of the "promotional allowances" and they had altered work papers to hide inconsistencies between USF management denials of vendor prepayments and the financial statements. In these and other actions, Hall and Meyer "improperly and repeatedly relied on management representations . . . even though these were contradicted by evidence from executed contracts and information from third parties." Hall and Meyer, charged the SEC, failed to comply with auditing standards by "unreasonably (i) failing to exercise due professional care, (ii) failing to maintain an attitude of professional skepticism" and by other failures in gathering evidence and for relying on management representations.[1]

As you can see, the charges against the auditors are connected to their failure to distance themselves from management misrepresentation of rebate payment as they conducted audits of USF's financial statements. This failure to exercise professional skepticism and to be impartial and objective in their audit investigation – as well as the alteration of their own work papers – demonstrates a violation of several ethical principles, including that of independence. Although it is not established that the auditors or their firm, KPMG, benefited financially from this misconduct, the improper conduct appears to have helped to hide various forms of criminal behavior for which Ahold managers and outside vendors were later penalized. Most certainly, publicity about this case in the United States and Europe had a negative impact on the market reputation of Ahold and the professional reputation of KPMG. In ethical terms, we can state that the individual auditors did not conduct themselves with due diligence; they did not uphold the good standing of their profession.

Arthur Andersen, Enron and before

When we consider negative impressions of the accounting profession in light of firms' misconduct in the late 1990s and early 2000s, no example looms larger than Arthur Andersen's relationship to Enron, which eventually lead to Andersen's criminal conviction and loss of its license in 2002: The criminal proceedings and conviction took place shortly after Enron declared bankruptcy because of its massive indebtedness which had come to light in 2001. There are several dimensions of the Enron case, with Arthur Andersen's improper conduct playing a significant role in key aspects of the scandal.

Prior to the Enron scandal, Arthur Andersen, with its audit work and consulting activity of non-audit services, faced serious criticism in the 1990s. These problems include: consulting advice given to Boston Chicken in the early 1990s about the parent company's relationship to its franchises, consulting pressures exerted on Waste Management and Andersen's overlooking of that company's earnings overstatements during the late 1990s (which cost the firm a $7 million civil fine), and the giving of an unqualified audit opinion to Sunbeam, when the company had overstated earnings in 1996–1998 (accounting misconduct for which Andersen had to pay Sunbeam shareholders $110 million in fees and interest payments).

Andersen's troubles in the 1990s occurred against a backdrop of tension generated by the firm's offering of both audit and tax services and a vast array of non-audit counseling services. Pressures to grow the firm's earnings by aggressive selling of these services and the sharp competition between the audit and the non-audit divisions of the firm dominated its internal culture in this period. Partners throughout the firm were expected to increase firm earnings, and structural arrangements within the firm pitted divisions against one another for a share of company profits. And throughout this period, Arthur Andersen was the auditor for the rapidly growing natural gas trader/energy giant Enron Corporation.

We focus specifically on Enron's arrangements with limited partnerships and the creation of hundreds of these so-called "Special Purpose Entities" (SPEs) as Enron tried to increase its access to capital and keep its share prices growing. Arthur Andersen's consulting advice on structuring a large portion of these arrangements enabled Enron to "hide debt" and to move poorly performing assets from Enron into the SPEs. Andersen assisted the SPEs in borrowing large amounts of money (with Enron collateralization) and advised Enron on various techniques that kept a massive amount of debt off Enron's books. Struggling to understand these financial arrangements, many outside commentators criticized Enron's financial reports for being obscure and virtually incomprehensible. Others challenged Enron for taking advantage of ownership rules established by the SEC and the Financial Standards Accounting Board (FASB). These rules and their manipulation by the company permitted Enron to create "partnerships" that can best be construed as Enron-owned structures whose primary purpose was to enhance Enron's earnings, rather than to stand as independent companies with distinct missions of their own.

Not only did Arthur Andersen make more money from non-auditing service fees than audit fees during some years in this period, it offered continuous advice on Enron's internal accounting procedures which it also audits. Firm accountants and lawyers shared office space in the Enron company headquarters, and they often socialized with their Enron counterparts. Most importantly, Arthur Andersen audited the corporate structures (the limited partnerships and Enron Corporation) and the financial transactions between Enron and the SPEs. The audit/consultant firm also gave advice on many of the complex financing arrangements made between Enron, the SPEs, and outside providers of capital. And then Andersen audited economic activities for which it had given Enron counsel!

A principal source of evidence about this cozy arrangement between Arthur Andersen and Enron is an internal report authorized by Enron's own Board of Directors in 2001. This report shows numerous examples of Andersen's failure to fulfill professional responsibilities in Enron audits. Andersen did not provide "objective accounting judgment," ". . . permitting questionable accounting treatment" of SPE transactions. This so-called "Powers Report" further criticized Andersen for not providing a sufficient check on the disclosure approach of the company and cited Andersen's negligence in not reporting its misgivings about Enron's internal controls. The report criticizes Andersen because the firm did not take these and other concerns to Enron's Audit Committee: the list goes on and on (Powers, Troubh & Winokur, 2004).

To bring this to a close: the fact is that one might fill an entire book of comparable examples from the past quarter century, where major firms (and small ones) violate the principle of independence and the related principles of objectivity and impartiality and fail in due diligence by not upholding the high ideals of accounting professionalism – Parmalat (Italy), WorldCom (US), Satyam (India). Given the accounting failures of the recent past, it is no wonder that some critics think that accounting faces a major crisis of legitimacy. The profession is challenged to maintain public trust and is endangered by the threat of losing a measure of its privilege of self-regulation to a more extensive and stringent government regulation.

MISREPRESENTATION: NOT A TRUE PICTURE

In June 2013, Andrew Fastow, former Enron CFO, spoke at the Association of Certified Fraud Examiners' Global Fraud Conference. Fastow had been prosecuted and spent several years in prison for not following specific SEC securities rules related to the way Enron financed its business operation. He said that was not the most important reason why he was guilty. The most important aspect of his guilt, he claimed, was that he engaged in transactions to misrepresent the financial position of Enron and this misrepresentation permitted Enron to appear to outsiders different than it really was.

Fastow admitted that his job at Enron was to engage in financial transactions that intentionally created a false impression of Enron's financial position. According to Fastow, accounting rules are vague, complex, and even sometimes nonexistent for particular circumstances, and people have to make decisions under such conditions. The accountants at Enron thought complexity was not a problem but an opportunity. The main decision rule used at Enron was whether the accounting and securities rules could be interpreted to allow the treatment Enron preferred. According to Fastow, the difficulty with making decisions based on whether the rules can be interpreted to allow a given desirable treatment is that it is difficult to know where to stop. If the rules are complex or vague, the proper question is to consider the purpose of the transaction. Rather than considering the purpose of the transaction, Enron manipulated the rules and then obtained approval for the transaction from management, the board, the lawyers, and the accountants. If an interpretation of the rules would allow the transaction and experts linked to Enron approved the transaction, then the company would make use of the transaction. The financial officers and deal-makers failed to consider whether the purpose of the transaction was clearly disclosed by the way the transaction was recorded. As a result of this attitude toward rules and their interpretation, Enron accountants prepared financial statements that misrepresented the company's financial position. The financial statements did not faithfully represent the financial reality of the company.[2]

THE MIXED GOOD OF ACCOUNTING DISCOURSE: MARKET VALUES AND ACCOUNTING ETHICS

We have assumed that accounting is an instrumental good for society, that its goal of describing economic events, "communicating what is going on" in the financial activities of companies, will contribute to the material good of individuals and organizations. Contemporary accounting practice, a technically sophisticated and ethics-guided discourse, projects itself as a socially beneficial enterprise. We believe this is a good and reasonable description of accounting. Given this view of accounting in society, we can (from the perspective of virtue ethics) ask two pointed questions about accounting goals and achievements. "Does accounting discourse project a substantive goal for society; that is, does accounting support a flourishing life and the possibilities of a happy, well-lived existence?" "Do the regulative ideals – the principles, rules, and the intellectual and moral traits of character – the guidelines for accounting practice actually support a life well-lived, a flourishing, human society?"

We believe accounting does indeed contribute to the material well-being of large numbers of people and to thriving organizations by supporting the movement of capital in the market. Yet we must remain sober in our assessment, because economic production and the distribution of goods create serious social costs and human suffering (as well as opportunities for prosperity and the satisfaction of many needs and preferences). In addition, the process of moving capital by investors, lenders, and customer/clients sometimes harms people and disrupts their communities (in addition to producing great benefits and genuine human gain). It cannot simply be stated that the economy, the market, or accounting practice which supports the market and economy do, in fact, lead to a rich and humane existence – a flourishing and satisfying life. Social costs, suffering, and injustice are significant aspects of modern social existence. Because of this: it is best to say that prosperity and the material good of the economy, as supported by the function of accounting, is a mixed good. And we can assert this sober judgment, even before we discuss whether or not material good and prosperity has been extended to the citizenry to a sufficient degree, or prior to debating about the just allocation of goods and services or determining some acceptable limit or another for suffering and social cost.

We can, of course, discuss the "role of accounting in society" as an elaboration of its fundamental goals and their realization in practice. We should recognize, however, that this topic immediately draws us into a debate about the principal values, the institutional structures and processes of the modern economy and the financial market. In fact, we have already begun such a discussion. Earlier in this chapter, we expanded beyond our book-long treatment of decision making to acknowledge the social power of economics language and the educational challenge of the "technicist" training of accountants. This critique expressed our own accounting theory which presupposes a moral, as well as a technical, component of accounting. Because of this assumption, we are willing to entertain the two virtue ethics questions asked in the preceding paragraph. Most certainly, these are to be legitimate topics for discussion in an accounting ethics text.

Our treatment of auditor independence also prompts a consideration of the values and workings of the modern economy, along with the operational norms that influence market exchanges and the organizational dynamics of large-scale corporations. The complexities of the market and the sharp competition between professional and commercial values have had significant impact on accountants' motivations, distracting them from preparing objective, impartial and truthful financial statements for their large corporate clients. These complexities and intense rivalries within the market shaped the workaday contexts for accounting firms and set the stage for their violations of the principle of professional independence.

MARKET VALUES AND ACCOUNTING VALUES: THE SOCIAL DOMAIN OF ACCOUNTING ETHICS

The earlier chapters focused on the accountant's decision making in the preparation and auditing of financial statements. We concentrated on the ethics of communicating high-quality information to stakeholders. Most of our examples and cases considered the ethical challenges of serving shareholders, potential investors and creditors in preparing trustworthy accounts of the financial positions and performances of companies. These particular stakeholders want measurements of previous performance and of current financial obligations, as they try to predict future cash flows in order to make rational choices to allocate their capital resources to one company or another. To a large extent, these discussions presumed that by serving these stakeholders, "market needs" are served and somehow "the public is served". Chapter Ten now expands this perspective. We analyze the roles played by accounting institutions and the profession in society and as comprehensive questions about the morality of accounting discourse with its regulative ideals (the standards of accounting and auditing). These concerns push us toward a more elaborate treatment of stakeholders in the economy other than current stockholders and potential investors. By treating a wide variety of stakeholders, this section expands the agenda of accounting ethics. Accounting ethics must deal with those who are not the main providers of capital – with laborers, customers, government regulators, and bureaucrats.

This shift in perspective puts the spotlight on these "others" including those who may be marginalized in modern economies, future generations who may "have a stake" in the outcomes of current decisions, and those who pay unusually high social costs and seek redress for economic "grievances." By doing this, accounting ethics conversation joins the long history of debate over theories of macroeconomics and competing theories of political organization, national polities, and international law. The ethicists who ask "the big questions" of accounting in society discover a vast field of play.

If you recall the difficulty of addressing the accounting and ethical issues of de-commissioning a nuclear power plant and recognizing the expenses of a safe storage of radioactive waste for an indefinite period; if you were perplexed about the close ties of accounting issues with immigration policies and market competition in the Joe's Taco case; if you caught a hint of the complex interplay of genetic research, audit rules of confidentiality, investment brokerage (and parent–child relationships within a single family) as these issues were presented in the Amgen case – then you might be convinced that the ethics domain of accounting discourse does, in fact, extend across the economic sphere, into politics and the family. And there is more.

For example, there is a long historical debate between socialistic theories of political economy and capitalist theories, the new interpretations of globalism and the intensity of the recent debate, not only in theoretical exchanges but in urban streets and halls of government. There is public distress over environmental disasters and the emergence of "environmental accounting," international conflicts over intellectual property (who owns the music of the airwaves and Internet?), and perplexing complexity over accounting for "intellectual capital" (how will the market account for my university degrees and continuing education?). There are other efforts to do accounting so that decisions can represent "corporate social responsibility" and support "ethical investment." All these complicated matters point toward realms of decision making that stretch beyond "keeping the books for the company" and merely "auditing for the stock market investor".

MARKET VALUES AND THE FUNCTION OF ACCOUNTING

The Market

The market is a metaphor that conveys the idea that individuals and companies own private property and use this property to engage in commerce. These property owners (individuals and companies) labor to produce goods or provide services, the sale of which may enhance the value of their holdings. The sale of these goods and services generates revenues – hopefully exceeding the cost of production and marketing – where a profit is realized and new capital is raised.

Capital is also raised by persuading other individuals and/or companies to invest or lend money to the company and its owner(s). Some of these providers of capital may buy shares in the company and become owners, while others will lend money, hoping to profit in the arrangement. In the market, risk-taking (the focus of creativity, labor, and organizational skill to produce and market or venture into capital-raising arrangements) is supported by the incentive of gaining profits and/or attracting new sources of capital. This capital can then finance new activities of production, marketing, and finance.

Considering other companies and individuals to be producers and sellers, customer-clients, and investors, the "participant-players" in the market engage in numerous forms of competition, cooperation, and negotiation as they produce, sell goods and services, and try to attract capital. Making use of material resources, channeling their own creative energies and harnessing the labor of others, the players in the market build and reshape the world; they alter the material and human landscape. They produce and sell and they deal – all the while engaging with one another.

Market relationships call for wariness and suspicion, for all players pursue their own self-interests, the quality of goods is never certain, and the reliability of services is never guaranteed. Inequalities of economic power are manifest in the market; every player has vulnerabilities; and there is greed. The players compete. Vital resources are limited, and some transactions leave losers (as well as winners). Yet market relations also presume trust and levels of honesty. Buyers and sellers often presuppose continuing relationships with each other. Accordingly, mutual gain and satisfaction pave the way to future deals. Good will is sought, and good reputations have high market value. And in many deals, there are only winners. While negotiations may seem to be only contests for self-interested gain at another's expense, many deals are, in fact, the fruits of cooperation, marked by genuine "handshakes of agreement" and mutual advantage. And the market game is not anarchy; there are laws and rules, constraints of many types. There are unacceptable forms of competition and even types of cooperation that are not allowed. There are sanctions, rewards for playing by the rules and punishments for rule violations.

Giving Accounts

Amidst these activities, whether as competitive rivals or cooperating colleagues, market participants attempt to keep track of what they are doing. They examine and reflect on their own activities and try to understand what the other players are doing. Taking account of these activities and communicating the sense of these events are vital to market relationships and necessary for the continuation of market exchanges. Owner-producers, marketing agents and service-consultants, deal-makers and the providers or recipients of capital – all of them try to determine "what is going on" in the economic events relevant to production, distribution, and finance. Market participants seek measurements of the costs and revenues of past activity, assessments of current obligations and predictions of future cash flows.

Contemporary accounting discourse selects some but not all features of the market. The discourse focuses on selected activities of the "players" and chooses to communicate only about certain types of events within the processes of production, distribution and capitalization. The formal discourse of accounting communicates knowledge of these features, activities and events through prescribed patterns and standardized formats. The discourse of accounting is guided by linguistic codes (standards encompassing fundamental purposes, regulative ideals, and constraining rules). Accounting discourse is directed to interested market players (stakeholders) and monitored by governmental and professional regulators who can even determine whether the accounts are legitimate or not. It is critical that these patterns of accounting disclosure provide clear and transparent information that keeps abreast of innovative business practices. This discourse should adhere not only to accounting rules but also to the spirit of professional principles, for this is vital for maintaining investor confidence and public trust in the market (Levitt, 1998).

Keeping in mind this sketch of the market and accounting as the keeping track of market events, we can continue our inquiry into the social context of accounting. First, we can consider the accounting ethics issue of standards setting processes at the international level, noting efforts to establish one set of accounting standards around the world. Next we consider the ethical implications of accounting professionals trying to influence the governmental monitoring of accounting firms and the legislation of public accounting.

A movement toward a common global set of accounting standards has a 40 year history. Currently two boards, the International Accounting Standards Board (IASB) and the International Auditing and Assurance Standards Board (IAASB), establish international standards for accounting and auditing. In the US, the Financial Accounting Standards Board (FASB) sets accounting standards, while auditing standards for public companies are set by the Public Company Accounting Oversight Board (PCAOB) and auditing standards for private companies by the American Institute of Certified Public Accountants (AICPA). In the past two decades, the SEC in the US, these three boards, and professional and government bodies in many other countries have taken important steps to establish common accounting and auditing standards. Numerous issues have prompted this movement, but clearly expanding international trade, the increase in the number of internationally-oriented companies, the economic power of multinational corporations, and the movements of investment monies across national boundaries play prominent roles.

The task of establishing a common set of standards is both crucial and daunting. As stakeholders including management, investors and creditors deal with financial reports prepared and audited under a wide variety of national and international standards, they face both accounting and ethical problems. Can the stakeholders trust judgments and decisions made under differing accounting "regimes". Can economic events described in various technical terms or estimates made according to differing standards of measurement be trustworthy? Will accounting information presented according different criteria of "reliability," "representative faithfulness," and "relevance" be comparable, "express the truth" or be "decision-useful"? The difficulties of moving toward a global set of standards are formidable, but market needs are great. This suggests that movement toward common global standards may be crucial (e.g., Mintz & Morris, 2011, pp. 378–80, 385–6).

One comprehensive ethics issue that is linked to the globalization of accounting standards is itself complicated and abstract. There has long been debate on whether accounting standards ought to be oriented toward stated principles or primarily based on rules. In a frequent assessment, US standards are characterized as rules-based, while most international standards are described as principles-based. This debate is important in the movement toward a global standard and re-surfaces in the writing and interpretation of the Sarbanes–Oxley legislation designed to reform public accounting after the major scandals in the early 2000s (e.g., Mintz & Morris, 2011; Schipper, 2003).

Consider our next issue: auditors' efforts to influence government policy regarding accounting regulation. In the late 1990s, Arthur Levitt, chairman of the SEC, campaigned to change rules about audit firms offering non-audit services (especially the offering of internal audit services to their own audit clients) and to reduce the firms' non-audit revenues. Levitt claimed to promote auditor independence. The Big Five major firms and their Congressional allies resisted Leavitt's efforts and defeated many of his proposals. During his tenure, Levitt also spoke often of the threat of "earnings management" and the influence of the "business climate" (the consensus of business attitudes) in supporting or resisting the preparation of transparent and comparable financial statements (Levitt, 1998).

In another example, one can review testimony in Congressional hearings on reform legislation in response to the major business scandals. Senior audit firm partners and high-level management of financial institutions seemed to work together to limit government oversight and strenuously resisted legal changes in auditing rules, especially by opposing mandates that the SEC interfere with professional self-regulation. We can consider the powerful influence of the major accounting firms on professional standards-setting and take note of the intense lobbying by audit firms as the SEC tried to regulate the firms in their offering of non-audit consulting services. There was lengthy testimony by audit firm executives and high-ranking managers of financial institutions during hearings as the US Congress debated the Sarbanes-Oxley legislation as a specific audit reform measure. These lobbying efforts continued even after the passage of the legislation, as the executives tried to delay implementation, influence the interpretations of specific rules, probe for loopholes and seek exemptions for certain constraints (Hochberg, Sapienza & Vissing-Jorgensen, 2008). The self-regulating power of the profession is at stake in these discussions. The debates have serious implications for the firms' fundamental task of serving not only their clients but also their maintenance of independence and performing due diligence. These debates concern the public interest and whether market players will receive useful financial statements that have been independently audited.

Consider these matters of a global set of accounting standards, government efforts to monitor accounting procedures, firms' lobbying efforts to influence government policies and standards setting. These issues demonstrate that accounting ethics has an important dimension beyond concerns for the individual accountant's decision making. Exploration of these matters opens a rich field of inquiry into the impact of the market innovation, international business needs and governmental activity on accounting discourse. These disrupt the previous patterns of disclosure and complicate the task of demonstrating technical proficiency and ethical sensibility in accounting performance.

SOCIAL CONTRACT THEORY

The modern political theory of the social contract provides an explanation of the origins of civil society and offers a justification of the state and the authority of government over individual members of society. Owing its modern development to English philosophers, Thomas Hobbes (1991) and John Locke (1988), and a French philosopher, Jean Jacques Rousseau (1997), there are a number of variations of this theory. We introduce some of the key elements.

In this philosophical tradition, all individuals are conceived to be comparable in their material needs, seeking their satisfaction in a competitive struggle for scarce resources with their personal survival at stake. Each person in body and spirit is presumed to be free, while each struggles for the basic physical necessities – food, clothing, shelter. However strong, talented or resourceful, and whatever inequalities of inheritance, merit or fortune, each individual is thought to be essentially equal to everyone else in his or her finitude and vulnerability. All are threatened by potential and actual violence as they try to secure their own existence.

Using their intellectual and physical abilities, people draw material resources from the natural world. They work to create material conditions and shape a world that will sustain their lives amidst other individuals and groups. This self-interested quest for material well-being is a competitive struggle for existence. Life is insecure and people are vulnerable; the material things one might gain can well be lost – snatched away by force and the aggressive assault of a neighbor, or secreted away by a thief in the night. Given such negative possibilities, individuals choose to cooperate with one another. They "give consent" (agree) to form a civil society, which affords a measure of protection for life and security for property – for each member of the community. In this agreement, their *social contract*, these individuals bind themselves to one another for mutual protection and to limit the life-threatening violence which each faces. In the social contract, individuals limit their own freedom for the mutual benefit of protecting one another. They freely consent; in so doing, they promise not to harm one another. They oblige themselves to protect each and every member of the society. They constrain their own aggressive tendencies and even direct some of their energy to watch over their neighbors' safety. For the sake of mutual protection, each individual also cedes a measure of his/her freedom to the state, recognizing it as the dominant power in the territory where they live. In effect, the individual citizens of the state (the fellow members of the contractual society) grant authority to its government. That is, the consenting members of a civil society legitimize the government's exercise of power over the society. These freely consenting individuals agree to obey the laws and rules of the government which they have authorized.

The social contract is construed as a rational agreement, freely assumed for mutual benefit – so that citizens do not harm one another. Each citizen limits his or her own freedom in order to preserve the life, the liberty and the property of fellow citizens, with each individual acknowledging a duty of protecting other people and property. Such a social pledge has a reciprocal dimension: "I will respect and protect you, on the condition that you respect and protect me. I will do you no harm, so long as you do me no harm." This reciprocity becomes the operating dynamic for the mutual benefits of communal existence, the basis for an "all for one and one for all" protective society. To further enhance the society's capacity to protect its members, the individuals entrust power to their government, on the condition (or with the assumption) that its laws and rules will protect the people and the property under the jurisdiction of the state. (Thomas Hobbes, 1991; John Locke, 1988).

In a contemporary version of this social thought, business organizations are (like individual people) conceived as particular members of society. These corporate "individuals" have a stake in an orderly, peaceful society. Engaged in their own struggle for continued existence, corporations compete for resources as they take ownership of property, use capital and market goods and services. In social contract terms: they acknowledge others (individual persons and corporate organizations) as fellow members of society. As members of society, these customers, clients, investors and even competing businesses can make claims, along with any corporation within the society – to share in the mutual protections of the social contract.

In this context, as "citizens" of a community and under the jurisdiction of its government, accounting institutions (firms, professional bodies, and standards-setting boards) pursue their own interests. They are also obligated not to harm others. From this perspective, as accountants and audit firms "give account" of companies by preparing financial statements and attesting to their representative faithfulness, they can be understood as watching over the financial interests of fellow citizens. By communicating high-quality information that describes a company's economic activities, the accounting institutions participate in an ethical discourse. Such an ethical discourse safeguards the reputation of the company because the financial reports correspond to the company's actual performance. The high-quality ethical discourse demonstrates respect for the freedom, rationality and autonomy of the stakeholders that receive its message. Clear, impartial and fair-minded reports permit the stakeholders to use their decision processes to pursue their own interests (because the information that is communicated does not deceive or manipulate them; it does not harm them). Of course, the preparation of financial reports and their audit – paid for by the company itself – is intended to advance a particular company's interests by showing off its performance and hopefully its worthiness for new infusions of capital – investments, loans, higher stock prices. But there is also an element of altruism in this process. The giving of the account provides information to many stakeholders, some of whom will not buy that company's stock, invest in it or extend credit to it. The communication of high-quality accounting knowledge can be described as a public good – even beyond the immediate interests of any given company or any particular stakeholder. In the framework of a social contract, it is reasonable to believe that the society benefits (its members are not harmed but rather are protected) by receiving high-quality accounting information.

The accounting institutions, working within the conceptual framework, standards and codes that support the production and communication of high-quality information, are duty-bound to function as responsible citizens of the community. In social contract language: the accounting organizations collectively and their individual accounting members honor the promise not to harm fellow members of the society. Taking on professional roles, working with due care and diligence within an accounting firm or making ethical decisions as a company accountant can be understood as civic duties. These are opportunities to serve one's fellow citizens by meeting their need for high-quality financial information, supporting their decision processes, and enhancing their chances for economic well-being. The success of accounting institutions contributes to the well-being of society.

Imagine a social contract perspective to assess recent audit failures. We have already reviewed examples of auditors' failure to remain independent of clients and their neglect of public service. In recent years, we have seen the international landscape littered with business disasters and the fallout from audit firm failure. These can be interpreted as civic failures. The business corporations and accounting firms did not fulfill their civic duties, as they broke laws and ignored their ethical responsibilities. Accounting fraud, misrepresentation in financial statements, and the communication of falsified information to investors and creditors caused real damage to many stakeholders and the general public, to the civil society formed by the social contract.

These firms ignored the moral structure of accounting discourse (Arrington, 2007; Schweiker, 1993). They demonstrated a lack of discipline and opportunism – an untrammeled pursuit of corporate interest in violation of laws and contrary to principled behavior – did serious harm in the market and caused major damage to public trust. What is more, as violations of the social contract, corporate greed and corruption undermines the stability of a community and disrupts the very order and peace of civil society. Dishonesty and fraud expresses disdain for the public, harms fellow members of society, and even threatens the social contract itself.

CORPORATE SOCIAL RESPONSIBILITY

Social contract theory, as we have seen, originated as a political philosophy to explain the nature of society and to justify the political authority of the state. Variations of this theory have been modified to examine business organizations as entities in civil society and explore questions regarding the nature of businesses' responsibility within the societies where they market goods and services and compete for investment capital. In this modification of political philosophy, corporate organizations (including businesses, accounting firms and professional bodies) are construed as individual members of civil society. These corporations have rights and responsibilities and hold a significant stake in the order and wellbeing of human community.

Benefiting from the social order and peace that is sustained whenever members of a given society restrain themselves from violence and agree not to harm each other, corporations can be assessed in terms of their ethical responsibility in society. They are to be held accountable for contributing to social wellbeing. Since the late 1950s, business ethics spokespersons have focused on evaluating business organizations in terms of "corporate social responsibility" (CSR). This broad-based movement offers many strategies and techniques for calling attention to and measuring how business organizations address their place in society. These ethicists are especially concerned to evaluate businesses with regard to ethical standards and norms. They discuss various forms of corporate "citizenship" in treating corporate responsibilities in society (Garriga & Melé, 2004).

Advocates of these CSR approaches to organizational behavior assume that corporations have responsibilities that extend beyond their provision of goods and services and beyond concerns for the company's earning a fair return for stockholders on the investment of capital. Considering, for example, companies' "triple bottom line" (people, production/environmental impact, and profit), the advocates of corporate social responsibility express concern for the spirit of the laws, the ethical norms and standards of national cultures and key values of the global business environment. They encourage companies to employ techniques that serve the general society and limit the social harm that may result from business activities. For example, they want businesses to engage in philanthropic activities, use "fair trade products," examine supply chains to ensure fair labor practices, develop self-audit procedures to determine their own "social accountability" for workplace safety, equitable manager–employee relations, and company morale, and to guard against environmental degradation in the production and marketing processes.

Most advocates of corporate social responsibility emphasize business self-regulation, but some also approve of trends in government legislation and bureaucratic oversight that hold businesses to various forms of accountability for business impact on the environment and the high ideal of sustainability for a healthy and vibrant community life to pass on to future generations. In 1997, an independent, non-profit organization called the Global Reporting Initiative, was started to support economic sustainability. The organization, established as a large international network of business, civil, academic, and non-profit groups, has developed a Sustainability Reporting Framework to set guidelines for reporting on businesses' performances in social and environmental sustainability. In 2011 an independent standards board, The Sustainability Accounting Standards Board, was also established in the US to support accountability for business organizations in dealing with a wide variety of environmental, social and governance issues. This board also develops standards for business self-assessment of organizational ethics; these assessments are called "corporate responsibility reports." These voluntary "corporate social reporting" efforts focus on human rights, company hiring and fair labor practices, product safety and how products and services may be "socially beneficial". There is special emphasis on how company policies may impact both the social and natural environments, with the assumption that businesses' personnel, production and marketing activities have local and global impacts.

To be sure, there is much controversy surrounding this movement, as critics debate whether or not business corporations by their very nature ought to be concerned beyond matters of rational efficiency, increasing their stockholders' wealth, or a prudent measure of public goodwill sufficient to continue doing business. Some critics argue that business self-regulation is of limited value, whatever the social goals or community purposes, while others claim that many practices of "responsibility" are simply window-dressing for publicity sake. In addition, there are important discussions on whether accounting techniques can adequately define and measure these "social" and "intangible" intellectual elements of company performance. It is asked, "How can ethics-related attitudes and behavior be identified and measured, categorized and quantified?"

A significant portion of the "corporate social responsibility" discussion dovetails into our treatment of "social contract theory," especially those aspects of discussion that Garriga and Melé call the "Integrative Social Contract Theory" (Garriga and Melé, 2004) and the ideas of "corporate citizenship" as elaborated by Thomas Donaldson and Thomas W. Dunfee (1999). Business organizations can rightfully be construed as "individuals" who enjoy the benefits of social order and exist within legal frameworks while being constrained to follow governmental laws and regulatory policies. It is not a stretch, then, to think that corporate leaders with social awareness and "good conscience" might direct their organizations (which are citizens of civil society) to respect and protect that society with its many diverse members. These business leaders can envision and work for the ideal of a peaceful, well-ordered society where individual and corporate citizens thrive and flourish (to use virtue ethics terminology). These

CSR efforts might well coexist with the drive for profit and the goal of stockholder well-being!

As we have seen, public concerns over business social responsibility and institutional developments to support corporate social responsibility and make use of corporate responsibility reporting pose significant challenges for accounting institutions – standards-setting bodies, professional associations and accounting firms. If corporations are to give accounts of their performance with regard to so many different issues, these accounts must be codified and regularized so that stakeholders can understand and use their information. Concepts, definitions, and technical vocabularies must be developed; new accounting standards must be established – to deal with intellectual and ethical issues, long-term environmental impacts, aspects of company moral and public trust. These sweeping corporate reports need to gain public credibility. Given the vast and diverse data: collection procedures, standards of measurement and reliable patterns of analysis must be proposed, tested and undergo a process of adoption by those who do the accounting. It is likely that new types of reporting statements (financial and "social-natural environmental") and new roles for company accountants and public auditors may be created to expand the accounting discourse. In a word: there will be new accounting standards and new roles for accountants and new ethical challenges to be addressed!

CHAPTER REVIEW QUESTIONS

1. (LO3) Explain the following: "The meaning of economic events can be communicated through a moral discourse."

2. (LO9) What is a social contract?

3. (LO5, LO8) Why is auditor independence important for the market?

4. (LO10) What is Corporate Social Responsibility? What is corporate social reporting?

5. (LO9) What does this mean: "Corporations can be considered as citizens of a society"?

6. LO10) Are stockholders the only important stakeholders in accounting discourse? Explain your answer.

7. (LO9, LO10) Why is the role played by accounting institutions in society considered as aspect of accounting ethics?

NOTES

1. *Wall Street Journal*, "SEC says two KPMG auditors ignored Ahold unit's red flags," February 17, 2006; SEC: "In the matter of Kevin Hall, CPA, and Rosemary Meyer, CPA," Administrative Proceeding, file number 3-12208, February 16, 2006; *Wall Street Journal*, "Ahold and SEC settle with no fine: Move caps investigation into accounting practices of supermarket operator," October 14, 2004; *Wall Street Journal*, "Former

Ahold officials are found guilty of fraud," May 23, 2006; *Wall Street Journal*, "U.S. Foodservice settles fraud charges for $30 million," September 2010.

2. Michael Cohn, "Former Enron CFO Andrew Fastow confronts the fraud examiners," *Accounting Today*, June 27, 2013.

REFERENCES

Arrington, C. (2007) A prolegomenon to the relation between accounting, language and ethics. *The Australasian Accounting and Finance Journal*, 1(2): 1–12.

Cowton. C. (2008) Accounting and the ethics challenge: Re-membering the professional body. *Accounting and Business Research*, 39(3): 177–190.

Donaldson, T. & Dunfee, T.W. (1999) *The Ties That Bind: A Social Contract Approach to Business Ethics*. Cambridge, MA: Harvard University Press.

Duska, R., Duska, B. & Ragatz, J. (2011) *Accounting Ethics*, 2nd edn. Chichester, UK: Wiley-Blackwell.

Garriga, E. & Melé, D. (2004) Corporate social responsibility: Mapping the territory. *Journal of Business Ethics*, 53: 51–71.

Hines, R. (1988) Financial accounting: In communicating reality, we construct reality. *Accounting, Organizations and Society*, 13(3): 251–261.

Hobbes, T. (1991) *Leviathan*, edited by Richard Tuck. Cambridge: Cambridge University Press.

Hochberg, Y., Sapienza, P. & Vissing-Jorgensen, A. (2008) Lobbyist speak in numbers: Evaluating the Sarbanes–Oxley Act of 2002. northwestern.edu/article.

Kaidonis, M. (2008) The accounting profession: Serving the public interest or capital interest? *Australasian Accounting Business and Finance Journal*, 2(4): 1–5.

Levitt, A. (1998) *The Numbers Game*, speech given at the NYU Center for Law and Business, September 28. sec.gov/speech archive 1998.

Locke, J. (1988) *Two Treatises on Government*, edited by P. Laslet. Cambridge: Cambridge University Press.

Mayper, A., Hoops, W., Pavur, R. & Merino, B. (2000) Accounting: A moral discipline? *Proceedings of the Interdisciplinary Perspective on Accounting Conference*, Manchester, 1–20.

Mayper, A., Pavur, R. & Merino, B. (2005) The impact of accounting education on ethical values: an institutional perspective. *Accounting and the Public Interest*, 5(1): 32–55.

McPhail, K. & Walters, D. (2009) *Accounting and Business Ethic: An Introduction*. London: Routledge.

Melé, D. (2005) Ethical education in accounting: Integrating rules, values and virtues. *Journal of Business Ethics*, 57(1): 97–109.

Mintz, S. & Morris, R. (2011) *Ethical Obligations and Decision Making in Accounting*, 2nd edn. New York: McGraw-Hill.

Pakaluk, M. & Cheffers, M. (2011) *Accounting Ethics and the Near Collapse of the World's Financial System*. Sutton, MA: Allen David Press.

Powers, W., Troubh, R. & Winkour, H. (2004) Report of Investigation by the Special Investigative Committee of the Board of Directors of Enron Corporation. In Knapp, M. (ed.) *Contemporary Auditing: Real Issues and Cases*, 5th edn. Mason, OH: Thomson, South-Western.

Rousseau, Jean Jacques (1997) *The Social Contract and Other Political Writings*, edited by V. Gourevitch. Cambridge: Cambridge University Press.

Schipper, K. (2003) Principles-based accounting standards. *Accounting Horizons*, 17: 61–72.

Schweiker, W. (1993) Accounting for ourselves: Accounting practice and the discourse of ethics. *Accounting, Organizations and Society*, 18(2–3): 231–252.

Suddaby, R., Gendron, Y. & Lam, H. (2009) The organizational context of professionalism in accounting. *Accounting, Organizations and Society*, 34: 409–427.

US v. Arthur Young, 465 U.S. 805 (1984) Cited in Pakaluk, M.& Cheffers, M., *Accounting Ethics and the Near Collapse of the World's Financial System*. Sutton, MA: Allen Davis Press.

Williams, P. (2004) You reap what you sow: The ethical discourse of professional accounting. *Critical Perspectives on Accounting*, 15(6–7): 995–1001.

INDEX